Advances in Explainable Artificial Intelligence

Advances in Explainable Artificial Intelligence

Editors

**Gabriele Gianini
Pierre-Edouard Portier**

Basel • Beijing • Wuhan • Barcelona • Belgrade • Novi Sad • Cluj • Manchester

Editors
Gabriele Gianini
Università degli Studi di
Milano-Bicocca
Milan
Italy

Pierre-Edouard Portier
INSA Lyon
Lyon
France

Editorial Office
MDPI
St. Alban-Anlage 66
4052 Basel, Switzerland

This is a reprint of articles from the Special Issue published online in the open access journal *Information* (ISSN 2078-2489) (available at: https://www.mdpi.com/journal/information/special_issues/advance_explain_AI).

For citation purposes, cite each article independently as indicated on the article page online and as indicated below:

Lastname, A.A.; Lastname, B.B. Article Title. *Journal Name* **Year**, *Volume Number*, Page Range.

ISBN 978-3-7258-0283-8 (Hbk)
ISBN 978-3-7258-0284-5 (PDF)
doi.org/10.3390/books978-3-7258-0284-5

© 2024 by the authors. Articles in this book are Open Access and distributed under the Creative Commons Attribution (CC BY) license. The book as a whole is distributed by MDPI under the terms and conditions of the Creative Commons Attribution-NonCommercial-NoDerivs (CC BY-NC-ND) license.

Contents

Roberta De Fazio, Rosy Di Giovannantonio, Emanuele Bellini and Stefano Marrone
Explainabilty Comparison between Random Forests and Neural Networks—Case Study of Amino Acid Volume Prediction
Reprinted from: *Information* **2023**, *14*, 21, doi:10.3390/info14010021 1

Youmna Abdelwahab, Mohamed Kholief and Ahmed Ahmed Hesham Sedky
Justifying Arabic Text Sentiment Analysis Using Explainable AI (XAI): LASIK Surgeries Case Study
Reprinted from: *Information* **2022**, *13*, 536, doi:10.3390/info13110536 20

Shailza Jolly, Pepa Atanasova and Isabelle Augenstein
Generating Fluent Fact Checking Explanations with Unsupervised Post-Editing
Reprinted from: *Information* **2022**, *13*, 500, doi:10.3390/info13100500 32

Vladimir Estivill-Castro, Eugene Gilmore and René Hexel
Constructing Explainable Classifiers from the Start—Enabling Human-in-the Loop Machine Learning
Reprinted from: *Information* **2022**, *13*, 464, doi:10.3390/info13100464 50

Alessandro Renda, Pietro Ducange, Francesco Marcelloni, Dario Sabella, Miltiadis C. Filippou, Giovanni Nardini, et al.
Federated Learning of Explainable AI Models in 6G Systems: Towards Secure and Automated Vehicle Networking
Reprinted from: *Information* **2022**, *13*, 395, doi:10.3390/info13080395 75

Pablo Mosteiro, Jesse Kuiper, Judith Masthoff, Floortje Scheepers and Marco Spruit
Bias Discovery in Machine Learning Modelsfor Mental Health
Reprinted from: *Information* **2022**, *13*, 237, doi:10.3390/info13050237 89

Yanou Ramon, R.A. Farrokhnia, Sandra C. Matz and David Martens
Explainable AI for Psychological Profiling from Behavioral Data: An Application to Big Five Personality Predictions from Financial Transaction Records
Reprinted from: *Information* **2021**, *12*, 518, doi:10.3390/info12120518 104

Andreas Maniatopoulos and Nikolaos Mitianoudis
Learnable Leaky ReLU (LeLeLU): An Alternative Accuracy-Optimized Activation Function
Reprinted from: *Information* **2021**, *12*, 513, doi:10.3390/info12120513 133

Taufique Ahmed and Luca Longo
Interpreting Disentangled Representations of Person-Specific Convolutional Variational Autoencoders of Spatially Preserving EEG Topographic Maps via Clustering and Visual Plausibility
Reprinted from: *Information* **2023**, *14*, 489, doi:10.3390/info14090489 149

Andreas Nugaard Holm, Dustin Wright and Isabelle Augenstein
Revisiting Softmax for Uncertainty Approximation in Text Classification
Reprinted from: *Information* **2023**, *14*, 420, doi:10.3390/info14070420 168

Martina Saletta and Claudio Ferretti
Exploring Neural Dynamics in Source Code Processing Domain
Reprinted from: *Information* **2023**, *14*, 251, doi:10.3390/info14040251 184

Article

Explainabilty Comparison between Random Forests and Neural Networks—Case Study of Amino Acid Volume Prediction

Roberta De Fazio [1,†], Rosy Di Giovannantonio [1,†], Emanuele Bellini [2,†] and Stefano Marrone [1,*,†]

1. Dipartimento di Matematica e Fisica, Università degli Studi della Campania "Luigi Vanvitelli", Viale Lincoln, 5-81100 Caserta, Italy
2. Dipartimento di Studi Umanistici, Università degli Studi Roma Tre, Via Ostiense, 234-00146 Roma, Italy
* Correspondence: stefano.marrone@unicampania.it; Tel.: +39-0823-27-5101
† All the authors contributed equally to this work.

Abstract: As explainability seems to be the driver for a wiser adoption of Artificial Intelligence in healthcare and in critical applications, in general, a comprehensive study of this field is far from being completed. On one hand, a final definition and theoretical measurements of explainability have not been assessed, yet, on the other hand, some tools and frameworks for the practical evaluation of this feature are now present. This paper aims to present a concrete experience in using some of these explainability-related techniques in the problem of predicting the size of amino acids in real-world protein structures. In particular, the feature importance calculation embedded in Random Forest (RF) training is compared with the results of the Eli-5 tool applied to the Neural Network (NN) model. Both the predictors are trained on the same dataset, which is extracted from Protein Data Bank (PDB), considering 446 myoglobins structures and process it with several tools to implement a geometrical model and perform analyses on it. The comparison between the two models draws different conclusions about the residues' geometry and their biological properties.

Keywords: random forest; multi-layer perceptron; explainable AI; protein data bank; neural network; machine learning

1. Introduction

Modern society and industry are demanding more and more smart applications, based on the paradigm of Artificial Intelligence (AI) [1]; the advantages span from a higher competitiveness of companies to the possibility of building more sustainable smart cities [2]. In particular, the Machine Learning (ML) paradigm is promising for solving problems whose solution is too difficult to be expressed in traditional algorithms: the availability of a sufficient amount of data can—in theory—allow solving complex problems with "zero-knowledge". As hunger for smart applications increases, critical domains are starting to be affected by this new software engineering paradigm: autonomous driving [3], Clinical Decision Support System (CDSS) [4] and financing-related applications [5] are just a few of these critical domains.

Notwithstanding the push of the market and the society, the applications of such a paradigm in critical domains is far from being simple; this is because the operation of safety-critical, business-critical and privacy-critical applications is based on rigorous and repeatable Verification & Validation (V&V) processes [6,7]. Such processes are mainly based on modelling, static and dynamic analyses of software, which require having a clear view of the actual behaviour of the code. In contrast, in ML-based code the application emerges from the weights between model parts. Explainability has risen in these years as a must for critical applications of AI; since NNs appear like black box phenomena, the behaviour of algorithms needs to be explained and rebuilt to make sense of the results [8]. As defined in [9], given an audience, an explainable Artificial Intelligence is one that produces details or reasons that make its functioning clear or easy to understand .

The objective of the paper is to report an experience in comparing two of the most widespread ML models under the lens of explainability. In particular, the models of RFs and NNs have been chosen and tested on a challenging case study: the prediction of volume of protein residues. The experience described, starts with the extraction of a subset from the PDB, including the group of myoglobin proteins—that will be preprocessed according to a method already present in the literature [10–12]—and then fed to the two different ML models, according to a set of geometric and non-geometric features. The performances of trained models are then analyzed with existing tools to explore which are—according to the different explainability tools—the most impactful and important features for the prediction task.

> It is important to underline that this paper focuses on the ML approaches and has the primary and sole purpose of comparing the presented approaches on the base of a replicable case study. The case study is taken as a driver to demonstrate the results of such a comparison: the authors are aware that the protein volume prediction—as taken as a problem itself—would need a more complex approach and the application of sophisticated methods and techniques that are not in the scope of the present paper.

The most valuable contribution of this paper is constituted by dealing with a challenging real case study. Many scientific papers report theoretical evaluations of the different ML-based explainability techniques [13,14]. The approach followed in this paper is different, preferring to focus on the reporting of a practical but repeatable experience in comparing off-the-shelf methods and technologies, rather than defining ad hoc solutions. Such a comparison is then conducted on a real-world case study.

This paper is structured as follows: Section 2 gives some background information about PDB, the used ML models and the related mechanisms to provide explainability facilities. Section 3 describes the methodology followed. Section 4 focuses on the preprocessing phase—which is always a foundational and crucial phase in every ML-based approach—highlighting the critical steps. Section 5 reports the results of the models training, while Section 6 compares the results under the different considered aspects. Section 7 gives a brief review of the related works, while Section 8 ends the paper and lays out future research lines.

2. Background

This section recalls some background concepts, reported for clarity. Section 2.1 reports the main concepts of the PDB and related manipulating software libraries, Section 2.2 recalls the base concepts of the used ML models and techniques, Section 2.3 gives some elements of the Eli-5 software library.

2.1. Protein Data Bank

PDB is a key resource in structural biology; it was created in 1971 and, since that date, it has been extensively used in international research projects [15]. It contains information about the exact location of all the atoms in more than 195,565 protein structures identified by a four-letter alphanumeric code. The structures are determined using different methods—e.g., electron microscopy, X-ray diffraction—and coded using a file format, considering information as name and function of the protein, the organism to which it belongs, crystallographic properties, quality of the structure, bibliographic references of the study, classification.

One of the most used notations concerning which the proteins contained in PDB can benefit is the textual notation. Each line protein is called a record; the different types of records are arranged in a specific order to describe a structure. Listing 1 reports an excerpt of the PDB structure of the Ferric Horse Heart Myoglobin; H64V/V67R Mutant (PDB code: 3HEN) [16].

Listing 1. PDB code: 3HEN protein file excerpt.

```
HEADER      OXYGEN TRANSPORT                        09-MAY-09   3HEN
TITLE       FERRIC HORSE HEART MYOGLOBIN; H64V/V67R MUTANT
COMPND      MOL_ID: 1;
COMPND     2 MOLECULE: MYOGLOBIN;
SOURCE     2 ORGANISM_SCIENTIFIC: EQUUS CABALLUS;
SOURCE     3 ORGANISM_COMMON: DOMESTIC HORSE, EQUINE;
SEQRES     1 A  153  GLY LEU SER ASP GLY GLU TRP GLN GLN VAL LEU ASN VAL
SEQRES     2 A  153  TRP GLY LYS VAL GLU ALA ASP ILE ALA GLY HIS GLY GLN
SEQRES     3 A  153  GLU VAL LEU ILE ARG LEU PHE THR GLY HIS PRO GLU THR
SEQRES     4 A  153  LEU GLU LYS PHE ASP LYS PHE LYS HIS LEU LYS THR GLU
SEQRES     5 A  153  ALA GLU MET LYS ALA SER GLU ASP LEU LYS LYS VAL GLY
SEQRES     6 A  153  THR ARG VAL LEU THR ALA LEU GLY GLY ILE LEU LYS LYS
SEQRES     7 A  153  LYS GLY HIS HIS GLU ALA GLU LEU LYS PRO LEU ALA GLN
SEQRES     8 A  153  SER HIS ALA THR LYS HIS LYS ILE PRO ILE LYS TYR LEU
SEQRES     9 A  153  GLU PHE ILE SER ASP ALA ILE ILE HIS VAL LEU HIS SER
SEQRES    10 A  153  LYS HIS PRO GLY ASP PHE GLY ALA ASP ALA GLN GLY ALA
SEQRES    11 A  153  MET THR LYS ALA LEU GLU LEU PHE ARG ASN ASP ILE ALA
SEQRES    12 A  153  ALA LYS TYR LYS GLU LEU GLY PHE GLN GLY
ATOM       1  N   GLY A  1      -1.476  41.015 -11.482  1.00 40.53           N
ATOM       2  CA  GLY A  1      -2.113  40.213 -12.574  1.00 40.50           C
ATOM       3  C   GLY A  1      -1.163  40.052 -13.757  1.00 38.97           C
ATOM       4  O   GLY A  1      -0.026  40.555 -13.734  1.00 40.91           O
```

As an example, each ATOM record represents the location, represented by x, y, z orthogonal coordinates, occupancy and temperature factor of each atom of the protein. HELIX and SHEET indicate the location and type of helices or sheet in the secondary structure. SEQRES, instead, contains the primary sequence of amino acids that belong to the protein.

2.2. Random Forest and MLP

The RF technique, extension of the construction approach of decision trees, belongs to the class of Average Ensemble methods [17]. The idea is based on the construction of several different independent estimators and, for all of them, to calculate an average of all predictions. The combined estimator indeed is often better than any single estimator, since it will have a reduced variance.

To overcome the limits of the perceptron, a more complex structure was introduced. One or more intermediate levels were added within Neural Networks, creating a class called Multilayer Perceptron Neural Network (MLP) [18]. The new model has three layers: input layer, output layer and hidden layer; in these networks, the signals travel from the input layer to the output layer and therefore they are also called multi-layer feedforward networks. Each neuron, in a generic layer, is connected with all those of the next layer, so the propagation of the signal occurs forward in an acyclic way and without transverse connections.

2.3. The Eli-5 Tool

The most controversial aspect of using MLP concerns the problem of the network behaviour interpretability. Neural Networks have always been considered like a sort of black box: they use an advanced technique in pattern recognition based on a strong algorithm of optimization, but they are not based on a structured model, so their results have to be explained. Eli-5 is a Python library that allows one to rebuilt the network behaviour using the Mean Decrease Accuracy algorithm [19–21]. This algorithm is based on the calculation and comparison of several scores achieved by the network in data prediction during some training, each of which is performed without a particular feature of the dataset. At the end of the algorithm, every feature will have its score of importance in the prediction of the target variable; that is, the higher it is, the lower the score of prediction performed by the network without that feature in the dataset. The only con of this algorithm is the required computational cost because it needs retraining of the network for each feature of the dataset.

3. Description of the Methodology

Figure 1 sketches the schema of the methodology followed.

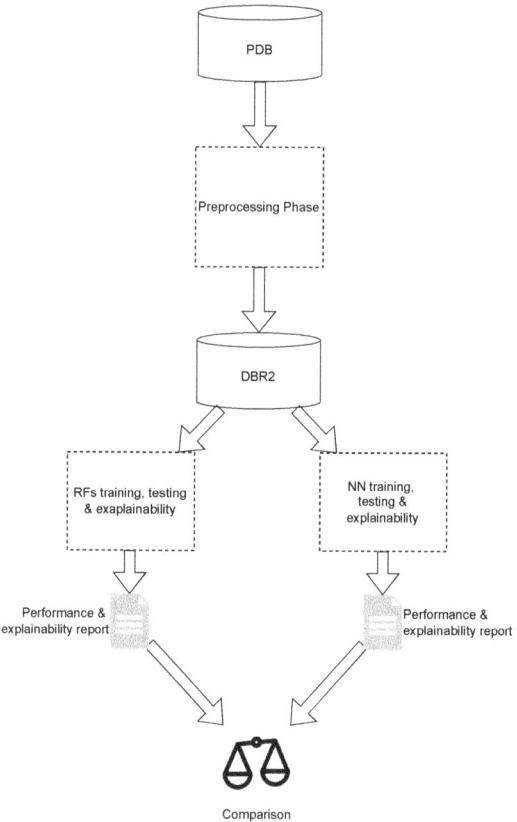

Figure 1. The schema of the methodology.

The main goal of this paper is comparing different analysis techniques in a particular case of study, in the field of bioinformatics. To pursue such goal, it is necessary to understand the background, explained in Section 2. The first phase concerns the study of the whole PDB, performing a qualitative analysis to define the subset of such a database that is the subject of the study.

The second phase sees a set of pre-processing tasks oriented to engineer and organize data from the PDB to extract the most meaningful features for the proposed analysis. The most meaningful tasks of such a phase are the definition and the design of a relational data base (DB) schema, the extraction and population processes oriented to import data from PDB files into such a DB, the transformation of such data to extract geometrical features. The tools used to face these challenges are the DBMS PostgreSQL and the Python libraries BioPython [22] and DSSP [23]. The technical details and the results of such a phase are reported in Section 4. Such results are contained in the Rosy and Roberta Database (DBR^2) database (both schema and instance).

Then the third phase involves two parallel activities that use the feature set defined during the first phase, to train two different amino acid volume predictors: the first using the RF model and the second using the MLP. Both the models are trained and tested starting from data contained in DBR^2 and all the details are explained in Section 5. On the trained model, explainability tools are used to obtain the most important features. The results of these activities are contained in two performance and explainability reports.

The final step of the approach consists in a comparison between the two methods, discussing the differences and the common points. Section 6 is devoted to this step.

4. From PDB to Geometrical Data

4.1. Data Preparation Process

In a general overview of the work done, the collection of the initial data and the careful study of these constitute the most important starting point. In this case study, information comes from the same source, the PDB. It was decided to focus on a particular biological family of proteins: the myoglobins. The initial design phase produces a conceptual schema, implemented in the form of a physical schema. The first population is based on data extraction from PDB files, using the Python library called BioPython. Then, an appropriate geometric model is constructed to describe the spatial properties of the protein primary sequence. Using this model, data are manipulated to proceed with a second population. Figure 2 illustrates these steps.

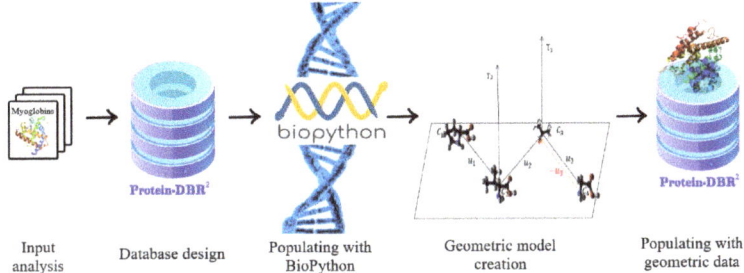

Figure 2. Process to realize the database management system.

4.2. Protein Geometrical Modelling

This study is based on a mathematical model designed for the description and prediction of the spatial structure of a protein. New mathematical tools were introduced to adequately represent one-dimensional and three-dimensional structures of proteins, so these can be regarded as mathematical objects. For further details or explanations, please refer to the publication [10,12].

As is well known, the notion of curvature is characteristic of continuous curves; in this particular case, it was necessary to introduce a discretized version of this parameter for the interpretation of a protein in its natural configuration as a folded chain. Thanks to this, it was possible to re-define torsion as a vectorial product between two curvatures as follows:

Definition 1. $\forall h \in (1, \ldots, n-1)$ consider the box B_h of the h-th amino acid s_p^h of a given protein P. The geometric centre vector:

$$C_h \equiv \left(\frac{x_i^* + x_{*i}}{2}, \frac{y_i^* + y_{*i}}{2}, \frac{z_i^* + z_{*i}}{2} \right) \quad (1)$$

is related to the α-Carbon position in the residue.

The vector that links geometric centres of two following amino acids s_p^h, s_p^{h+1} is given by:

$$\mathbf{u}_h \equiv C_{h+1} - C_h \equiv \quad (2)$$

$$\equiv \left(\frac{x_{h+1}^* + x_{*h+1}}{2} - \frac{x_h^* + x_{*h}}{2}, \frac{y_{h+1}^* + y_{*h+1}}{2} - \frac{y_h^* + y_{*h}}{2}, \frac{z_{h+1}^* + z_{*h+1}}{2} - \frac{z_h^* + z_{*h}}{2} \right)$$

So now it is possible to define curvature and torsion as follows:

Definition 2. For any $h \in (1, \ldots, n-1)$, the vector:

$$\mathbf{K_h} = \mathbf{u_{h-1}} \times \mathbf{u_h} \qquad (3)$$

is called **vectorial curvature** of the h-th amino acid of P.

Definition 3. For any $h \in (1, \ldots, n-1)$, the vector:

$$\mathbf{T_h} = \mathbf{K_h} \times \mathbf{K_{h+1}} \qquad (4)$$

is called **vectorial torsion** related to amino acid couple (s_P^h, s_P^{h+1}) of the h-th and (h+1)-th amino acids of P.

This theory allows one to obtain the necessary information on the geometric structure of each consecutive amino acid quadruplet of a given protein P:

- Three distances $|C_i - C_{i+1}|, i \in \{h-1, h, h+1\}$;
- The angles φ_h, φ_{h+1} determined by the vectors joining the centres;
- The angle θ_h corresponding to the two curvature vectors.

4.3. DBR² Scheme Definition

For the composition of an appropriate relational scheme, the use of a mixed strategy was chosen, combining the advantages of the top-down strategy with those of the bottom-up strategy. As a result of several phases of refinement, the Entity-Relationship (E-R) scheme realized is shown in Figure 3.

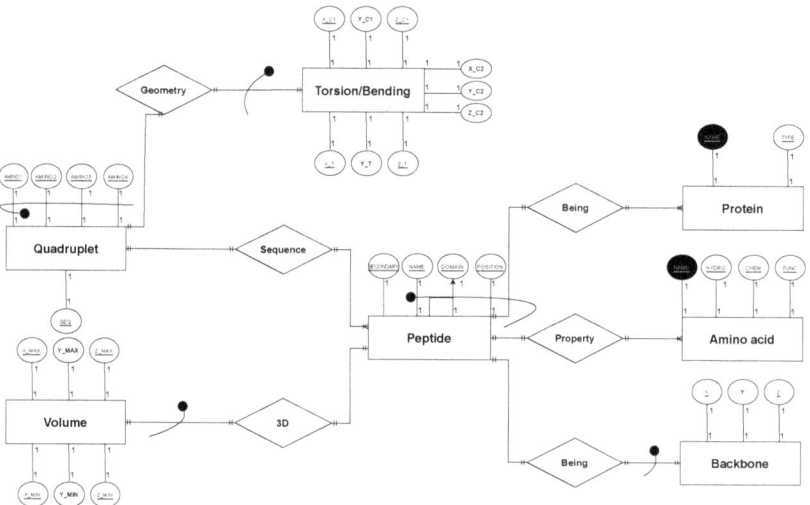

Figure 3. DBR2 ER scheme.

It shows a principal entity (Peptide) related to another six entities, four of these introducing geometric properties and mathematical models—these properties are fully described in [12] (Volume, Quadruplet, Torsion/Bending and Backbone)—and the other two describing amino acids' properties (Protein and Amino acid).

Moving from a conceptual to a logical schema is quite straightforward. The translation generates a schema composed of seven tables, as reported in Figure 4.

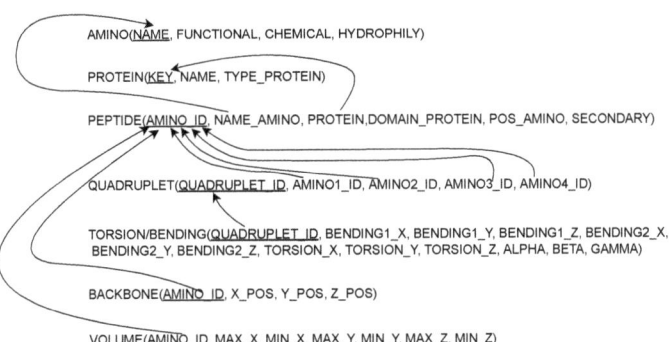

Figure 4. Conceptual scheme translation in logical scheme.

The last step consists of a physical implementation of the database called DBR^2 using PostGreSQL.

It is necessary to clarify an aspect of this implementation: as the logical scheme shows, the entity `Quadruplet` is linked to the entity `Peptide` using four foreign key constraints, but these are not implemented in the physical scheme. This choice is taken into account to avoid an error of referential integrity constraint violation due to a particular manipulation of control flows established while populating the database to simplify the operations. Indeed, the record related to the i-th amino of the chain is put in table `Peptide`, but during the same iteration of the 'for' cycle the record is also inserted that shows the i-th amino as the first of the quadruplet, and consequently the codes of the aminos (i+1)-th, (i+2)-th, (i+3)-th are required for this record, even if they have not already been inserted in the principle table `Peptide`.

4.4. DBR^2 Instance Population

The populating procedure has been very well articulated as shown in Figure 5. The number of the required steps is huge, as well as the processed items.

As already mentioned, population starts with the selection of the PDB files, available online at https://www.rcsb.org/ (accessed on 28 December 2022). As previously mentioned, the selection considers 446 Myoglobin proteins, and they are parsed one by one through the BioPython library. Thus, protein secondary structures are extracted from PDB files. Once all the information has been collected, they are inserted in the DBR^2. The information of interest is extracted to populate all the tables: `Protein`, `Peptide`, `Backbone`, `Volume` and `Quadruplet`. The remaining table `Torsion/Bending` is populated through several queries and calculations returning the geometrical parameter values. All these issues are addressed using the tool described earlier, following the schema described in Figure 5. This phase required a great effort and it is necessary to pursue the goal of the paper; since the data as initially presented in PDB show a lot of information that is not useful for our purposes and are not well interconnected to each other, it is not possible to easily manipulate them and represent the geometric model formulated. Therefore, it is necessary to use a software to simplify the manipulation of the data and the construction of the datasets for the analysis.

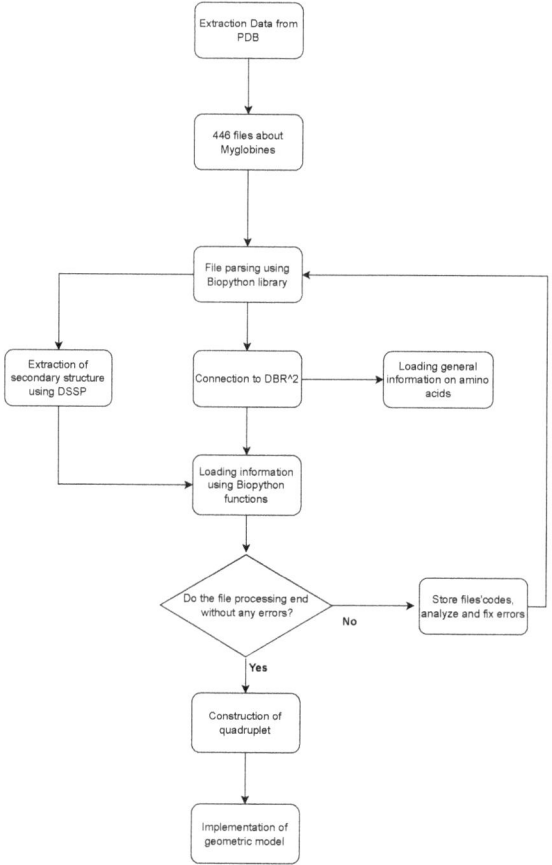

Figure 5. Illustrative schema of the DBR^2 population procedure.

5. Building the ML Models

5.1. Experiment Description

To conduct an analysis on DBR^2, it was necessary to build some additional tables, in which data were grouped and arranged in a way in which they could be more easily analyzed. It was decided to not insert such tables into the database schema but rather to store them in Comma Separated Value (CSV) files, processed through libraries offered by Python language, in subsequent scripts. The initial phase provides for the choice of features to be analyzed: in this case study, the target variable is the **amino acid volume**. The idea is to determine the different characteristics on which it depends. The fixed amino acid to be analyzed is named *Amino acid 0 (AA_0)*.

The features of interest are:

- Volume of the amino acid located in position $-3, -2, -1, 1, 2, 3$ from AA_0;
- Functional class of the amino acid located in position $-3, -2, -1, 1, 2, 3$ from AA_0;
- Chemical class of the amino acid located in position $-3, -2, -1, 1, 2, 3$ from AA_0;
- Hydrophilic class of the amino acid located in position $-3, -2, -1, 1, 2, 3$ from AA_0;
- Relative position of AA_0 in the chain;
- Norm of the 1st and 2nd curvature of the quadruplet in which AA_0 is in position 1;
- Norm of the 1st and 2nd curvature of the quadruplet in which AA_0 is in position 4;
- Norm of the torsion of the quadruplet in which AA_0 is in position 1;
- Norm of the torsion of the quadruplet in which AA_0 is in position 4;

- Volume of AA_0

At a later stage, the dataset is extended considering also the properties of the amino acids that reside in AA_0, comprising six and then nine residues that precede and follow it. To better clarify which are the features selected, how they have been processed and what is their geometrical meaning, it is possible to analyze the following schema Figure 6. Here is shown, as an example, what the steps are that allow one to populate the CSV file for the analyses. In this example, the amino acid Aspartic Acid (ASP) was considered in all the primary structures loaded in DBR^2. In particular, during STEP 1, the algorithm will detect its presence in the protein PDB code: 3HEN Listing 1, in position 4/153, 20/153 and so on. Then, in STEP 2, for each of these occurrences, the algorithm will also detect the two quadruplets—i.e., those in which ASP is in first and last position—and subsequently, during STEP 3, it will extract the geometrical features—according to the model presented in [12]—and the biological ones. Finally, in STEP 4, for every occurrence of ASP, a row, including all the information extracted, will be added to the CSV file.

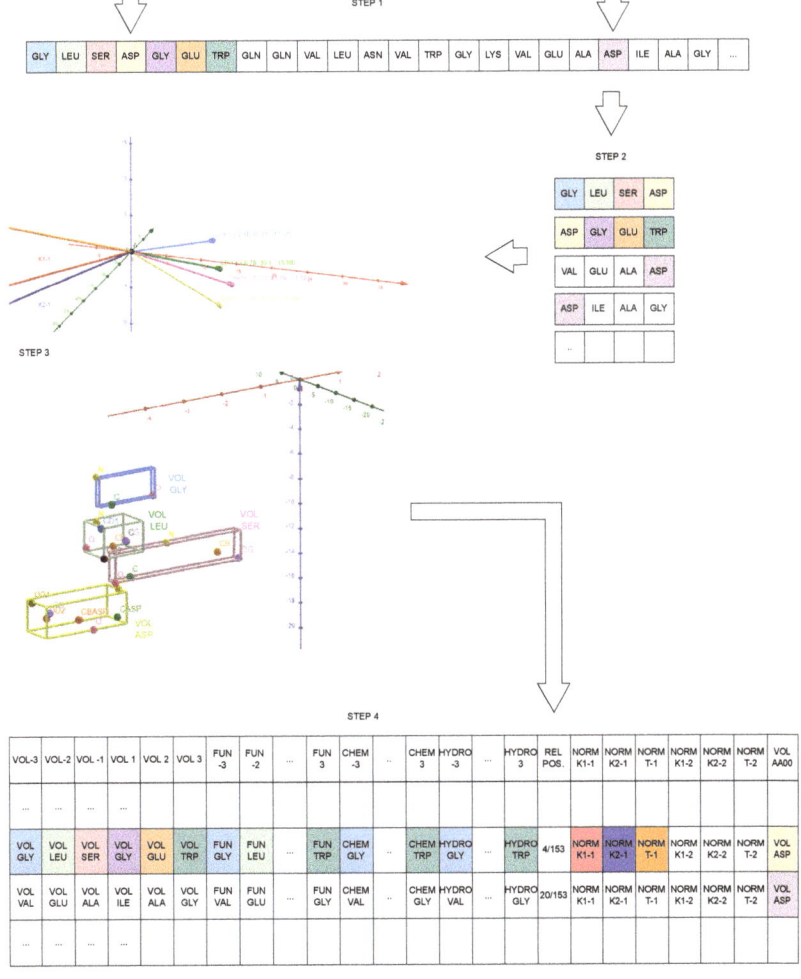

Figure 6. The schema of the dataset construction. The colors of the cells highlight the connection between the amino acids and the relative features with the same colors.

5.1.1. Lysine Analysis

Initially, attention was paid, for statistical and computational reasons, to the most frequent amino acid found in the myoglobins: lysine (LYS).

5.1.2. All Aminos, Separated

At the end of this phase, in order to make the analysis more complete, to generalize the results, obtained for LYS, to all the amino acids and to test the calculation capabilities of the server used, new CSV files are generated, one for each of the 20 amino acids. In all, repeating the same procedure described, 60 tables were created to conduct the analysis. In other words, for each amino acid—whatever it is, not only the Lysine—three files were analyzed, storing features of the residues in its surroundings, including the 3, 6 and 9 that precede and follow it.

5.1.3. All Aminos

Finally, the same approach was applied to create a unique big CSV file that stores the described information about all the amino acids of each myoglobin, without subdividing them. For reason of computational costs, this kind of analysis is limited to the features of three residues that precede and follow every AA_0.

5.2. Analyzing Data with RF

To ensure a high network performance, a preliminary analysis was conducted on the parameters of the algorithm. An automatic model generally has several parameters that are not trained by the learning set and they control the accuracy of the model. Thanks to the `GridSearchCV()` function of the SKlearn library, it is possible to train the model on a grid built combining the different parameters with each other in all possible ways to find the best match of them, assuring the highest accuracy on target variable prediction.

This test was repeated for all the datasets described:

- Table that contains features about 3 amino acids preceding and following LYS;
- Table that contains features about 6 amino acids preceding and following LYS;
- Table that contains features about 9 amino acids preceding and following LYS;
- Table that contains features about 3 amino acids preceding and following each residue;

Of course, the kinds of parameters depend on the algorithm considered.

In the case of RF, it was decided to train the model by varying:

- The number of estimators: Random Forest trees may vary from 50 to 500, with step 10;
- The depth of the tree: the maximum number of children from root to node further leaf, can range from 5 to 12. The value None was also attached to the list, which means default maximum depth was not chosen.

For each parameter combination, the `evaluate()` function returns the model accuracy, so is possible to detect the best combination, Listing 2 presents such a situation.

Listing 2. RF hyperparameter optimization results.

```
LYS-3: {'max_depth': None, 'n_estimators': 300}
    Model Performance
    Average Error: 9.1795 degrees.
    Accuracy = 81.75%

LYS-6 : {'max_depth': None, 'n_estimators': 300}
    Model Performance
    Average Error: 8.6356 degrees.
    Accuracy = 82.04%

LYS-9: {'max_depth': None, 'n_estimators': 300}
    Model Performance
    Average Error: 8.5398 degrees.
    Accuracy = 83.39%
```

Since this process is long and expensive, the tuning of the hyperparameters was carried out only on the Lysine tables. It was chosen, however, to evaluate the model with the fixed hyperparameters obtained on Lysine, on all other tables. This process has reported excellent results in terms of accuracy, shown in Table 1:

Table 1. Table showing that for every amino acids the results, in terms of accuracy and average error, were performed training the RF with the hyperparameters found with the stress test.

Amino Acids	Features about 3 Amino Acids Preceding and Following AA_0		Features about 6 Amino Acids Preceding and Following AA_0		Features about 9 Amino Acids Preceding and Following AA_0	
	Average Error	Accuracy	Average Error	Accuracy	Average Error	Accuracy
GLY	0.5385	75.54%	0.5151	70.97%	0.4468	78.68%
ALA	0.7402	93.28 %	0.6254	93.97 %	0.6009	94.01%
VAL	1.8636	92.94%	1.4999	94.18%	1.5162	93.98%
LEU	2.8407	93.65%	2.5713	94.23%	2.4643	94.42%
ILE	2.6804	93.02%	2.4010	93.74%	2.2002	94.25%
MET	3.8676	92.29%	2.8892	94.59%	3.0405	94.29%
SER	1.0704	93.76%	1.0899	93.05%	1.0885	93.25%
PRO	1.6259	91.33%	1.4459	92.46%	1.3758	92.71%
THR	1.6654	93.65%	1.4738	94.31%	1.4648	94.33%
CYS	4.3423	71.34%	3.4113	77.39%	1.6509	93.66%
ASN	2.4039	93.87%	2.0666	94.81%	1.8991	94.69%
GLN	5.9150	88.48%	4.4296	91.30%	5.1124	91.34%
PHE	4.6112	93.14%	3.5674	94.76%	3.4181	94.65%
TYR	5.1439	94.54%	4.0024	95.63%	4.6987	95.48%
TRP	4.8437	95.60%	4.3107	95.98%	4.2929	95.80%
LYS	9.1833	81.72%	8.5886	82.15%	8.5366	83.39%
HIS	3.3231	93.25%	3.1346	93.60%	2.8392	94.33%
ARG	10.5045	69.72%	10.1136	68.02%	10.1957	68.46%
ASP	2.8097	92.15%	2.5156	93.04%	2.5252	93.00%
GLU	5.2578	88.68%	5.1794	88.16%	4.9968	89.58%

In a first approach to the analysis, through the use of RF, it was chosen to predict the volume of each occurrence of 8821 Lysine stored in DBR^2, using features as its relative position within the chain, volumes and functional, chemical and hydrophilic properties of the 3, 6 or 9 previous and subsequent amino acids.

The created function, `random_forest(csvfilename)`, requires as input name the ray value of the AA_0 around it to be analyzed. Using the `train_test_split()` function allows splitting the dataset into a training set and a test set; in particular, having set the value of the parameter test size on 0.25, 70% of the set will be devoted to training and 30% to phase testing. After training the regressor on the training set, the `predict` method uses the predictor on the X_test to derive the y_test and, by means of the `evaluate()` function, the goodness of the model is estimated. In addition to the information on the goodness of the model, other information was searched for and saved: mean absolute error (MAE), mean squared error (MSE), root mean squared error (RMSE), the minimum between the max_depth of the RF trees, its number of nodes and arcs, the iterations made and the time taken to calculate such details. Listing 3 reports this case.

Because hyperparameter research led to the choice of training the regressor without imposing conditions on the maximum depth of forest decision trees, the graphical representation of the latter is very complicated: it is not presented in this paper, even if all the material can be sourced from the supplementary section of the paper and downloaded from the GitHub repository.

Listing 3. RF performance results.

```
LYS-3 {'max_depth': None, 'n_estimators': 300}:
    Average Error: 9.1833 degrees.
    Accuracy = 81.72%.
    Means absolute error    9.183323451548308
    Means squared error    186.71606785645264
    Root means squared error    13.664408800107402
    Minimum max depth of tree = 30
    16737 nodes 25068 edges 8420 iter 13.43~sec

LYS-6 {'max_depth': None, 'n_estimators': 300}:
    Average Error: 8.5886 degrees.
    Accuracy = 82.15%.
    Means absolute error    8.588595380071665
    Means squared error    166.42968189426642
    Root means squared error    12.900762841563534
    Minimum max depth of tree = 32
    16789 nodes 25137 edges 8155 iter 13.78~sec

LYS-9 {'max_depth': None, 'n_estimators': 300}:
    Average Error: 8.5366 degrees.
    Accuracy = 83.39%.
    Means absolute error    8.536609032254626
    Means squared error    165.80542920374762
    Root means squared error    12.876545701536093
    Minimum max depth of tree = 31
    14937 nodes 22372 edges 7057 iter 8.21 sec
```

5.3. Analyzing Data with MLP

The first step, mandatory to ensuring a high accuracy, is the hyperparameter research, as described in Section 5.2. In the case of MLP, it was decided to train the network by varying:

- The size of the hidden layers, from 100 to 1000 with step 300;
- The activation function, deleting from the grid those that did not carry, in any case, to the algorithm convergence;
- The solver, choosing the one compatible with the activation functions defined;
- The maximum number of iterations, from 100 to 1000 with step 200.

At the end of the process, the best_estimator() function returns the best combination detected, reported in Listing 4.

Listing 4. MLP hyperparameter optimization results.

```
LYS-3
    Parameters:
    {'activation': logistic, 'hidden_layer_sizes': 700,
    'max_iter':900, 'solver': 'adam'}
    Accuracy = 79.22%

LYS-6
    Parameters:
    {'activation': logistic, 'hidden_layer_sizes': 700,
    'max_iter':900, 'solver': 'adam'}
    Accuracy = 80.35%

LYS-9
    Parameters:
    {'activation': logistic, 'hidden_layer_sizes': 700,
    'max_iter':900, 'solver': 'adam'}
    Accuracy = 81.27%
```

This test required an expensive computational effort and an hour and half of computing for every file, but it was necessary to ensure the best fit to the algorithm. For this reason, the same approach used for RF was performed: it was chosen to apply the hyperparameters found for the LYS to all the amino acids to avoid performing the stress test many times, even because the results of accuracy reached were reasonable, as expected. The results are shown in Table 2.

Table 2. MLP performance table.

Amino Acids	Features about 3 Amino Acids Preceding and Following AA_0		Features about 6 Amino Acids Preceding and Following AA_0		Features about 9 Amino Acids Preceding and Following AA_0	
	Average Error	Accuracy	Average Error	Accuracy	Average Error	Accuracy
GLY	0.4813	74.08%	1.5946	30.03%	1.6121	10.36%
ALA	0.6569	93.62%	2.1218	78.64%	1.8956	80.09%
VAL	1.7685	93.14%	4.8140	80.44%	4.1212	83.52%
LEU	3.2014	92.66%	6.8586	85.08%	6.7312	84.92%
ILE	2.6705	92.96%	6.8473	82.38%	6.8182	82.39%
MET	4.1665	92.59%	7.8958	84.33%	7.6145	86.10%
SER	1.0998	93.36%	2.7085	83.28%	2.8237	82.77%
PRO	1.5146	92.02%	3.9080	79.57%	3.7529	81.58%
THR	1.7111	93.39%	3.8131	85.29%	3.7133	85.47%
CYS	1.2494	95.18%	3.4752	80.31%	2.0410	91.85%
ASN	2.1876	93.87%	4.1435	89.31%	3.9476	89.00%
GLN	5.6628	90.25%	11.1820	77.89%	10.7624	81.91%
PHE	3.8403	94.11%	11.4726	83.08%	12.1458	81.15%
TYR	7.1454	93.21%	12.9676	86.32%	14.0738	85.72%
TRP	5.5169	94.84%	15.7977	85.43%	8.6417	91.98%
LYS	9.4384	81.81%	16.5806	67.33%	15.6154	70.29%
HIS	3.3458	93.27%	8.5671	83.00%	7.5599	85.21%
ARG	10.2835	71.13%	17.4146	60.54%	15.9363	61.93%
ASP	2.7899	92.36%	5.6960	84.28%	5.1691	85.76%
GLU	5.4416	88.77%	10.4980	78.21%	9.7335	79.30%

6. Explainability Analysis and Discussion

6.1. Lysine Analysis

As mentioned in Section 5.1, the first step of the analysis is focused on training the two analysis algorithms on the files concerning the LYS. This script requires a parameter input, which can be '3', '6' or '9'.

In fact, based on this choice, one of the three files related to the LYS—containing the characteristics of the 3, 6 or 9 amino acids, respectively, previous and subsequent—are processed. The first instructions aim to select the features to be considered, based on the input indicated. In the case of using MLP, after training the network, to determine the feature importance, it was necessary to use the Python tool Eli-5 to rebuild the network behaviour as described in Section 2.3. The results of this stage are three graphs for both the methods, which show which characteristics most influence the prediction of the Lysine volume, assigning them a score of importance between 0 and 1.

The graph resulting from the analysis with RF shows a close dependence of the Lysine volume on the volumes of the surrounding amino acids. The same conclusions can be drawn even using the MLP algorithm. In addition, the increase in the number of surrounding amino acids considered confirms this pattern, at least in the case of Lysine, considering the results of analysis on files with the features of 6 and 9 residues around it.

However, there is a certain influence of the relative position feature in the prediction of the target variable. This sharp prevalence of volumes has caused some suspicions. A transitive dependence has been proposed: such volumes could depend on a third characteristic, which in this type of approach, however, does not emerge clearly and is put in the background.

Therefore, a speculative analysis was proposed, considering all the amino acids, in order to generalize the conclusions reached for the LYS and also to repeat the procedure, but eliminating all data concerning the volumes of the surrounding amino acids.

6.2. All Aminos, Separated

In order to dive deeply into the studies conducted on Lysine, it was immediately proposed to repeat the same procedure on each amino acid. The only difference involved in relation to the code allowing the analysis of the LYS is the introduction of an additional function that allows one to process one amino acid at a time rather simply by running a cycle. In the present case, it was decided not to use the graphic presentation of the results, because producing 20 different graphs does not make it easy to understand and compare them. It was decided to keep the scores of the six most important features for each amino acid and store them in a table containing the columns MAE, MSE and RMSE. These tables are present in the Supplementary Materials. From a careful analysis of these results, the volumes of the surrounding amino acids always emerge as the features that strongly influence the prediction of the target variable; however, it is possible to underline some different conclusions drawn using the two different methods. The results of the analysis carried out with RF lead to the following considerations:

- When the amino acid is considered in its configuration with three previous and subsequent residues, the variable that most affects the prediction is always one of the volumes of the surrounding residues, except in the case of aspartic acid in which the chemical property of a residue emerges previously. The following variables also apply for the greater part of the volumes.
- Even considering the information on the six residues prior to and after the AA_0, the volumes are the features that mostly influence the prediction. However, in the case of Aspartic Acid and Glutamine, their relative position in the chain acquires the role of main Features Importance (FI).
- Finally, considering a round of the AA_0 of 9 amino acid ray, the analysis reports, again, as first FI, one of the volumes of the surrounding amino acids, for almost all residues. In the case of aspartic acid and cysteine, in fact, the relative position is confirmed as the main FI and in the case of isoleucine the functional characteristic is of one of the following residues.

Despite that, something different emerges from the results of MLP analysis:

- When the amino acid is considered in its configuration with three previous and subsequent residues, the variable that most affects the prediction is always one of the volumes of the surrounding residues, with an exception made for cystein which shows the highest score in prediction for the geometric feature torsion of the first quadruplet. The following FIs are also, for the most part, volumes, but features related to the geometry still emerge.
- Even when considering the information on the six residues prior to and after the AA_0, the volumes are the most influential features of the prediction. This is the case even with the greater impact as compared to the previous case. However, in the case of proline and serine, torsion of a quadruplet in the chain acquires the role of the main FI.
- Finally, considering the surroundings of the AA_0 of the 9 amino acid ray, the analysis confirms the pattern established by the previous cases, reporting, again, as first in FI, one of the volumes of the surrounding amino acids, for almost all residues, without any exceptions. The geometrical features seem to appear as the third or following, in the classification of FI.

Considering, therefore, the hypothesis of a multiple dependence, it has been decided to repeat the analyses, eliminating all the data relating to the volumes of the surrounding residues—be they 3, 6 or 9—from the features on which to train the network. Even in that case, some analogies and some differences come out from the comparison of the two approaches. The tables, obtained with RF and MLP analysis—presented in full in the Supplementary Materials—lead to the following considerations:

- On the one hand, the role of the relative position of the AA_0 stands out, as the main feature, showing its fundamental role in this type of analysis;
- On the other hand, contrary to what might be expected, the main FI that emerges when excluding volumes is not the characteristics of the amino acids (chemical, functional or hydrophobic), but the geometric ones, formulated ad hoc for the problem in examination. This has enhanced and supported the validity and correctness of the model created.

The results of MLP confirm the hypothesis, showing:

- Clear predominance of the geometric features related only to the torsion parameters, which decreases slightly only in the analysis of feature 9 residues in the surroundings.
- On the other hand, contrary to what might be expected—in complete disagreement with the same analysis conducted with RF—the other features that emerge when excluding volumes are not the other geometric characteristics—i.e., curvatures—but both relative position and the amino acid properties (chemical, functional or hydrophobic).

6.3. All Aminos

Considering only information about the three previous and subsequent amino acids from AA_0, the generated CSV file counted 68.613 rows and the analysis took several hours. Optimization of the hyperparameters, in the case of analysis with RF, produced the optimal accuracy in the case of max_depth = None and n_estimators = 200. With this setting, the RandomForestRegressor(), in a code completely analogous to the previous one, produced the following results:

```
TOT-3 {'max_depth': None, 'n_estimators': 200}:
    Average Error: 4.0070 degrees.
    Accuracy = 86.91%.
    Means absolute error:   4.010753088384853
    Means squared error:   62.97177931847423
    Root means squared error:   7.935475998229358
    Max_depth min =   42
    129749 nodes 194571 edges 70263 iter 1524.40 sec
```

As you can see, the accuracy is 86%, so you can consider the model very reliable. Also in this case, the FI are graphically represented. Concerning the analysis conducted with MLP, using the hyperparameters found with the stress test of Section 5.3, the degree of accuracy was lower but surely more than acceptable:

```
TOT-3: {'activation': 'logistic',
    'hidden_layer_sizes': 700, 'max_iter': 1000, 'solver': 'adam'}
    Average Error: 5.8446 degrees.
    Accuracy = 73.19%.
```

Both came to an unexpected and different conclusion from the previous one: the volume prediction of amino acid belonging to myoglobins, without distinction by type, is mostly influenced by its relative position within the domain. It reports a significantly higher score than that of the other features. It is clear that there is a close dependence of the volume of an amino acid on its relative position. All the characteristics concerning the volumes, indeed, have scores similar to each other, but barely more than half of the relative position. Despite what has been concluded for the relative position, this result is quite in disagreement with that reported in the analysis with RF, which shows a mix between volumes and amino acid chemical properties firmly among the first positions. As already happened at the end of the analysis carried out on the individual amino acids (see Section 6.2, second step comparison), curiosity has given rise to a final proposal for analysis. In complete analogy to the case study of the amino acids treated singularly, it was decided, in the end, to repeat the analysis, excluding the predominant feature: the relative position. Eliminating the main feature, will the volumes return to the top of the FI?

Using the optimal hyperparameters, the RF and the MLP, respectively, returned the following results:

```
TOT NO POS 3 {'max_depth': None, 'n_estimators': 200}:
    Average Error: 4.0616 degrees.
    Accuracy = 86.43%.
    Means absolute error:   4.07168620428757
    Means squared error:   64.37940508449833
    Root means squared error:   8.023677777958081
    Max_depth min =  42
    129765 nodes 194598 edges 69420 iter 1516.01 sec
```

```
TOT NO POS 3: {'activation': 'logistic',
    'hidden_layer_sizes': 700,'max_iter': 1000, 'solver': 'adam'}
    Average Error: 6.3096 degrees.
    Accuracy = 67.55%.
```

A key conclusion of FI was exactly the one expected. The results show that the main variables influencing volume prediction, using the RF model, excluding relative position, are still the volumes of the surrounding amino acids. Even the results obtained with MLP confirm the previous conclusions: there is a dependence of the volume of an amino acid from that of the surrounding residues. In this case, there is no clear distinction between the best feature score and that of the subsequent one. In addition, at volumes, the biological characteristics of amino acids and data related to torsion follow. This final result brought us to a twofold consideration:

- On one hand both, the models confirm the predominance of relative positions and volumes, so the main features seem to be well detached by the different approach.
- On the other hand, analysis with RF seems to underline the strength of the mathematical model; instead, analysis with MLP emphasizes the role of the torsion in determining the target variable and a quite significant impact of chemical properties.

7. Related Works

The scientific literature counts several works on eXplainable Artificial Intelligence (XAI): such works can be summarized in some comprehensive surveys, among which are [8,24].

While the comparison of ML approaches under the lens of performance and accuracy is a process that is quite often assessed in the scientific literature, there is a need for a unified and shared framework for measuring and comparing [25]. This need is motivated by the growing demand for a trustworthy AI [26]. Furthermore, the necessity of finding a good trade-off between accuracy and explainability is well known [27].

The present paper does not contribute to this theoretical discussion; rather, it presents a practical experience in determining the most meaningful features in a concrete, real-world case study; some of these papers are presented here.

- A comparative analysis of different Natural Language Processing (NLP) models in sentiment analysis of single domain Twitter messages [28]. In this paper, some ML models are analyzed and a comparison is made against classification accuracy and explainability capabilities.
- A study on the explainability in Deep Neural Network (DNN)s for image-based mammography analysis is reported in [29]. The paper makes a contribution with the introduction of an explainability method (named oriented, modified integrated gradients, OMIG) and its application to image analysis.
- The authors in [30] carry out a concrete analysis concerning the explainability of glaucoma prediction by merging the information coming from two different sources (tomography images and medical data).

The presented paper differs from the cited ones since it focuses on wide-ranging ML models and uses standard off-the-shelf technologies.

8. Conclusions and Future Developments

This paper presents a vertical experience, related to a biological problem, with a comparison between two mainstream ML models and explainability technologies.

The study confirms the presence of a trade-off between performance and explainability, as stated in [9]. RFs are highly explainable, while the accuracy of MLPs is better. The usage of the Eli-5 tool gives "non-natively explainable" formalisms—as MLPs—the same explainability power as other models. The usability of such a library is high.

As the discussion concerning the results of the experimentation reveals, there is a clear dependency of the predicted volume from the volumes of the surrounding amino acids and from its relative position in the chain, while there is not a meaningful dependency from the other geometrical features (e.g., torsion, bending, etc.). These features, of course, are expected to enter in case there are other problems to tackle, e.g., predicting the protein shape.

Another valuable result is that there are not, for the considered problems, meaningful differences between the two considered classifiers: RFs and MLPs. Differences are expected to arise in cases of more challenging problems and for another kind of model, i.e., DNNs.

This, however, constitutes a valuable result concerning the understanding of the minor differences of the FI mechanisms: one present in RFs and the other one coming from the usage of eli-5.

This notwithstanding, the results reported in this paper are limited to the scope of the paper itself, which is a study of the effects of XAI techniques. Such limitations can be summarized as follows:

1. The members of the chosen protein family—i.e., myoglobin—are very similar in their sequences (85–99% identity): this similarity implies that trained predictors exhibit high performance that is not met in reality; Otherwise, it was decided to perform this kind of analysis—aware of such similarity—because all the proteins belonging to the same family have similar functions. This similitude is intentional and allows one to study how geometrical features can vary within a similar primary structure. Moreover, it is clear that this has no impact on the results: the most important features are not directly related to the primary structure but to an amino acid's properties and its relative position in the chain (there could be multiple within the same structure).
2. The present work is based on the mathematical model reported in [10], which has its limited scope and constraining hypotheses: in particular, it does not explicitly consider gaps in the protein structure and does not use sophisticated bioinformatics methods for the evaluation of the protein structure.

Concerning such limitations, the validity of the results of the work is minorly impacted, not only due to the above-mentioned limitation of the scope of the work. In fact, the high-performance baseline for the prediction algorithm can exalt the differences between the two approaches (the first point); furthermore, the used mathematical model is fast and facilitates the computation of the population of the database.

Future research efforts will be devoted to using other explainability tools and libraries. A more formal framework to measure the explainability of trained models will also be considered in further analyses.

Author Contributions: Conceptualization, S.M.; methodology, S.M.; validation, E.B. and S.M.; investigation, data curation, software R.D.F. and R.D.G.; writing, R.D.F., R.d.G., E.B. and S.M. All authors have read and agreed to the published version of the manuscript.

Funding: This research received no external funding.

Institutional Review Board Statement: Not applicable because the work does not involve the use of animals or humans.

Informed Consent Statement: Not applicable because the work does not involve the use of humans.

Data Availability Statement: All the material is available on GitHub repository: https://github.com/robidfz/ProteinAnalysis.

Acknowledgments: The authors wants to thank the anonymous reviewers who spent a great effort in improving the paper with their continuous and competent remarks.

Conflicts of Interest: The authors declare no conflict of interest.

Abbreviations/Code

The following abbreviations/codes are used in this manuscript:

3HEN	Ferric Horse Heart Myoglobin; H64V/V67R Mutant
AA_0	Amino acid 0
AI	Artificial Intelligence
CSV	Comma Separated Value
DBR^2	Rosy and Roberta Database
DNN	Deep Neural Network
FI	Features Importance
LYS	Lysine
MAE	mean absolute error
ML	Machine Learning
MLP	Multilayer Perceptron Neural Network
MSE	mean squared error
NLP	Natural Language Processing
NN	Neural Network
PDB	Protein Data Bank
RF	Random Forest
RMSE	root mean squared error
V&V	Verification & Validation
XAI	eXplainable Artificial Intelligence

References

1. Aceto, G.; Persico, V.; Pescapé, A. Industry 4.0 and Health: Internet of Things, Big Data and Cloud Computing for Healthcare 4.0. *J. Ind. Inf. Integr.* **2020**, *18*, 100129. [CrossRef]
2. Allam, Z.; Dhunny, Z.A. On big data, Artificial Intelligence and smart cities. *Cities* **2019**, *89*, 80–91. [CrossRef]
3. El Sallab, A.; Abdou, M.; Perot, E.; Yogamani, S. Deep reinforcement learning framework for autonomous driving. *Electron. Imaging* **2017**, *2017*, 70–76. [CrossRef]
4. Murdoch, T.B.; Detsky, A.S. The inevitable application of big data to health care. *JAMA* **2013**, *309*, 1351–1352. [CrossRef] [PubMed]
5. Cao, L.; Tay, F.E. Support vector machine with adaptive parameters in financial time series forecasting. *IEEE Trans. Neural Netw.* **2003**, *14*, 1506–1518. [CrossRef] [PubMed]
6. Martinelli, F.; Marulli, F.; Mercaldo, F.; Marrone, S.; Santone, A. Enhanced Privacy and Data Protection using Natural Language Processing and Artificial Intelligence. In Proceedings of the 2020 International Joint Conference on Neural Networks (IJCNN), Glasgow, UK, 19–24 July 2020; pp. 1–8.
7. Antão, L.; Pinto, R.; Reis, J.; Gonçalves, G. Requirements for testing and validating the industrial internet of things. In Proceedings of the 2018 IEEE International Conference on Software Testing, Verification and Validation Workshops (ICSTW), Vasteras, Sweden, 9–13 April 2018; pp. 110–115. [CrossRef]
8. Zhou, J.; Gandomi, A.H.; Chen, F.; Holzinger, A. Evaluating the quality of Machine Learning explanations: A survey on methods and metrics. *Electronics* **2021**, *10*, 593. [CrossRef]
9. Barredo Arrieta, A.; Díaz-Rodríguez, N.; Del Ser, J.; Bennetot, A.; Tabik, S.; Barbado, A.; Garcia, S.; Gil-Lopez, S.; Molina, D.; Benjamins, R.; et al. Explainable Artificial Intelligence (XAI): Concepts, taxonomies, opportunities and challenges toward responsible AI. *Inf. Fusion* **2020**, *58*, 82–115. [CrossRef]
10. Vitale, F. On statistically meaningful geometric properties of digital three-dimensional structures of proteins. *Math. Comput. Model.* **2008**, *48*, 141–160. [CrossRef]
11. Vitale, F. A topology for the space of protein chains and a notion of local statistical stability for their three-dimensional structures. *Math. Comput. Model.* **2008**, *48*, 610–620. [CrossRef]
12. On a 3D-matrix representation of the tertiary structure of a protein. *Math. Comput. Model.* **2006**, *43*, 1434–1464. [CrossRef]
13. Gilpin, L.H.; Bau, D.; Yuan, B.Z.; Bajwa, A.; Specter, M.; Kagal, L. Explaining explanations: An overview of interpretability of machine learning. In Proceedings of the 2018 IEEE 5th International Conference on Data Science and Advanced Analytics (DSAA), Turin, Italy, 1–3 October 2018; pp. 80–89. [CrossRef]

14. Miller, T. Explanation in Artificial Intelligence: Insights from the social sciences. *Artif. Intell.* **2019**, *267*, 1–38. [CrossRef]
15. Berman, H.; Westbrook, J.; Feng, Z.; Gilliland, G.; Bhat, T.; Weissig, H.; Shindyalov, I.; Bourne, P. The Protein Data Bank. *Nucleic Acids Res.* **2000**, *28*, 235–242. [CrossRef] [PubMed]
16. Yi, J.; Heinecke, J.; Tan, H.; Ford, P.C.; Richter-Addo, G.B. The Distal Pocket Histidine Residue in Horse Heart Myoglobin Directs the O-Binding Mode of Nitrite to the Heme Iron. *J. Am. Chem. Soc.* **2009**, *131*, 18119–18128. [CrossRef] [PubMed]
17. Breiman, L. Random Forests. *Mach. Learn.* **2001**, *45*, 5–32. [CrossRef]
18. Nassif, A.B.; Ho, D.; Capretz, L.F. Towards an early software estimation using log-linear regression and a multilayer perceptron model. *J. Syst. Softw.* **2013**, *86*, 144–160. [CrossRef]
19. Kuzlu, M.; Cali, U.; Sharma, V.; Güler, Ö. Gaining insight into solar photovoltaic power generation forecasting utilizing explainable Artificial Intelligence tools. *IEEE Access* **2020**, *8*, 187814–187823. [CrossRef]
20. Sarp, S.; Knzlu, M.; Cali, U.; Elma, O.; Guler, O. An interpretable solar photovoltaic power generation forecasting approach using an explainable Artificial Intelligence tool. In Proceedings of the 2021 IEEE Power & Energy Society Innovative Smart Grid Technologies Conference (ISGT), Washington, DC, USA, 16–18 February 2021. [CrossRef]
21. Vij, A.; Nanjundan, P. Comparing Strategies for Post-Hoc Explanations in Machine Learning Models. *Lect. Notes Data Eng. Commun. Technol.* **2022**, *68*, 585–592. [CrossRef]
22. Cock, P.J.; Antao, T.; Chang, J.T.; Chapman, B.A.; Cox, C.J.; Dalke, A.; Friedberg, I.; Hamelryck, T.; Kauff, F.; Wilczynski, B.; et al. BioPython: Freely available Python tools for computational molecular biology and bioinformatics. *Bioinformatics* **2009**, *25*, 1422–1423. [CrossRef]
23. Touw, W.G.; Baakman, C.; Black, J.; Te Beek, T.A.H.; Krieger, E.; Joosten, R.P.; Vriend, G. A series of PDB-related databanks for everyday needs. *Nucleic Acids Res.* **2015**, *43*, D364–D368. [CrossRef]
24. Xu, F.; Uszkoreit, H.; Du, Y.; Fan, W.; Zhao, D.; Zhu, J. Explainable AI: A Brief Survey on History, Research Areas, Approaches and Challenges. In Proceedings of the CCF International Conference on Natural Language Processing and Chinese Computing, Dunhuang, China, 9–14 October 2019; Volume 11839 LNAI, pp. 563–574. [CrossRef]
25. De Mulder, W.; Valcke, P. The need for a numeric measure of explainability. In Proceedings of the 2021 IEEE International Conference on Big Data, Orlando, FL, USA, 15–18 December 2021; pp. 2712–2720. [CrossRef]
26. Bedué, P.; Fritzsche, A. Can we trust AI? An empirical investigation of trust requirements and guide to successful AI adoption. *J. Enterp. Inf. Manag.* **2022**, *35*, 530–549. [CrossRef]
27. London, A.J. Artificial Intelligence and Black-Box Medical Decisions: Accuracy versus Explainability. *Hastings Cent. Rep.* **2019**, *49*, 15–21. [CrossRef] [PubMed]
28. Fiok, K.; Karwowski, W.; Gutierrez, E.; Wilamowski, M. Analysis of sentiment in tweets addressed to a single domain-specific Twitter account: Comparison of model performance and explainability of predictions. *Expert Syst. Appl.* **2021**, *186*, 115771. [CrossRef]
29. Amanova, N.; Martin, J.; Elster, C. Explainability for deep learning in mammography image quality assessment. *Mach. Learn. Sci. Technol.* **2022**, *3*, 025015. [CrossRef]
30. Kamal, M.S.; Dey, N.; Chowdhury, L.; Hasan, S.I.; Santosh, K. Explainable AI for Glaucoma Prediction Analysis to Understand Risk Factors in Treatment Planning. *IEEE Trans. Instrum. Meas.* **2022**, *71*, 1–9. [CrossRef]

Disclaimer/Publisher's Note: The statements, opinions and data contained in all publications are solely those of the individual author(s) and contributor(s) and not of MDPI and/or the editor(s). MDPI and/or the editor(s) disclaim responsibility for any injury to people or property resulting from any ideas, methods, instructions or products referred to in the content.

Article

Justifying Arabic Text Sentiment Analysis Using Explainable AI (XAI): LASIK Surgeries Case Study

Youmna Abdelwahab *, Mohamed Kholief and Ahmed Ahmed Hesham Sedky

College of Computing, Arab Academy for Science, Technology, and Maritime Transport, Alexandria 1029, Egypt
* Correspondence: Youmna.Abdelfattah5@student.aast.edu

Abstract: With the increasing use of machine learning across various fields to address several aims and goals, the complexity of the ML and Deep Learning (DL) approaches used to provide solutions has also increased. In the last few years, Explainable AI (XAI) methods to further justify and interpret deep learning models have been introduced across several domains and fields. While most papers have applied XAI to English and other Latin-based languages, this paper aims to explain attention-based long short-term memory (LSTM) results across Arabic Sentiment Analysis (ASA), which is considered an uncharted area in previous research. With the use of Local Interpretable Model-agnostic Explanation (LIME), we intend to further justify and demonstrate how the LSTM leads to the prediction of sentiment polarity within ASA in domain-specific Arabic texts regarding medical insights on LASIK surgery across Twitter users. In our research, the LSTM reached an accuracy of 79.1% on the proposed data set. Throughout the representation of sentiments using LIME, it demonstrated accurate results regarding how specific words contributed to the overall sentiment polarity classification. Furthermore, we compared the word count with the probability weights given across the examples, in order to further validate the LIME results in the context of ASA.

Keywords: deep learning; LSTM; Arabic sentiment analysis; Explainable AI; text mining

Citation: Abdelwahab, Y.; Kholief, M.; Sedky, A.A.H. Justifying Arabic Text Sentiment Analysis Using Explainable AI (XAI): LASIK Surgeries Case Study. *Information* 2022, 13, 536. https://doi.org/10.3390/info13110536

Academic Editor: Gabriele Gianini

Received: 9 October 2022
Accepted: 8 November 2022
Published: 11 November 2022

Publisher's Note: MDPI stays neutral with regard to jurisdictional claims in published maps and institutional affiliations.

Copyright: © 2022 by the authors. Licensee MDPI, Basel, Switzerland. This article is an open access article distributed under the terms and conditions of the Creative Commons Attribution (CC BY) license (https://creativecommons.org/licenses/by/4.0/).

1. Introduction

In the last couple of years, machine learning approaches have been applied successfully throughout a wide range of applications, such as medical diagnostics, hospitality, and other domain-specific fields. While the associated models have been improving over time, the complexity of each model has also continued to increase. Furthermore, despite these models increasing in popularity, many still lack explanation. As has been stated in [1], the main purpose of applying XAI is to answer one or more of the main seven goals, including reliability, usability, trust, fairness, privacy, causality, and transparency. Therefore, XAI has been used across different deep learning models in order to further justify the proposed classification within a specific domain's functionality, as well as the overall reliability of Deep Learning and Machine Learning [2]. As previously stated, machine learning has been applied for various purposes. One such application—sentiment analysis—involves determining the polarity of a text as negative, neutral, or positive [3].

Throughout previous research, sentiment analysis has been applied through the use of ML and DL models for accurate polarity classification in different domains and languages. For example, in [4], the authors have proposed a sentiment analysis model to classify the polarity of customer reviews on a Chinese-based e-commerce website. They collected about 100,000 customer reviews to perform the testing and training. Meanwhile, in [5], the authors used sentiment analysis to measure the destination carrying capacity targeted at a specific city in Europe, using online reviews from TripAdvisor.

Even though most research papers have targeted the English language, some studies have considered Arabic text sentiment analysis (ASA) as well. In a previous review on ASA [6], it has been stated that ASA is challenging due to the different dialects and morphology of the Arabic language, as well as the imitation faced along the process. Some studies have been implemented in Arabic; for example, in [7], the authors implemented sentiment analysis to assess various Twitter data regarding COVID-19. The authors of this particular study used the proposed model as a precautionary measure, rather than a measure of being a potential COVID-19 patient, which was adjusted to predict the individual perceptions of Arabian users. In all of these studies, the researcher's main goal was to create an advanced model for the purpose of accurately classifying the polarity of text across social media services. The proposed models do not provide a comprehensible justification of how classification into different polarities is carried out. Therefore, some studies have begun to apply XAI methods to further justify the DL model results.

Throughout our previous works, several experiments have been carried out on several DL models across different sentiment levels, which led us to conclude that the attention-based LSTM has the best performance across the Arabic data set in terms of word-level sentiment analysis [8]. Therefore, in this paper, we propose the application of an XAI method—LIME—to the attention-based LSTM model on an Arabic text data set concerning LASIK surgeries across Twitter users. The general approach used in this study is depicted in Figure 1.

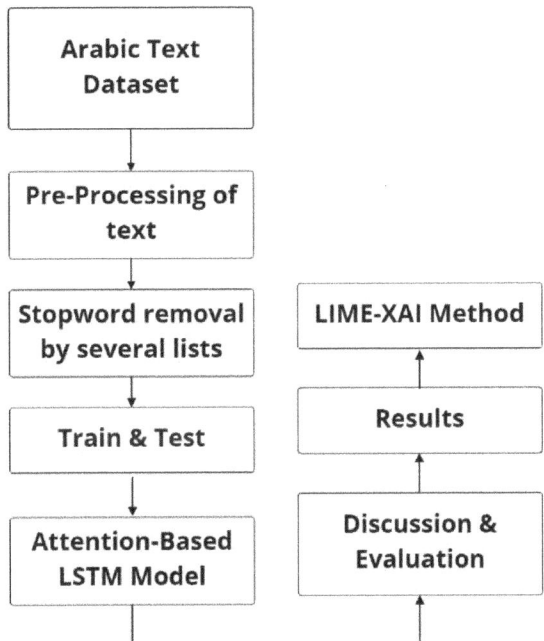

Figure 1. Flowchart of Applied Approach.

The remainder of this paper is structured as follows: In Section 2, we provide the literature review, while Section 3 gives the background related to this study. Section 4 details the methodology used. Finally, Sections 5 and 6 are dedicated to the discussion and conclusion, respectively.

2. Literature Review

In previous studies on sentiment analysis, the use of DL models has been proposed. For example, in [7], a DL model was developed for COVID-19-related tweets; however, this study lacked an XAI model to further interpret the model classification process. Meanwhile, the authors in [9] have proposed an XAI-based NB model to better explain the results for COVID-19, by looking at the symptoms that were disclosed in Twitter tweets based in

Turkey in order to determine the approximate numbers of infected people and predict possible virus breakouts. In [10], the authors have provided a comparison of the XAI methods LIME and LRP through simulatability tests on English text, which led to the conclusion that both methods can help in increasing the understanding of the DL model.

Moreover, XAI has been used across different domains; for example, in [11], XAI methods on ML combined with LSTM have been used to predict stocks and further explain the sentiments of headlines that influence users, using LIME to enhance stock prediction. Meanwhile, in [12], the researchers have used LIME and SHAP (Shapley Additive explanations) values to validate the features used in order to defend a specific sentiment polarity obtained by LSTM and hybrid LSTM-based models on customer reviews of food services during the COVID-19 crisis. In another study, they aimed to further explain the sentiments of Twitter users by using the XAI method LIME on a proposed BI-LSTM model, in order to interpret public perception in several domains [13]. Within the NLP domain, such a model has been used to detect sarcasm, due to its complexity within the English text data set, by applying LIME and SHAP values on an ensemble-supervised learning algorithm, in order to elaborate how the model with selected features detects whether the text contains sarcasm [14]. Meanwhile, the authors in [15] have aimed to classify IT jobs using attention-based LSTM and finalized their work by comparing the word frequency outcome with the LIME prediction, which led to the conclusion that LIME helped in discovering a new way of identifying job descriptions.

Moreover, the authors in [16] have used LIME to clearly justify the classification of source code vulnerability detection by applying both ML and DL models on LIME. This led to the conclusion that LIME works well in vulnerability detection, with the limitation of not identifying the second IF condition in a code sample. In [17], XAI has been utilized for the classification of offensive text across topics in Bangla, which resulted in a graphical presentation of the topics that contained the majority of the offensive text. Finally, in [18], the authors have utilized an XAI method to help in understanding why a tweet text would be considered xenophobic/racist, in order to prevent xenophobic acts or events. Throughout the previous studies across several domains, LIME was utilized and presented accurate results when paired with LSTM and attention-based LSTM when a low-resource language was used [17], or for the detection of racism [18]. According to [6], a lot of challenges are faced in ASA due to variant dialects and slang used across social media services, which makes it hard to emphasize which word has the largest contribution when considering the polarity of each sentiment. While most papers have aimed to use the LIME approach for their proposed LSTM model concerning different domains within the English language, due to the enormous number of data sets and accessible corpus (see Table 1), fewer studies have applied it to lower-resource languages, specifically Arabic text. Given that the overall performance of LIME in previous studies was promising, in terms of justifying DL models, enhancing human interpretation of the model, and indicating its important features, in this study we apply LIME to an Arabic text sentiment analysis approach. To the best of our knowledge, this paper is one of the first works to apply an XAI approach to Arabic text. This paper aims to do so by applying it to a domain-specific data set regarding LASIK surgery, further justifying the sentiment analysis classification by applying the XAI model LIME to justify why certain features have been specified to a particular polarity. This paper contributes to the area by applying XAI to Twitter, carrying out Arabic sentiment analysis using an Arabic text data set, as well as through the creation of a data set on LASIK surgery in Arabic text across Twitter users.

Table 1. Previous work in which LIME was applied to DL Models.

Reference	Year	Scope	Classifiers	XAI Algorithm	Accuracy
In Hyeok Choi et al. [15]	2020	IT Job classification	LSTM, Attention-based LSTM	LIME	76%/91%
Aljameel et al. [9]	2021	Predict the possible outbreak of COVID-19 patients in turkey	NB	Probabilistic methods	93.6%
Gite et al. [11]	2021	Stock Prediction	ML and LSTM	LIME	NA
Chowdhury et al. [13]	2021	Interpret Sentiments across several domains of Twitter users	BI-LSTM	LIME	72%
Kumar et al. [14]	2021	Detecting Sarcasm	XGBoost	SHAP, LIME	NA
Tang, G. et al. [16]	2021	Source code vulnerability detection	LR, DT, SVM, and Bi-LSTM.	LIME	NA
Rathore et al. [10]	2022	Better classification of tweets in the English language	ANN	LIME, LRP	85%/90%
Adak A et al. [12]	2022	Validate features used to defend a specific sentiment polarity on food reviews	LSTM, Bi-LSTM, Bi-Gru-LSTM-CNN	SHAP LIME	96.7%, 95.85%, 96.33%
Aporna et al. [17]	2022	Classifying offensive speech in Bangla text	SVM, CNN, Bi-LSTM, Conv-LSTM	Graphical representation	67%/73%/75%/78%

3. Background
3.1. XAI Tools

For the application of XAI across different fields and domains, the two most commonly used algorithms are LIME and SHAP. First, Local Interpretable Model-agnostic Explanation (LIME) is an open-source framework used to describe individual predictions of a machine learning model, first introduced in [19], which aimed to concentrate on the decision-making of complex ML algorithms and how humans can trust their predictions. Local means that the framework analyzes a specific observation. Interpretable means that the user should be able to understand the behavior of the model. Explanation indicates the output that the LIME framework produces. Meanwhile, Shapley Additive Explanation (SHAP) methods are used to describe how each feature affects the model and how it enables the global analysis of data sets, which is based on a game-theoretic approach, in order to explain the output of machine learning models [20]. ContrXT is a global proposed approach that traces the decision criteria of text classifiers by encoding changes in the decision logic and provides a global model agonistic Time contrastive explanation in natural language processing [21]. In this paper, they proposed a novel self-explaining architecture for neural network text classifiers based on both local and global interpretability in a single framework on sentences rather than words, which resulted in promising results [22]. In this paper, they proposed an approach to measure how correct the explanations provided by the local explanation method are in relation to the synthetic ground truth explanation. Experimental results demonstrate how the proposed approach can easily assess the local explanation of a site and characterize the quality of the local explanation method. Throughout their evaluation, this was tested across text, image and tabular data returning features and rules. The results of the local explanation of the word importance explanation on text stated that LIME extracts more stable explanation and resulted in higher recall and precision compared to SHAP. Moreover, the results returned the best explanation according to the words identified with respect to the number of words used as a vocabulary [23]. Additionally, the variations of dialects within the Arabic language that are used across the social media platforms will result in better explanation across the Arabic language.

Throughout previous works, we have observed that LIME works well with text data sets within the English language across different domains, which led to its usage in this research across Arabic text. LIME was chosen to further explain how the attention-based LSTM model classifies the polarity of ASA text, due to its nature as a Local Explainer, which is very helpful when using it across a language with a complex morphology and variant dialects. In the result, the representation can emphasize the importance of a word in a single sentiment and explain how it was classified as a specific polarity, which is important since—in the case of Arabic words—a lot of variance in meaning may occur across dialects.

3.2. LASIK Surgeries

LASIK is a form of refractive surgery that can correct vision in people with near-sightedness, far-sightedness, or astigmatism. This is one of many vision correction surgeries that involves re-shaping the cornea—the clear area in front of the eye—so that light is focused on the retina (at the back of the eye) [24]. This surgery is popular among relevant patients across the world, particularly in Arabic-speaking countries. This has led to many questions regarding detailed information, recommendations, and sharing of previous experiences with LASIK surgery procedures, in order to further understand and prepare for the surgery, including asking optometrists about the variations in the LASIK Surgeries available for patients and which is more suitable.

4. Materials and Methods

4.1. Data Set Creation

For this research, we created a data set that was used throughout the experiments. Twitter provides different types of application programming interfaces (APIs). We used the Full Archive API, which is a premium service provided by Twitter. By using the Tweepy Python module, 10,000 Arabic tweets were successfully scraped for further processing and analysis. The scraping operation targeted the timeframe between January 2017 and December 2021. The number of records was narrowed down to 4201 after precise cleaning and initial pre-processing of retweets, unrelated tweets, and spam. The resulting remainder were records that consisted of text, written mainly in the Egyptian and Saudi dialects, MSA, and other dialects within Arabic-speaking countries. This was collected regarding a specific topic—LASIK Surgeries—using specific keywords. The first keyword was "ليزك", and the second keyword was "تصحيح". This particular topic was chosen due to its importance across the Middle East and the satisfactory nature of associated results across medical studies [25]. Furthermore, this provides a basis for the creation of an Arabic data set for common eye surgeries in the Middle East, which can be used across future studies, rather than Arabic-text data sets without a specific context. This data set is concentrated on Arabic-speaking Twitter users, and the data were labeled positive, negative, or neutral using a script and by manual curation for further accuracy. Furthermore, the data set is publicly available [26]. Table 2 shows the number of tweets per label in the created data set.

Table 2. Tweets per label in LASIK Surgery Data set.

	Positive	Negative	Neutral
Data set [21]	2355	1040	807

4.2. Data Pre-Processing

To fit our proposed approach, data pre-processing was conducted to clean the input tweet data. To simplify and standardize our text, we first removed all English and other Latin-based characters. Second, as URLs and links— which do not provide any necessary information—are commonly used to refer to any uniform resource or other Twitter users on the internet, they were removed using regular expressions (regex). Third, some common Arabic stop words, which do not contribute much information in the overall sentence, were removed. To filter and avoid these stop words, we used the NLTK package for Arabic text on the collected data set. Fourth, all punctuation was removed, except for the question and exclamation marks, due to their use in changing the overall meaning and conveying the message. Fifth, when dealing with texts, numbers may not add much information; as such, we eliminated them utilizing the re.sub module. Finally, repeated characters were not removed, due to their use in emphasizing or showing a particular feeling. For example, the word "عايزة", which means "want," could be written as "عاييييزة" to emphasize the feeling of urgently wanting that particular object.

4.3. Feature Selection

In this part, we look at the details of tweets in depth. We applied the text to padding sequencing, such that each tweet was represented by a vector. For this, we implemented the tokenizer method from the Keras library offered by Python [27], which is often used to vectorize a corpus of text by converting each text into a set of integers (each integer is the index of the token in the dictionary), where all of the text has the same length. Across this work, we used the 2000 words most commonly used across the LASIK surgeries Arabic data set. Figure 2 shows the word count across the collected data set. This data set is used in some examples with the XAI LIME method, in order to further explain the ASA.

Figure 2. Word Cloud across collected LASIK surgery data set.

4.4. LSTM Model

In our prior research, as indicated previously, we explored a deep learning approach for Arabic sentiment analysis using LSTM word-level models [8], in order to explore how they perform across multi-dialect Arabic text and two benchmark data sets. The results indicated that the attention-based LSTM worked the best across word-level Arabic sentiment analysis. Therefore, we intend to extend upon this study by applying LIME to the attention-based LSTM while considering the LASIK surgery Arabic text data set model, in order to provide enhanced sentiment classification explanation. For this research, the data set was split into training and testing sets at an 80:20 ratio. The attention-based LSTM model was used at word level, in which each word within an Arabic text tweet was then taken as a token within the input layer. Figure 3 depicts the proposed approach, where the learning phase is made up of several embedding layers, where the input length is the maximum length of words, and the vocabulary size is 2000 (the most commonly used words). The rest of the process includes LSTM layers including 1024 and 256 filters, with a dropout rate of 0.5, an attention layer, and a single neuron. Finally, a dense layer with a Softmax activation function was applied for multi-class classification. Meanwhile, an accuracy of 79.1% was achieved by the proposed attention-based LSTM model through the addition of an attention layer, which improved the classification accuracy within the Arabic-text data set. This proved to be a challenging process, due to its complex morphology. We focused on how the approach can pay attention to each word by applying a word count within the embedding layer.

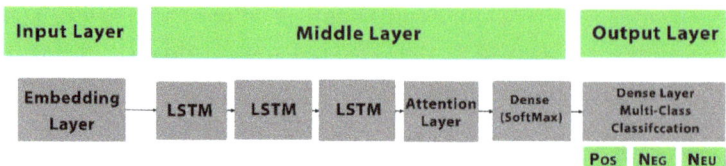

Figure 3. LSTM Model Framework.

4.5. Applying LIME XAI Method

XAI was applied to further explain and provide transparency for the applied sentiment analysis carried out on the data set. Similar approaches have been reported in previous works, such as in [8], where they used information about the symptoms written in Twitter posts to determine whether a user had potentially been exposed to the COVID-19 virus, in order to estimate places where a viral breakout could occur. To the best of our knowledge, this paper is the first of its kind to implement such an approach to ASA. Furthermore, the LIME (Local interpretable model-agnostic explanations) XAI model [28] was applied, due to its model-agnostic nature, which makes it suitable for use with various other models. This approach acts as an approximation technique for the DL model, using a local, interpretable model to explain each prediction. First, we applied it to the Arabic text data set that specifically targets the general opinion of users regarding LASIK surgeries with positive sentiment, in order to further understand some of the potential concerns and thoughts of users across social media. As previously mentioned, the data set consisted of posts with positive, negative, and neutral labels, for a total of 4202 texts. In the experiments previously carried out, the attention-based LSTM achieved higher accuracy. We applied the XAI method, which randomly sampled from the LSTM model to further explain why they were classified with a specific sentiment, considering the representation of sentiments that could be easy for non-native speakers to comprehend when translated and interpreted. Figure 4 shows an illustration of a sentence that was originally classified as having positive sentiment. The original sentence states that "his eyesight was weak and soon he will gain back his full eyesight." Even though the LASIK surgery keyword was not mentioned within the sentence, it indicated the perceived recovery of his eyesight after performing the surgery. This is represented in the illustration below where the words "نظره" and "يشوف" were categorized as positive and, even though the words "يرجع", "هيعمل", and "ضعف" were classified as negative, within the Arabic morphology, they could have a double meaning, depending on other words within the text (as shown below).

Figure 4. LIME results for LASIK surgery Positive sentiment.

Meanwhile, Figure 5 shows an illustration of a sentence that was originally classified as having neutral sentiment, as it is initially a sentence regarding what a clinic offers; the text states "Offers on eye deficiency with the latest technologies, great price, free checkup and consultation". The word "باحدث" is classified as neutral, because it means "Latest" which can be used in a positive or negative context, based on its usage within this sentence. In this case, it is neutral, as it simply describes the latest technologies offered by the clinic. Other words, such as "الإبصار" and "لعلاج", are used to represent eyesight and provide a cure for eyesight problems but are mentioned in a casual way to be read by users across social media. By applying XAI as a proposed approach, words and their importance can be better indicated. For example, the words used within the LASIK surgery data set can be assessed to further provide more useful insights about what concerns the potential patients may have before undergoing the surgery. These keywords may also be used as main search keywords within marketing campaigns used by clinics and hospitals, potentially leading to an increase in their reach to a wide range of potential patients. This can also be used to generate a safety index for the variations of LASIK surgeries, as determined by the experience of previous patients across Twitter users. Furthermore, we compared the count of words that appeared in the sentiments in Figure 5 with the probability weights of the words in Table 3, which indicated that some of the word counts were low. Words such as "باحدث" (which means "latest") had a larger probability of 0.46 and a word count of 12 times, while "الإبصار" ("eyesight") had a probability of 0.18 and a word count of 21. Even though the second word had a higher word count, a higher probability was given to the word "latest" due to its usage across sentences specifically emphasizing the latest technologies used. Furthermore, words such as "فحص" and "التقنيات" had the same word count but different weights, due to the main subject of the sentence itself being eyesight.

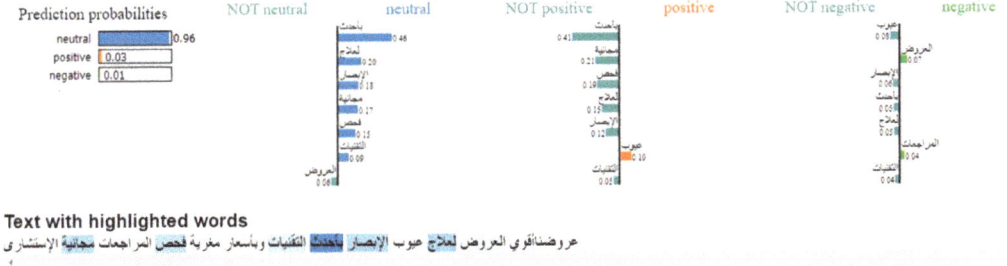

Figure 5. LIME results for LASIK surgery neutral sentiment.

Table 3. Word counts and LIME-based weights of words.

Word	Weight	Word Count
الإبصار	0.18	21
باحدث	0.46	12
لعلاج	0.20	9
فحص	0.15	18
التقنيات	0.09	18

While some words had a lower word occurrence, LIME also gave them significance according to their appearance with respect to the single sentiment itself, considering the occurrence of several variants of the same word with the same meaning. Therefore, LIME elaborates and works significantly well with Arabic text. According to [1], the utilized LIME XAI method for LASIK surgeries satisfied two out of the seven purposes stated as the main reasons for XAI applications: transparency, allowing users and decision-makers to further apply compatible decisions, and reliability, regarding the attention-based LSTM model, which can be proven according to the model performance on the data set.

Finally, an example of a Negative sentiment within the applied case study is shown in Figure 6. The sentiment involves the statement of the regret of a user after having the LASIK surgery: "I should go back to my eyeglasses". The words "ارجع" ("go back"), "النضارة" ("eyeglasses"), and "لازم" ("Must") are considered indicators of a negative experience here regarding the surgery, which made the user consider going back to wearing eyeglasses. Even though the words equivalent to "Must" and "go back" could have a positive impact within the Arabic language itself, according to the context of this particular sentiment, LIME was able to emphasize that these words were the main reason for the negative classification of this sentiment.

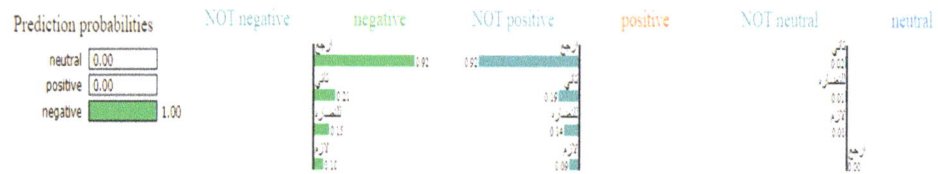

Text with highlighted words

Figure 6. LIME results for LASIK surgery negative sentiment.

5. Discussion

An evaluation of the LSTM on the proposed data set was conducted, due to its size and nature. We measured the Recall, Precision, F1-score, and Accuracy. Table 4 shows the results across the data set, indicating an accuracy of 79.1%. As the data were unbalanced, the F1-score is a valuable metric to take into consideration, which reached 0.71 for the model. This can be considered a promising result, considering the nature of the data set. The recall measures the extent to which the model correctly classifies sentiment polarities. For our model and data set, the recall reached 0.76. On the other hand, the precision reached 0.71, which is also a promising result. Finally, Figure 7 illustrates how the model performed across the epochs within training and validation phases. While it achieved high accuracy in the Arabic text data set, we did not only aim for accuracy, but also good justification performance, regarding how well the model classified sentiments into negative, positive, and neutral.

Table 4. Evaluation Results.

Data Set	Accuracy	Precision	Recall	F1-Score
[23]	79.1%	0.71	0.76	0.71

In this work, we demonstrated several experiments following on from our previous work [8], which showed that the attention-based model had the best performance in word-level ASA. Furthermore, due to the complexity of the LSTM as well as the Arabic text, here we aimed to further justify how the attention-based LSTM classified the sentiments within Arabic text. We demonstrated our work on a domain-specific Arabic data set. First, we created a domain-specific data set for LASIK surgery feedback across Twitter users. The data set was labeled manually by two annotators. Subsequently, the proposed data set went through pre-processing and feature selection.

We then applied the XAI LIME method, due to its great performance across different studies in various fields, which led us to further examine its potential regarding Arabic, due to its high complexity and variations. In this study, we observed that in the application of ASA with the help of an attention-based LSTM and using LIME as a post hoc explanation method, we could determine the sentiment classification based on specific words within the context of LASIK surgery Arabic texts; as such, we could conclude that LIME works well in the face of the complexity of Arabic text, especially with respect to its various dialects used across social media services (which led to challenges and considerations in the labelling and pre-processing steps). For this study, many trials were carried out, with the consideration of keeping the collected text closer to what was originally written by users. Therefore, not applying normalization and not removing repetitive characters were essential points that helped to improve the performance of both the attention-based model and LIME, as well as how words were classified according to their importance, regardless of the variation in the same words. In this line, we presented specific examples for the sake of explaining how the DL model classified the sentiments across the Arabic text. Second, we aimed to gain further insights into the main concerns of potential LASIK surgery patients, which could be helpful in developing a safety index for a future marketing campaign or another targeted promotion approach for future potential patients. Finally, the LIME results were promising, in terms of both presented examples of positive and neutral tweets. We then demonstrated a comparison and described how LIME classified words according to their significance within the sentiment analysis context, indicating that it works well both within the domain-specific Arabic text data set as well as for further evaluation of the Attention-based LSTM model across the domain-specific LASIK surgery Arabic text data set [26].

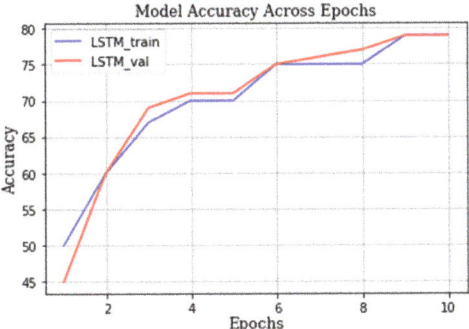

Figure 7. Performance Assessment.

6. Conclusions

In this study, an LSTM approach based on an attention layer and word count in the embedding layer was applied. For further analysis and comprehension of results, LIME (which is an XAI method) was applied to the attention-based LSTM model, even though it did not reach the expected accuracy. We were able to achieve an accuracy of 79.1%, which can be considered good due to the complexity and nature of Arabic text. The end goals here were primarily to further explain the classification of sentiments by the DL model, as they are considered black-box models. We have confirmed that the previously mentioned attention-based LSTM Model performed the best across different data sets in a previous work [8]. Subsequently, we used this model on a domain-specific data set composed of the opinions of LASIK surgery patients across Twitter, in order to clarify how the sentiments were classified into the corresponding classes, which were proposed based on word count. Furthermore, we applied LIME across three examples relating to the three sentiments in Arabic text about LASIK surgery, in order to further understand the concerns of the patients when trying to commit to an eye surgery based on Twitter posts, as well as how these words were output with their corresponding probabilities. This, in turn, is expected to help in choosing better keywords when targeting patients in future marketing campaigns, which may lead to a higher rate of coverage of an event. We deduced that LIME works well concerning Arabic text, due to its nature of checking the words within a local sentiment, according to the complex morphology of Arabic language and the variant dialects used across users, where a word can have different sentimental impact depending on where it is placed within the Arabic sentence. These results can help in further trusting the outcomes presented by deep learning models for non-expert users and decision-makers. Finally, our future work will consist of applying XAI methods to multi-dialect Arabic data sets, which are considered challenging due to the variety and variations of words with exact meanings, in order to evaluate how LIME works in a multi-dialect data set as well as considering several other sentiment levels, such as character- and document-level.

Author Contributions: Conceptualization, M.K. and A.A.H.S.; Supervision, Y.A.; methodology, software, validation, formal analysis, and visualization, Y.A; data curation, Investigation, writing—original draft preparation. M.K., A.A.H.S. and Y.A.; writing—review and editing. All authors have read and agreed to the published version of the manuscript.

Funding: This research received no external funding.

Data Availability Statement: Data set publicly available via Abdelfattah Youmna. lasikSurgery-arabic-text-dataset.Kaggle.com.10.34740/kaggle/dsv/42722722022 (accessed on 1 October 2022). Available from https://www.kaggle.com/datasets/youmnahabdelfattah/lasik-surgery-arabic-text-dataset (accessed on 1 October 2022).

Conflicts of Interest: The authors declare no conflict of interest.

Abbreviations

Abbreviation	Terminology
DL	Deep learning
ML	Machine Learning
LIME	Local Interpretable Model-agnostic Explanations
LSTM	Long Short-Term Memory
SHAP	SHapley Additive exPlanations
ASA	Arabic Sentiment Analysis

References

1. Fiok, K.; Farahani, F.V.; Karwowski, W.; Ahram, T. Explainable artificial intelligence for education and training. *J. Def. Model. Simul. Appl. Methodol. Technol.* **2021**, *19*, 133–144. [CrossRef]
2. Arrieta, A.B.; Díaz-Rodríguez, N.; del Ser, J.; Bennetot, A.; Tabik, S.; Barbado, A.; García, S.; Gil-López, S.; Molina, D.; Benjamins, R.; et al. Explainable Artificial Intelligence (XAI): Concepts, taxonomies, opportunities and challenges toward responsible AI. *Inf. Fusion* **2020**, *58*, 82–115. [CrossRef]
3. Feldman, R. Techniques and applications for sentiment analysis. *Commun. ACM* **2013**, *56*, 82–89. [CrossRef]
4. Yang, L.; Li, Y.; Wang, J.; Sherratt, R.S. Sentiment analysis for E-commerce product reviews in Chinese based on sentiment lexicon and deep learning. *IEEE Access* **2020**, *8*, 23522–23530. [CrossRef]
5. Kim, H.; So, K.K.; Wirtz, J. Service robots: Applying social exchange theory to better understand human–robot interactions. *Tour. Manag.* **2022**, *92*, 104537. [CrossRef]
6. Oueslati, O.; Cambria, E.; HajHmida, M.B.; Ounelli, H. A review of sentiment analysis research in Arabic language. *Future Gener. Comput. Syst.* **2020**, *112*, 408–430. [CrossRef]
7. Aljameel, S.S.; Alabbad, D.A.; Alzahrani, N.A.; Alqarni, S.M.; Alamoudi, F.A.; Babili, L.M.; Aljaafary, S.K.; Alshamrani, F.M. A sentiment analysis approach to predict an individual's awareness of the precautionary procedures to prevent COVID-19 outbreaks in Saudi Arabia. *Int. J. Environ. Res. Public Health* **2021**, *18*, 218. [CrossRef] [PubMed]
8. Abdelwahab, Y.; Kholief, M.; Sedky, A. An experimental survey of ASA on DL classifiers using multi-dialect arabic texts. In Proceedings of the Future of Information and Communication Conference 2022, San Francisco, CA, USA, 3–4 March 2022.
9. Alaff, A.J.; Mukhairez, H.H.; Kose, U. An explainable artificial intelligence model for detecting COVID-19 with twitter text classification: Turkey case. In Proceedings of the International Conference on Computing and Communication Systems 2021, Shillong, India, 28–30 April 2020; Springer: Singapore, 2020; pp. 87–97.
10. Rathore, R.K.; Kolonin, A. Explorative study of explainable artificial intelligence techniques for sentiment analysis applied for english language. In Proceedings of the International Conference on Paradigms of Communication, Computing and Data Sciences 2022, Kurukshetra, India, 7–9 May 2021; Springer: Singapore, 2021; pp. 861–868.
11. Gite, S.; Khatavkar, H.; Srivastava, S.; Maheshwari, P.; Pandey, N. Stock prices prediction from financial news articles using LSTM and XAI. In Proceedings of the Second International Conference on Computing, Communications, and Cyber-Security 2021, Delhi, India, 3–4 October 2020; Springer: Singapore, 2020; pp. 153–161.

12. Adak, A.; Pradhan, B.; Shukla, N.; Alamri, A. Unboxing deep learning model of food delivery service reviews using explainable artificial intelligence (XAI) technique. *Foods* **2022**, *11*, 2019. [CrossRef] [PubMed]
13. Chowdhury, K.R.; Sil, A.; Shukla, S.R. Explaining a black-box sentiment analysis model with local interpretable model diagnostics explanation (LIME). In *Advances in Computing and Data Sciences, Proceedings of the 5th International Conference on Advances in Computing and Data Sciences, Nashik, India, 23–24 April 2021*; Springer: Cham, Switzerland, 2021; pp. 90–101.
14. Kumar, A.; Dikshit, S.; Albuquerque, V.H. Explainable artificial intelligence for sarcasm detection in dialogues. *Wirel. Commun. Mob. Comput.* **2021**, *2021*, 2939334. [CrossRef]
15. Choi, I.H.; Kim, Y.S.; Lee, C.K. A Study of the classification of IT jobs using LSTM and LIME. In Proceedings of the 9th International Conference on Smart Media and Applications, Jeju, Korea, 17–19 September 2020; pp. 248–252.
16. Tang, G.; Zhang, L.; Yang, F.; Meng, L.; Cao, W.; Qiu, M.; Ren, S.; Yang, L.; Wang, H. Interpretation of learning-based automatic source code vulnerability detection model using LIME. In *Knowledge Science, Engineering and Management, Proceedings of the International Conference on Knowledge Science, Engineering and Management, Tokyo, Japan, 14–16 August 2021*; Springer: Cham, Switzerland, 2021; pp. 275–286.
17. Aporna, A.A.; Azad, I.; Amlan, N.S.; Mehedi, M.H.; Mahbub, M.J.; Rasel, A.A. Classifying offensive speech of bangla text and analysis using explainable AI. In *Advances in Computing and Data Sciences, Proceedings of the 6th International Conference on Advances in Computing and Data Sciences, Kurnool, India, 22–23 April 2022*; Springer: Cham, Switzerland, 2022; pp. 133–144.
18. Pérez-Landa, G.I.; Loyola-González, O.; Medina-Pérez, M.A. An Explainable Artificial Intelligence Model for Detecting Xenophobic Tweets. *Appl. Sci.* **2021**, *11*, 10801. [CrossRef]
19. Ribeiro, M.T.; Singh, S.; Guestrin, C. "Why should i trust you?" Explaining the predictions of any classifier. In Proceedings of the 22nd ACM SIGKDD International Conference on Knowledge Discovery and Data Mining, San Francisco, CA, USA, 13–17 August 2016; pp. 1135–1144.
20. Lundberg, S.M.; Lee, S.I. A unified approach to interpreting model predictions. *Adv. Neural Inf. Process. Syst.* **2017**, *30*, 4768–4777.
21. Malandri, L.; Mercorio, F.; Mezzanzanica, M.; Nobani, N.; Seveso, A. ContrXT: Generating contrastive explanations from any text classifier. *Inf. Fusion* **2022**, *81*, 103–115. [CrossRef]
22. Rajagopal, D.; Balachandran, V.; Hovy, E.; Tsvetkov, Y. Selfexplain: A self-explaining architecture for neural text classifiers. *arXiv* **2021**, arXiv:2103.12279.
23. Guidotti, R. Evaluating local explanation methods on ground truth. *Artif. Intell.* **2021**, *291*, 103428. [CrossRef]
24. Alsabaani, N.; Alshehri, M.S.; AlFlan, M.A.; Awadalla, N.J. Prevalence of laser refractive surgery among ophthalmologists in Saudi Arabia. *Saudi J. Ophthalmol.* **2020**, *34*, 116. [CrossRef] [PubMed]
25. Boyd, K. LASIK—Laser Eye Surgery. American Academy of Ophthalmology. 23 August 2022. Available online: https://www.aao.org/eye-health/treatments/lasik (accessed on 23 August 2022).
26. Abdelfattah Youmna. LasikSurgery-Arabic-Text-Dataset. *Kaggle.com*. 10.34740/kaggle/dsv/4272272. (Dataset). 2022. Available online: https://www.kaggle.com/datasets/youmnahabdelfattah/lasik-surgery-arabic-text-dataset (accessed on 1 October 2022).
27. TensorFlow Core v2.9.1. TensorFlow. Available online: https://www.tensorflow.org/api_docs/python/tf/keras/preprocessing/text/Tokenizer (accessed on 7 June 2022).
28. Local Interpretable Model-Agnostic Explanations (Lime)—Lime0.1 Documentation. Available online: https://lime-ml.readthedocs.io/en/latest/ (accessed on 27 October 2022).

Article

Generating Fluent Fact Checking Explanations with Unsupervised Post-Editing

Shailza Jolly [1,*,†], Pepa Atanasova [2] and Isabelle Augenstein [2]

1. Amazon Alexa AI, 10117 Berlin, Germany
2. Department of Computer Science, University of Copenhagen, 1050 Copenhagen, Denmark
* Correspondene: shailzj@amazon.com
† Work was done prior to joining Amazon.

Abstract: Fact-checking systems have become important tools to verify fake and misguiding news. These systems become more trustworthy when human-readable explanations accompany the veracity labels. However, manual collection of these explanations is expensive and time-consuming. Recent work has used extractive summarization to select a sufficient subset of the most important facts from the ruling comments (RCs) of a professional journalist to obtain fact-checking explanations. However, these explanations lack fluency and sentence coherence. In this work, we present an iterative edit-based algorithm that uses only phrase-level edits to perform unsupervised post-editing of disconnected RCs. To regulate our editing algorithm, we use a scoring function with components including fluency and semantic preservation. In addition, we show the applicability of our approach in a completely unsupervised setting. We experiment with two benchmark datasets, namely LIAR-PLUS and PubHealth. We show that our model generates explanations that are fluent, readable, non-redundant, and cover important information for the fact check.

Keywords: natural language generation; fact-checking; explainable AI

Citation: Jolly, S.; Atanasova, P.; Augenstein, I. Generating Fluent Fact Checking Explanations with Unsupervised Post-Editing. *Information* **2022**, *13*, 500. https://doi.org/10.3390/info13100500

Academic Editors: Gabriele Gianini and Pierre-Edouard Portier

Received: 29 August 2022
Accepted: 12 October 2022
Published: 17 October 2022

Publisher's Note: MDPI stays neutral with regard to jurisdictional claims in published maps and institutional affiliations.

Copyright: © 2022 by the authors. Licensee MDPI, Basel, Switzerland. This article is an open access article distributed under the terms and conditions of the Creative Commons Attribution (CC BY) license (https://creativecommons.org/licenses/by/4.0/).

1. Introduction

In today's era of social media, the spread of news is a click away, regardless of if it is fake or real. However, the quick propagation of fake news has repercussions on peoples' lives. To alleviate these consequences, independent teams of professional fact checkers manually verify the veracity and credibility of news, which is time and labor-intensive, making the process expensive and less scalable. Therefore, the need for accurate, scalable, and explainable automatic fact-checking systems is inevitable [1].

Current automatic fact-checking systems perform veracity prediction for given claims based on evidence documents (Thorne et al. [2], Augenstein et al. [3], inter alia), or based on long lists of supporting ruling comments (RCs, Wang [4], Alhindi et al. [5]). RCs are in-depth explanations for predicted veracity labels, but they are challenging to read and not useful as explanations for human readers due to their sizable content.

Recent work [6,7] has thus proposed to use automatic summarization to select a subset of sentences from long RCs and used them as short layman explanations. However, using a purely extractive approach [6] means sentences are cherry-picked from different parts of the corresponding RCs, and as a result, explanations are often disjoint and non-fluent.

While a Seq2Seq model trained on parallel data can partially alleviate these problems, as Kotonya and Toni [7] propose, it is an expensive affair in terms of the large amount of data and compute required to train these models. Therefore, in this work, we focus on unsupervised post-editing of explanations extracted from RCs. In recent studies, researchers have addressed unsupervised post-editing to generate paraphrases [8] and sentence simplifications [9]. However, they use small single sentences and perform exhaustive word-level or a combination of word and phrase-level edits, which has limited applicability for longer text inputs with multiple sentences, e.g., veracity explanations, due to prohibitive convergence times.

Hence, we present a *novel iterative edit-based algorithm* that performs three edit operations (insertion, deletion, reorder), all at the phrase level. Figure 1 presents a qualitative example from the PubHealth dataset [7], which illustrates how each post-editing step contributes to creating explanations that are more readable, fluent, and creates a coherent story, while also preserving the information important for the fact check.

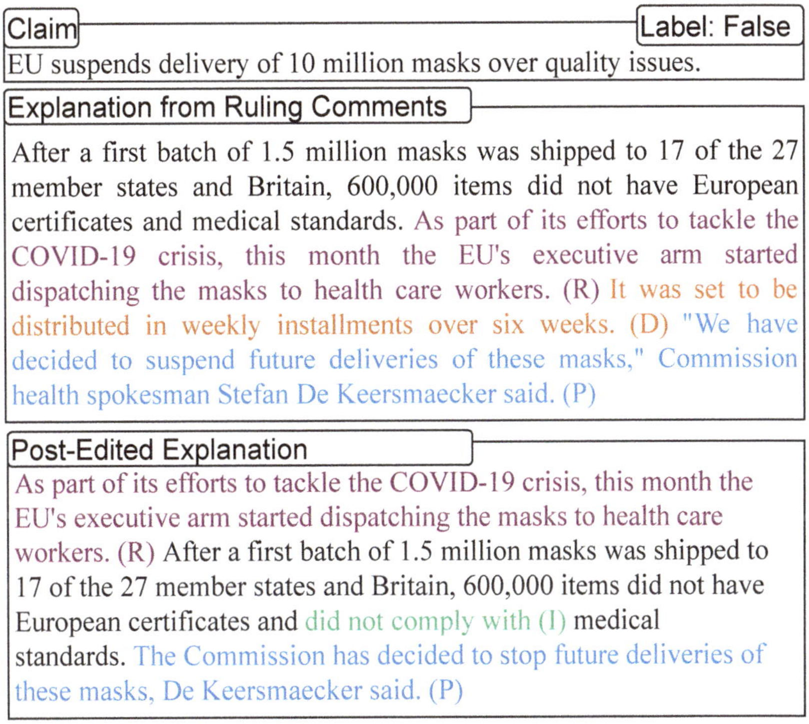

Claim — **Label: False**
EU suspends delivery of 10 million masks over quality issues.

Explanation from Ruling Comments
After a first batch of 1.5 million masks was shipped to 17 of the 27 member states and Britain, 600,000 items did not have European certificates and medical standards. As part of its efforts to tackle the COVID-19 crisis, this month the EU's executive arm started dispatching the masks to health care workers. (R) It was set to be distributed in weekly installments over six weeks. (D) "We have decided to suspend future deliveries of these masks," Commission health spokesman Stefan De Keersmaecker said. (P)

Post-Edited Explanation
As part of its efforts to tackle the COVID-19 crisis, this month the EU's executive arm started dispatching the masks to health care workers. (R) After a first batch of 1.5 million masks was shipped to 17 of the 27 member states and Britain, 600,000 items did not have European certificates and did not comply with (I) medical standards. The Commission has decided to stop future deliveries of these masks, De Keersmaecker said. (P)

Figure 1. Example of a post-edited explanation from PubHealth that was initially extracted from ruling comments. We illustrate four post-editing steps: insertion (I), reordering (R), deletion (D), and paraphrasing (P).

Our proposed method finds the best post-edited explanation candidate according to a scoring function, ensuring the quality of explanations in fluency, semantic similarity, and semantic preservation. To ensure that the sentences are grammatically correct, we also perform grammar checking of the candidate explanations. As a second step, we apply paraphrasing to further improve the conciseness and human readability of the explanations.

In summary, our main contributions include:
- To the best of our knowledge, this work is the first to explore an iterative unsupervised edit-based algorithm using only phrase-level edits. The proposed algorithm also leads to the first computationally feasible solutions for unsupervised post-editing of long text inputs, such as veracity ruling comments.
- We show how combining an iterative algorithm with grammatical corrections, and paraphrasing-based post-processing leads to fluent and easy-to-read explanations.
- We conduct extensive experiments on the LIAR-PLUS [4] and PubHealth [7] fact-checking datasets. Our manual evaluation confirms that our approach improves the fluency and conciseness of explanations.

2. Related Work

The most closely related streams of approaches to our work are explainable fact checking, generative approaches to explainability and post-editing for language generation.

2.1. Explainable Fact Checking

Recent work has produced fact-checking explanations by highlighting words in tweets using neural attention [10]. However, their explanations are used only to evaluate and compare the proposed model with other baselines without neural attention. Wu et al. [11] propose to model evidence documents with decision trees, which are inherently interpretable ML models. In a recent study, Atanasova et al. [6] present a multi-task approach to generate free-text explanations for political claims jointly with predicting the veracity of claims. They formulate an extractive summarization task to select a few important sentences from a long fact-checking report. Atanasova et al. [12] also perform extractive explanation generation guided by a set of diagnostic properties of explanations and evaluate on the FEVER [2] fact-checking dataset, where explanation sentences have to be extracted from Wikipedia documents.

In the domain of public health claims, Kotonya and Toni [7] propose to generate explanations separately from the task of veracity prediction. Mishra et al. [13] generate summaries of evidence documents from the Web using an attention-based mechanism. They show that their summaries perform better than using the original evidence documents directly. Similarly to Atanasova et al. [6], Kotonya and Toni [7], we present a generative approach for creating fact-checking explanations. In contrast to related work, we propose an unsupervised post-editing approach to improve the fluency and readability of previously extracted fact-checking explanations.

2.2. Generative Approaches to Explainability

Explainable AI [14] is important to encourage trust of blackbox model's decisions and increase their acceptability among users. While most work on explanation generation propose methods to highlight portions of inputs (Camburu et al. [15], DeYoung et al. [16], inter alia), some work focuses on generative approaches to explainability. Ref Camburu et al. [15] propose combining an explanation generation and a target prediction model in a pipeline or a joint model for Natural Language Inference with abstractive explanations about the entailment of two sentences. They find that first explaining and then predicting based on the explanation achieves better trust as the prediction is based on the right reasons. Stammbach and Ash [17] propose few-shot training for the GPT-3 [18] model to explain a fact check from retrieved evidence snippets. GPT-3, however, is a limited-access model with high computational costs. As in our work, Kotonya and Toni [7] first extract evidence sentences, which are then summarised by an abstractive summarisation model. The latter is trained on the PubHealth dataset. In contrast, we are the first to focus on unsupervised post-editing of explanations produced using automatic summarization.

2.3. Post-Editing for Language Generation

Previous work has addressed unsupervised post-editing for multiple tasks such as paraphrase generation [8], sentence simplification [9] or sentence summarization [19]. However, all these tasks handle shorter inputs in comparison to the long multi-sentence extractive explanations that we have. Furthermore, they perform exhaustive edit operations at the word level and sometimes additionally at the phrase level, both of which increase computation and inference complexity. Therefore, we present a novel approach that performs a fixed number of edits only at the phrase level followed by grammar correction and paraphrasing.

3. Method

Our method is comprised of two steps. First, we select sentences from RCs that serve as extractive explanations for verifying claims (Section 3.1). We then apply a post-editing algorithm on the extractive explanations in order to improve their fluency and coherence (Section 3.2).

3.1. Selecting Sentences for Post-Editing

Supervised Selection. To produce supervised extractive explanations, we use the method implemented by Atanasova et al. [20] for the LIAR-PLUS dataset. We then adapt the supervised method for the PubHealth dataset using the same pre-trained model as used by Kotonya and Toni [7] for the dataset. The models used for the extractive explanations are based on DistilBERT [21] for LIAR-PLUS, and SciBERT [22] for PubHealth, which allows for direct comparison with Kotonya and Toni [7], Atanasova et al. [20].

We supervise explanation generation by k greedily selected sentences from each claim's RCs that achieve the highest ROUGE-2 F1 score when compared to the gold justification. We choose $k = 4$ for LIAR-PLUS and $k = 3$ for PubHealth, the average number of sentences in the veracity justifications in the corresponding datasets. The selected sentences are positive gold labels, $\mathbf{y}^E \in \{0,1\}^N$, where N is the number of sentences in the RCs. We also use the veracity labels $\mathbf{y}^F \in Y_F$ for supervision.

Following Atanasova et al. [20], we then learn a multi-task model $g(X) = (\mathbf{p}^E, \mathbf{p}^F)$. Given the input X, comprised of a claim and the RCs, it predicts jointly the veracity explanation $\mathbf{p}^E$ and the veracity label $\mathbf{p}^F$, where $\mathbf{p}^E \in \mathbb{R}^{1,N}$ selects sentences for explanation, i.e., $\{0,1\}$, and $\mathbf{p}^F \in \mathbb{R}^m$, with $m = 6$ for LIAR-PLUS, and $m = 4$ for PubHealth. Finally, we optimise the joint cross-entropy loss function $\mathcal{L}_{MT} = \mathcal{H}(\mathbf{p}^E, \mathbf{y}^E) + \mathcal{H}(\mathbf{p}^F, \mathbf{y}^F)$.

Unsupervised selection. We also experiment with unsupervised selection of sentences to test the possibility to construct fluent fact-checking explanations in an entirely unsupervised way. We use a Longformer [23] model, which was introduced for tasks with longer input, instead of the sliding-window approach also used in Atanasova et al. [20], which is without cross-window attention. We train a model $h(X) = \mathbf{p}^F$ to predict the veracity of a claim. We optimise a cross-entropy loss function $\mathcal{L}_F = \mathcal{H}(\mathbf{p}^F, \mathbf{y}^F)$ and select k sentences $\mathbf{p}^{E'} \in \mathbb{R}^{1,N}$, $\{0, 1\}$, with the highest saliency scores. The saliency score of a sentence is the sum of the saliency scores of its tokens. The saliency of a token is the gradient of the input token w.r.t. the output [24]. We selected sentences using the raw gradients as Atanasova et al. [25] show that different gradient-based methods yield similar results. As the selection could be noisy [26], we consider these experiments as only complementary to the main supervised results.

3.2. Post-Editing

Our post-editing is completely unsupervised and operates on sentences obtained in Section 3.1. It is a search algorithm that evaluates the candidate sequence $\mathbf{p}^C$ for a given input sequence, where the input sequence is either $\mathbf{p}^E$ for supervised selection or $\mathbf{p}^{E'}$ for unsupervised selection. Below, we use $\mathbf{p}^E$ as a representative of both $\mathbf{p}^E$ and $\mathbf{p}^{E'}$.

Given $\mathbf{p}^E$, we iteratively generate multiple candidates by performing phrase-level edits as defined in Section 3.2.1. To evaluate a candidate explanation, we define a scoring function, which is a product of multiple scorers, also known as a product-of-experts model [27]. Our scoring function includes fluency and semantic preservation, and controls the length of the candidate explanation (Section 3.2.2). We repeat the process for n steps and select the last best-scoring candidate as our final output. We then use grammar correction (Section 3.2.4) and paraphrasing (Section 3.2.5) to further ensure conciseness and human readability.

3.2.1. Candidate Sequence Generation

We generate candidate sequences by phrase-level edits. We use the off-the-shelf syntactic parser from CoreNLP [28] to obtain the constituency tree of a candidate sequence $\mathbf{p}^C$. As $\mathbf{p}^C$ is long, we perform all operations at the phrase level. At each step t, our algorithm first randomly picks one operation—insertion, deletion, or reordering, and then randomly selects a phrase. For **insertion**, our algorithm inserts a <MASK> token before the randomly selected phrase, and use RoBERTa to evaluate the posterior probability of a candidate word [29]. This functionality allows us to leverage the pre-training capabilities of RoBERTa and inserts high-quality words that support the context of the overall explanation. Furthermore, inserting a <MASK> token before a phrase prevents breaking other phrases within the explanation, thus preserving their fluency.

The **deletion** operation deletes the randomly selected phrase, For the **reorder** operation we randomly select one phrase, which we call *reorder phrase*, and randomly select m phrases, which we call *anchor phrases*. We **reorder** each *anchor phrase* with a *reorder phrase* and obtain m candidate sequences. We feed these candidates to GPT2 and select the most fluent candidate based on the fluency score given by Equation (1).

3.2.2. Scoring Functions

The scoring functions employed for our post-editing algorithm rely on pre-trained models, such as RoBERTa [30] for semantic preservation, and GPT-2 [31] for fluency preservation. Similar to our approach, most contemporary natural language processing methods rely on pre-trained models. Related work also uses pre-trained models to improve fluency and semantic similarity [9,32,33].

The **fluency score** (f_{flu}) measures the language fluency of a candidate sequence. We use pre-trained GPT2 model [31]. We use the joint likelihood of candidate $\mathbf{p}^C$:

$$f_{flu}(\mathbf{p}^C) = \prod_{i=1}^{n} P(\mathbf{p}_i^C | \mathbf{p}_1^C, ..., \mathbf{p}_{i-1}^C) \quad (1)$$

For **semantic preservation**, we compute similarities at both word and explanation level between our source explanation ($\mathbf{p}^E$) and candidate sequence ($\mathbf{p}^C$) at time-step t. The word-level semantic scorer evaluates the preserved amount of keyword information in the candidate sequence. Similarly to Li et al. [29], we use RoBERTa (R) [30], a pre-trained masked language model, to compute a contextual representation of the ith word in an explanation as $R(\mathbf{p}_i^E, \mathbf{p}^E)$. Here, $\mathbf{p}^E = (\mathbf{p}_1^E \ldots \mathbf{p}_m^E)$ is an input sequence of words. We then extract keywords from $\mathbf{p}^E$ using Rake [34] and compute a **word-level semantic similarity score**:

$$f_w(\mathbf{p}^E, \mathbf{p}^C) = \min_{k \in kw(\mathbf{p}^E)} \max_{\mathbf{p}_i^C \in \mathbf{p}^C} R(k, \mathbf{p}^E)^\top R(\mathbf{p}_i^C, \mathbf{p}^C) \quad (2)$$

which is the lowest cosine similarity among all keywords i.e., the least matched keyword of $\mathbf{p}^E$.

The **explanation-level semantic preservation scorer** evaluates the cosine similarity of two explanation vectors:

$$f_e(\mathbf{p}^E, \mathbf{p}^C) = \frac{(\mathbf{p}^C)^\top \mathbf{p}^E}{||\mathbf{p}^C|| ||\mathbf{p}^E||} \quad (3)$$

We use SBERT [35] for obtaining embeddings for both $\mathbf{p}^E$, $\mathbf{p}^C$. Our overall semantic score is the product of the word level and the explanation-level semantics scores:

$$f_{sem}(\mathbf{p}^E, \mathbf{p}^C) = f_w(\mathbf{p}^E, \mathbf{p}^C)^\beta \cdot f_e(\mathbf{p}^E, \mathbf{p}^C)^\eta \quad (4)$$

where β, and η are hyperparameter weights for the separate scores.

Length score (f_{len}) This score encourages the generation of shorter sentences. It is proportional to the inverse of the sequence length, i.e., the higher the length of a candidate sentence, the lower its score. To control over-shortening, we reject explanations with fewer than 40 tokens.

Named entity (NE) score (f_{ent}) This score is a proxy for meaning preservation, since NEs hold the key information within a sentence. We first identify NEs using an off-the-shelf entity tagger (https://spacy.io/, accessed on 3 February 2021) and then count their number in a given explanation.

Overall scoring Our overall scoring function is the product of individual scores:

$$f_(\mathbf{p}^C) = f_{flu}(\mathbf{p}^C)^\alpha \cdot f_{sem}(\mathbf{p}^E, \mathbf{p}^C) \cdot f_{len}(\mathbf{p}^C)^\gamma \cdot f_{ent}(\mathbf{p}^C)^\delta \quad (5)$$

where α, γ, and δ are hyperparameter weights for the different scores.

3.2.3. Iterative Edit-Based Algorithm

Given input explanations, our algorithm iteratively performs edit operations for n steps to search for a highly scored candidate ($\mathbf{p}^C$). At each search step, it computes scores for the previous sequence ($\mathbf{p}^{C-1}$) and candidate sequence using Equation (5). It selects a candidate sequence if its score is larger than the previous one by a multiplicative factor r_{op}:

$$f_{\mathbf{p}^C}/f_{\mathbf{p}^{C-1}} > r_{op} \qquad (6)$$

For each edit operation, we use a separate threshold value r_{op}. r_{op} allows controlling specific operations, as for the reorder operation, if $\mathbf{p}^C$ gets a lower score than $\mathbf{p}^{C-1}$ then a lower value of r_{op} will enable selection of $\mathbf{p}^C$. In particular, it controls the exploration vs. the overall score of the selected candidates stemming from the particular operation. In other words, having a higher value for r_{op} would lead to selecting candidates with higher overall scores, but might lead to none or only a few operations of that type being selected. We pick values of r_{op} that result in selecting candidates with high scores, while also leading to a similar number of selected candidates per operation type. We tune all hyperparameters, including r_{op}, n, etc., using the validation split of the LIAR-PLUS dataset.

3.2.4. Grammatical Correction

Once the best candidate explanation is selected, we apply a language toolkit over the candidate explanation (https://github.com/jxmorris12/language_tool_python, accessed on 2 April 2021), which detects grammatical errors such as capitalization and irrelevant punctuation, and returns a corrected version of the explanation. Furthermore, to ensure that we have no incomplete sentences, we remove sentences without verbs in the explanation.

3.2.5. Paraphrasing

Finally, to improve fluency and readability further, we use Pegasus [36], a model pre-trained with an abstractive text summarization objective. It focuses on relevant input parts to summarize the input semantics in a concise and more readable way. Since we want our explanations to be both fluent and human-readable, we leverage this pre-trained model without fine-tuning on downstream tasks. This way, after applying our iterative edit-based algorithm with grammatical error correction and paraphrasing, we obtain explanations that are fluent, coherent, and non-redundant.

4. Experiments

4.1. Datasets

We use two fact-checking datasets, LIAR-PLUS [4] and PubHealth [7]. These are the only two available real-world fact-checking datasets that provide short veracity justifications along with claims, ruling comments, and veracity labels. LIAR-PLUS contains 10,146 training, 1278 validation, and 1255 test data points from the political domain. PubHealth contains 9817 training, 1227 validation, and 1235 test data points from the health domain, including 447 claims about COVID-19. The labels used in LIAR-PLUS are {true, false, half-true, barely-true, mostly-true, pants-on-fire}, and in PubHealth, {true, false, mixture, unproven}.

While claims in LIAR-PLUS are only from PolitiFact, PubHealth contains claims from eight fact-checking sources. PubHealth has also been manually curated, e.g., to exclude poorly defined claims. Finally, the claims in PubHealth are more challenging to read than those in LIAR-PLUS and other real-world fact-checking datasets.

4.2. Models

Our experiments include the following models; their hyperparameters are given in Appendix F.

(Un)Supervised Top-N extracts sentences from the RCs, which are later used as input to our algorithm. The sentences are extracted in either a supervised or unsupervised way (see Section 3.1).

(Un)Supervised Top-N+Edits-N generates explanations with the iterative edit-based algorithm (Section 3.2.3) and grammar correction (Section 3.2.4). The model is fed with sentences extracted from RCs in an (un)supervised way.

(Un)Supervised Top-N+Edits-N+Para generates explanations by paraphrasing the explanations produced by Edits-N - (Un)Supervised (see Section 3.2.5).

Atanasova et al. [20] is a reference model that trains a multi-task system to predict veracity labels and extract explanation sentences. The model extracts N sentences, where N is the average number of the sentences in the justifications of each dataset. Kotonya and Toni [7] is a baseline model that generates abstractive explanations with an average sentence length of 3.

Lead-K [37] is a common lower-bound baseline for summarisation models, which selects the first K sentences from the RCs.

4.3. Iterative Edit-Based Algorithm

The proposed scoring functions (Section 3.2.2) and the iterative edit-based algorithm (Section 3.2.3) introduce hyper-parameters for controlling the importance of the individual post-editing scores as well as the efficiency and effectiveness trade-off of the iterative post-editing algorithm. We choose the hyper-parameter values with a standard hyper-parameter search over several values over a held-out validation set (Appendix B). The hyper-parameters enhance the proposed algorithm by making it adaptable to the specifics of the downstream application task. For example, one can easily select the hyper-parameter values depending on the required length, fluency, and semantic preservation of the produced explanations.

We select the editing target and the editing operation at random as the space of the possible operations and targets is computationally prohibitive, especially given long textual inputs, such as veracity explanations. While we follow related work [8] by selecting these at random, the scoring functions, as well as the threshold (r_{op}) used in the interactive edit-based algorithm, ensure that only fluent and semantically coherent sentences are selected at each step.

4.4. Evaluation Overview

We perform both automatic and manual evaluations of the models above. We include automatic ROUGE F1 scores (overlap of the generated explanations with the gold ones, Section 5.1) for compatibility with prior work. We further include automatic measures for assessing readability (see Section 5.2). While the latter was not included in prior work, we consider readability an essential quality of an explanation, and thus report it. We note, however, that the employed automatic measures are limited as they are based on word-level statistics. Especially ROUGE F1 scores should be taken with a grain of salt, as only exact matches of words are rewarded with higher scores, where paraphrases or synonyms of words in the gold summary are not scored. Hence, we also conduct a manual evaluation following Atanasova et al. [20] to further assess the quality of the generated explanations with a user study. As manual evaluation is expensive to obtain, the latter is, however, usually estimated based on small samples.

5. Automatic Evaluation and Results

As mentioned above, we use ROUGE F1 scores to compute overlap between the generated explanations and the gold ones, and compute readability scores to assess how challenging the produced explanations are to read.

5.1. Automatic ROUGE Scores

Metrics. To evaluate the generated explanations w.r.t. the gold justifications, we follow Kotonya and Toni [7], Atanasova et al. [20] and use measures from automatic text summarisation – ROUGE-1, ROUGE-2, and ROUGE-L F1 scores. These account for n-gram (1/2) and longest (L) overlap between generated and gold justification. The scores are recall-oriented, i.e., they calculate how many of the n-grams in the gold text appear in the generated one.

Caveats. Here, automatic evaluation with ROUGE scores is used to verify that the generated explanations preserve information important for the fact check, as opposed to generating completely unrelated text. Thus, we are interested in whether the ROUGE scores of the post-edited explanations are close but not necessarily higher than the ROUGE scores of the selected sentences from the RCs given as input. This work includes paraphrasing and insertion of new words to improve the readability of the explanation, which, while bearing the same meaning, necessarily results in lower ROUGE scores.

Results. In Table 1, we present the ROUGE score results. First, comparing the results for the input Top-N sentences with the intermediate and final explanations generated by our system, we see that, while very close, the ROUGE scores tend to decrease. For PubHealth, we also see that the intermediate explanations always have higher ROUGE scores compared to the final explanations from our system. These observations corroborate two main assumptions about our system. First, our system manages to preserve a large portion of the information important for explaining the veracity label, which is also present in the justification. This is further corroborated by observing that the decrease in the ROUGE scores is often not statistically significant ($p < 0.05$, except for some ROUGE-2 and one ROUGE-L score). Second, the operations in the iterative editing and the subsequent paraphrasing allow for the introduction of novel n-grams, which, while preserving the meaning of the text, are not explicitly present in the gold justification, thus, affecting the word-level ROUGE scores. We further discuss this in Section 7 and the Appendix E.

The ROUGE scores of the explanations generated by our post-editing algorithm when fed with sentences selected in an unsupervised way are considerably lower than with the supervised models. The latter illustrates that supervision for extracting the most important sentences is important to obtain explanations close to the gold ones. Finally, the systems' results are mostly above the LEAD-N scores, with a few exceptions for the unsupervised explanations for LIAR-PLUS.

Table 1. ROUGE-1/2/L F1 scores (see Section 5.1), and readability measures (see Section 5.2) over the test splits (for validation and ablations, see the Table A3 in appendix). Readability measures include sample variance. In *italics*, we report results reported from prior work, where we do not always have the outputs to compute readability. Underlined ROUGE scores of the Top-N+Edits-N and Top-N+Edits-N+Para are statistically significant ($p < 0.05$) compared to the input Top-N ROUGE scores, N = {5, 6}. Readability scores for Top-N+Edits-N and Top-N+Edits-N+Para are statistically significant ($p < 0.05$) compared to Top-N, and to Atanasova et al. [6]-3/4, except for the score in purple.

	Method	R-1 ↗	R-2 ↗	R-L ↗	Flesch ↗	Dale–Chall ↘
		LIAR-PLUS				
Baselines	Lead-4	28.11	6.96	24.38	51.70 ± 14.85	8.72 ± 0.95
	Lead-6	29.15	8.28	25.84	53.24 ± 12.18	8.42 ± 0.78
Supervised	Top-6 (Supervised)	34.42	12.36	30.58	58.39 ± 12.11	7.88 ± 0.80
	Top-6+Edits-6	33.92	11.73	30.01	60.20 ± 12.08	7.74 ± 0.86
	Top-6+Edits-6+Para	33.94	<u>11.25</u>	30.08	66.33 ± 11.09	7.41 ± 0.91
Unsupervised	Top-6 (Unsupervised)	29.63	7.58	25.86	53.32 ± 10.86	8.50 ± 0.73
	Top-6+Edits-6	28.93	<u>7.06</u>	25.14	55.25 ± 12.03	8.46 ± 0.85
	Top-6+Edits-6+Para	28.98	<u>6.84</u>	25.39	62.13 ± 11.16	8.10 ± 0.89
	Atanasova et al. [6]-4	*35.70*	*13.51*	*31.58*	58.55 ± 13.70	7.97 ± 1.05
	Justification	*-*	*-*	*-*	58.81 ± 13.33	8.22 ± 1.07

Table 1. Cont.

	Method	R-1 ↗	R-2 ↗	R-L ↗	Flesch ↗	Dale–Chall ↘
		PubHealth				
Baselines	Lead-3	29.01	10.24	24.18	-	-
	Lead-3	23.05	6.28	19.27	44.43 ± 22.97	9.10 ± 1.32
	Lead-5	23.73	6.86	20.67	45.95 ± 18.77	8.85 ± 1.03
Supervised	Top-5 (Supervised)	29.93	12.42	26.24	48.63 ± 14.14	8.67 ± 0.89
	Top-5+Edits-5	29.38	11.16	25.41	53.79 ± 14.56	8.36 ± 0.97
	Top-5+Edits-5+Para	28.40	9.56	24.37	61.38 ± 12.69	7.96 ± 0.98
Unsupervised	Top-5 (Unsupervised)	23.52	6.12	19.93	45.20 ± 14.36	8.94 ± 0.88
	Top-5+Edits-5	23.09	5.56	19.44	50.74 ± 14.92	8.62 ± 0.99
	Top-5+Edits-5+Para	23.35	5.38	19.56	60.06 ± 12.97	8.14 ± 0.95
	Kotonya and Toni [7]-3	32.30	13.46	26.99	-	-
	Atanasova et al. [6]-3	33.55	13.12	29.41	48.72 ± 16.38	8.87 ± 1.09
	Justification	-	-	-	49.28 ± 19.08	9.15 ± 1.61

Overall observations. We note that while automatic measures can serve as sanity checks and point to major discrepancies between generated explanations and gold ones, related work in generating fact-checking explanations [20] has shown that the automatic scores to some extent disagree with human evaluation studies, as they only capture word-level overlap and cannot reflect improvements of explanation quality. Human evaluations are therefore conducted for most summarisation models [38,39], which we include in Section 6.

5.2. Readability Results

Metrics. Readability is a desirable property for fact-checking explanations, as explanations that are challenging to read would fail to convey the reasons for the chosen veracity label and would not improve the trust of end-users. To evaluate readability, we compute Flesch Reading Ease [40] and Dale–Chall Readability Score [41]. The Flesch Reading Ease metric gives a text a score between 1 and 100, where a score between 50 and 30 requires college education and is difficult to read, a score between 50 and 60 requires a 10th to 12th school grade and is still fairly difficult to read, a score between 60 and 70 is regarded as plain English, which is easily understood by 13- to 15-year-old students. The Dale–Chall Readability Score gives a text a score between 9.0 and 9.9 when it is easily understood by a 13th to 15-grade (college) student, a score between 8.0 and 8.9 when it is easily understood by an 11th or 12th-grade student, a score between 7.0 and 7.9 when it is easily understood by a 9th or 10th-grade student.

Results. Table 1 presents the readability results. We find that our iterative edit-based algorithm consistently improves the reading ease of the explanations by up to 5.16 points, and reduces the grade requirement by up to 0.32 points. Conducting paraphrasing further improves the reading ease of the text by up to 9.32 points, and reduces the grade requirement by up to 0.48 points. It is also worth noting that the explanations produced by Atanasova et al. [20] as well as the gold justifications are fairly difficult to read and can require even college education for grasping the explanation, while the explanations generated by our algorithm can be easily understood by 13- to 15-year-old students according to the Flesch Reading Ease score.

Overall observations. Our results show that our method makes fact-checking explanations less challenging to read and makes them accessible to a broader audience of up to 10th-grade students.

6. Manual Evaluation and Results

As automated ROUGE scores only account for word-level similarity between the generated and the gold explanation, and the readability scores account only for surface-level characteristics of the explanation, we further conduct a manual evaluation of the quality of the produced explanations.

6.1. Explanation Quality

We manually evaluate two explanations: the input Top-N sentences, and the final explanations produced after paraphrasing (Edits-N+Para). We perform a manual evaluation of the test explanations obtained from supervised selection for both datasets with two annotators for each. Both annotators have a university-level education in English.

Metrics. We show a claim, veracity label, and two explanations to each annotator and ask them to rank the explanations according to the following criteria. **Coverage** means the explanation contains important and salient information for the fact check. **Non-redundancy** implies the explanation does not contain any redundant/repeated/not relevant information to the claim and the fact check. **Non-contradiction** checks if there is information contradictory to the fact check. **Fluency** measures the grammatical correctness of the explanation and if there is a coherent story. **Overall** measures the overall explanation quality. Following Atanasova et al. [20], we allow annotators to give the same rank to both explanations. We randomly sample 40 instances and do not provide the annotators with information about the explanation type. We choose 40 instances following related work [20] and work in the domain of automated summarisation [42], which use this low number of annotators/annotations due to the incurring annotation costs.

Results. Table 2 presents the human evaluation results for the first task. Each row indicates the annotator number and the number of times they ranked an explanation higher for one criterion. *Both* refers to both explanations being equal. Our system's explanations achieve higher acceptance for non-redundancy and fluency for LIAR-PLUS. The results are more pronounced for the PubHealth dataset, where our system's explanations were preferred in almost all metrics by both annotators. We hypothesise that PubHealth being a manually curated dataset leads to overall cleaner post-editing explanations, which annotators prefer.

Table 2. Manual annotation results of explanation quality with two annotators for both datasets. Each value indicates the relative proportion of when an annotator preferred a justification for a criterion. The preferred method, out of the input Top-N and the output of our method, Top-N+Edits-N+Para, is emboldened, Both indicates no preference.

#	LIAR-PLUS			PubHealth		
	Top-L	E-N+P	Both	Top-L	E-N+P	Both
	Coverage					
1	**42.5**	0.0	57.5	27.5	**60.0**	12.5
2	40.0	5.0	55.0	22.5	20.0	57.5
	Non-redundancy					
1	10.0	**87.5**	2.5	10.0	**82.5**	7.5
2	7.5	10.0	82.5	7.5	**75.0**	17.5
	Non-contradictory					
1	32.5	5.0	62.5	7.5	10.0	82.5
2	10.0	7.5	82.5	**20.0**	15.0	65.0
	Fluency					
1	40.0	**57.5**	2.5	35.0	**52.5**	12.5
2	**77.5**	15.0	7.5	20.0	**72.5**	7.5
	Overall Quality					
1	**57.5**	42.5	0.0	35.0	**62.5**	2.5
2	**62.5**	15.0	22.5	25.0	**67.5**	7.5

6.2. Explanation Informativeness

Metrics. We also perform a manual evaluation for veracity prediction. We ask annotators to provide a veracity label for a claim and an explanation where, same as for the evaluation of Explanation Quality, the explanations are either our system's input or output. The annotators provide a veracity label for three-way classification; true, false, and insufficient (see map to original labels for both datasets in Appendix A. We use 30 instances of explanation type and perform evaluation for both datasets with two annotators for each dataset and instance.

Results. For the LIAR-PLUS dataset, one annotator gave the correct label 80% times for input and 67% times for the output explanations. The second annotator chose the correct label 56% times using output explanations and 44% times using input explanations. However, both annotators found at least 16% of explanations to be insufficient for the task of veracity prediction (Table A1 in Appendix A).

For PubHealth, both annotators found each explanation to be useful for the task. The first annotator chose the correct label 50% & 40% of the times for the given input & output explanations. The second annotator chose the correct label in 70% of the cases for both explanations. This corroborates that for a clean dataset such as PubHealth our explanations help for the task of veracity prediction.

7. Discussion

Results from our automatic and manual evaluation suggest two main implications of applying our post-editing algorithm over extracted RCs. First, with the automatic ROUGE evaluation, we confirmed that the post-editing preserves a large portion of important information that is contained in the gold explanation and is important for the fact check. This was further supported by our manual evaluation of veracity predictions, where the post-edited explanations have been most useful for predicting the correct label. We conjecture the above indicates that our post-editing can be applied more generally to summaries generated automatically for knowledge-intensive tasks, such as fact checking and question answering, where the information needed for prediction has to be preserved.

Second, with both the automatic and manual evaluation, we also corroborate that our proposed post-editing method improves several qualities of the generated explanations – fluency, conciseness, and readability. The latter are important prerequisites for building trust in automated fact-checking predictions as Thagard [43] find that people generally prefer simpler, more general explanations with fewer causes. They can also contribute to reaching a broader audience when conveying the veracity of the claim. Conciseness and readability are also the downsides of current professional long and in-depth ruling comments, which some leading fact-checking organisations, e.g., PolitiFact, (https://www.politifact.com/, accessed on 1 April 2021) have slowly started addressing by including short overview sections for the RCs.

8. Conclusions

In this work, we present an unsupervised post-editing approach to improve extractive explanations for fact-checking. Our novel approach is based on an iterative edit-based algorithm and rephrasing-based post-processing. In our experiments on two fact-checking benchmarking datasets, we observe, in both the manual & automatic evaluation, that our approaches generate fluent, coherent, and semantically preserved explanations.

For future work, an obvious next step is to investigate the applicability of our approach for other downstream tasks, such as machine summarisation, where the requirements for length and readability could vary depending on the end-user specifics. Furthermore, future work could explore additional improvements regarding the computational complexity of the proposed approach. For example, generative models trained with few-shot learning from a few post-editing examples could be employed to perform efficiently and effectively different editing operations. This would reduce the space of possible target positions and editing operations, especially for long input texts, such as veracity ruling comments. Finally, future work could explore other editing scores, e.g., scores optimising properties of natural language explanations, such as whether the explanation can be used to simulate the veracity prediction of the model.

Author Contributions: Conceptualization, S.J., P.A. and I.A.; Data curation, S.J. and P.A., Formal analysis, S.J.; Methodology, S.J. and P.A.; Software, S.J. and P.A.; Writing—original draft, S.J. and P.A.; Writing—review and editing, S.J., P.A. and I.A.; Supervision, I.A. All authors have read and agreed to the published version of the manuscript.

Funding: Shailza Jolly was supported by the TU Kaiserslautern CS Ph.D. scholarship program, the BMBF project XAINES (Grant 01IW20005), a STSM grant from the COST project Multi3Generation (CA18231), and the NVIDIA AI Lab (NVAIL) program. Pepa Atanasova has received funding from the European Union's Horizon 2020 research and innovation programme under the Marie Skłodowska-Curie grant agreement No 801199. Isabelle Augenstein's research is further partially funded by a DFF Sapere Aude research leader grant.

Institutional Review Board Statement: Not applicable.

Informed Consent Statement: Not applicable.

Data Availability Statement: We use open-source datasets that can be accessed from the referenced papers introducing the corresponding datasets.

Conflicts of Interest: The authors declare no conflict of interest.

Appendix A. Manual Evaluation

As explained in the Section 6 of the main paper, we mapped user inputs (TRUE/FALSE) for task two to the original labels for each dataset. For Liar, we map "true", "mostly-true", "half-true" to TRUE and "false", "pants-on-fire", and "barely-true" to FALSE. In the PubHealth dataset, we map "true" to TRUE, "false" to FALSE. The "insufficient" label is mapped to UNPROVEN. This way, once the mapping is done, we then compute the number of matches and non-matches to obtain an overall accuracy for this subset.

We appointed annotators with a university-level education in English.

Table A1. Results of manual evaluation for second task, i.e., predicting veracity label. DT refers to data type, # refers to annotator number, M/NM refers to number of matches/non-matches between annotator labels and original labels and I refers to number of times annotators found an explanation not sufficient to predict a label.

#	DT	LIAR-PLUS			PubHealth		
		M	NM	I	M	NM	I
1	Top-L	20	5	5	15	15	0
1	Edits-N+Para	14	7	9	12	18	0
2	Top-L	11	14	5	21	9	0
2	Edits-N+Para	13	10	7	21	9	0

Appendix B. Iterative Edit-Based Algorithm

We used the validation split of LIAR-PLUS to select the best hyperparameters for both datasets. We use the weight of 1.5, 1.2, 1.4, 0.95 for $\alpha, \eta, \gamma, \delta$ and 1.0 for β in our scoring function. We set the thresholds as 0.94 for reordering, 0.97 for deletion, and 1.10 for insertion. We keep all models – GPT-2, RoBERTa, and Pegasus, fixed and do not finetune them on any in-house dataset. We run our search algorithm on a single V100-32 GB GPU for 220 steps, which takes around 13 h for each split for both datasets.

Appendix C. Automatic Evaluation

In Tables A2 and A3, we provide results over both dev and test splits of the dataset for the ROUGE and readability automatic evaluation. We additionally provide ablation results for components of our approach. First, applying Pegasus directly on the extracted sentences preserves a slightly larger amount of information when compared to applying Pegasus on top of the iterative editing approach—up to 0.96 ROUGE-L scores, but the readability scores are still lower—up to 4.28 Flesch Reading Ease points. We also show results of the two parts included in the Edits step—the iterative editing and the grammar correction. We find that the grammar correction improves the ROUGE scores with up to 8 ROUGE-L score points and up to 8 Flesch Reading Ease points.

Table A2. Flesch Reading Ease (Flesch) and Dale–Chall Readability Score (Dale–Chall) for Validation (V) and Test (T) sets. Ablations are provided for the method as well – input selected sentences of Top-6, iterative-editing (Edits-IE), grammatical corrections (Edits-Gram), paraphrasing (Para).

	Method	Flesch-V ↗	Flesch-T ↗	Dale-Chall-V ↘	Dale-Chall-T ↘
		LIAR-PLUS			
	Justification	58.90 ± 13.38	58.81 ± 13.33	8.26 ± 1.08	8.22 ± 1.07
	Atanasova et al. [6]-4	54.76 ± 11.53	58.55 ± 13.70	8.38 ± 0.76	7.97 ± 1.05
Sup.	Top-6	57.77 ± 11.54	58.39 ± 12.11	7.90 ± 0.81	7.88 ± 0.80
	Top 6+Para	63.87 ± 10.60	64.44 ± 10.78	7.55 ± 0.76	7.52 ± 0.78
	Top 6+Edits	55.70 ± 12.40	56.26 ± 14.12	6.50 ± 0.69	6.46 ± 0.80
	Top 6+Edits+Gram	59.52 ± 11.98	60.20 ± 12.08	7.77 ± 0.88	7.74 ± 0.86
	Top 6+Edits+Gram+Para	66.04 ± 10.74	66.33 ± 11.09	7.44 ± 0.85	7.41 ± 0.91
Unsup.	Top-6	52.84 ± 10.37	53.32 ± 10.86	8.51 ± 0.69	8.50 ± 0.73
	Top 6+Para	59.33 ± 10.43	59.82 ± 10.58	8.13 ± 0.70	8.20 ± 0.80
	Top 6+Edits	50.70 ± 11.09	50.92 ± 12.54	6.91 ± 0.50	6.96 ± 0.62
	Top 6+Edits+Gram	54.76 ± 11.53	55.25 ± 12.03	8.38 ± 0.76	8.46 ± 0.85
	Top 6+Edits+Gram+Para	61.80 ± 11.11	62.13 ± 11.16	8.01 ± 0.77	8.10 ± 0.89
		PubHealth			
	Justification	48.19 ± 17.77	49.28 ± 19.08	9.21 ± 1.53	9.15 ± 1.61
	Atanasova et al. [6]-3	49.68 ± 15.96	48.72 ± 16.38	8.81 ± 1.09	8.87 ± 1.09
Sup.	Top-5	49.56 ± 13.48	48.63 ± 14.14	8.63 ± 0.88	8.67 ± 0.89
	Top 5+Para	57.52 ± 12.07	57.28 ± 12.35	8.18 ± 0.87	8.20 ± 0.88
	Top 5+Edits	47.38 ± 14.61	46.22 ± 15.95	7.06 ± 0.67	7.10 ± 0.75
	Top 5+Edits+Gram	54.30 ± 13.01	53.79 ± 14.56	8.32 ± 0.92	8.36 ± 0.97
	Top 5+Edits+Gram+Para	61.51 ± 11.28	61.38 ± 12.69	7.95 ± 0.92	7.96 ± 0.98
Unsup.	Top-5	43.54 ± 17.96	45.20 ± 14.36	9.25 ± 1.13	8.94 ± 0.88
	Top 5+Para	56.32 ± 11.41	55.78 ± 11.91	8.35 ± 0.83	8.39 ± 0.84
	Top 5+Edits	42.70 ± 17.01	42.29 ± 17.34	7.34 ± 0.79	7.36 ± 0.80
	Top 5+Edits+Gram	50.45 ± 14.45	50.74 ± 14.92	8.64 ± 0.95	8.62 ± 0.99
	Top 5+Edits+Gram+Para	60.24 ± 11.77	60.06 ± 12.97	8.12 ± 0.93	8.14 ± 0.95

Table A3. ROUGE-1/2/L F1 scores (see Section 5.1) for the edited justifications, higher results are better. Results in *italics* are those reported in the corresponding related work. Ablations are provided for the method as well – input selected sentences of Top-6, iterative-editing (Edits-IE), grammatical corrections (Edits-Gram), paraphrasing (Para).

	Method	Validation			Test		
		R-1	R-2	R-L	R-1	R-2	R-L
		LIAR-PLUS					
Baseline	Lead-4	27.92	6.94	24.26	28.11	6.96	24.38
	Lead-6	28.92	8.33	25.69	29.15	8.28	25.84
Supervised	Top-6	34.30	12.20	30.51	34.42	12.36	30.58
	Top 6 + Para	34.49	11.51	30.72	34.60	11.79	30.79
	Top 6 + Edits-IE	25.17	8.60	22.07	25.49	8.76	22.28
	Top 6 + Edits-IE + Edits-Gram	34.07	11.59	30.14	33.92	11.73	30.01
	Top-6 + Edits-IE + Edits-Gram + Para	34.20	11.05	30.29	33.94	11.25	30.08
Unsupervised	Top-6	29.24	7.99	25.83	29.63	7.58	25.86
	Top 6 + Para	29.94	7.72	26.40	29.92	7.35	26.24
	Top-6 + Edits-IE	21.49	5.67	18.77	22.73	5.56	19.51
	Top 6 + Edits-IE + Edits-Gram	29.00	7.46	25.51	28.93	7.06	25.14
	Top 6 + Edits-IE + Edits-Gram + Para	29.40	7.25	25.90	28.98	6.84	25.39
SOTA	Atanasova et al. [6]-4	*35.64*	*13.50*	*31.44*	*35.70*	*13.51*	*31.58*

Table A3. Cont.

	Method	Validation			Test		
		R-1	R-2	R-L	R-1	R-2	R-L
	PubHealth						
Baseline	Lead-3				29.01	10.24	24.18
	Lead-3	23.11	5.93	19.04	23.05	6.28	19.27
	Lead-5	24.20	6.83	20.89	23.73	6.86	20.67
Supervised	Top-6	30.35	12.63	26.43	29.93	12.42	26.24
	Top 5 + Para	29.76	10.75	25.47	29.43	10.69	25.51
	Top 5 + Edits-IE	22.49	8.94	19.70	22.11	8.72	19.49
	Top 5 + Edits-IE + Edits-Gram	29.58	11.18	25.54	29.38	11.16	25.41
	Top 5 + Edits-IE + Edits-Gram + Para	28.82	9.68	24.51	28.40	9.56	24.37
Unsupervised	Top-5	23.94	6.13	20.04	23.52	6.12	19.93
	Top 5 + Para	24.45	5.96	20.53	24.10	6.01	20.43
	Top-5 + Edits-IE	18.26	4.49	15.50	18.09	4.41	15.48
	Top 5 + Edits-IE + Edits-Gram	23.75	5.71	19.77	23.09	5.56	19.44
	Top-5 + Edits-IE + Edits-Gram + Para	23.97	5.46	19.98	23.35	5.38	19.56
SOTA	Kotonya and Toni [7]-3				32.30	13.46	26.99

Appendix D. Examples

Table A4 shows a qualitative example from the PubHealth dataset. We find that the final post-processed explanation is more readable, fluent, and concise in comparison to the originally selected explanation from RCs.

Table A4. Example explanations from Ruling Comments, Our iterative edit-based algorithm, and a combination of our algorithm and post-processing from test split of Pubhealth dataset. Each color presents an edit operation with **Reordering**, deletion, insertion, and paraphrasing.

Explanation from Ruling comments: Heavily-armed Muslims shouting "Allahu Akbar" open fire campers and hikers in a park. A heavily armed group of Middle Eastern looking Muslim men was arrested outside Los Angeles after opening fire upon hikers and campers in a large State Park in the area. There was no evidence found that a crime had been committed by any of the subjects who were detained and they were released. Moreover, the police report described the men only as "males," not "Middle Eastern males" or "Muslim males." The web site that started this rumor was Superstation95, which is not a "superstation" at all but rather a repository of misinformation from Hal Turner, who in 2010 was sentenced to 33 months in prison for making death threats against three federal judges. No credible news reports made any mention of the "Allahu Akbar" claim, and no witnesses stated they had been "shot at" by the men while hiking or camping.

Explanation from iterative algorithm: Heavily-armed Muslims males shouting "Allahu Akbar" open fire in a park. A heavily armed group of Middle Eastern looking Muslim men was arrested after opening fire upon hikers and campers in a large State Park outside Los Angeles. There was no evidence found that a crime had been committed by any of the subjects on campers and hikers. Furthermore, the police report described the men only as ",", not "Middle Eastern" or "Muslim." The website that started this rumor was Superstation95, which is not a "superstation" at all but rather a repository of misinformation from Hal Turner, who in 2010 was sentenced to 33 months in prison for making death threats against three federal judges. No credible news reports made any mention of the "Allahu Akbar" claim, and no witnesses stated they had been "shot at".

Explanation from iterative algorithm + Post-processing: Muslims shout "Allahu Akbar" open fire in a park. A heavily armed group of Middle Eastern looking Muslim men was arrested after opening fire on hikers and campers in a large State Park outside Los Angeles. There was no evidence that a crime had been committed by any of the campers or hikers. The website that started this rumor was Superstation95, which is not a "superstation" at all but rather a repository of misinformation from Hal Turner, who in 2010 was sentenced to 33 months in prison. There were no credible news reports that mentioned the Allahu Akbar claim, and no witnesses that said they had been shot at.

Claim: The media covered up an incident in San Bernardino during which several Muslim men fired upon a number of Californian hikers.

Label False

Appendix E. Novelty and Copy Rate

Table A5 presents additional statistics for the generated explanations from the test sets of both datasets. First, we compute how many of the words from the input Top-N Ruling Comments are preserved in the final explanation. We find that with the final step of the post-editing process, up to 8% of the tokens from the Ruling comments are not found in the final explanation. On the other hand, our post-editing approach generates up to 10% novel words that are not previously found in the RCs. This could explain the lower results for the ROUGE scores, which account only for exact token overlaps. Finally, while ROUGE scores are recall-oriented, i.e., they compute how many of the words in the gold explanation can be found in the candidate one, we compute a precision-oriented statistic of the words in the candidate that can be found in the gold explanation. Surprisingly, while ROUGE scores of our generated explanations decrease after post-processing, the reverse score increases, pointing to improvements in the precision-oriented overlap with our method.

Table A5. Copy rate from the Ruling Comments, Novelty w.r.t the Ruling comments, and Coverage % of words in the explanation that are found in the justification.

Method	Copy Rate	Novelty	Gold Coverage
LIAR-PLUS			
Top-6 Sup.	100	0	29.2 ± 11.4
Justification	41.4 ± 13.0	58.6 ± 13.0	100
Top-6+Edits-6 Sup.	98.5 ± 1.8	1.5 ± 1.8	30.7 ± 12.1
Top-6+Edits-6+Para Sup.	90.8 ± 4.8	9.2 ± 4.8	32.5 ± 12.6
PubHealth			
Top-5 Sup.	100	0	26.3 ± 21.2
Justification	47.1 ± 21.0	52.9 ± 21.0	100
Top-5+Edits-6 Sup.	98.1 ± 3.4	1.8 ± 2.0	27.8 ± 21.3
Top-5+Edits-6+Para Sup.	90.4 ± 5.8	9.5 ± 5.2	28.5 ± 20.2

In addition, in LIAR/PubHealth, the average summary length is 136/142 tokens for the extracted RCs, 89/86 for the gold justifications, 118.7/117.3 after iterative editing, and 98.5/94.7 after paraphrasing.

Appendix F. Experimental Setup

Selection of Ruling Comments

For the supervised selection of Ruling Comments, as described in Section 3.1, we follow the implementation of the multi-task model of Atanasova et al. [20]. For LIAR-PLUS, we do not conduct fine-tuning as the model is already optimised for the dataset. For PubHealth, we change the base model to SciBERT, as the claims in PubHealth are from the health domain and previous work [7] has shown that SciBERT outperforms BERTs for the domain. In Table A6, we show the results for the fine-tuning we performed over the multi-task architecture with a grid-search over the maximum length limit of the text and the weight for the positive sentences in the explanation extraction training objective. We finally select and use explanations generated with the multi-task model with a maximum text length of 1700, and a positive sentence weight of 5.

For the unsupervised selection of explanation sentences, we employ a Longformer model. We construct the Longformer model with BERT as a base architecture and conduct 2000 additional fine-tuning steps for the newly added cross-attention weights to be optimised. We then train models for both datasets supervised by veracity prediction. The most salient sentences are selected as the sentences that have the highest sum of token saliencies.

Table A6. Fine-tuning for PubHealth supervised multi-task model over positive sentence loss weight, base model and maximum length.

Method	Validation			Test		
	R-1	R-2	R-L	R-1	R-2	R-L
SciBERT, w-1, l-1200	26.00	7.29	21.41	25.78	7.71	21.42
SciBERT, w-1, l-1500	27.78	9.81	23.32	27.37	9.62	23.07
SciBERT, w-1, l-1700	28.73	11.27	24.42	28.45	11.32	24.21
SciBERT, w-2, l-1700	30.15	12.32	25.66	29.71	12.04	25.35
SciBERT, w-5, l-1700	30.96	12.59	26.54	30.79	12.31	26.38

Finally, we remove long sentences and questions from the Ruling Comments, where the ROUGE score changes after filtering are illustrated in Table A7, which results in the Top-N sentences, that are used as input for the post-editing method.

Table A7. Sentence clean-up of long sentences for LIAR-PLUS and PubHealth.

Method	Validation			Test		
	R-1	R-2	R-L	R-1	R-2	R-L
LIAR-PLUS Unsup						
Top-6	29.26	7.98	25.83	29.62	7.94	26.04
Filtered Top-6	29.52	7.90	25.98	29.60	7.96	25.94
LIAR-PLUS SUP						
Top-6	34.42	12.35	30.64	34.49	12.54	30.67
Filtered Top-6	34.30	12.20	30.51	34.42	12.36	30.58
PubHealth Unsup						
Top-5	23.78	6.23	19.95	23.13	6.08	19.63
Filtered Top-5	23.94	6.13	20.04	23.52	6.12	19.93
PubHealth SUP						
Top-5	30.24	12.61	26.36	29.78	12.50	26.18
Filtered Top-5	30.35	12.63	26.43	29.93	12.42	26.24

These experiments were run on a single NVIDIA TitanRTX GPU with 24 GB memory and 4 Intel Xeon Silver 4110 CPUs. Model training took ∼3 h.

References

1. Kotonya, N.; Toni, F. Explainable Automated Fact-Checking: A Survey. In Proceedings of the 28th International Conference on Computational Linguistics, Barcelona, Spain, 8–13 December 2020; pp. 5430–5443. [CrossRef]
2. Thorne, J.; Vlachos, A.; Christodoulopoulos, C.; Mittal, A. FEVER: A Large-scale Dataset for Fact Extraction and VERification. In Proceedings of the 2018 Conference of the North American Chapter of the Association for Computational Linguistics: Human Language Technologies, Volume 1 (Long Papers), New Orleans, LA, USA, 1–6 June 2018; pp. 809–819. [CrossRef]
3. Augenstein, I.; Lioma, C.; Wang, D.; Lima, L.C.; Hansen, C.; Hansen, C.; Simonsen, J.G. MultiFC: A Real-World Multi-Domain Dataset for Evidence-Based Fact Checking of Claims. In Proceedings of the 2019 Conference on Empirical Methods in Natural Language Processing and the 9th International Joint Conference on Natural Language Processing (EMNLP-IJCNLP), Hong Kong, China, 3–7 November 2019; pp. 4677–4691.
4. Wang, W.Y. "Liar, Liar Pants on Fire": A New Benchmark Dataset for Fake News Detection. In Proceedings of the 55th Annual Meeting of the Association for Computational Linguistics (Volume 2: Short Papers), Vancouver, BC, Canada, 30 July–4 August 2017; pp. 422–426.
5. Alhindi, T.; Petridis, S.; Muresan, S. Where is Your Evidence: Improving Fact-checking by Justification Modeling. In Proceedings of the First Workshop on Fact Extraction and VERification (FEVER), Brussels, Belgium, 1 November 2018; pp. 85–90. [CrossRef]
6. Atanasova, P.; Wright, D.; Augenstein, I. Generating Label Cohesive and Well-Formed Adversarial Claims. In Proceedings of the 2020 Conference on Empirical Methods in Natural Language Processing (EMNLP), Online, 16–18 November 2020; pp. 3168–3177. [CrossRef]
7. Kotonya, N.; Toni, F. Explainable Automated Fact-Checking for Public Health Claims. In Proceedings of the 2020 Conference on Empirical Methods in Natural Language Processing (EMNLP), Online, 16–18 November 2020; pp. 7740–7754. [CrossRef]
8. Liu, X.; Mou, L.; Meng, F.; Zhou, H.; Zhou, J.; Song, S. Unsupervised Paraphrasing by Simulated Annealing. In Proceedings of the 58th Annual Meeting of the Association for Computational Linguistics, Online, 5–10 July 2020; pp. 302–312.

9. Kumar, D.; Mou, L.; Golab, L.; Vechtomova, O. Iterative Edit-Based Unsupervised Sentence Simplification. In Proceedings of the 58th Annual Meeting of the Association for Computational Linguistics, Online, 5–10 July 2020; pp. 7918–7928.
10. Lu, Y.J.; Li, C.T. GCAN: Graph-aware Co-Attention Networks for Explainable Fake News Detection on Social Media. In Proceedings of the 58th Annual Meeting of the Association for Computational Linguistics, Online, 5–10 July 2020; pp. 505–514. [CrossRef]
11. Wu, L.; Rao, Y.; Zhao, Y.; Liang, H.; Nazir, A. DTCA: Decision Tree-based Co-Attention Networks for Explainable Claim Verification. In Proceedings of the 58th Annual Meeting of the Association for Computational Linguistics, Online, 5–10 July 2020; pp. 1024–1035. [CrossRef]
12. Atanasova, P.; Simonsen, J.G.; Lioma, C.; Augenstein, I. Diagnostics-Guided Explanation Generation. In Proceedings of the Thirty-Sixth AAAI Conference on Artificial Intelligence (AAAI'21), Virtually, 2–9 February 2021.
13. Mishra, R.; Gupta, D.; Leippold, M. Generating Fact Checking Summaries for Web Claims. In Proceedings of the Sixth Workshop on Noisy User-generated Text (W-NUT 2020), Online, 19 November 2020; pp. 81–90. [CrossRef]
14. Gunning, D. *Explainable Artificial Intelligence (xai)*; Defense Advanced Research Projects Agency (DARPA): Arlington County, VA, USA, 2017; Volume 2.
15. Camburu, O.M.; Rocktäschel, T.; Lukasiewicz, T.; Blunsom, P. e-SNLI: Natural Language Inference with Natural Language Explanations. In *Advances in Neural Information Processing Systems 31*; Bengio, S., Wallach, H., Larochelle, H., Grauman, K., Cesa-Bianchi, N., Garnett, R., Eds.; Curran Associates, Inc.: Red Hook, NY, USA, 2018; pp. 9539–9549.
16. DeYoung, J.; Jain, S.; Rajani, N.F.; Lehman, E.; Xiong, C.; Socher, R.; Wallace, B.C. ERASER: A Benchmark to Evaluate Rationalized NLP Models. In Proceedings of the 58th Annual Meeting of the Association for Computational Linguistics, Online, 5–10 July 2020; pp. 4443–4458. [CrossRef]
17. Stammbach, D.; Ash, E. e-FEVER: Explanations and Summaries for Automated Fact Checking. In Proceedings of the 2020 Truth and Trust Online Conference (TTO 2020), Virtual, 16–17 October 2020, p. 32.
18. Brown, T.; Mann, B.; Ryder, N.; Subbiah, M.; Kaplan, J.D.; Dhariwal, P.; Neelakantan, A.; Shyam, P.; Sastry, G.; Askell, A.; et al. Language Models are Few-Shot Learners. In *Proceedings of the Advances in Neural Information Processing Systems*; Larochelle, H., Ranzato, M., Hadsell, R., Balcan, M.F., Lin, H., Eds.; Curran Associates, Inc.: Red Hook, NY, USA, 2020; Volume 33, pp. 1877–1901.
19. Schumann, R.; Mou, L.; Lu, Y.; Vechtomova, O.; Markert, K. Discrete Optimization for Unsupervised Sentence Summarization with Word-Level Extraction. In Proceedings of the 58th Annual Meeting of the Association for Computational Linguistics, Online, 5–10 July 2020; pp. 5032–5042.
20. Atanasova, P.; Simonsen, J.G.; Lioma, C.; Augenstein, I. Generating Fact Checking Explanations. In Proceedings of the 58th Annual Meeting of the Association for Computational Linguistics, Online, 5–10 July 2020; pp. 7352–7364. [CrossRef]
21. Sanh, V.; Debut, L.; Chaumond, J.; Wolf, T. DistilBERT, a distilled version of BERT: Smaller, faster, cheaper and lighter. *arXiv* **2020**, arXiv:1910.01108.
22. Beltagy, I.; Lo, K.; Cohan, A. SciBERT: A Pretrained Language Model for Scientific Text. In Proceedings of the 2019 Conference on Empirical Methods in Natural Language Processing and the 9th International Joint Conference on Natural Language Processing (EMNLP-IJCNLP), Hong Kong, China, 3–7 November 2019; pp. 3615–3620. [CrossRef]
23. Beltagy, I.; Peters, M.E.; Cohan, A. Longformer: The Long-Document Transformer. *arXiv* **2020**, arXiv:2004.05150.
24. Simonyan, K.; Vedaldi, A.; Zisserman, A. Deep Inside Convolutional Networks: Visualising Image Classification Models and Saliency Maps. *arXiv* **2014**, arXiv:1312.6034.
25. Atanasova, P.; Simonsen, J.G.; Lioma, C.; Augenstein, I. A Diagnostic Study of Explainability Techniques for Text Classification. In Proceedings of the 2020 Conference on Empirical Methods in Natural Language Processing (EMNLP), Online, 5–10 July 2020; pp. 3256–3274. [CrossRef]
26. Kindermans, P.J.; Hooker, S.; Adebayo, J.; Alber, M.; Schütt, K.T.; Dähne, S.; Erhan, D.; Kim, B. The (un) reliability of saliency methods. In *Explainable AI: Interpreting, Explaining and Visualizing Deep Learning*; Springer: Berlin, Germany, 2019; pp. 267–280.
27. Hinton, G.E. Training products of experts by minimizing contrastive divergence. *Neural Comput.* **2002**, *14*, 1771–1800. [CrossRef] [PubMed]
28. Manning, C.D.; Surdeanu, M.; Bauer, J.; Finkel, J.R.; Bethard, S.; McClosky, D. The Stanford CoreNLP natural language processing toolkit. In Proceedings of the 52nd Annual Meeting of the Association for Computational Linguistics: System Demonstrations, Baltimore, MD, USA, 22–27 June 2014; pp. 55–60.
29. Li, J.; Li, Z.; Mou, L.; Jiang, X.; Lyu, M.; King, I. Unsupervised Text Generation by Learning from Search. In *Proceedings of the Advances in Neural Information Processing Systems*; Larochelle, H., Ranzato, M., Hadsell, R., Balcan, M.F., Lin, H., Eds.; Curran Associates, Inc.: Red Hook, NY, USA, 2020; Volume 33, pp. 10820–10831.
30. Liu, Y.; Ott, M.; Goyal, N.; Du, J.; Joshi, M.; Chen, D.; Levy, O.; Lewis, M.; Zettlemoyer, L.; Stoyanov, V. RoBERTa: A Robustly Optimized BERT Pretraining Approach. *arXiv* **2019**, arXiv:1907.11692.
31. Radford, A.; Wu, J.; Child, R.; Luan, D.; Amodei, D.; Sutskever, I. Language models are unsupervised multitask learners. *OpenAI Blog* **2019**, *1*, 9.
32. Zhang, X.; Lapata, M. Sentence Simplification with Deep Reinforcement Learning. In Proceedings of the 2017 Conference on Empirical Methods in Natural Language Processing, Copenhagen, Denmark, 7–11 September 2017; pp. 584–594. [CrossRef]

33. Kriz, R.; Sedoc, J.; Apidianaki, M.; Zheng, C.; Kumar, G.; Miltsakaki, E.; Callison-Burch, C. Complexity-Weighted Loss and Diverse Reranking for Sentence Simplification. In Proceedings of the 2019 Conference of the North American Chapter of the Association for Computational Linguistics: Human Language Technologies, Volume 1 (Long and Short Papers), Minneapolis, MN, USA, 2–7 June 2019; pp. 3137–3147. [CrossRef]
34. Rose, S.; Engel, D.; Cramer, N.; Cowley, W. Automatic keyword extraction from individual documents. *Text Min. Appl. Theory* **2010**, *1*, 1–20.
35. Reimers, N.; Gurevych, I.; Reimers, N.; Gurevych, I.; Thakur, N.; Reimers, N.; Daxenberger, J.; Gurevych, I. Sentence-BERT: Sentence Embeddings using Siamese BERT-Networks. In Proceedings of the 2019 Conference on Empirical Methods in Natural Language Processing, Hong Kong, China, 3–7 November 2019.
36. Zhang, J.; Zhao, Y.; Saleh, M.; Liu, P. Pegasus: Pre-training with extracted gap-sentences for abstractive summarization. In Proceedings of the International Conference on Machine Learning. PMLR, Virtual Event, 13–18 July 2020; pp. 11328–11339.
37. Nallapati, R.; Zhai, F.; Zhou, B. SummaRuNNer: A Recurrent Neural Network Based Sequence Model for Extractive Summarization of Documents. In Proceedings of the Thirty-First AAAI Conference on Artificial Intelligence (AAAI'17), San Francisco, CA, USA, 4–9 February 2017; pp. 3075–3081.
38. Chen, Y.C.; Bansal, M. Fast Abstractive Summarization with Reinforce-Selected Sentence Rewriting. In Proceedings of the 56th Annual Meeting of the Association for Computational Linguistics (Volume 1: Long Papers), Melbourne, Australia, 15–20 July 2018; pp. 675–686. [CrossRef]
39. Tan, J.; Wan, X.; Xiao, J. Abstractive Document Summarization with a Graph-Based Attentional Neural Model. In Proceedings of the 55th Annual Meeting of the Association for Computational Linguistics (Volume 1: Long Papers), Vancouver, BC, Canada, 30 July–4 August 2017; pp. 1171–1181.
40. Kincaid, J.P.; Fishburne, R.P., Jr.; Rogers, R.L.; Chissom, B.S. *Derivation of New Readability Formulas (Automated Readability Index, Fog Count and Flesch Reading Ease Formula) for Navy Enlisted Personnel*; Technical report; Naval Technical Training Command Millington TN Research Branch: Millington, TN, USA, 1975.
41. Powers, R.D.; Sumner, W.A.; Kearl, B.E. A recalculation of four adult readability formulas. *J. Educ. Psychol.* **1958**, *49*, 99. [CrossRef]
42. Liu, Y.; Lapata, M. Text Summarization with Pretrained Encoders. In Proceedings of the 2019 Conference on Empirical Methods in Natural Language Processing and the 9th International Joint Conference on Natural Language Processing (EMNLP-IJCNLP), Hong Kong, China, 3–7 November 2019; pp. 3730–3740. [CrossRef]
43. Thagard, P. Explanatory coherence. *Behav. Brain Sci.* **1989**, *12*, 435–467. [CrossRef]

Article

Constructing Explainable Classifiers from the Start—Enabling Human-in-the Loop Machine Learning

Vladimir Estivill-Castro [1], Eugene Gilmore [2,*] and René Hexel [2]

[1] Department of Information and Communications Technologies, Universitat Pompeu Fabra, 08018 Barcelona, Spain
[2] School of Information and Communication Technology, Griffith University, Brisbane 4111, Australia
* Correspondence: eugene.gilmore@alumni.griffithuni.edu.au

Abstract: Interactive machine learning (IML) enables the incorporation of human expertise because the human participates in the construction of the learned model. Moreover, with human-in-the-loop machine learning (HITL-ML), the human experts drive the learning, and they can steer the learning objective not only for accuracy but perhaps for characterisation and discrimination rules, where separating one class from others is the primary objective. Moreover, this interaction enables humans to explore and gain insights into the dataset as well as validate the learned models. Validation requires transparency and interpretable classifiers. The huge relevance of understandable classification has been recently emphasised for many applications under the banner of explainable artificial intelligence (XAI). We use parallel coordinates to deploy an IML system that enables the visualisation of decision tree classifiers but also the generation of interpretable splits beyond parallel axis splits. Moreover, we show that characterisation and discrimination rules are also well communicated using parallel coordinates. In particular, we report results from the largest usability study of a IML system, confirming the merits of our approach.

Keywords: interactive machine learning; decision tree classifiers; transparent-by-design; parallel coordinates

Citation: Estivill-Castro, V.; Gilmore, E.; Hexel, R. Constructing Explainable Classifiers from the Start—Enabling Human-in-the Loop Machine Learning. *Information* **2022**, *13*, 464. https://doi.org/10.3390/info13100464

Academic Editors: Gabriele Gianini and Pierre-Edouard Portier

Received: 24 August 2022
Accepted: 23 September 2022
Published: 29 September 2022

Publisher's Note: MDPI stays neutral with regard to jurisdictional claims in published maps and institutional affiliations.

Copyright: © 2022 by the authors. Licensee MDPI, Basel, Switzerland. This article is an open access article distributed under the terms and conditions of the Creative Commons Attribution (CC BY) license (https://creativecommons.org/licenses/by/4.0/).

1. Introduction

Humans' trust in the recommendations by artificial intelligence [1] (even with knowledge engineered expert systems) has required explanations in human understandable terms [2–5]. Even in heterogeneous robot–human teams, robots delivering explanations of their decisions are crucial to humans [6]. For instance, in the domain of power systems applications, experts mistrust the results of machine learning when they do not understand the outputs [7], which is an issue that has been ameliorated by applying Explainable AI (XAI). It could be argued that machine learning (ML) was fuelled by the need to decrease the cost of transferring human expertise into decision support systems and reducing the high cost of knowledge engineering and deploying such systems [8].

"It is obvious that the interactive approach to knowledge acquisition cannot keep pace with the burgeoning demand for expert systems; Feigenbaum terms this the 'bottleneck problem'. This perception has stimulated the investigation of machine learning as a means of explicating knowledge." [9]

From early reviews on the progress of ML, the understandability (then named comprehensibility) of the classification delivered by learned models was considered vital [10].

"A definite loss of any communication abilities is contrary to the spirit of AI. AI systems are open to their user who must understand them" [11].

There is so much to gain from incorporating Human-In-the-Loop Learning (HILL) into ML tasks. Early research identified validation or new knowledge elicitation [12–15] as advantages for Human-In-the Loop Machine Learning (HITL-ML). Today, the partnership between the fast heuristic search for classifiers, leveraging of visual analytics for ML [16], and HITL-ML has received the name of Interactive Machine Learning (IML) [17,18] because not only are datasets the source of knowledge, but IML also captures the experience of human experts [19]. The characteristics of IML that we emphasise here are that humans are assigned tasks in the learning loop [13,15] with specific roles, typically as experts, iteratively and incrementally updating the model, in a setting where the user interface is particularly important in influencing how the learning takes place [18]. We should point out that IML within the terminology of visual analytics [20] also has received the name of visualisation for model understanding, and in particular, visualisation for iterative steering model construction [16].

However, the immense progress in ML to tackle accuracy has resulted in the deployment of classifiers in enormous data sets and diverse domains. Supervised learning is part of many sophisticated integration applications, but the extraordinary predictive power and the superb accuracy have sacrificed the transparency and interpretability of the predictions. There is a revived interest in considering other criteria besides predictive accuracy [21,22], particularly in domains such as medicine [23], credit scoring [24], churn prediction [25], and bio-informatics [26].

Deep learning (considered a sub-area of machine learning [27]) offers Convolutional Neural Networks (CNNs) as supervised learning techniques that are regarded as superior for object classification, face recognition, and automatic handwriting understanding [27]. Similarly, Support Vector Machines (SVMs) are considered immensely potent for pattern recognition [28]. CNNs, ensembles [29], and SVMs output models that are considered "black box" models, since they are difficult to interpret by domain experts [21,30]. Thus, delivering understandable classification models is an urgent research topic [21,22]. The most common approach is to follow the production of accurate black-box models with methods to extract explanations [31,32]. There are two lines of work for delivering explainable models. The first line builds interpretable surrogate models that learn to closely reproduce the output of the black-box model while regulating aspects such as cluster size for explanation [33,34]. The second path is to produce an explanation for the classification of a specific instance [35] or to identify cases belonging to a subset of the feature space where descriptions are suitable [36] and trustworthy [37]. However, there are strong arguments that suggest that real interpretable models must be learned from the beginning [34,38].

Learning decision trees from data is one of the pioneer methods that produces understandable models [21,39]. Decision tree learning is now ubiquitous in big data, statistics, data mining, and ML. It is listed first among the top 10 most-used algorithms in data mining [40] is C4.5 [41] (a method based on a recursive approach incorporated into CLS [42] and ID3 [43]). Another representative of decision-tree learning is CART (Classification and Regression Trees) [44], and it also appears among the top 10 algorithms in data mining.

Earlier [45], we incorporated HITL-ML and used visualisation with parallel coordinates [46] to interactively build accurate and interpretable models with explainable outputs. We reviewed earlier evaluations of HITL-ML in machine learning tasks [45]. In particular, we provided an in-depth evaluation [45] of the WEKA [14] package for IML. Since the three fundamental aspects of IML are users, data, and interface [47], in this paper, we turn our attention to the interface and evaluate it with users who could play the primary roles of data scientists (but not domain experts) [48]. We have now incorporated parallel coordinates for the exploration of datasets and HITL-ML into a software prototype for the deployment of decision-tree classifiers (DTCs).

In this paper, we discuss how this prototype exhibits improvements over numerous other HITL-ML systems. We emphasise that our prototype not only achieves high accuracy [49] but enables (1) understanding of learnt classifiers, (2) exploration and insight into datasets, and (3) meaningful exploration by humans. In particular, we present here how parallel coordinates can provide a visualisation of specific rules and support an operator's interaction with the dataset even further to scrutinise specific rules. This enables the construction of characterisation and discrimination rules [50], which focus on one class above the others. We will show that users gain understanding through visualisation [24], presenting the experimental design, survey questions and results [51] of a detailed usability study for HITL-ML. We note that despite the increased interest in explainable outcomes from machine learning, a recent study [52] has found that from more than 600 publications between 2014 and 2020, one out of three exclusively use anecdotal evidence for their findings. The same study found that only one in five papers ever provided a case study. Thus, our contribution is not only the inclusion of a detailed user case study and the interface of our prototype, but the case study itself provides a model for a systematic evaluation of tools and systems for IML.

The paper is organised as follows. In Section 2, we review salient HITL-ML systems where learning classifiers involves dataset visualisations. We highlight the advantages of using parallel coordinates, noting that our review of HITL-ML systems reveals that there is almost no experimental evaluation of the effectiveness of HITL-ML. So far, the largest study was our reproduction [45] with 50 users, while the original WEKA `UserClassifier` paper reported a study with only five participants [14]. Section 3 explains our algorithms and system for HITL-ML. We proceed in Section 4 to provide the details of our study that consists of three experiments. Then, Section 5 reports on our own experiments with over 100 users on our proposed system. We highlight how our system overcomes a number of the shortcomings of the HITL-ML systems we reviewed in Section 2.

2. Dataset Visualisations for Involving Experts in Classifier Construction

Perhaps the earliest system to profit from the interpretability of decision trees for HITL-ML was the second version [53] of PCB [12], which introduced a coloured bar to illustrate an attribute. This bar is constructed by sorting the dataset on the attribute in question, representing each instance as a pixel (in the bar), which was coloured corresponding to its class. This allows a user to visually recognise clusters of a class on any one attribute. A DTC is visualised by showing bars with cuts to represent a split on an attribute. Each level of the tree can then be shown as a subset of an attribute bar with splits. A user participates in the learning the tree using this visualisation by themselves specifying where on a bar to split an attribute. The HITL-ML process has some algorithmic support to offer suggestions for splits and to finish subtrees. This type of visualisation appears particularly effective at showing a large dataset in a way that does not take much screen real estate.

However, the bar representation removes important human domain knowledge. For instance, all capability to see actual values of attributes (or the magnitude of value differences) disappears. This prevents experts from incorporating their knowledge. Moreover, the bar representation restricts classification rules to tests consisting of strictly univariate splits. There is no visualisation of attribute relationships (correlations, inverse correlations, or oblique correlations).

We discard bars, and inspired by the Nested Cavities (NC) algorithm [54,55], which is an approach to IML, we adopt parallel coordinates [46]. A parallel-coordinates visualisation draws a parallel axis for each attribute of the dataset. An instance of the dataset is then shown as a poly-line that crosses each axis at the normalised value for that attribute. Unlike most other visualisation techniques, parallel coordinates scale, and they are not restricted to datasets with a small number of dimensions. Parallel coordinates with 400 dimensions have been used [56] (Figure 14.21). More attributes are displayed by packing their axis on the side. However, decisions being based on over 100 variables are hardly interpretable and understandable [56]. Our method is an improvement over the NC algorithm [57]. Moreover, our prototype uses ML metrics to recommend attributes (and their order) in a visualisation. The operator still can select their preferred number of parallel axes to display.

The construction of classifiers with NC is similar to decision trees, because both approaches follow conditional focusing [58] (Figure 8.3) and recursive refinement [43] (p. 152, Chaper 4)that results in a decision tree structure [59] (p. 407). However, to the best of our knowledge, there are no user-focussed evaluations of IML with NC.

Other researchers have attempted star-coordinates for dataset visualisation and decision-tree construction [60,61]. With star-coordinates, each attribute is drawn as an axis on a 2D plane starting from the centre of the screen and projected outwards. Initially, all axes are evenly spaced so that they form a star shape. To map an instance onto the plane, all attribute values are first normalised (using linear scaling; that is $x' = (x - x_{\min})/(x_{\max} - x_{\min})$). Following this, the position of that instance on each axis is calculated. The final position of the instance is the average position from each axis. The user can interact with the visualisation by stretching and moving each axis, which recalculates the position of all the points displayed. However, star-coordinates displays suffer similar drawbacks as bar visualisations: users are unable to find subsets of predictive attributes, or ways to discriminate classes. In star-coordinates, the location for visualisation of an instance depends on the value of all attributes, making it impossible to identify boundaries between classes provided by a few (or even single) attributes. In contrast, with parallel coordinates, such separations are readily apparent.

With star coordinates, experts cannot explore and interchange attributes with other attributes, even if aware of subsets of predictive attributes. Users can only chose a projection emphasising influential attributes, losing any insight of one attribute's interaction with other attributes. There is no natural interaction with the star-coordinates visualisation where a user can also determine exactly what attribute(s) are contributing the most to the position of a point in the visualisation. PaintingClass [61] extends StarClass [60] so the expert can use visualisations of categorical attributes with parallel coordinates. However, the restriction persists for numerical attributes. PaintingClass uses parallel coordinates for categorical attributes where categorical values are evenly distributed along the axis as they appear in the dataset. This produces a visualisation with unintended bias. Because PaintingClass does not provide any machine learning support, and building the classifier is completely human-driven, it could be argued that it is not HITL-ML.

iVisClassifier [62] profits from parallel coordinates, but to reduce the attributes presented to the user, the dataset is presented only after using linear discriminant analysis (LDA) for feature reduction. The visualisation uses only the top LDA vectors. However, using this new LDA feature blocks the user's understanding of the visualisation since each LDA feature is a vector of coefficients over all the original attributes (or dimensions). Heat-maps are displayed in an attempt to help interpret component features, but they could possibly only have some semantics in the particular application of front-human-portrait face-recognition. A similar approach [20,63] uses techniques to visualise the high-dimensional feature space in two dimensions, so a human can draw a piece-wise linear boundary split in the 2D visualisation and iteratively construct the decision-tree classifier. This approach claims that some feature semantics are preserved, but it does not offer any user evaluation of this claim, neither when it comes to understandability nor accuracy.

As opposed to the earlier proposals, some empirical evaluation is reported in WEKA's UserClassifier [14]. UserClassifier is an IML system for DTCs that shows a scatter plot of only two attributes at a time (the user can pivot which two attributes appear in the visualisation). A display of small bars for each attribute provides some assistance for attribute relevance. The attribute bar presents the distribution of classes when sorted by that attribute. The user can review the current tree as a node-link diagram in one display, select, and expand a node. WEKA's UserClassifier is the only one reporting usability studies, and it involved only five participants [14]. Later, it was evaluated with 50 university students who had completed 7 weeks of material on machine learning and DTCs [45]. This study confirmed a number of limitations of WEKA's UserClassifier. For instance, the type of interaction (on the dataset and on the model) are restrictive in a number of ways.

- The visualisation displays only two attributes at a time; this is critically restrictive.
- The space to display region bars is minuscule, impeding users' observation of differences to decide which two attributes to display.

- Despite the immense literature on techniques for splitting a node to grow and construct a decision tree, the system does not provide any split-suggestion to the user.
- Unless users depart from the attribute visualisation window (losing context of the current splitting task), the tree under construction is not visible.
- Visualisation techniques (such as colour, or size) are not used. So, the user cannot inspect any properties of a node or an edge nor any relationship between a node and the dataset under analysis.

In summary, these issues limit a human's ability to gain a broader understanding of the datasets and of the classifiers. Nevertheless, we point out that a comparison of decision trees built by humans against decision trees built by machines resulted in humanly-built trees being superior in many aspects over those built by machines [64]. In that research [64], the technique for human-centred IML was parallel coordinates, which reinforces our approach to include this in our prototype and its evaluation.

3. Iterative Construction of DTCs Supported by Visualisations in Parallel Coordinates

We propose an HITL-ML system that uses parallel coordinates to visualise the training set, the decision tree, and also specific rules. We claim that our proposal addresses key shortcomings of the systems examined in Section 2 including those of the WEKA `UserClassifier`.

3.1. Using Parallel Coordinates

In a parallel-coordinates visualisation, a vertical axis is drawn for each dimension (each attribute). An instance $v = (a_1, a_2, \ldots, a_d)$ (a point in Cartesian coordinates) corresponds to a poly-line in parallel coordinates that visits value a_n on the axis for attribute A_n (for $n \in \{1, \ldots, d\}$). For HITL-ML, we assign a different colour to each class, and the labelled instances of the training set are painted using the colour of their label. Figure 1 shows two examples of the parallel coordinate visualisation and the corresponding partially-built decision tree.

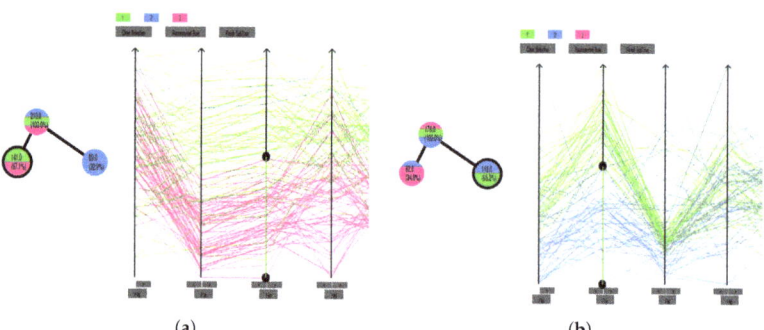

Figure 1. Two examples, each exploring a different dataset and focussing on different leaves. (a) Exploring the `seed` dataset. (b) Exploring the `wine` dataset.

If there are many attributes, a window with a projection onto a subset of the attributes is displayed. On-line Analytical Processing (OLAP) tools enable business intelligence practitioners to analyse multidimensional data interactively from multiple perspectives [65]. Our use of colour concentration allows the rapid selection and application of OLAP-type operations on the visible window. For instance, removing one attribute from visualisation and adding another one is a pivot operation. The information gain on an attribute or range within an attribute is used to suggest relevant attributes to the human operator. The visualisation enables domain experts to explore scenarios from their domain knowledge or spot new patterns and hypothesis.

For the specific task of IML, the user will build a DTC following Hunt's generic recursive construction [43] (p. 152, Chaper 4): the user picks a leaf-node T to further refine the current rule that terminates at T. However, our system provides support for this deeper growth of the tree from leaf T.

1. We colour the corresponding leaf T to illustrate the purity of T (this directly correlates with the classification accuracy of the rule terminating at T). For instance, the left leaf in the tree of Figure 1a indicates it containing an almost even split of two classes. However, the right leaf is practically pure. The depth of the leaf T inversely correlates with the applicability and generality of that rule terminating at T. Understandability and interpretability also inversely correlate with leaf depth.
2. The system allows the user to select whether to display values of predictability power of attributes, such as the information gain.

A tree is always a classifier because the decision at a leaf is the simple Naïve Bayes decision.

3.2. The Splits the User Shall Apply

The splits the user can apply were defined in our earlier work [49]. A split on one axis alone is commonly a range, and this is familiar to DTC construction as this is also the type of split evaluated by algorithms such as C4.5 [41] or J48 [66]. However, the parallel-coordinates visualisation allows an *oblique* split [67–69] that involves two attributes. Thus, the oblique test is interpretable particularly because of the point-line duality in parallel coordinates [46]. For instance, a rule that uses a point between two attributes in parallel coordinates means that instances in this split follow two types: first, those that closely follow some linear correlation between two attributes, and second, those that do not reflect such a linear correlation. If we use a rectangular region for the split, then we regulate a margin for the above-mentioned linear correlation. Figure 2 illustrates the types of splits users can introduce in our system.

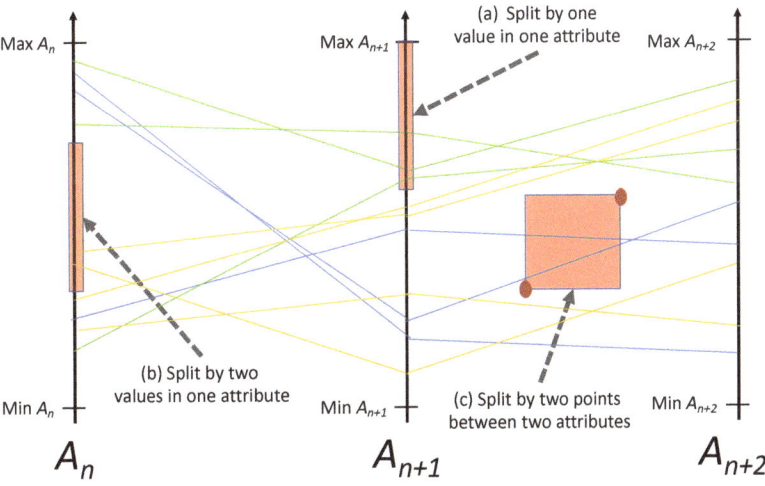

Figure 2. The types of splits that the user can apply to further a leaf to interactively refine a decision tree. Split (a) and split (b) are familiar from standard decision tree construction. However, a rectangular split (c) provides an excellent trade-off between interpretability and multivariate splits.

In addition to the interpretability of the splits based on rectangles between two parallel axes, these splits constitute a richer language to define DTCs than the standard splits of classical machine learning algorithms. Although not as powerful as the full *oblique* splits [67–69], this is appropriate, as full oblique splits are extremely hard to comprehend by humans. DTCs that use oblique splits are also called multivariate decision trees [70,71], and although learning multivariate decision trees results in shorter trees, they are rarely used because the tests (and thus their rules) are incomprehensible by humans.

3.3. Information That Supports Interaction

Our HITL-ML system supports interaction is several ways. For instance, when the user selects a node in the tree, the visualisation restricts the instances displayed in the parallel coordinates' canvas to those that satisfy the splits of the selected node's ancestors.

The user can elect several algorithms for ordering attributes in the parallel coordinates' canvas, which, by default, are sorted by criteria of discriminative power, and among these, the default is information gain. Then, if a user selects an attribute for the next split, the system also offers suggestions for the split on the axis, and again, diverse algorithms are available (again, information gain, gini index, etc.) Moreover, the user can opt for a proposal for a split from the system. Such proposals are rectangular splits computed using evolutionary strategies [49]. The use can accept or modify the rectangle suggested by the system. The automatic construction can be restricted to a node or to a subtree. As the user explores proposed subtrees, the user gains an understanding of the attributes and interaction between attributes. We argue that the algorithms supporting the HITL-ML provide adequate balance between number-crunching and machine learning support, and user's intervention and interaction to incorporate human expertise, or for users to discover new insights in the data.

We highlight here the crucial role that human pattern spotting has on some of the split selections. For example, Figure 3 represents a setting where humans easily chose better splits than machine learning indicators (such as information gain, gini index). The user can also intervene when machine learning indicators are offering similar values, but some attributes are easier to capture or much more readily available than others.

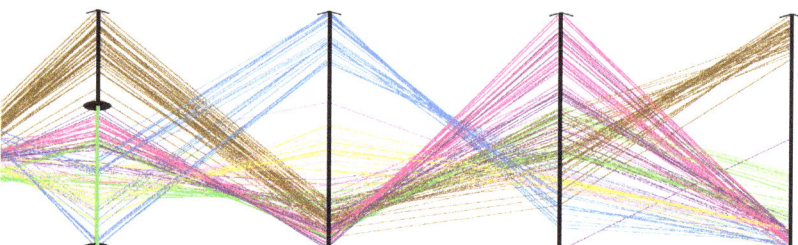

Figure 3. The use of ML metrics of discrimination (in this case, both, information gain or gini ratio) sorts the attributes from left to right and elects the highlighted split. However, a human would chose a better (more purifying) split, such as the second attribute that isolates the blue class with a robust gap, or the fourth attribute, which isolates the brown class with also a wide gap. This situation illustrates how HITL-ML can deliver better models.

3.4. Visualising the Tree

As illustrated by the two examples in Figure 1 and those in Figure 4, an interactive display of the tree under construction can be presented on the left of the parallel coordinates' canvas. As we mentioned, the nodes of the tree are coloured with a histogram that informs the user of the number of instances of each class in the training set that reached the node. We emphasise that this rapidly shows the user the purity (and thus accuracy) of rules reaching a node. The user can also obtain feedback information about the support (percentage of the training set instances that reach the node) and confidence (percent of correct-class classification) for the rule at the node.

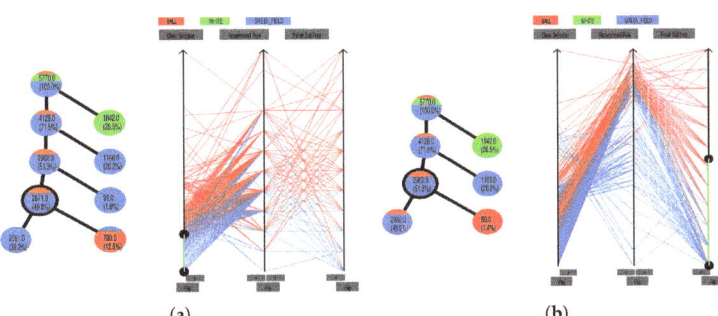

Figure 4. Illustrations of the HITL-ML systems used for IML to build DTCs with either a high precision or high recall for the "black" class (coloured red). (**a**) High recall DTC. (**b**) High precision DTC.

3.5. Visualising Rules

So far, we have shown how our HITL-ML system uses parallel coordinates to effectively assist a user in the interactive learning phase of constructing a DTC. We now demonstrate how we can also use parallel coordinates to allow a user to understand a particular classification made by a learnt DTC. Our approach here supports explorative data mining, where experts are seeking to find characteristic rules or discriminant rules [50]. One of the features of DTCs is their ability to be converted into a decision list. Such a decision list is composed of a series of if–else rules that can be followed to determine the classification of a particular instance. We use a similar idea to visualise the decision path for a single leaf in a DTC. Instead of a textual representation of such a rule, however, we can again use parallel coordinates to graphically represent this decision path. We argue that parallel coordinates are ideally suited to this task, as we can use a series of axes to visualise each component of the rule in the one visualisation. Depending on the depth of the rule and available screen real estate, we may even be able to visualise the entire decision path on one screen. Not only this, but in our graphical representation, we can visualise the training data and the effect that each component of the decision path has on the resulting subset of selected data. When used in conjunction with our visualisation of the entire DTC and its accompanying statistics for each node, we argue that this gives a human user a profound, intuitive and interpretable explanation of a DTC's classification.

Figure 5 shows an example of how we use parallel coordinates to visualise the decision path to a leaf node in a DTC. Here, the left-most axis is used to represent the split of the root node in the DTC, which will always be the first component in any decision path. In this example, the split for the root node of the decision tree is a simple single attribute split on attribute A_1 and is visualised as such with the highlighted range. Between the first and second axes, the start of poly-lines for every instance in the training set is shown. From the second axis, only instances in the training set continue on that matched the split from the previous axis. This allows the user to easily see what subset of data is selected by each split. The visualisation continues in this manner with poly-lines being terminated once they no longer match a split in the decision path. In this example, the final split in the decision path is a parallel coordinates region split and is visualised using the last two axes.

Another advantage of visualising a particular leaf of a DTC in this way is allowing the user to assess the likelihood that a specific classification is accurate. While traditional performance metrics such as accuracy, ROC, and F1 score capture the performance of the entire tree, it is possible that accuracy varies between individual sections of the model. Using our visualisation, a user can view the amount of the majority class in a leaf node as well as how significant this majority is. When looking at the classification of a particular instance, the user can also see how close to the margins of each split that instance is.

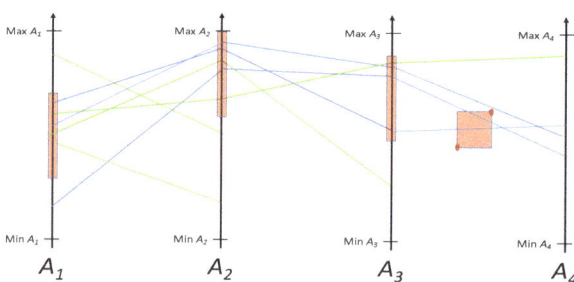

Figure 5. Example of how our HITL-ML system using parallel coordinates to visualise the decision path of a single leaf in a DTC.

3.5.1. Condensing the Decision Path

In cases where an attribute (or attribute pair in the case of our parallel coordinates region splits) appears more than once in a decision path, we have the opportunity to reduce the number of attributes required to display the decision path by taking the union of both splits. If using only a single attribute split, we can create an upper bound on the number of axes required to visualise any decision path equal to the number of attributes in the dataset. When not condensing the decision path in this way, the ordering of axes in parallel coordinates allows the user to see the depth of each rule in the DTC. For this reason, we provide the user with the option of turning this feature on or off in our HITL-ML system.

3.5.2. Visualising Negated Splits

When visualising a decision path, we need to consider how negated splits are handled. This is important, since half of the sum of all path components are negated splits, i.e., we traverse to the child node that represents the path to take when not matching the node's split. For single attribute splits of the form $l \leq A_n$, the negated split becomes $A_n < l$ and can be represented on a parallel coordinates axis by simply swapping the highlighted region with the region not highlighted. For a single attribute test with two split points of the form $l \leq A_n \leq r$, our negated split becomes $A_n < l \vee r < A_n$. This can again be represented on a parallel coordinates axis by swapping the highlighted region with the region not highlighted. Although the representation of this two-value split may seem complicated (particularly, when we consider condensing a decision path that contains the same attributes multiple times), swapping of highlighted regions is simplified using De Morgan Laws [72]. Consider a decision path that includes two components using attribute A_n. The first component is of the form $l_1 \leq A_n \leq r_1$, and the second is the negated form of the split $l_2 \leq A_n \leq r_2$, i.e., $A_n < l_2 \vee r_2 < A_n$. Suppose we have the situation where $l_1 < l_2 \wedge r_1 > r_2$. In this case, our condensed split becomes $l_1 \leq A_n \leq l_2 \vee r_2 \leq A_n \leq r_1$. To represent this condensed split on a parallel coordinates axis, we now need to highlight multiple disconnected sections of the axis.

Figure 6 illustrates this situation. In a case where the same attribute is used many times in a decision path, the resulting axis consists of several disconnected sections of the axis, which are highlighted (these are disjunctions of intervals). Interestingly, this effect is only possible when using tests containing two split points. Although we have shown in our previous work that using such splits appears to produce less accurate trees, we argue that in an HITL-ML system, it is only natural that a user will want to use these splits containing two split points to isolate certain sections of data, and as such, our system supports the visualisation of condensed rules of this form.

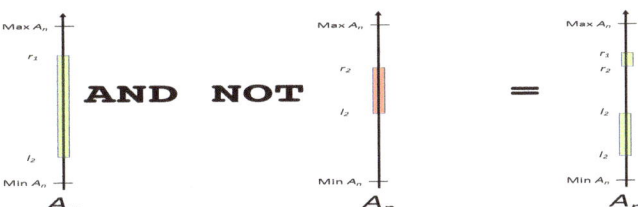

Figure 6. Disconnected sections on a single axis through negated split condensing rules. The green and negated red selections result in two selected ranges (third axis).

4. Materials and Methods

We now report on the design, materials and methods for a comprehensive study evaluating our prototype. We obtain quantitative data on the effectiveness of our visualisation techniques from an online survey using the custom built survey platform Prolific [73]. The quantitative data are from 104 participants who performed timed tasks using variants of our new visualisation techniques and HITL-ML approach, resulting in 8944 data points.

Our survey starts by reviewing three concepts applicable to HITL-ML. These three concepts are (1) DTC (2) PC, and (3) scatter-plot based visualisation techniques. This refresher practice ensures we can rank the expertise with ML topics of our participants and exclude any not fluent with DTC construction. Then, the survey requires users to complete tasks building DTC on a platform for automatic data collection [73]. In addition to the facility to animate aspects of the visualisations, the online platform allowed us to select participants who had experience in ML.

4.1. Recruiting Participants

Research studies using Prolific [73] commonly use the capability to enable participation to only specific demographics. We also selected participants whose answers to demographic questions were as follows.

Which of the following best describes the sector you primarily work in? Information Technology, Science, Technology, Engineering and Mathematics;
What is your first language? English;
Which of these is the highest level of education you have completed? Undergraduate degree (BA/BSc/other);
Do you have computer programming skills? Yes/No.

4.2. Survey Design

The online survey consists of three different experiments and offers participants user interaction as if they were performing tasks in a system for HITL-ML. Not only does the system display videos and allow users to click on images to experiment, while moving forward and back through explanations, it also enables interactivity in all components when building DTC, including display, the selection of nodes, and their expansion. In addition, the system allows users to configure some parameters of these visualisations.

The first experiment examines the effectiveness of visualising a DTC using a node-link diagram with coloured nodes (see Figure 1). The second experiment examines participants' ability to understand the classification of individual instances, comparing the traditional method of traversal of a DTC against the PC-based visualisation of the path to a leaf node. In the third experiment, pairs of videos are played to the participants, contrasting two different HITL-ML systems. Showing videos removes the participants' need to gain sufficient expertise with GUI aspects that are not the core of the visualisation. Nevertheless, participants can evaluate how well a system supports the user to perform a HITL-ML task.

Before starting the survey, each participant is randomly placed in one of two evenly sized groups (Group A and Group B). Participants from each group are shown slightly different visualisations when completing tasks in Experiment 1 and Experiment 2 with the aim of evaluating what effect these visualisations have on a participant's ability to complete the tasks in each experiment. This also requires that the sections introducing participants to visualisation techniques be presented and ordered slightly differently. The arrows in Figure 7 show the sections displayed to each group in the order (work-flow) from the perspective of participants. We now detail the exact composition of each experiment and the introductory section of the survey.

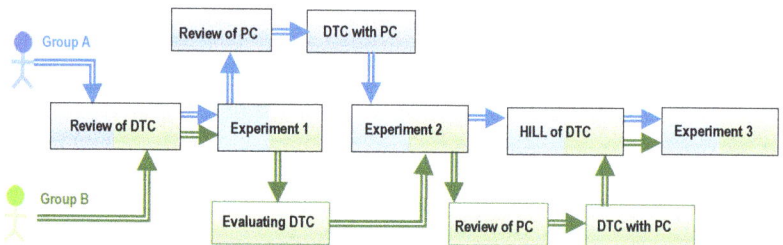

Figure 7. Composition of DTC and HITL-ML survey for participants in Group A and Group B.

4.2.1. Experiment 1—DTC Node Colouring

Experiment 1 examines the effect that colouring the nodes of a DTC has on a participant's ability to interpret the tree. Specifically, this experiment looks at the ability to use a visualisation of a DTC to estimate the accuracy of the entire tree as well as subsections thereof. Participants are shown several different DTC and are required to complete two tasks for each DTC. The first task requires participants to estimate the accuracy of the DTC. Then, participants must select a single leaf node that they believe 'is most in need of further refinement to improve the accuracy of the classifier'. Figure 8 shows the layout of this experiment. The objective of these tasks is to provide evidence for the following hypotheses.

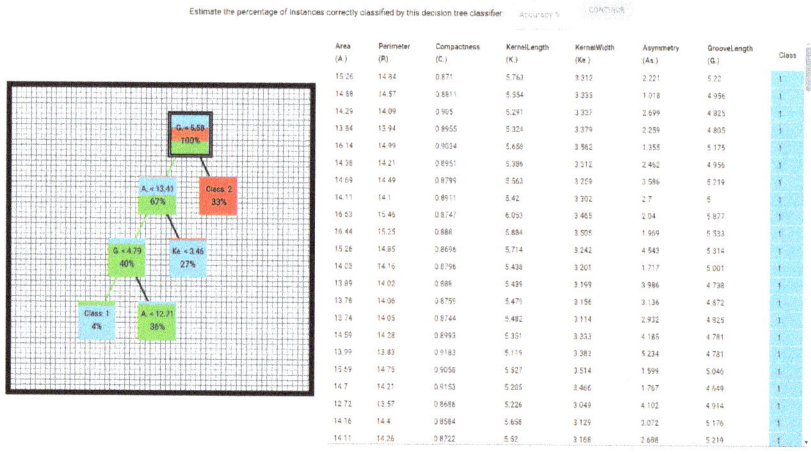

Figure 8. Layout of survey for Experiment 1. The table on the right shows instances reaching the selected node. The class column colours instances with a distinctive colour for the class. The top instances show up as blue boxes on the table, the users would need to scroll down to find those instances belonging to the red class and to the green class.

Hypothesis 1. *The technique of colouring nodes will allow a user to more accurately estimate the predictive power of a DTC.*

Hypothesis 2. *The technique of colouring nodes will allow a user to more quickly estimate the predictive power of a DTC.*

Hypothesis 3. *The technique of colouring nodes will allow a user to more accurately identify the most impure nodes in a DTC.*

Hypothesis 4. *The technique of colouring nodes will allow a user to more quickly identify the most impure nodes in a DTC.*

On the left of the screen, the system presents a visualisation of a DTC to both groups of participants (there is no difference in this aspect for Group A and Group B). The right half of the screen shows a table containing the training data used to learn the DTC. This table also has a colour coding for the class column for both Group A and Group B. For participants in Group B, the nodes of the DTC are also coloured. For each tree, participants are first asked to estimate the accuracy of the tree by entering an integer between 0 and 100. Using accuracy rather than the F-measure ensured that all participants were familiar with the statistic used. Given that accuracy is a much simpler statistic to calculate than F-measure, asking for accuracy also ensures that the cognitive load on the participant is reduced as much as possible.

After estimating the accuracy of each DTC, participants are asked to select the leaf node they *'believe is most in need of further refinement to improve the accuracy of the classifier'*. To quantify the accuracy of a user's choice, we use a metric $RImp(n)$, describing the impurity of a node in a DTC relative to the most impure node in the tree. Let n be defined as a leaf node in a DTC containing N leaf nodes. Furthermore, let $I(n)$ be the number of instances of training data that reach n, whose class is not the majority class of instances reaching n.

Definition 1. *We can then define $I_{max}(N)$ as follows:*

$$I_{max}(N) = \max\{I(n) \mid n \in N\}.$$

The following now defines our evaluation metric.

Definition 2. *We define $RImp(n)$, the relative impurity of a node, as*

$$RImp(n) = \frac{(I_{max}(N) - I(n))}{I_{max}(N)}.$$

Each participant is shown eight different DTCs that were constructed from three datasets. We use three datasets available from the UCI-repository [74], the Wine (Available online: https://archive.ics.uci.edu/ml/datasets/Wine, accessed on 3 April 2020), Cryotherapy (Available online: https://archive.ics.uci.edu/ml/datasets/Cryotherapy+Dataset+, accessed on 3 April 2020) and Seeds (Available online: https://archive.ics.uci.edu/ml/datasets/seeds, accessed on 3 April 2020) datasets. These three datasets exhibit the following relevant properties.
- A reasonably accurate (>90% accuracy) DTC can be learnt for each dataset with small trees sizes that remain interpretable to a human.
- All attributes have humanly understandable names and semantic meaning.

Using these three datasets, eight DTCs were built with a range of different accuracies for two reasons. First, having different accuracies for each DTC ensures that there are no patterns in the survey that participants can use to help them assess the accuracy of any individual tree. Second, having a range of accuracies ensures that participants' ability to assess the accuracy of a DTC is not dependent on the DTC having a particularly low or high accuracy. Table 1 shows the true accuracy of each DTC presented to participants. For each participant, we record the following information.

- Their prediction of the accuracy of each DTC.
- The time taken to predict the accuracy of each DTC.
- The leaf node selected by the participant as most impure for each DTC.
- The time taken to select the most impure leaf node in each DTC.

Table 1. Training set accuracy of each DTC presented to participants.

Tree No.	Dataset	Accuracy
1	Wine	69
2	Wine	99
3	Wine	90
4	Cryotherapy	72
5	Cryotherapy	92
6	Seeds	72
7	Seeds	95
8	Seeds	82

4.2.2. Experiment 2—Rule Visualisation

This experiment evaluates the effectiveness of representing the path from a root node to a leaf node using PC. Figure 9 shows the layout of this experiment. For this experiment, participants must determine whether a given instance reaches a particular leaf node in a DTC. Participants in Group A and Group B are shown two different visualisations while performing this task. For participants in Group A, this visualisation consists of a DTC on the left half of the screen and a table on the right half of the screen. The DTC on the left is represented as a simple node-link diagram with the split criteria for each internal node represented textually within the node. As part of this visualisation, a green arrow points to one of the nodes in the DTC. The table on the right contains a single row with the attribute values of one instance. Group A participants are required to manually traverse the DTC for the instance shown in the table and determine whether it arrives at the node indicated by the green arrow. Group A participants are also shown a table with a single instance containing the attribute values to be used to traverse the tree.

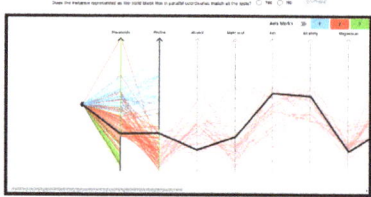

Figure 9. The layout of Experiment 2 for users in Group A (**left**) and Group B (**right**).

Group B participants are shown a PC visualisation of the path to a particular leaf node in a DTC. This PC visualisation shows the entire dataset as well as ranges on several of the PC axes to represent each of the univariate splits on the path to the leaf node. The polyline for one of the instances is shown as a distinct thick black line. Group B participants are required to determine if this instance arrives at the leaf node being visualised using PC.

Participants in both groups use the same set of instances and DTC. The DTCs used are the same as those in Experiment 1. For each DTC, participants must evaluate three instances from the dataset used to create the DTC. Participants answer whether they think this instance reaches the selected leaf node. This experiment tests the following hypotheses.

Hypothesis 5. *Participants visualising the path to a node using PC will more accurately determine whether an instance reaches a particular leaf node.*

Hypothesis 6. *Participants visualising the path to a node using PC will more quickly determine whether an instance reaches a particular leaf node.*

4.2.3. Experiment 3—Human-in-the-Loop Video Survey

This experiment evaluates several HITL-ML features proposed earlier. For each pair of videos, one video illustrates a particular HITL-ML task being performed using a system based on the techniques proposed earlier. The other video in each pair shows how the same task is carried out using Weka's `UserClassifier`. After viewing both videos, participants are required to express their preference on a five-point Likert scale. At the start of the experiment, the survey system randomly decides which HITL-ML system's video will be shown to each participant first. The order then remains the same for all video pairs for this participant. In total, five different pairs of videos demonstrate a variety of HITL-ML tasks. A description of each video pair and its questions are given below. Table 2 also shows a summary of the questions asked for each video pair. After answering the Likert-scale questions for each of the five pairs of videos, the survey system asks participants one final Likert scale question. This question asks participants, *'Based on the videos you've seen, which system would you prefer to use to build a decision tree classifier?'*

Table 2. Questions for Experiment 3.

Question No.	Question
Q1	Which system do you believe provides a better method of finding splits to build a decision tree classifier?
Q2	Which system allows you to better navigate and understand the current state of a decision tree classifier as it is being constructed?
Q3	Which system allows you to more easily determine how often a tree will predict the class correct class of an instance?
Q4	Which system allows you to more easily find nodes in a decision tree classifier that need additional splits?
Q5	Which system would provide better assistance to you when constructing a decision tree?
Q6	Based on the videos you have seen, which system would you prefer to use to build a decision tree classifier?

The tasks on the activities with videos are as follows.

1. The first pair of videos examines the ability of a user to find an effective split for a node in a DTC. In the `UserClassifier` video, survey participants are shown how the dataset is visualised using a two-dimensional scatter-plot as well as how a user can select attributes using the small bar visualisation of each attribute on the right of the screen. The video then demonstrates how a user can construct a split for a node by selecting a region on the two-dimensional scatter-plot. The PC-based video shows how a dataset is visualised using PC and how a user can create a split by selecting a range on an axis. This video also shows how a user can rearrange axes and remove axes that are not of interest. In addition, participants are shown how a user can ask the PC-based system to reorder axes so that interesting axes appear on the far left. This rearrangement is achieved by ordering axes based on the best gain ratio of each attribute, as discussed in Section 3.3. At the end of both videos, participants are asked, *'Which system do you believe provides a better method of finding splits to build a decision tree classifier?'*

2. The next pair of videos examines a user's ability to navigate and understand a DTC in each HITL-ML system. The `UserClassifier` video shows how a user can switch to a separate tab from the training set visualisation to observe the current state of the DTC being constructed. Participants are shown how internal and leaf nodes are displayed as grey circles and rectangles, respectively. This video also shows how splits for each internal node can be observed by selecting the node and switching tabs to see the selected region in the dataset visualisation tab. The PC-based video demonstrates how the system splits one window into two sections. The video shows how the left

section visualises the DTC using the coloured nodes. This video also demonstrates how a user can interact with this DTC and select a node, at which point any split for that node is shown on the far left axis in PC. After viewing both videos, the survey system asks participants, *'Which system allows you to better navigate and understand the current state of a decision tree classifier as it is being constructed?'*

3. The third set of videos looks at a user's ability to estimate the accuracy of a DTC using each HITL-ML system. The `UserClassifier` video shows participants how a user can look at the counts of instances shown in each leaf node to determine the majority class and how often this leaf misclassified training instances. This video also demonstrates how a user can assess the quality of a split for a node by visualising it with the training set in the second tab of the system. The PC-based video shows participants how a user can use the colouring of the nodes in the DTC to determine the accuracy of each leaf node. Participants are also shown how a user can assess the quality of a split using the visualisation of the split in PC. After both videos, participants are asked, *'Which system allows you to more easily determine how often a tree will predict the correct class of an instance?'*

4. The fourth pair of videos examines the ability of a user to locate nodes in a DTC that requires further refinement. In the `UserClassifier` video, participants are shown how a user can use the visualisation of the DTC and the numbers within each node to find leaf nodes with a large number of instances from multiple classes. The PC-based video shows participants how a user can use the colouring of nodes to determine which nodes require further refinement. Following these videos, participants are asked, *'Which system allows you to more easily find nodes in a decision tree classifier that need additional splits?'*

5. The final pair of videos look at the algorithmic assistance features offered by each system. In the `UserClassifier` video, participants are shown how a user can use an automated algorithm to complete a subtree. This video points out to participants that the user has no way of visualising the generated subtree or determining any of its characteristics. The PC-based video shows how a user can ask the system to suggest a test for a node in the tree and how this test can be visualised for the user. This video also shows how the system can complete a subtree for the user, which can be visualised and edited as deemed appropriate by the user. Following these videos, participants are asked, *'Which system would provide better assistance to you when constructing a decision tree?'*

4.3. Methods

4.3.1. Introduction to Decision Trees

As we explained, the first section of the survey provides users with an introduction to DTCs. This introduction is structured as a review that illustrates all examples with the Iris dataset. Figure 10 shows the layout of the user's window on the survey. Subjects are first presented with a scrollable table containing the complete Iris dataset. Using interactive prompts, the survey introduces participants to terminology, such as an instance in a dataset, what the class of an instance is, and the goals of a classification task.

After the introduction to the basic terminology about datasets, participants are introduced to DTCs. Subjects work through an interactive visualisation of a DTC for the Iris dataset. This DTC visualisation is similar to the node-link visualisation of a DTC described in Section 3.4. The participant is able to click on each node in the tree to filter the instances displayed in the tables of the Iris dataset. Interactive prompts guide the participants through the following concepts.

- The structure of a DTC.
- How to evaluate univariate splits on internal nodes in a DTC.
- How to traverse a DTC.
- How a DTC can be used to classify an instance.

- How the class label assigned to a leaf node is determined via the majority class of instances reaching that leaf.
- Examples of a DTC incorrectly classifying instances.
- How a user might use the presented visualisation of a DTC to estimate its accuracy.

Participants in Group B are additionally introduced to the concept of colouring nodes in the visualisation of the DTC in this section. This is the visualisation technique introduced in Section 3.4, where each node in the DTC is coloured such that the amount of each colour in a node is proportionate to the amount of the corresponding class reaching the node.

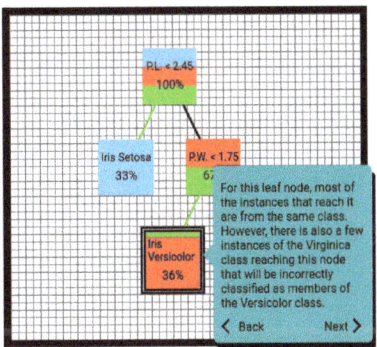

Figure 10. Layout of survey section introducing DTC. When the leaf node is selected, the data table is updated to those exemplars that arrive to this node. Since most of them are from a class coloured red, the class column shows most of them have a red box in this column.

Before moving to the next section in the survey, participants from Group A and Group B are shown how they can estimate the accuracy of a DTC by looking at the impurity of each leaf node. Participants from Group B are also shown how the colouring of nodes can help in this process.

4.3.2. Introduction to Parallel Coordinates

In this section, participants are given an introduction to PC. Similar to the first section of the survey, participants are shown a table containing the Iris dataset. Next to this table, users are shown a parallel coordinates representation of the Iris dataset. Figure 11 shows the layout of this section of the survey. We designed the survey system to require participants to click through several interactive prompts, highlighting the following features.

- How each instance is represented in parallel coordinates.
- The use of colour in each poly-line to indicate the class of an instance.
- The ability for a user to toggle a numerical scale for all axes on and off.
- Coloured buttons at the top of the PC visualisation which allow a user to show/hide individual classes.

To increase a participant's understanding of PC, an additional visualisation technique is included in this section. Participants are able to hover their mouse over an individual instance in the table of the Iris dataset. When a participant hovers their mouse over an instance, the corresponding polyline for the instance in PC is emphasised using a bold black colour. Participants are encouraged to explore how individual instances in the Iris dataset are mapped to the PC visualisation before moving to the next section.

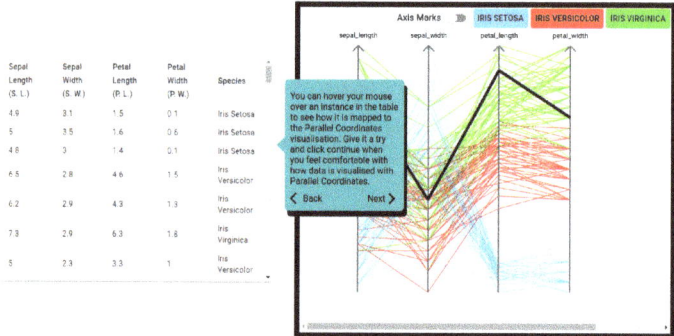

Figure 11. Layout of survey section introducing PC.

4.3.3. Decision Tree Classifiers with Parallel Coordinates

This section shows participants how PC and the DTC visualisation introduced in the previous sections can be combined into one system. This visualisation presented to participants is similar to the HITL-ML system introduced in Section 3.1, with the left half of the screen displaying the DTC and the right half of the screen visualising a dataset with PC. The Iris dataset is used again to introduce participants to this system. Participants are introduced to the following features of the combined visualisation.

- How selecting a node in the DTC filters the instances shown in PC.
- How univariate splits can be represented in PC as a range on an axis.

For participants in Group B, this section is also used to introduce the technique of using PC to visualise all splits in the path from the root node to a particular leaf node in a DTC. This is the visualisation technique introduced in Section 3.5. Group B participants are shown the following features of this visualisation technique.

- How the poly-lines for all instances in this visualisation originate from an origin point before passing through each axis in PC.
- How all splits in the path to a leaf node are shown as a series of ranges on PC axes.
- How axes are ordered to match the order of attributes appearing in the path to the leaf node.
- How the poly-line for each instance is terminated when it does not match the range on a PC axis.
- How each poly-line is dimmed after it passes through all required ranges to reach a leaf node.

This section of the survey appears directly before Experiment 2 for participants in Group B. In Experiment 2, Group B participants are required to use the PC visualisation of the path to a leaf node to determine if an instance reaches a particular leaf. This section explains to Group B participants the structure of questions in Experiment 2 and how to use the visualisation techniques introduced to complete Experiment 2.

For participants in Group A, this section introduces the node colouring technique that was shown previously (in the first section) to participants in Group B. This node colouring technique is shown here for participants in Group A to ensure that they have been introduced to all the same visualisation techniques as those in Group B before the start of the last section on HITL-ML. The only exception to this is the use of PC to visualise the path to a leaf node. Participants from Group A are not shown this visualisation technique, since it has no relevance to any of the content in the HITL-ML section of the survey.

4.3.4. Evaluating Decision Tree Classifiers

This section of the survey appears only for participants in Group A. It aims to prepare Group A participants for Experiment 2, where they will be asked to determine if a given instance reaches a particular leaf node in a DTC. No new visualisation techniques are introduced in this section. Instead, Group A participants are shown two examples of how to traverse a DTC for a given instance. Participants are shown a table with a single instance. An interactive tutorial guides participants through the traversal of a DTC for each instance. This tutorial shows participants an example of a situation where an instance does or does not reach a particular leaf node and how to answer questions of this nature.

4.3.5. Human-in-the-Loop-Learning of Decision Tree Classifiers

In this section of the survey, participants are given an introduction to the concepts behind HITL-ML. Figure 12 shows the layout of this survey section. The Iris dataset is again used to introduce these concepts. The section begins with several interactive prompts explaining how a user can build a DTC using HITL-ML. Participants are then encouraged to use a simplified HITL-ML system to create a DTC for the Iris dataset. This aims to ensure users understand the concepts behind HITL-ML, before providing feedback on the two HITL-ML systems presented in Experiment 3. To minimise bias towards one visualisation style, the HITL-ML system in this section allows a participant to select their preferred visualisation style to build a DTC using a two-dimensional scatter-plot and PC.

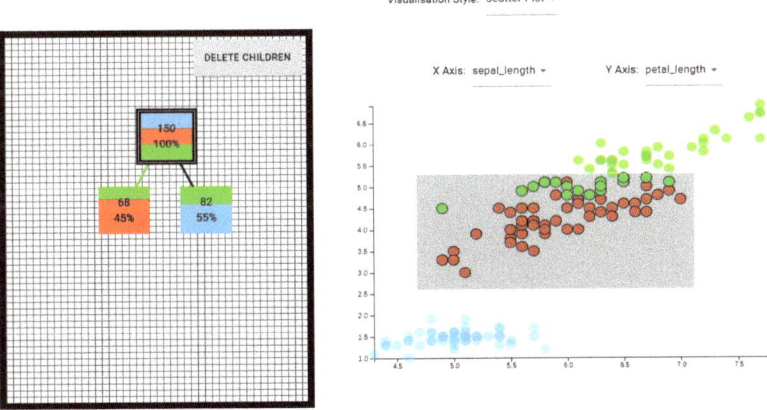

Figure 12. Layout of survey section introducing HITL-ML. The selection of the root node in the tree shows that there are three classes each with a different colour. The display on the right shows the exemplars of the three classes on the two attributes chosen by the user.

5. Results

5.1. Experiment 1

A total of 51 participants from Group A and 53 participants from Group B completed this experiment. Table 3 shows the average results for each group. From this table, we can see that when estimating the accuracy of a DTC, participants in Group B appear to be slightly less accurate than those in Group A, but they managed to make their estimation much faster. Similarly, when selecting the most impure leaf in a DTC, the mean relative impurity of leaf nodes selected by participants in Group B was slightly higher; however, the time to choose this leaf node was quicker than participants in Group A.

We now proceed to evaluate as to whether the results accounted for statistically significant differences in the results between Groups A and B. Since some of the results obtained in this experiment are not normally distributed as determined by the Shapiro–Wilk test [75], we use the Wilcoxon–Mann–Whitney test to check for statistically significant differences between Group A and Group B as opposed to a t-Test. The Wilcoxon–Mann–Whitney test is a nonparametric equivalent to the t-Test to compare independent samples [76]. Performing this statistical test on the accuracy differences and $RImp$ results in p-values of 0.196 and 0.311, respectively. As such, we cannot reject the null hypotheses that Group A and Group B perform equally in terms of ability to estimate the accuracy of a DTC and ability to find the most impure nodes in a DTC and must reject Hypotheses 1 and 3. Performing statistical tests on accuracy time and leaf selection time results in p-values of 3.65×10^{-10} and 0.006, respectively. Here, the differences in time for both tasks in this experiment are statistically significant. As such, we can accept Hypotheses 2 and 4. Although this experiment showed that colouring nodes does assist users to more quickly assess the predictive power of a DTC and find leaf nodes requiring further refinement, node colouring appears to have minimal impact on how accurately participants perform these tasks.

Table 3. Results for Experiment 1.

Group	Mean Accuracy Differences	Mean Accuracy Time (s)	Mean $RImp$	Mean Leaf Choice Time (s)
A	17.8%	80.2	0.259	17.6
B	19.0%	49.3	0.282	17.1

5.2. Experiment 2

Like Experiment 1, Experiment 2 consisted of 51 participants in Group A and 53 participants in Group B. For each participant, we calculate the percentage of questions where the participant provided the correct answer. Table 4 shows the average result from Group A and Group B for Experiment 2. These average accuracies show clear differences in the performance between the two groups. Using the PC-based visualisation, participants in Group B answered 86.7% of questions correctly. This is in contrast to Group A participants, who only achieved 77.5% accuracy. Group B participants also appear to be able to determine whether an instance reaches a leaf node faster than Group A participants. On average, Group B participants only required approximately one-quarter of the time to determine whether an instance reached a leaf as those in Group A. Using the Wilcoxon–Mann–Whitney Test, we confirm that the average accuracy and time results are statistically significant with p-values of 1.51×10^{-9} and $<2.2 \times 10^{-16}$, respectively. As such, Hypotheses 5 and 6 are accepted. We argue these results demonstrate a clear advantage to the use of PC to allow humans to interpret DTC. Using PC dramatically decreased the mistakes made when interpreting the splits for a DTC as well as allowing participants to more quickly interpret the series of splits leading to the classification of an instance.

Table 4. Results for Experiment 2.

Group	Mean Accuracy	Mean Time per Leaf (s)
A	77.5%	24.0
B	86.7%	6.7

5.3. Experiment 3

Experiment 3 was completed by 104 participants. Table 5 shows a summary of the responses received for each question in the experiment. Figure 13 also visualises the distribution of responses received for each question. We can see from these results that there is a clear preference for the PC-based system for all HITL-ML tasks examined. For each of the five pairs of videos, between 66.3% and 79.8% of participants had some preference for the PC-based system. In addition, participant responses from the last question showed 79.8% of participants had an overall preference for the PC-based system.

Table 5. Results for Experiment 3.

Question	Q1	Q2	Q3	Q4	Q5	Q6
Strongly PC-based system	38	42	39	44	58	57
Somewhat PC-based system	32	27	32	33	25	26
Strongly UserClassifier	7	7	6	4	5	7
Somewhat UserClassifier	23	21	21	13	8	7
No differences	4	7	6	10	8	7
Subtotal PC-based system	70	69	71	77	83	83
Subtotal UserClassifier	30	28	27	17	13	14

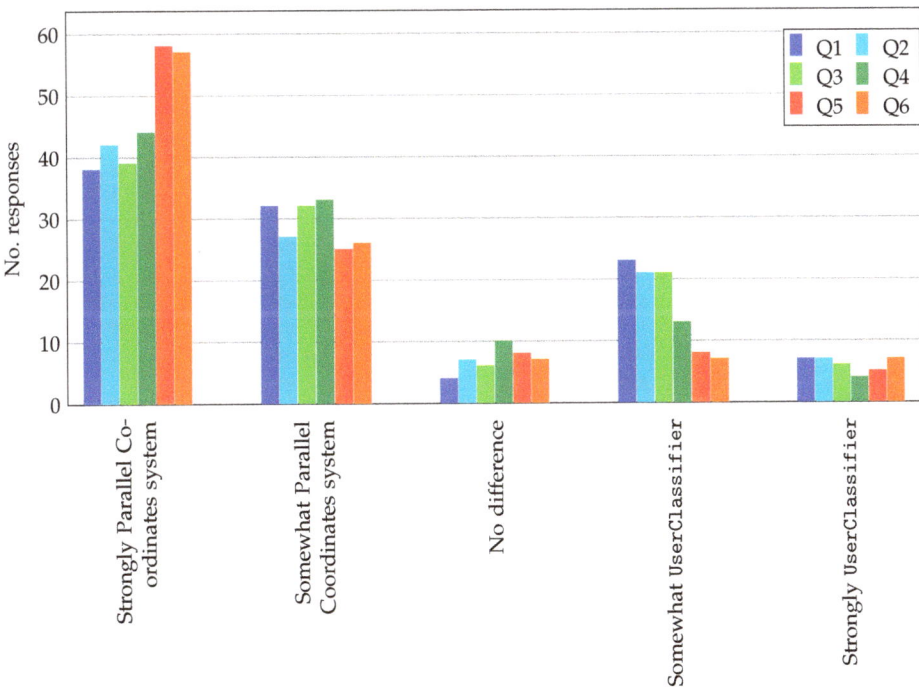

Figure 13. Graph of distribution of response from Experiment 3.

5.4. Validity Threats

We now discuss the internal and external validity of the results obtained from the experiments in this section. We note three possible threats to the internal validity of these experiments. First, as this survey was conducted online, participants could not be observed as they carried out these experiments. In both Experiment 1 and Experiment 2, the survey system records the time taken for participants to complete each task. These time measurements could be affected by participants taking breaks or being distracted while completing the survey. Second, we designed the interactive tutorials in this survey under the assumption that participants had limited experience with PC. Some intuition often needs to be built when using PC. Participants that did have previous experience using PC may have performed better on certain tasks in these experiments than participants that had no or limited experience using PC. Finally, we note that all participants completed this survey using their own computers. Given the importance of available screen real estate for any data visualisation, the size of the monitor a participant used may have affected their performance. While we made every effort to ensure that the survey system works well on a variety of screen sizes, participants with larger monitors may have found some visualisations presented in this survey easier to interpret.

Regarding external validity for this survey, we note that participation in the survey was restricted to participants with a bachelor's level education who are working in the STEM field. Participants with a higher level of expertise in ML or data visualisation may have found the visualisation techniques presented in this survey more intuitive to use and performed better at the tasks included in this survey.

6. Discussion

Many have argued that there are clear advantages of human-in-the-loop for machine learning tasks [12,14,17,19,60,61,77]. In particular, the structural breakdown of an IML system highlights that through the interface, the users not only interact with the data but also interact with and conceptualise the model [47], which goes far beyond what an after-the-fact interpretation of a black-box machine learning classification can achieve. We have explored here the effectiveness of our proposed interface for both of these aspects. Our prototype uses parallel coordinates to visualise and interact with the data, scaling into high levels of dimensionality while retaining the ability to re-order and focus on important attributes. Crucially, our proposal also delivers the modes of interaction with the model (the classifier) that are necessary for constructive conceptualisation. The oblique tests in particular are components of the model that directly benefit from the parallel coordinates layout and its ability to make an otherwise highly dimensional attribute space, that transcends human comprehension, accessible through re-ordering and focussing on individual as well as adjacent dimensions. These aspects are essential for the close interaction expected of IML, where users and learning systems are coupled by focussed and frequent interactions [18]. Our prototype and our analysis advances the crucial element in IML of how the model can be frequently and incrementally updated [48,78].

Our approach here shows how effective visualisation can involve a human expert in expeditiously guiding the construction of interpretable classification models. Moreover, our IML system not only contributes to explainable AI by producing conceptually understandable models; it also allows a user to revise the objective of classification accuracy when alternatives manifest themselves as important objectives. Furthermore, we have proposed how to visualise and elaborate on characterisation and discrimination rules where users are interested in one class above the others. We have also emphasised that while decision trees rank highly overall as a model for HITL-ML classification, by reordering attributes based on the importance perceived through our visualisation, we can strike a suitable balance between multi-variate decision tress and uni-variate decision trees. Users can propose bi-variate splits they visually discover between adjacent attribute axes, that remain understandable, even in high overall dimensionality, in our parallel coordinates canvas.

In the literature, IML has hardly been evaluated with human participants [52]. This paper also provides a large study and suggests a methodology for evaluation. As such, the experiments described here not only support our claims regarding the interface but constitute a model and a benchmark for the assessment of IML.

Author Contributions: Conceptualisation, V.E.-C., E.G. and R.H.; methodology, V.E.-C., E.G. and R.H.; software, E.G.; validation, V.E.-C., E.G. and R.H.; analysis, E.G.; investigation, V.E.-C., E.G. and R.H.; resources, E.G.; data curation, E.G.; writing—original draft preparation, V.E.-C. and R.H.; writing—review and editing, V.E.-C., E.G. and R.H.; visualisation, E.G.; supervision, V.E.-C. and R.H. All authors have read and agreed to the published version of the manuscript.

Funding: This research received no external funding.

Institutional Review Board Statement: The study was conducted in accordance with the Declaration of Helsinki, and approved by the Ethics Committee of Griffith University (protocol code 2021/538, March 2021) for studies involving humans.

Informed Consent Statement: Informed consent was obtained from all subjects involved in the study.

Data Availability Statement: The data presented in this study are openly available in https://github.com/eugene-gilmore/dtc-survey-results (accessed on 3 April 2020).

Acknowledgments: Eugene Gilmore is thankful to the Griffith Graduate Research School (Griffith University) for support during some of his PhD program through a Higher Degree Research Scholarship (Australian Postgraduate Award). All authors are thankful for the support of the School of ICT (Griffith University) that funded the cost of the survey in the survey platform Prolific [73].

Conflicts of Interest: The authors declare no conflict of interest.

Abbreviations

The following abbreviations are used in this manuscript:

CART	Classification and Regression Trees
DTC	Decision Tree Classifier
XAI	Explainable Artificial Intelligence
HITL-ML	Human-In-The-Loop Machine Learning
IML	Interactive Machine Learning
ML	Machine Learning
NC	Nested Cavities Algorithm
PC	Parallel Coordinates

References

1. Dzindolet, M.T.; Peterson, S.A.; Pomranky, R.A.; Pierce, L.G.; Beck, H.P. The role of trust in automation reliance. *Int. J. Hum.-Comput. Stud.* **2003**, *58*, 697–718. [CrossRef]
2. Darlington, K. Aspects of Intelligent Systems Explanation. *Univers. J. Control. Autom.* **2013**, *1*, 40–51. [CrossRef]
3. Dominguez-Jimenez, C. PROSE: An Architecture for Explanation in Expert Systems. In Proceedings of the Third COGNITIVA Symposium on at the Crossroads of Artificial Intelligence, Cognitive Science, and Neuroscience, COGNITIVA 90, Madrid, Spain, 20–23 November 1990; North-Holland Publishing Co.: Amsterdam, The Netherlands, 1991; pp. 305–312.
4. Swartout, W.R.; Moore, J.D. Explanation in Second Generation Expert Systems. In *Second Generation Expert Systems*; David, J.M., Krivine, J.P., Simmons, R., Eds.; Springer: Berlin/Heidelberg, Germany, 1993; pp. 543–585.
5. Ye, R.L.; Johnson, P.E. The Impact of Explanation Facilities on User Acceptance of Expert Systems Advice. *MIS Q.* **1995**, *19*, 157–172. [CrossRef]
6. Wang, N.; Pynadath, D.V.; Hill, S.G. Trust calibration within a human-robot team: Comparing automatically generated explanations. In Proceedings of the 2016 11th ACM/IEEE International Conference on Human-Robot Interaction (HRI), Christchurch, New Zealand, 7–10 March 2016; pp. 109–116. [CrossRef]
7. Machlev, R.; Perl, M.; Belikov, J.; Levy, K.Y.; Levron, Y. Measuring Explainability and Trustworthiness of Power Quality Disturbances Classifiers Using XAI—Explainable Artificial Intelligence. *IEEE Trans. Ind. Inform.* **2022**, *18*, 5127–5137. [CrossRef]
8. Weiss, S.M.; Kulikowski, C.A. *Computer Systems That Learn: Classification and Prediction Methods from Statistics, Neural Nets, Machine Learning, and Expert Systems*; Morgan Kaufmann Publishers Inc.: San Francisco, CA, USA, 1991.
9. Quinlan, J.R. Induction of Decision Trees. *Mach. Learn.* **1986**, *1*, 81–106. [CrossRef]
10. Henery, R.J. Chapter 2: Classification. In *Machine Learning, Neural and Statistical Classification*; Michie, D., Spiegelhalter, D.J., Taylor, C.C., Eds.; Ellis Horwood: New York, NY, USA, 1995; pp. 6–16.
11. Kodratoff, Y. Chapter 8: Machine Learning. In *Knowledge Engineering Volume I Fundamentals*; Adeli, H., Ed.; McGraw-Hill, Inc.: New York, NY, USA, 1990; pp. 226–255.
12. Ankerst, M.; Elsen, C.; Ester, M.; Kriegel, H.P. Visual Classification: An Interactive Approach to Decision Tree Construction. In Proceedings of the Fifth ACM SIGKDD International Conference on Knowledge Discovery and Data Mining, KDD'99, San Diego, CA, USA, 15–18 August 1999; ACM: New York, NY, USA, 1999; pp. 392–396. [CrossRef]
13. Estivill-Castro, V. Collaborative Knowledge Acquisition with a Genetic Algorithm. In Proceedings of the 9th International Conference on Tools with Artificial Intelligence, ICTAI'97, Newport Beach, CA, USA, 3–8 November 1997; IEEE Computer Society: Newport Beach, CA, USA, 1997; pp. 270–277. [CrossRef]
14. Ware, M.; Frank, E.; Holmes, G.; Hall, M.; Witten, I.H. Interactive machine learning: Letting users build classifiers. *Int. J. Hum.-Comput. Stud.* **2001**, *55*, 281–292. [CrossRef]

15. Webb, G.I. Integrating machine learning with knowledge acquisition through direct interaction with domain experts. *Knowl.-Based Syst.* **1996**, *9*, 253–266. [CrossRef]
16. Sacha, D.; Kraus, M.; Keim, D.A.; Chen, M. VIS4ML: An Ontology for Visual Analytics Assisted Machine Learning. *IEEE Trans. Vis. Comput. Graph.* **2019**, *25*, 385–395. [CrossRef]
17. Amershi, S.; Cakmak, M.; Knox, W.B.; Kulesza, T. Power to the People: The Role of Humans in Interactive Machine Learning. *AI Mag.* **2014**, *35*, 105–120. [CrossRef]
18. Mosqueira-Rey, E.; Hernández-Pereira, E.; Alonso-Ríos, D.; Bobes-Bascarán, J.; Fernández-Leal, A. Human-in-the-loop machine learning: A state of the art. *Artif. Intell. Rev.* **2022**, *35*, 1–19. [CrossRef]
19. Fails, J.A.; Olsen, D.R. Interactive Machine Learning. In Proceedings of the 8th International Conference on Intelligent User Interfaces, IUI'03, Miami, FL, USA, 12–15 January 2003; Association for Computing Machinery: New York, NY, USA, 2003; pp. 39–45. [CrossRef]
20. Krak, I.; Barmak, O.; Manziuk, E.; Kudin, H. Approach to Piecewise-Linear Classification in a Multi-dimensional Space of Features Based on Plane Visualization. In *Advances in Intelligent Systems and Computing, Proceedings of the International Scientific Conference "Intellectual Systems of Decision Making and Problem of Computational Intelligence", Kherson, Ukraine, 25–29 May 2020*; Lytvynenko, V., Babichev, S., Wójcik, W., Vynokurova, O., Vyshemyrskaya, S., Radetskaya, S., Eds.; Springer International Publishing: Cham, Switzerland, 2020; pp. 35–47. [CrossRef]
21. Freitas, A.A. Comprehensible classification models: A position paper. *SIGKDD Explor.* **2013**, *15*, 1–10. [CrossRef]
22. Guidotti, R.; Monreale, A.; Ruggieri, S.; Turini, F.; Giannotti, F.; Pedreschi, D. A survey of methods for explaining black box models. *ACM Comput. Surv. (CSUR)* **2018**, *51*, 1–42. [CrossRef]
23. Lavrač, N. Selected techniques for data mining in medicine. *Artif. Intell. Med.* **1999**, *16*, 3–23. [CrossRef]
24. Mues, C.; Huysmans, J.; Vanthienen, J.; Baesens, B. Comprehensible Credit-Scoring Knowledge Visualization Using Decision Tables and Diagrams. In *Enterprise Information Systems VI*; Springer: Dordrecht, The Netherlands, 2006; pp. 109–115. [CrossRef]
25. Verbeke, W.; Martens, D.; Mues, C.; Baesens, B. Building comprehensible customer churn prediction models with advanced rule induction techniques. *Expert Syst. Appl.* **2011**, *38*, 2354–2364. [CrossRef]
26. Freitas, A.A.; Wieser, D.; Apweiler, R. On the Importance of Comprehensible Classification Models for Protein Function Prediction. *IEEE/ACM Trans. Comput. Biol. Bioinform.* **2010**, *7*, 172–182. [CrossRef]
27. Sahu, M.; Dash, R. A Survey on Deep Learning: Convolution Neural Network (CNN). In *Smart Innovation, Systems and Technologies, Proceedings of the Intelligent and Cloud Computing, Smart Innovation, Systems and Technologies, Bhubaneswar, India, 22–23 October 2021*; Mishra, D., Buyya, R., Mohapatra, P., Patnaik, S., Eds.; Springer: Singapore, 2021; Volume 153. [CrossRef]
28. Cervantes, J.; Garcia-Lamont, F.; Rodríguez-Mazahua, L.; Lopez, A. A comprehensive survey on support vector machine classification: Applications, challenges and trends. *Neurocomputing* **2020**, *408*, 189–215. [CrossRef]
29. Dong, X.; Yu, Z.; Cao, W.; Shi, Y.; Ma, Q. A survey on ensemble learning. *Front. Comput. Sci.* **2020**, *14*, 241–258. [CrossRef]
30. Moore, A.; Murdock, V.; Cai, Y.; Jones, K. Transparent Tree Ensembles. In Proceedings of the 41st International ACM SIGIR Conference on Research & Development in Information Retrieval, SIGIR'18, Ann Arbor, MI, USA, 8–12 July 2018; Association for Computing Machinery: New York, NY, USA, 2018; pp. 1241–1244. [CrossRef]
31. Liao, Q.V.; Singh, M.; Zhang, Y.; Bellamy, R.K. Introduction to Explainable AI. In Proceedings of the Extended Abstracts of the 2020 CHI Conference on Human Factors in Computing Systems, CHI EA'20, Honolulu, HI, USA, 25–30 April 2020; Association for Computing Machinery: New York, NY, USA, 2020; pp. 1–4. [CrossRef]
32. Samek, W.; Müller, K.R. Towards Explainable Artificial Intelligence. In *Explainable AI: Interpreting, Explaining and Visualizing Deep Learning*; Springer International Publishing: Cham, Switzerland, 2019; pp. 5–22. [CrossRef]
33. Blanco-Justicia, A.; Domingo-Ferrer, J. Machine Learning Explainability through Comprehensible Decision Trees. In *Lecture Notes in Computer Science, Proceedings of the Machine Learning and Knowledge Extraction, Canterbury, UK, 26–29 August 2019*; Holzinger, A., Kieseberg, P., Tjoa, A.M., Weippl, E., Eds.; Springer International Publishing: Cham, Switzerland, 2019; pp. 15–26. [CrossRef]
34. Bourguin, G.; Lewandowski, A.; Bouneffa, M.; Ahmad, A. Towards Ontologically Explainable Classifiers. In *Lecture Notes in Computer Science, Proceedings of the Artificial Neural Networks and Machine Learning—ICANN 2021, Bratislava, Slovakia, 14–17 September 2021*; Farkaš, I., Masulli, P., Otte, S., Wermter, S., Eds.; Springer International Publishing: Cham, Switzerland, 2021; pp. 472–484.
35. Samek, W.; Binder, A.; Montavon, G.; Lapuschkin, S.; Müller, K. Evaluating the Visualization of What a Deep Neural Network Has Learned. *IEEE Trans. Neural Netw. Learn. Syst.* **2017**, *28*, 2660–2673. [CrossRef]
36. Lakkaraju, H.; Kamar, E.; Caruana, R.; Leskovec, J. Faithful and Customizable Explanations of Black Box Models. In Proceedings of the 2019 AAAI/ACM Conference on AI, Ethics, and Society, AIES'19, Honolulu, HI, USA, 27–28 January 2019; Association for Computing Machinery: New York, NY, USA, 2019; pp. 131–138. [CrossRef]
37. Ali, H.; Khan, M.S.; Al-Fuqaha, A.; Qadir, J. Tamp-X: Attacking Explainable Natural Language Classifiers through Tampered Activations. *Comput. Secur.* **2022**, *120*, 102791. [CrossRef]
38. Rudin, C. Stop explaining black box machine learning models for high stakes decisions and use interpretable models instead. *Nat. Mach. Intell.* **2019**, *1*, 206–215. [CrossRef]
39. Kingsford, C.; Salzberg, S.L. What are decision trees? *Nat. Biotechnol.* **2008**, *26*, 1011–1013. [CrossRef] [PubMed]
40. Wu, X.; Kumar, V.; Quinlan, J.R.; Ghosh, J.; Yang, Q.; Motoda, H.; McLachlan, G.; Ng, A.; Liu, B.; Yu, P.; et al. Top 10 algorithms in data mining. *Knowl. Inf. Syst.* **2008**, *14*, 1–37. [CrossRef]

41. Quinlan, J. *C4.5: Programs for Machine Learning*; Morgan Kaufmann Publishers: San Mateo, CA, USA, 1993.
42. Hunt, E.; Martin, J.; Stone, P. *Experiments in Induction*; Academic Press: New York, NY, USA, 1966.
43. Tan, P.N.; Steinbach, M.; Kumar, V. *Introduction to Data Mining*; Addison-Wesley Publishing Co.: Reading, MA, USA, 2006.
44. Breiman, L.; Friedman, J.; Olshen, R.; Stone, C. *Classification and Regression Trees*; Wadsworth and Brooks: Monterrey, CA, USA, 1984.
45. Estivill-Castro, V.; Gilmore, E.; Hexel, R. Human-In-The-Loop Construction of Decision Tree Classifiers with Parallel Coordinates. In Proceedings of the IEEE International Conference on Systems, Man, and Cybernetics, SMC, Toronto, ON, Canada, 11–14 October 2020; pp. 3852–3859. [CrossRef]
46. Inselberg, A. *Parallel Coordinates: Visual Multidimensional Geometry and Its Applications*; Springer: New York, NY, USA, 2009.
47. Dudley, J.J.; Kristensson, P.O. A Review of User Interface Design for Interactive Machine Learning. *ACM Trans. Interact. Intell. Syst.* **2018**, *8*, 1–37. [CrossRef]
48. Ramos, R.; Meek, C.; Simard, P.; Suh, J.; Ghorashi, S. Interactive machine teaching: A human-centered approach to building machine-learned models. *Hum.-Comput. Interact.* **2020**, *35*, 413–451. [CrossRef]
49. Estivill-Castro, V.; Gilmore, E.; Hexel, R. Constructing Interpretable Decision Trees Using Parallel Coordinates. In *Lecture Notes in Computer Science, Proceedings of the Artificial Intelligence and Soft Computing—19th International Conference, ICAISC, Part II, Zakopane, Poland, 12–14 October 2020*; Rutkowski, L., Scherer, R., Korytkowski, M., Pedrycz, W., Tadeusiewicz, R., Zurada, J.M., Eds.; Springer: Berlin/Heidelberg, Germany, 2020; Volume 12416, pp. 152–164. [CrossRef]
50. Han, J. Data Mining Tasks and Methods: Rule Discovery: Characteristic Rules. In *Handbook of Data Mining and Knowledge Discovery*; Oxford University Press, Inc.: New York, NY, USA, 2002; pp. 339–344.
51. Estivill-Castro, V.; Gilmore, E.; Hexel, R. Interpretable decisions trees via human-in-the-loop-learning. In Proceedings of the 20th Australasian Data Mining Conference (AusDM'22), Sydney, Australia, 12–16 December 2022.
52. Nauta, M.; Trienes, J.; Pathak, S.; Nguyen, E.; Peters, M.; Schmitt, Y.; Schlötterer, J.; van Keulen, M.; Seifert, C. From Anecdotal Evidence to Quantitative Evaluation Methods: A Systematic Review on Evaluating Explainable AI. *arXiv* **2022**, arXiv:2201.08164. [CrossRef]
53. Ankerst, M.; Ester, M.; Kriegel, H.P. Towards an Effective Cooperation of the User and the Computer for Classification. In Proceedings of the Sixth ACM SIGKDD International Conference on Knowledge Discovery and Data Mining, KDD'00, Boston, MA, USA, 20–23 August 2000; ACM: New York, NY, USA, 2000; pp. 179–188. [CrossRef]
54. Inselberg, A.; Avidan, T. Classification and visualization for high-dimensional data. In Proceedings of the Sixth ACM SIGKDD International Conference on Knowledge Discovery and Data Mining, Boston, MA, USA, 20–23 August 2000; ACM: Boston, MA, USA, 2000; pp. 370–374. [CrossRef]
55. Lai, P.L.; Liang, Y.J.; Inselberg, A. Geometric Divide and Conquer Classification for High-dimensional Data. In Proceedings of the DATA 2012—International Conference on Data Technologies and Applications, Rome, Italy, 25–27 July 2012; SciTePress: Setúbal, Portugal, 2012; pp. 79–82. [CrossRef]
56. Inselberg, A. III.14 Parallel Coordinates: Visualization, Exploration and Classification of High-Dimensional Data. In *Handbook of Data Visualization*; Springer: Berlin/Heidelberg, Germany, 2008. [CrossRef]
57. Gilmore, E.; Estivill-Castro, V.; Hexel, R. More Interpretable Decision Trees. In *Lecture Notes in Computer Science, Proceedings of the Hybrid Artificial Intelligent Systems—16th International Conference, HAIS 2021, Bilbao, Spain, 22–24 September 2021*; Sanjurjo-González, H., Pastor-López, I., García Bringas, P., Quintián, H., Corchado, E., Eds.; Springer: Berlin/Heidelberg, Germany, 2021; Volume 12886, pp. 280–292. [CrossRef]
58. Hunt, E. *Concept Learning—An Information Processing Problem*, 2nd ed.; John Wiley: New York, NY, USA, 1962.
59. Cohen, P.R.; Feigenbaum, E.A. *The Handbook of Artificial Intelligence, Volume III*; HeurisTech Press: Stanford, CA, USA, 1982.
60. Teoh, S.T.; Ma, K. StarClass: Interactive Visual Classification using Star Coordinates. In Proceedings of the Third SIAM International Conference on Data Mining, SIAM, San Francisco, CA, USA, 1–3 May 2003; Volume 112, pp. 178–185. [CrossRef]
61. Teoh, S.T.; Ma, K.L. PaintingClass: Interactive Construction, Visualization and Exploration of Decision Trees. In Proceedings of the Ninth ACM SIGKDD International Conference on Knowledge Discovery and Data Mining, KDD'03, Washington, DC, USA, 24–27 August 2003; Association for Computing Machinery: New York, NY, USA, 2003; pp. 667–672. [CrossRef]
62. Choo, J.; Lee, H.; Kihm, J.; Park, H. iVisClassifier: An interactive visual analytics system for classification based on supervised dimension reduction. In Proceedings of the 2010 IEEE Symposium on Visual Analytics Science and Technology, Salt Lake City, UT, USA, 25–26 October 2010; pp. 27–34. [CrossRef]
63. Krak, I.; Barmak, O.; Manziuk, E. Using visual analytics to develop human and machine-centric models: A review of approaches and proposed information technology. *Comput. Intell.* **2022**, *38*, 921–946. [CrossRef]
64. Tam, G.K.L.; Kothari, V.; Chen, M. An Analysis of Machine- and Human-Analytics in Classification. *IEEE Trans. Vis. Comput. Graph.* **2017**, *23*, 71–80. [CrossRef]
65. Chaudhuri, S.; Dayal, U. An Overview of Data Warehousing and OLAP Technology. *SIGMOD Rec.* **1997**, *26*, 65–74. [CrossRef]
66. Hall, M.; Frank, E.; Holmes, G.; Pfahringer, B.; Reutemann, P.; Witten, I.H. The WEKA data mining software: An update. *SIGKDD Explor.* **2009**, *11*, 10–18. [CrossRef]
67. Cantú-Paz, E.; Kamath, C. Inducing oblique decision trees with evolutionary algorithms. *IEEE Trans. Evol. Comput.* **2003**, *7*, 54–68. [CrossRef]

68. Heath, D.; Kasif, S.; Salzberg, S. Induction of Oblique Decision Trees. In Proceedings of the 13th International Joint Conference on Artificial Intelligence, Chambery, France, 28 August–3 September 1993; Morgan Kaufmann: Chambéry, France, 1993; pp. 1002–1007.
69. Murthy, S.K.; Kasif, S.; Salzberg, S. A System for Induction of Oblique Decision Trees. *J. Artif. Int. Res.* **1994**, *2*, 1–32. [CrossRef]
70. Brodley, C.E.; Utgoff, P.E. Multivariate Decision Trees. *Mach. Learn.* **1995**, *19*, 45–77. [CrossRef]
71. Koziol, M.; Wozniak, M. Multivariate Decision Trees vs. Univariate Ones. In *Computer Recognition Systems 3*; Kurzynski, M., Wozniak, M., Eds.; Advances in Intelligent and Soft Computing; Springer: Berlin/Heidelberg, Germany, 2009; Volume 57, pp. 275–284. [CrossRef]
72. Hurley, P.J. *A Concise Introduction to Logic*, 12th ed.; Cengage: Boston, MA, USA, 2015.
73. Palan, S.; Schitter, C. Prolific.ac—A subject pool for online experiments. *J. Behav. Exp. Financ.* **2018**, *17*, 22–27. [CrossRef]
74. Dua, D.; Graff, C. *UCI Machine Learning Repository*; University of California, School of Information and Computer Science: Irvine, CA, USA, 2017. Available online: http://archive.ics.uci.edu/ml (accessed on 3 April 2020).
75. Shapiro, S.S.; Wilk, M.B. An analysis of variance test for normality (complete samples). *Biometrika* **1965**, *LII*, 591–611. [CrossRef]
76. Hui, E.G.M. *Learn R for Applied Statistics: With Data Visualizations, Regressions, and Statistics*; Springer: Berkeley, CA, USA, 2019.
77. Nguyen, T.D.; Ho, T.; Shimodaira, H. Interactive Visualization in Mining Large Decision Trees. In *Lecture Notes in Computer Science, Proceedings of the Knowledge Discovery and Data Mining, Current Issues and New Applications, 4th Pacific-Asia Conference PADKK 2000, Kyoto, Japan, 18–20 April 2000*; Springer: Kyoto, Japan, 2000; Volume 1805, pp. 345–348. [CrossRef]
78. Jiang, L.; Liu, S.; Chen, C. Recent research advances on interactive machine learning. *J. Vis.* **2019**, *22*, 401–417. [CrossRef]

Article

Federated Learning of Explainable AI Models in 6G Systems: Towards Secure and Automated Vehicle Networking

Alessandro Renda [1,*], Pietro Ducange [1], Francesco Marcelloni [1], Dario Sabella [2], Miltiadis C. Filippou [3], Giovanni Nardini [1], Giovanni Stea [1], Antonio Virdis [1], Davide Micheli [4], Damiano Rapone [4] and Leonardo Gomes Baltar [3]

1 Department of Information Engineering, University of Pisa, 56122 Pisa, Italy
2 Intel Corporation Italia SpA, 20094 Milan, Italy
3 Intel Deutschland GmbH, 85579 Neubiberg, Germany
4 Telecom Italia S.p.a., 00198 Roma, Italy
* Correspondence: alessandro.renda@unipi.it

Abstract: This article presents the concept of federated learning (FL) of eXplainable Artificial Intelligence (XAI) models as an enabling technology in advanced 5G towards 6G systems and discusses its applicability to the automated vehicle networking use case. Although the FL of neural networks has been widely investigated exploiting variants of stochastic gradient descent as the optimization method, it has not yet been adequately studied in the context of inherently explainable models. On the one side, XAI permits improving user experience of the offered communication services by helping end users trust (by design) that in-network AI functionality issues appropriate action recommendations. On the other side, FL ensures security and privacy of both vehicular and user data across the whole system. These desiderata are often ignored in existing AI-based solutions for wireless network planning, design and operation. In this perspective, the article provides a detailed description of relevant 6G use cases, with a focus on vehicle-to-everything (V2X) environments: we describe a framework to evaluate the proposed approach involving online training based on real data from live networks. FL of XAI models is expected to bring benefits as a methodology for achieving seamless availability of decentralized, lightweight and communication efficient intelligence. Impacts of the proposed approach (including standardization perspectives) consist in a better trustworthiness of operations, e.g., via explainability of quality of experience (QoE) predictions, along with security and privacy-preserving management of data from sensors, terminals, users and applications.

Keywords: explainable artificial intelligence; federated learning; 6G; vehicle-to-everything (V2X); quality of service; quality of experience

Citation: Renda, A.; Ducange, P.; Marcelloni, F.; Sabella, D.; Filippou, M.C.; Nardini, G.; Stea, G.; Virdis, A.; Micheli, D.; Rapone, D.; et al. Federated Learning of Explainable AI Models in 6G Systems: Towards Secure and Automated Vehicle Networking. *Information* 2022, 13, 395. https://doi.org/10.3390/info13080395

Academic Editors: Pierre-Edouard Portier and Gabriele Gianini

Received: 7 July 2022
Accepted: 17 August 2022
Published: 20 August 2022

Publisher's Note: MDPI stays neutral with regard to jurisdictional claims in published maps and institutional affiliations.

Copyright: © 2022 by the authors. Licensee MDPI, Basel, Switzerland. This article is an open access article distributed under the terms and conditions of the Creative Commons Attribution (CC BY) license (https://creativecommons.org/licenses/by/4.0/).

1. Introduction

Artificial Intelligence (AI), along with Machine Learning (ML) as one of its core building blocks, is entering many market domains at a fast pace and will not only leverage advanced communication networks but also shape the definition of next-generation networks themselves. In particular, AI is expected to play a crucial role in the design, operation and management of future beyond-5G (B5G)/6G networks and in a plethora of applications [1]. However, the introduction of in-network AI comes with growing concerns on privacy, security and trust for citizens and users; for this reason, the adoption of eXplainable AI (XAI) models is an emerging trend considered for the design of transparent AI-based solutions. Moreover, future service scenarios, especially in the automotive domain, will be characterized by the deployment of connected vehicular systems from heterogeneous car manufacturers, connected via different Mobile Network Operators (MNOs) and different technology infrastructures [2]. In such complex setups, it will be imperative for service providers to consider federated network environments including multiple administrative and technical domains as a working assumption for the design of innovative applications. It is worth noting that the automated driving use case of "Teleoperated Driving (ToD) for Remote Steering" [3] requires a throughput of up to 36 Mbps per single stream, along with a positioning accuracy of 0.1 m and a reliability of 99.999% for the service to be considered available to the end customer. Such stringent requirements call for new technical enablers, to be introduced as part of the 6G network design. Considering the above-mentioned challenges, in this article we envision the use of the federated learning (FL) concept applied jointly with XAI models and discuss its applicability to automated vehicle networking use cases to be encountered in B5G/6G setups. In fact, although FL has recently been widely investigated in the context of Neural Networks and Deep Learning models (due to their gradient based optimization strategy), much less attention has been devoted so far to FL of XAI models.

The main contributions of this article can be summarized as follows:

- We propose the integration of FL with XAI for performing quality of experience (QoE) predictions in B5G/6G networks, by providing a detailed discussion about the benefits it can bring and the main challenges that need to be addressed;
- Considering vehicle-to-everything (V2X) applications as relevant use cases, we present the design of a framework to evaluate the benefits of the proposed approach and provide the guidelines to implement a realistic B5G/6G network testbed supporting the training of XAI models in a federated fashion, as well as the issuance of explainable QoE predictions;
- We shed light on the impact that the proposed FL approach with XAI models will have on both the industrial and standardization sectors.

While the following subsections provide an overview of XAI and FL, respectively, Section 2 describes the FL of XAI models applied to advanced 5G systems towards 6G. Section 3 elaborates on some relevant V2X use cases and provides more details on the proposed FED-XAI framework, focusing on a QoE prediction task. In Section 4, the impact of such solutions to the automotive vertical segment is discussed: in particular, the benefits of predicted QoE explanations useful for decision making are detailed for both car Original Equipment Manufacturers (OEMs) and MNOs. Standardization impacts are also analysed to provide interoperable and globally applicable solutions, and some challenges of FL of XAI models are discussed. Finally, Section 5 draws some conclusions.

1.1. The Need for XAI

The adoption of AI techniques cannot disregard the fundamental value of trustworthiness, which, along with inclusiveness and sustainability, represents the three core values of the European Union Flagship Hexa-X (www.hexa-x.eu (accessed on 16 August 2022)) vision for the upcoming 6G era [1]. Trustworthiness has become paramount for both users and government entities, as witnessed by the "right to explanation" described in the General Data Protection Regulation (GDPR) and by the European Commission's (EC) Technical Report on "Ethics guidelines for trustworthy AI" [4]. According to these, explainability represents a key requirement towards trustworthiness. Thus, industry and academia are placing increasing attention on XAI, that is, an AI "that produces details or reasons to make its functioning clear or easy to understand" [5].

In this context, two strategies for achieving explainability can be identified [5]: the adoption of post-hoc explainability techniques (i.e., the "explaining black-box" strategy) and the design of inherently interpretable models (i.e., "transparent box design" strategy). In this article, we focus on this latter class of approaches, noting that certain applications may tolerate a limited performance degradation to achieve fully trustworthy operation. In fact, performance and transparency are typically considered conflicting objectives [5,6]. However, this trade-off holds as long as the target task entails a certain complexity and the data available are many and high quality. In this case, complex models, such as Deep Neural Networks (DNNs), which are hard to interpret due to their huge number of parameters and non-linear modelling, have proven to achieve high levels of accuracy; conversely, decision trees and rule-based models may feature lower modelling capability but are typically considered "highly interpretable".

The importance of explainability has been recently highlighted in the context of Secure Smart Vehicles [7]: on one hand, explanation is crucial in safety-critical AI-based algorithms, designed to extend some widely available capabilities (e.g., lane-keeping and braking assistants) towards fully automated driving; on the other hand, explainability is needed at the design stage to perform model debugging and knowledge discovery, thus positively impacting system security by reducing model vulnerabilities against external attacks. Explainability of AI models will be crucial for 6G-enabled V2X systems. A prime example is an AI service consumer requesting in-advance notifications on QoS predictions, as studied in Hexa-X [1] and the 5G Automotive Association (5GAA) [8]. Accurate and timely predictions should support very demanding use cases, with a horizon ranging from extremely short to longer time windows. Better explainability of such predictions and any consequent decision will provide benefits not only for technology and service providers (see Section 4), but also for end-customers, who will become more receptive to AI-based solutions.

1.2. Federated Learning

Exploiting data from multiple sources can enhance the performance (i.e., high accuracy based on reduced bias) of AI models. However, wirelessly collecting and storing peripheral data for processing on a centralized server has become increasingly impractical due to two main reasons: first, it typically introduces severe communication and computation overhead due to the transmission and storage of large training data sets, respectively; second, it violates the privacy and security requirements imposed by data owners by expanding the surface of possible over-the-air attacks towards biased decision making. In other words, the preservation of data privacy represents an urgent requirement of today's AI/ML systems, because data owners are often reluctant to share their data with other parties; in some jurisdictions, users have the ability to consent or not with the sharing of privacy-sensitive data (e.g., per the General Data Protection Regulation—GDPR in European Union). Such a need to preserve privacy of data owners, however, clashes with the need to collect data to train accurate ML models, which are typically data hungry in their learning stage. To overcome these limitations, FL has been proposed as a privacy-preserving paradigm for collaboratively training AI models. In an FL system, participants iteratively learn a shared model by only transferring local model updates and receiving an aggregated shared model update, without sharing raw data.

The main opportunities of FL in the context of Intelligent Transportation Systems (ITS) have been recently discussed in [9]: FL is expected to support both vehicle management (i.e., automated driving) and traffic management (i.e., infotainment and route planning) applications. Furthermore, FL has been applied in the context of Ultra-Reliable Low-Latency Communications for Vehicle-to-Vehicle scenarios, allowing vehicular users to estimate the distribution of extreme events (i.e., network-wide packet queue lengths exceeding a predefined threshold) with a model learned in a decentralized manner [10]. The model parameters are obtained by executing maximum likelihood estimation in a federated fashion, without sharing the local queue state information data. The concept of Federated Vehicular Network (FVN) has been recently introduced [11], as an architecture with decentralized components that natively support applications, such as entertainment at sport venues and distributed ML. However, FVN is a stationary vehicular network and relies on the assumption that vehicles remain at a fixed location, e.g., parking lots, so that the wireless connection is stable.

In most of the work on FL, the strategy for model aggregation was inspired by the federated averaging protocol (FedAvg), which enables collaborative Stochastic Gradient Descent (SGD) optimization in a federated manner. Thus, FL has been extensively investigated for models implementing SGD as their optimization method, such as Neural Networks (NNs), but has not yet been adequately studied in the context of inherently explainable models. The following section introduces how XAI models can be generated by FL, a new approach which appears very promising for future 6G systems.

2. FED-XAI: Bringing together Federated Learning and Explainable AI

Existing AI-based solutions for wireless network planning, design and operation ignore either or both of the following aspects: (i) the need to preserve data privacy at all times, including wireless transfer and storage, and (ii) the explainability of the involved models. Furthermore, latency and reliability requirements of safety-critical automotive communications call for seamless availability of decentralized and lightweight intelligence, where data are generated—and decisions made—anytime and anywhere.

Current FL approaches only address the first requirement. Explainability has been given less attention, having been approached primarily by exploiting post-hoc techniques, e.g., Shapley values to measure feature importance [12]. There is a substantial lack of approaches for FL of inherently explainable models. On the other hand, a federated approach for learning interpretable-by-design models, in which transparency is guaranteed for every decision made, would represent a significant leap towards trustworthy AI. Therefore, we introduce the concept of FL of XAI (FED-XAI) models, as a framework with a twofold objective: first, to leverage FL for privacy preservation during collaborative training of AI models, especially suitable in heterogeneous B5G/6G scenarios; second, to ensure an adequate degree of explainability of the models themselves (including the obtained aggregated model as a result of FL).

In the following, we provide some insights into how inherently explainable models (e.g., decision trees or rule-based) can be learned, employing an FL paradigm. First, it is worth noting that standard algorithms for learning such models typically adopt a heuristic approach; in fact, gradient descent-based optimization methods, widely used in FL, cannot be immediately applied, as they require the formulation of a global objective function. The greedy induction of decision trees, for example, recursively partitions the feature space by selecting for each decision node the most suitable attribute. The major challenge of the FED-XAI approach, therefore, consists in generating XAI models, whose FL is not based on the optimization of a differentiable global objective function.

The proposed FED-XAI approach relies on orchestration by a central entity but ensures that local data are not exposed beyond source devices: each data owner learns a model by elaborating locally acquired raw data and shares such a model with the central server, which merges the received models to produce a global model (Figure 1). Notably, our envisioned approach for federated learning of explainable AI models ensures data privacy regardless of the data sample size. As per the advantages of the FED-XAI approach, we expect that the global aggregated model performs better than the local models because it exploits the overall information stored and managed by all data owners, without compromising model interpretability.

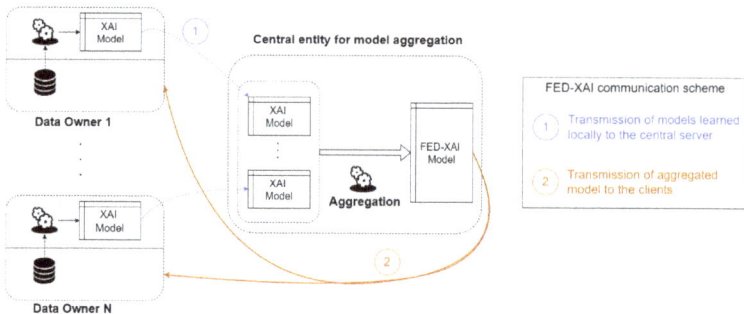

Figure 1. Illustration of federated learning of XAI models.

Our approach differs from classical FL in two aspects: first, it entails a one-shot communication scheme for each model update and not an iterative algorithm. As a consequence, the communication overhead is reduced, and the system is more robust to possible connectivity problems. Second, merging decision trees and rule-based models requires defining appropriate procedures, necessarily different from the simple weighted average of models of the FedAvg protocol applied, for example, to NNs. In more detail, the XAI models we consider can be represented as collections of "IF *antecedent* THEN *consequent*" rules, (natively in a rule-based system, and easily obtainable also from a decision tree). This representation is applicable regardless of the target task (regression or classification) and the type of the attributes (e.g., nominal or numeric). The aggregation procedure consists in juxtaposing rules collected from data owners, and resolving possible *conflicts*, which emerge when rules from different models, having antecedents referring to identical or overlapping regions of the attribute space, have different consequents. In one of our recent works [13], we presented a novel approach for FL of Takagi-Sugeno-Kang (TSK) fuzzy rule based systems [14], which can be considered as XAI models in regression problems. In a TSK model, the antecedent of a rule identifies a specific region of the attribute space, whereas the corresponding consequent allows for the evaluation of the predicted output within such a region as a linear combination of the input variables. When two rules, generated by different clients, share the same antecedent, the aggregation strategy for generating the FED-XAI model involves combining the two rules into a single one with the same antecedent: the coefficients of the linear model of the new consequent are evaluated as the weighted average of the coefficients of the original rules, where the weight of each rule depends on its support and confidence values. Research efforts in the FED-XAI domain, however, are still in their embryonic stage: as for tree-based models, a preliminary investigation of the trade-off between accuracy and interpretability has been recently carried out [15], but learning strategies compliant with the federated setting still need to be sharpened.

The FED-XAI approach may find immediate applicability in the automated vehicle networking domain, and, specifically, within the exemplary scenario described in Section 1: a model for QoS prediction which is explainable by a wide set of service consumers may be learned in a federated manner, reaping the benefits of collaborative training and privacy protection.

Main Challenges of the FED-XAI Approach

There are also challenges related to the FED-XAI approach, especially for time-critical operations in automated driving setups. For example, the computation (and, therefore, energy) footprint of FED-XAI needs to be pre-evaluated before implementation to identify the scalability potential of the solution. A clear distinction should be made between the stages of *training* and *inference*. For most ML models, including decision tree and rule-based systems, the inference time (critical from automated driving service standpoint) is negligible compared to the training time and, in any case, model complexity can be tuned to ensure that time constraints are satisfied. A larger computational overhead is required in the training stage, but it does not affect the application (e.g., learning can be performed in idle state). Another challenge is FED-XAI system resilience to attackers trying to benefit from the access to explanations of QoE predictions (e.g., towards increasing automated driving service outages for all or targeted vehicles). Finally, the approach will also need to address some additional challenges that are typical of FL and are likely to characterize 6G network-based intelligent transportation applications: (i) multi-source data may have different distributions and volumes, (ii) the number of participants can grow fast and their participation to FL may be unstable due to insufficiency of radio and computational resources, and (iii) learned models will need to be agilely updated in scenarios where concept drift alters the characteristics of data distributions over time.

3. The Proposed FED-XAI Framework for QoE Predictions in V2X Environments

This section describes some V2X use cases for which the FED-XAI approach is expected to be beneficial. Furthermore, we discuss a framework for QoE prediction in B5G/6G systems along with realistic sourcing of live data from an MNO network.

3.1. Exemplary 6G Use Cases in V2X Environments

The use of Information and Communication Technology, and especially AI techniques, in the automotive sector is gaining increasing attention [16]. Given the large amount of data generated by multiple, distributed sources, AI is one of the key technologies to enable innovative use cases, such as autonomous driving [17,18], improved safety [19] and platooning [20].

In the Hexa-X project, a general AI-assisted V2X use case is described ([1], Section 4.2.7.3). In future enhanced automotive uses cases or services, collecting a high volume of contextual and sensor data from traffic participants and road infrastructure will be common practice. With these data, a Digital Twin (DT) of the traffic environment can be created in the cloud or the edge of future mobile networks. This DT can be distributed across multiple edge nodes corresponding to a coverage area or to higher hierarchical edge-cloud nodes in different locations of the network and employed to optimize vehicle traffic by generating inputs to traffic management as well as driving or manoeuvring instructions to traffic participants. Moreover, DTs can be used to support ToD, by providing real-time information and predictions of road traffic information, as well as predictions for the QoS of the radio access network (e.g., radio signal quality). Real-time management of DTs is very challenging and requires network capabilities not available today. To guarantee safety, system operation requires extremely low latency, high reliability and ultra-high location accuracy along with efficient and explainable AI algorithms. Multiple edge nodes can be part of MNO or road infrastructure, and, at a given time, geographically proximate nodes might contain similar AI models which are either part of the same learning federation or updated by applying knowledge sharing. Moreover, when it comes to safety-related V2X services for automated and connected vehicles, most of the use cases analysed by 5GAA [2], e.g., See Through, Vulnerable Road User protection, Intersection Movement Assist, or In-Vehicle Entertainment, are evaluated, attributing great significance to security and privacy. In this perspective, the FED-XAI approach provides an intrinsic benefit, compared to its centralized learning counterparts.

In [1] authors proposed to further improve the ToD use case by applying the AI-as-a-Service approach: a driver planning to perform a journey would like to be informed of any V2X service degradations along the planned route by means of in-advance QoS predictions based on a plurality of data, gathered, e.g., from the Uu and PC5 interfaces but also from vehicle sensors (RADAR, LiDAR, etc.). Such notifications will allow for the decision upon activation of other V2X-related functionalities: for instance, automated driving features should be avoided if the predicted QoS in a certain part of the route would not allow such features to be used; hence, the driver should take control of the car until new, favourable QoS predictions suggest switching to automated driving mode. Moreover, QoS predictions could also be used to schedule the execution of non-V2X functionalities, e.g., software over-the-air downloads. In addition, in this scenario, the various data owners are encouraged to participate in the FED-XAI procedure, because the collaborative model will blend the knowledge extracted from all data rather than only from local data.

In the following section, we describe an illustrative automotive scenario, which can be the basis of evaluating the performance of the FED-XAI concept.

3.2. Details of the Proposed FED-XAI Framework

We consider an application where several instances of vehicular User Equipment (UE) connected to a B5G/6G Base Station (BS) receive a video stream whose quality plays a decisive role in the safety of remote driving. The quality of experience (QoE) perceived by UEs depends on the QoS provided by the network. This can be mapped, for instance, to a see-through use-case, where the receiving UE is a car using a live feed from the camera of another car (e.g., to make overtaking safer in the presence of visual impairments for the driver), or to ToD, where the sender is the car being driven and the receiver is the driving operator. In either case, operations may be supported by a DT of the traffic area at the edge. From an implementation perspective, Multi-access Edge Computing (MEC) infrastructure can be leveraged as an intrinsic facilitator for the segregation of data, as requested by international regulation in the matter of ITS services. Furthermore, state-of-the-art MEC technologies are defined by considering MEC security with an end-to-end approach, leveraging existing standards relevant in the area, e.g., ETSI-NFV-SEC (European Telecommunications Standards Institute—Network Functions Virtualisation—Security), TC CYBER (Technical Committee Cybersecurity), 3GPP (Third Generation Partnership Project), carefully selected to be applicable in edge computing systems.

The objective of the envisioned application is to employ XAI models, learnt (and updated) in a federated fashion based on QoS/QoE data, to predict the QoE perceived by UEs in the near future. Notably, it has been recently shown that highly interpretable tree-based models are able to achieve competitive performance in this specific task [21]. In the following, we describe how the FED-XAI approach can be deployed on a MEC-enabled B5G/6G architecture (see Figure 2). A FED-XAI computation engine (CE) instantiated within an edge/cloud node (also called a MEC host) is the central entity responsible for model aggregation. With reference to the see-through scenario in Figure 2, each UE measures QoS and QoE metrics, while receiving the video stream, possibly enhanced by the DT. Examples of relevant metrics are: received throughput, jitter, packet error rate (QoS), startup delay, number of stall events and rebuffering ratio (QoE). The collected values of such QoS/QoE metrics are securely transmitted by each (vehicular) UE to a corresponding MEC application, called FED-XAI manager (FM), possibly together with any other relevant information for the FED-XAI learning algorithm. Each UE communicates with its dedicated FM, which acts as an interface to the CE in the MEC system and provides all the functionalities to allow the UE to participate in the federation, e.g., join/leave, transmit/obtain model to/from the CE, etc. Alternatively, an FM can be hosted directly at the UE (instead of the MEC host).

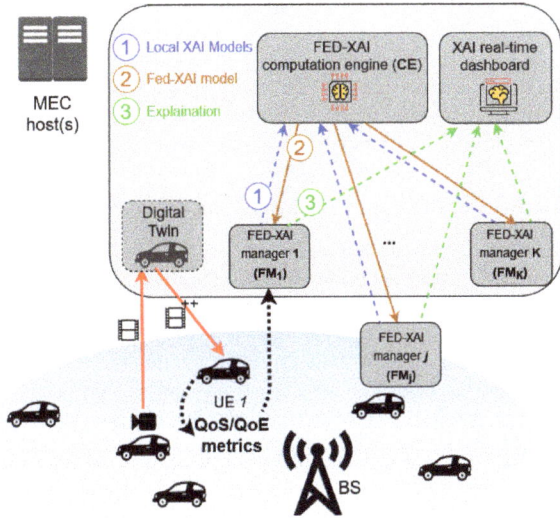

Figure 2. Example of video flow (red arrows) and related QoS/QoE metrics reporting (dashed black arrows) in a MEC-enabled FED-XAI architecture. Interaction among FM, CE and a real time XAI dashboard is also shown.

We divide time in periods, as shown in Figure 3. During each period, a UE measures both QoS and QoE metrics. We call $\mathbf{QOS}_k(i)$ and $\mathbf{QOE}_k(i)$ the vectors of QoS and QoE metrics measured by UE_k during period i. Both vectors are sent to the FM of UE_k, FM_k. At $t = n$, FM_k uses the XAI model obtained by the CE to predict the QoE that UE_k will perceive in the next period, i.e., $QOE_k(n+1)$.

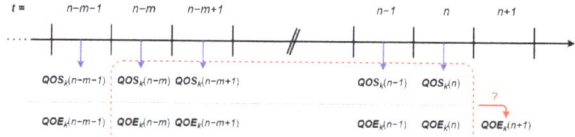

Figure 3. QoE prediction based on previous QoS/QoE samples.

For building (or updating) the FED-XAI model, the involved FMs train (or update) the local model based on recent data ($\mathbf{QOS}(i)$ and $\mathbf{QOE}(i)$ for each $i = n - m, n - m + 1, \ldots, n$, where m is a predefined time window), and share it with the CE. Once the CE produces the aggregated FED-XAI model, the latter is sent back to the FMs that will use it to perform the QoE prediction for their corresponding UE. The results of the prediction feed a dashboard that displays them in real time and explains how they were obtained.

The above scenario will be evaluated in a real-time distributed testbed, which embodies both the communication and computation aspects of the system, as well as the application logic. The communication is realized by Simu5G, a modular simulator of 3GPP-compliant New Radio based on OMNeT++ [22], which also works in real time and interfaces with external applications [23]. The MEC subsystem is realized using Intel's OpenNESS open-source framework (www.openness.org (accessed on 16 August 2022)). Moreover, QoS information is taken in real time from Simu5G, also through its MEC service interface, that can be queried by MEC applications. In order to make the aforementioned testbed more realistic, the network scenario implemented by Simu5G is designed considering data taken from TIM's live network as input, such as base stations position and user data volume, extracted using the techniques described in Section 3.3.

We have recently carried out a preliminary experimental analysis focused on QoE forecasting in B5G/6G networks [24]: we have presented a novel data set (QoE forecasting data set: http://www.iet.unipi.it/g.nardini/ai6g_qoe_dataset.html (accessed on 16 August 2022)) obtained through realistic network simulations and showed how decision trees as an inherently explainable model can be considered a valid baseline for the prediction task. Specifically, the data set consists of time-tagged contextual (e.g., UE position), QoS (e.g., Signal to Interference plus Noise Ratio (SINR) value measured at packet reception) and QoE (e.g., percentage of a frame arrived at the time of its display) metrics from 24 repetitions of a scenario in which 15 instances of UE experiment with a video for approximately 120 s. The prediction task has been formulated as a regression problem. The preprocessing and feature extraction steps are extensively described in [24]; in a nutshell, for each UE we collected the timeseries related to 12 metrics (QoS, QoE and contextual) and obtained any record of the preprocessed data set as follows: for a timestamp t, the input variables consist of 11 statistics (i.e., mean, median, max, min, variance, standard deviation, kurtosis, skewness, Q1 and Q3, number of samples) measured for each metric in the time window $[t - W, t]$ (with $W = 10$ s), whereas the output variable consists in the mean of the target QoE metric over the time horizon of one second (i.e., in $[t, t + H]$, with $H = 1$ s). For the preliminary experimental analysis, we considered the *centralized* setting, i.e., all data available on a single node, and resorted to the decision tree for regression available in scikit-learn (https://scikit-learn.org/stable/modules/generated/sklearn.tree.DecisionTreeRegressor.html (accessed on 16 August 2022)). Figure 4 reports an example of real and predicted timeseries for a given QoE metric. Although our final goal is to learn XAI models in a *federated* fashion, such a preliminary analysis allowed us to set a baseline for the *centralized* setting and to assess the performance of an XAI model in a prediction task on realistic B5G/6G network simulations.

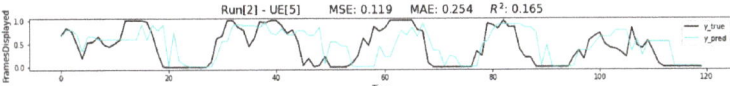

Figure 4. Real and predicted values of QoE for an example UE of the test set (Figure from [24]).

3.3. Feeding Models with Real Network Data

AI-based algorithms need to be fed with real data and collecting live measurements from the MNO network is critical for the reliability of the produced output. In that perspective, the Minimization of Drive Tests (MDT) functionality is applied on TIM Radio Access Network (RAN) to acquire geolocated real data from live RAN. MDT is a 3GPP standard feature (TS 37.320) which allows collecting geolocated radio measurements from UEs in both idle and connected states [25]. This enables UEs to periodically send a large set of measurements from Layer 2—MAC (3GPP TS 36.321), and Layer 3—Radio Resource Control (3GPP TS 36.331). UEs take those measurements for standard procedures, such as cell re-selection, handovers, quality reporting, etc. With MDT, UEs keep measuring the same quantities but share their measurements periodically with the network. If a Global Positioning System (GPS) receiver is enabled, UE measurements are geolocated, which allows anonymous data collection for statistical analysis. MDT paves the way for replacing traditional time-consuming drive tests, made by few test UEs, with thousands or millions of measurements, reported by most devices in the network. Moreover, MDT data come from several customers and UE types, thus allowing a realistic insight into user QoE. MDT measurements in this work mainly refer to geolocated UE throughput and data volume metrics. Examples of MDT georeferenced data from the TIM live network are reported in Figure 5 for the area around Venice, where every pixel represents 1 m^2 of the area, and MDT data in each pixel are averaged and normalized to all MDT data collected in all pixels.

Most MDT data are geolocated in the sea and Venice channels too. This highlights the capability of MDT data to represent the real traffic scenario. The real radio coverage map of several cells in the 1800 MHz frequency band is reported with different colours. MDT data are completely anonymous because neither customer nor UE identity data are monitored or gathered. In particular, MDT data are only geolocated radio measurements reported by UE. The MDT data on TIM's RAN are gathered by using a Nokia system called Geosynthesis.

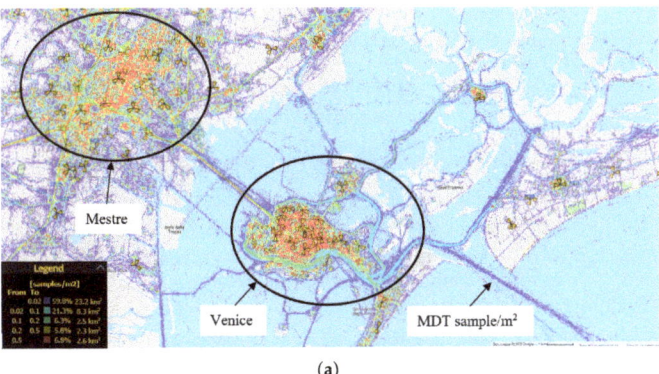

(a)

Figure 5. *Cont.*

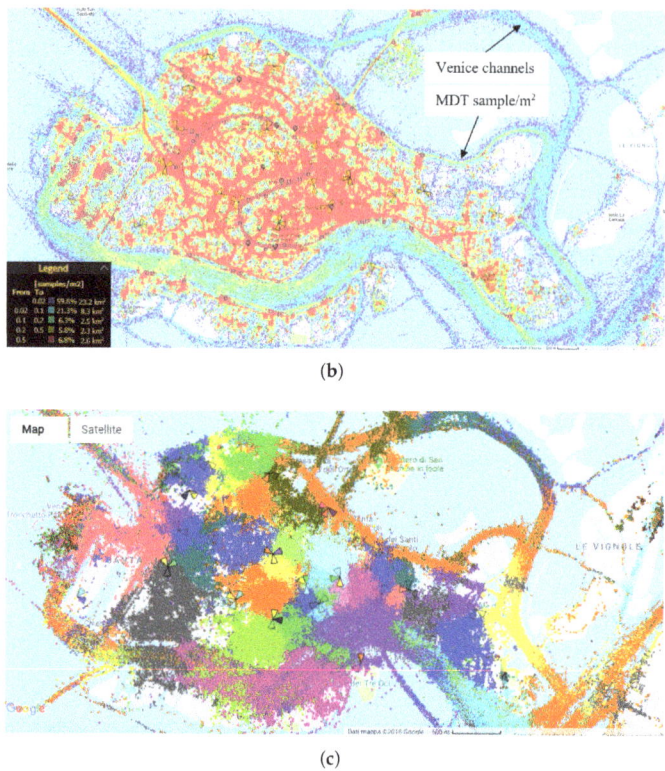

(b)

(c)

Figure 5. MDT georeferenced data from TIM live network on the area of Mestre and Venice cities. (**a**) MDT sample density (MDT sample/m^2) in the area of Mestre and Venice Cities (Italy) averaged over 24 h. On the map, each single visible point is a square pixel with 1 m side. (**b**) MDT sample density on Venice city. (**c**) MDT Best Serving Cell radio coverage of Venice Cities (Italy). Each colour identifies a single cell in the 1800 MHz frequency band. On the map, each single visible point is a square pixel with 1 m side.

4. Impacts of the Proposed FED-XAI Approach on V2X Applications in B5G/6G Networks

The practical use value (or benefit) of FL for the considered V2X use cases, involving various local models instantiated at vehicles, roadside units and edge cloud infrastructure is that the QoE predictions issued by the resulting global aggregated model will be characterized by a higher generalization capability in space and in time than local models. In other words, when a QoE prediction request is issued by a (new) vehicle entering the area of interest, the QoE prediction value to be returned in response will be more accurate and of higher confidence than the one generated by a local model trained by using only the data acquired in the vehicle. On top of the increased generalization capability, a second benefit of the FED-XAI approach is the increase in trust in AI for 6G-enabled services. This has an immediate business impact on 6G business entities. This increase in trust is beneficial for all system entities, from end users to operators and service providers, edge-computing providers and other vertical market players (e.g., automotive, industrial automation, etc.), as it better instils collaboration, starting from a business level. For instance, the exemplary V2X applications described in Section 3.1 are typical cases where a collaboration (and related business agreement) is needed between MNOs, possibly in partnership with edge-computing service providers and car OEMs. Both car OEMs and MNOs can benefit from explanations about such predictions and any consequent decision making: MNOs can provide a more explainable set of 6G functionalities (e.g., FL agents enabling QoE predictions) and expose them to their customers (including car OEMs but also application developers and system integrators); OEMs can also benefit from more information on network predictions, exploitable to improve automated driving features offered to their end customers (i.e., the actual drivers).

Figure 6 shows the same V2X service scenario, characterized by a fundamentally different view, depending on the perspective considered: a car dashboard (from the point of view of the user) shows the set of enabled V2X functionalities and their respective space and time availability. Instead, the view of a network operator (providing the needed communication and computation infrastructure) embeds more complexity, including the management and operation of the network infrastructure and the FED-XAI functionalities needed to provide QoE predictions for the offered V2X services. The boundary between these two worlds is typically governed by a set of Service Level Requirements (SLRs), defining the terms and conditions of the agreement between these two stakeholders (see 5GAA reports for the V2X cases [2]). These SLRs are service-specific and can be defined in terms of minimum throughput, maximum delay, but also availability and reliability of the guaranteed KPIs (defined, e.g., in a certain time window). In this perspective, moving towards 6G, accurate and timely predictions (supported by XAI models) are key to providing advanced and very demanding use cases, with a horizon ranging from extremely short to long time windows. Therefore, it is evident how FED-XAI is paramount for improving the understanding and mutual trust among 6G business entities (i.e., MNOs and OEMs here).

Moreover, the industry is moving towards the adoption of MEC Federations, characterized by a multi-MNO environment, where each operator can provide and share with the other federating entities its own edge-computing infrastructure and services to third parties, also in collaboration with other operators. Dually, operators can consume the resources of other operators (e.g., in countries where they do not have a network infrastructure), offering a seamless user experience to their own customers. Again, the FED-XAI approach is particularly beneficial in such challenging scenarios, which are likely to become widely adopted in B5G and 6G systems.

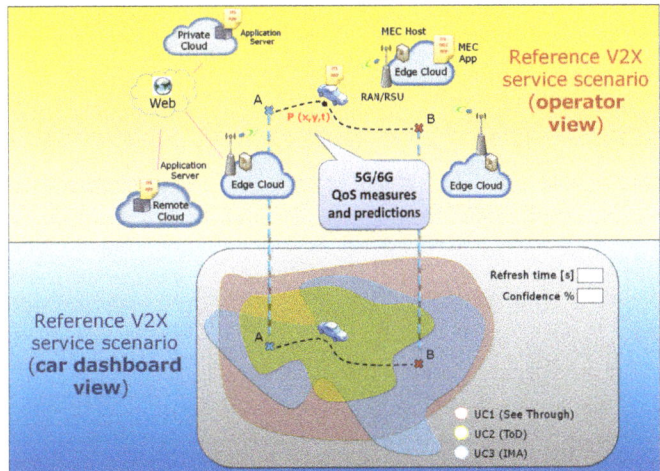

Figure 6. Reference V2X service scenarios, with MNO perspective and customer/car OEM perspective.

Standardization Impact of an Interoperable FED-XAI Implementation

An interoperable implementation of the FED-XAI concept with a focus on an automotive scenario is expected to stimulate discussion within Standards Development Organizations (SDOs) on specifying the involved architectural entities (e.g., FED-XAI CE and FMs), communication interfaces and service protocols including the exchanged data structures. For instance, the International Telecommunication Union (ITU) Focus Group on AI for Autonomous and Assisted Driving (FG-AI4AD) aims to internationally harmonize the definition of a minimal performance threshold for AI "on the road". Additionally, the ETSI Industry Specification Group on Securing AI (ISG SAI) has introduced a new work item on explainability and transparency of AI processing (June 2021). AI platform design issues aiming to provide assurance of explainability and transparency of decisions and allowing independent determination of biases are in scope. ETSI ISG MEC is also of relevance, as one of its specifications (GS MEC 030) focuses on defining the V2X Information Service (VIS) for MEC systems: one of VIS functionalities is to facilitate issuing journey-aware QoS predictions.

5. Conclusions

The aim of this article was to provide a comprehensive vision of AI-pervasive 6G networks that will be extremely high performing, intelligent and trustworthy by design, with a particular applicability to automated vehicle networking. We have introduced the FED-XAI concept, proposing federated learning of XAI models. The FED-XAI concept, applied to advanced 5G systems towards 6G, is expected to improve the user experience of the offered communication services by helping end users trust in-network AI functionality. Benefits of the proposed approach (that could also include standardization) consist in better trustworthiness of operations, e.g., via explainability of QoE predictions, along with security and privacy-preserving management of data from sensors, terminals, users and applications for a range of automotive use cases.

Author Contributions: Conceptualization, A.R., P.D., F.M., D.S., M.C.F., G.N., G.S., A.V., D.M., D.R. and L.G.B.; Investigation, A.R., P.D., F.M., D.S., M.C.F., G.N., G.S., A.V., D.M., D.R. and L.G.B.; Writing—original draft, A.R., P.D., F.M., D.S., M.C.F., G.N., G.S., A.V., D.M., D.R. and L.G.B.; Writing—review and editing, A.R. and P.D. All authors have read and agreed to the published version of the manuscript.

Funding: Part of this work was funded from the European Union's Horizon 2020 research and innovation programme under grant agreement No 101015956 Hexa-X.

Institutional Review Board Statement: Not applicable

Informed Consent Statement: Not applicable

Conflicts of Interest: M.C.F. and L.G.B. are employed by Intel Deutschland GmbH, part of Intel Corporation. D.S. is employed by Intel Corporation Italia SpA, part of Intel Corporation. The authors declare no conflict of interest.

Abbreviations

The following abbreviations are used in this manuscript:

3GPP	Third Generation Partnership Project
AI	Artificial Intelligence
B5G	Beyond 5G
CE	Computation Engine
DNN	Deep Neural Network
DT	Digital Twin
ETSI	European Telecommunications Standards Institute
FedAvg	Federated Averaging
FED-XAI	Federated learning of explainable Artificial Intelligence
FL	Federated Learning
FM	FED-XAI Manager
FVN	Federated Vehicular Network
GPS	Global Positioning System

ISG	Industry Specification Group
ITS	Intelligent Transportation Systems
MDT	Minimization of Drive Tests
MEC	Multi-access Edge Computing
ML	Machine Learning
MNO	Mobile Network Operators
NFV	Network Functions Virtualisation
NN	Neural Network
OEM	Original Equipment Manufacturers
QoE	Quality-of-Experience
QoS	Quality-of-Service
RAN	Radio Access Network
SGD	Stochastic Gradient Descent
SINR	Signal to Interference plus Noise Ratio
SLR	Service Level Requirements
ToD	Teleoperated Driving
TSK	Takagi-Sugeno-Kang
UE	User Equipment
V2X	Vehicle-to-Everything
XAI	Explainable Artificial Intelligence

References

1. Hexa-X Deliverable D1.2—Expanded 6G Vision, Use Cases and Societal Values—Including Aspects of Sustainability, Security and Spectrum. Available online: https://hexa-x.eu/d1-2-expanded-6g-vision-use-cases-and-societal-values-including-aspects-of-sustainability-security-and-spectrum/ (accessed on 3 May 2021).
2. 5GAA Working Item MEC4AUTO. Technical Report Use Cases and Initial Test Specifications Review. Available online: https://5gaa.org/news/working-item-mec4auto/ (accessed on 19 July 2021).
3. 5GAA Technical Report. Tele-Operated Driving (ToD): System Requirements Analysis and Architecture. Available online: https://5gaa.org/news/tele-operated-driving-tod-system-requirements-analysis-and-architecture/ (accessed on 15 September 2021).
4. Ethics Guidelines for Trustworthy AI, Technical Report. European Commission. High Level Expert Group on AI. 2019. Available online: https://ec.europa.eu/digital-single-market/en/news/ethics-guidelines-trustworthy-ai (accessed on 16 August 2022).
5. Barredo Arrieta, A.; Díaz-Rodríguez, N.; Del Ser, J.; Bennetot, A.; Tabik, S.; Barbado, A.; Garcia, S.; Gil-Lopez, S.; Molina, D.; Benjamins, R.; et al. Explainable Artificial Intelligence (XAI): Concepts, taxonomies, opportunities and challenges toward responsible AI. *Inf. Fusion* **2020**, *58*, 82–115. [CrossRef]
6. Fernandez, A.; Herrera, F.; Cordon, O.; Jose del Jesus, M.; Marcelloni, F. Evolutionary Fuzzy Systems for Explainable Artificial Intelligence: Why, When, What for, and Where to? *IEEE Comput. Intell. Mag.* **2019**, *14*, 69–81. [CrossRef]
7. Scalas, M.; Giacinto, G. On the Role of Explainable Machine Learning for Secure Smart Vehicles. In Proceedings of the 2020 AEIT International Conference of Electrical and Electronic Technologies for Automotive (AEIT AUTOMOTIVE), Turin, Italy, 18–20 November 2020; pp. 1–6. [CrossRef]
8. 5GAA White Paper: Making 5G Proactive and Predictive for the Automotive Industry. White Paper. Available online: https://5gaa.org/news/5gaa-releases-white-paper-on-making-5g-proactive-and-predictive-for-the-automotive-industry/ (accessed on 8 January 2020).
9. Elbir, A.M.; Soner, B.; Coleri, S. Federated learning in vehicular networks. *arXiv* **2020**, arXiv:2006.01412.
10. Samarakoon, S.; Bennis, M.; Saad, W.; Debbah, M. Federated Learning for Ultra-Reliable Low-Latency V2V Communications. In Proceedings of the 2018 IEEE Global Communications Conference (GLOBECOM), Abu Dhabi, United Arab Emirates, 9–13 December 2018; pp. 1–7. [CrossRef]
11. Posner, J.; Tseng, L.; Aloqaily, M.; Jararweh, Y. Federated Learning in Vehicular Networks: Opportunities and Solutions. *IEEE Netw.* **2021**, *35*, 152–159. [CrossRef]
12. Salim, S.; Turnbull, B.; Moustafa, N. A Blockchain-Enabled Explainable Federated Learning for Securing Internet-of-Things-Based Social Media 3.0 Networks. *IEEE Trans. Comput. Soc. Syst.* **2021**, 1–17. [CrossRef]
13. Corcuera Bárcena, J.L.; Ducange, P.; Ercolani, A.; Marcelloni, F.; Renda, A. An Approach to Federated Learning of Explainable Fuzzy Regression Models. In Proceedings of the IEEE WCCI 2022 (World Congress on Computational Intelligence), Padua, Italy, 18–23 July 2022.
14. Takagi, T.; Sugeno, M. Fuzzy identification of systems and its applications to modeling and control. *IEEE Trans. Syst. Man Cybern.* **1985**, *SMC-15*, 116–132. [CrossRef]
15. Bechini, A.; Corcuera Bárcena, J.L.; Ducange, P.; Marcelloni, F.; Renda, A. Increasing Accuracy and Explainability in Fuzzy Regression Trees: An Experimental Analysis. In Proceedings of the IEEE WCCI 2022 (World Congress on Computational Intelligence), Padua, Italy, 18–23 July 2022.

16. Tong, W.; Hussain, A.; Bo, W.X.; Maharjan, S. Artificial Intelligence for Vehicle-to-Everything: A Survey. *IEEE Access* **2019**, *7*, 10823–10843. [CrossRef]
17. Dong, L.; Sun, D.; Han, G.; Li, X.; Hu, Q.; Shu, L. Velocity-Free Localization of Autonomous Driverless Vehicles in Underground Intelligent Mines. *IEEE Trans. Veh. Technol.* **2020**, *69*, 9292–9303. [CrossRef]
18. Wu, Y.; Liao, S.; Liu, X.; Li, Z.; Lu, R. Deep Reinforcement Learning on Autonomous Driving Policy with Auxiliary Critic Network. *IEEE Trans. Neural Netw. Learn. Syst.* **2021**, 1–11. [CrossRef]
19. Peng, Z.; Gao, S.; Li, Z.; Xiao, B.; Qian, Y. Vehicle Safety Improvement through Deep Learning and Mobile Sensing. *IEEE Netw.* **2018**, *32*, 28–33. [CrossRef]
20. Zhan, J.; Ma, Z.; Zhang, L. Data-Driven Modeling and Distributed Predictive Control of Mixed Vehicle Platoons. *IEEE Trans. Intell. Veh.* **2022**, 1. [CrossRef]
21. Renda, A.; Ducange, P.; Gallo, G.; Marcelloni, F. XAI Models for Quality of Experience Prediction in Wireless Networks. In Proceedings of the 2021 IEEE International Conference on Fuzzy Systems (FUZZ-IEEE), Luxembourg, 11–14 July 2021; pp. 1–6. [CrossRef]
22. Nardini, G.; Sabella, D.; Stea, G.; Thakkar, P.; Virdis, A. Simu5G—An OMNeT++ Library for End-to-End Performance Evaluation of 5G Networks. *IEEE Access* **2020**, *8*, 181176–181191. [CrossRef]
23. Nardini, G.; Stea, G.; Virdis, A.; Sabella, D.; Thakkar, P. Using Simu5G as a Realtime Network Emulator to Test MEC Apps in an End-to-End 5G Testbed. In Proceedings of the 2020 IEEE 31st Annual International Symposium on Personal, Indoor and Mobile Radio Communications, London, UK, 31 August–3 September 2020; pp. 1–7. [CrossRef]
24. Corcuera Bárcena, J.L.; Ducange, P.; Marcelloni, F.; Nardini, G.; Noferi, A.; Renda, A.; Stea, G.; Virdis, A. Towards Trustworthy AI for QoE prediction in B5G/6G Networks. In Proceedings of the First International Workshop on Artificial Intelligence in beyond 5G and 6G Wireless Networks (AI6G 2022), Padua, Italy, 18–23 July 2022.
25. Micheli, D.; Muratore, G.; Vannelli, A.; Scaloni, A.; Sgheiz, M.; Cirella, P. Rain Effect on 4G LTE In-Car Electromagnetic Propagation Analyzed Through MDT Radio Data Measurement Reported by Mobile Phones. *IEEE Trans. Antennas Propag.* **2021**, *69*, 8641–8651. [CrossRef]

Article

Bias Discovery in Machine Learning Models for Mental Health

Pablo Mosteiro [1,*], Jesse Kuiper [1], Judith Masthoff [1], Floortje Scheepers [2] and Marco Spruit [1,3,4]

[1] Department of Information and Computing Sciences, Utrecht University, 3584 CS Utrecht, The Netherlands; jesse94kuiper@gmail.com (J.K.); j.f.m.masthoff@uu.nl (J.M.); m.r.spruit@lumc.nl (M.S.)
[2] Afdeling Psychiatrie, University Medical Center Utrecht, 3584 CX Utrecht, The Netherlands; f.e.scheepers-2@umcutrecht.nl
[3] Department of Public Health and Primary Care, Leiden University Medical Center, 2333 ZA Leiden, The Netherlands
[4] Leiden Institute of Advanced Computer Science, Leiden University, 2311 EZ Leiden, The Netherlands
* Correspondence: p.mosteiro@uu.nl

Abstract: Fairness and bias are crucial concepts in artificial intelligence, yet they are relatively ignored in machine learning applications in clinical psychiatry. We computed fairness metrics and present bias mitigation strategies using a model trained on clinical mental health data. We collected structured data related to the admission, diagnosis, and treatment of patients in the psychiatry department of the University Medical Center Utrecht. We trained a machine learning model to predict future administrations of benzodiazepines on the basis of past data. We found that gender plays an unexpected role in the predictions—this constitutes bias. Using the AI Fairness 360 package, we implemented reweighing and discrimination-aware regularization as bias mitigation strategies, and we explored their implications for model performance. This is the first application of bias exploration and mitigation in a machine learning model trained on real clinical psychiatry data.

Keywords: fairness; bias; artificial intelligence; machine learning; psychiatry; health; mental health

Citation: Mosteiro, P.; Kuiper, J.; Masthoff, J.; Scheepers, F.; Spruit, M. Bias Discovery in Machine Learning Models for Mental Health. *Information* **2022**, *13*, 237. https://doi.org/10.3390/info13050237

Academic Editors: Gabriele Gianini and Pierre-Edouard Portier

Received: 23 March 2022
Accepted: 3 May 2022
Published: 5 May 2022

Publisher's Note: MDPI stays neutral with regard to jurisdictional claims in published maps and institutional affiliations.

Copyright: © 2022 by the authors. Licensee MDPI, Basel, Switzerland. This article is an open access article distributed under the terms and conditions of the Creative Commons Attribution (CC BY) license (https://creativecommons.org/licenses/by/4.0/).

1. Introduction

For over ten years, there has been increasing interest in the psychiatry domain for using machine learning (ML) to aid psychiatrists and nurses [1]. Recently, multiple approaches have been tested for violence risk assessment (VRA) [2–4], suicidal behaviour prediction [5], and the prediction of involuntary admissions [6], among others.

Using ML for clinical psychiatry is appealing both as a time-saving instrument and as a way to provide insights to clinicians that might otherwise remain unexploited. Clinical ML models are usually trained on patient data, which includes some protected attributes, such as gender or ethnicity. We desire models to give equivalent outputs for equivalent patients that differ only in the value of a protected attribute [7]. Yet, a systematic assessment of the fairness of ML models used for clinical psychiatry is lacking in the literature.

As a case study, we focused on the task of predicting future administrations of benzodiazepines. Benzodiazepines are prescription drugs used in the treatment of, for example, anxiety and insomnia. Long-term use of benzodiazepines is associated with increased medical risks, such as cancer [8]. In addition, benzodiazepines in high doses are addictive, with complicated withdrawal [9]. From a clinical perspective, gender should not play a role in the prescription of benzodiazepines [10,11]. Yet, biases in the prescription of benzodiazepines have been explored extensively in the literature; some protected attributes that contributed to bias were prescriber gender [12], patient ethnicity [13,14], and patient gender [15], as well as interaction effects between some of these protected attributes [16,17]. There is no conclusive consensus regarding these correlations, with some studies finding no correlations between sociodemographic factors and benzodiazepines prescriptions [18].

We explored the effects of gender fairness bias on a model trained to predict the future administration of benzodiazepines to psychiatric patients based on past data, including past doses of benzodiazepines. A possible use case of this model is to identify patients that are at risk of taking benzodiazepines for too long. We hypothesized that our model is likely to unfairly use the patient's gender in making predictions. If that is the case, then mitigation strategies must be put in place to reduce this bias. We expect that there will be a cost to predictive performance.

Our research questions are:

1. For a model trained to predict future administrations of benzodiazepines based on past data, does gender unfairly influence the decisions of the model?
2. If gender does influence the decisions of said model, how much model performance is sacrificed when applying mitigation strategies to avoid the bias?

To answer these questions, we employed a patient dataset from the University Medical Center (UMC) Utrecht and trained a model to predict future administrations of benzodiazepines. We applied the bias discovery and mitigation toolbox AI Fairness 360 [19]. Whenever we found that gender bias was present in our model, we presented an appropriate way to mitigate this bias. Our main contribution is a first implementation of a fairness evaluation and mitigation framework on real-world clinical data from the psychiatry domain. We present a way to mitigate a real and well-known bias in benzodiazepine prescriptions, without loss of performance.

In Section 2, we describe our materials and methods, including a review of previous work in the field. In Section 3, we present our results, which we discuss in Section 4. We present our conclusions in Section 5.

2. Materials and Methods

2.1. Related Work

The study of bias in machine learning has garnered attention for several years [20]. The authors in [21] outlined the dangers of selection bias. Even when researchers attempt to be unbiased, problems might arise, such as bias from an earlier work trickling down into a new model [22] or implicit bias from variables correlated with protected attributes [23,24]. The authors in [25] reviewed bias in machine learning, noting also that there is no industry standard for the definition of *fairness*. The authors in [26] evaluated bias in a machine learning model used for university admissions; they also point out the difference between *individual* and *group* fairness, as do [27]. The authors in [28,29] provided theoretical frameworks for the study of fairness. Along the same lines, refs. [30,31] provided metrics for the evaluation of fairness. The authors in [32,33] recommend methods for mitigating bias.

As for particular applications, refs. [34–36] studied race and gender bias in facial analysis systems. The authors in [37] evaluated fairness in dialogue systems, and while they did not actually evaluate ML models, ref. [38] highlighted the importance of bias mitigation in AI for education.

In the medical domain, ref. [39] pointed out the importance of bias mitigation. Indeed, ref. [40] uncovered bias in post-operative complication predictions. The authors in [41] found that disparities metrics change when transferring models across hospitals. Finally, ref. [42] explored the impact of random seeds on the fairness of classifiers using clinical data from MIMIC-III, and found that small sample sizes can also introduce bias.

No previous study on ML fairness or bias focuses on the psychiatry domain. This domain is interesting because bias seems to be present in the daily practice. We have already discussed in the introduction how bias is present in the prescription of benzodiazepines. There are also gender disparities in the prescription of zolpidem [43] and in the act of seeking psychological help [44]. The authors in [45] also found racial disparities in clinical diagnoses of mania. Furthermore, psychiatry is a domain where a large amount of data is in the form of unstructured text, which is starting to be exploited for ML solutions [46,47]. Previous work has also focused on the explainability of text-based computational support systems in the psychiatry domain [48]. It will be crucial—as these text-based models begin to be applied in the clinical practice—to ensure that they too are unbiased towards protected attributes.

2.2. Data

We employed de-identified patient data from the Electronic Health Records (EHRs) from the psychiatry department at the UMC Utrecht. Patients in the dataset were admitted to the psychiatry department between June 2011 and May 2021. The five database tables included were: admissions, patient information, medication administered, diagnoses, and violence incidents. Table 1 shows the variables present in each of the tables.

Table 1. Datasets retrieved from the psychiatry department of the UMC Utrecht, with the variables present in each dataset that are used for this study. Psychiatry is divided into four *nursing wards*. For the "medication" dataset, the "Administered" and "Not administered" variables contain, in principle, the same information; however, sometimes only one of them is filled.

Dataset	Variable	Type
Admissions	Admission ID	Identifier
	Patient ID	Identifier
	Nursing ward ID	Identifier
	Admission date	Date
	Discharge date	Date
	Admission time	Time
	Discharge time	Time
	Emergency	Boolean
	First admission	Boolean
	Gender	Man/Woman
	Age at admission	Integer
	Admission status	Ongoing/Discharged
	Duration in days	Integer
Medication	Patient ID	Identifier
	Prescription ID	Identifier
	ATC code (medication ID)	String
	Medication name	String
	Dose	Float
	Unit (for dose)	String
	Administration date	Date
	Administration time	Time
	Administered	Boolean
	Dose used	Float
	Original dose	Float
	Continuation After Suspension	Boolean
	Not administered	Boolean
Diagnoses	Patient ID	Identifier
	Diagnosis number	Identifier
	Start date	Date
	End date	Date
	Main diagnosis group	Categorical
	Level of care demand	Numeric
	Multiple problem	Boolean
	Personality disorder	Boolean
	Admission	Boolean
	Diagnosis date	Date
Aggression	Patient ID	Identifier
	Date of incident	Date
	Start time	Time
Patient	Patient ID	Identifier
	Age at start of dossier	Integer

We constructed a dataset where each data point was 14 days after the admission of a patient. We selected only completed admissions (admission status = "discharged") that lasted at least 14 days (duration in days ≥ 14). A total of 3192 admissions (i.e., data points) were included in our dataset. These were coupled with data from the other four tables mentioned above. The nursing ward ID was converted to four binary variables; some rows did not belong to any nursing ward ID (because, for example, the patient was admitted outside of psychiatry and then transferred to psychiatry); these rows have zeros for all four nursing ward ID columns.

For diagnoses, the diagnosis date was not always present in the dataset. In that case, we used the end date of the treatment trajectory. If that was also not present, we used the start date of the treatment trajectory. One of the entries in the administered medication table had no date of administration; this entry was removed. We only consider administered medication (administered = True). Doses of various tranquillizers were converted to an equivalent dose of diazepam, according to Table 2 [49]. (This is the normal procedure when investigating benzodiazepine use. All benzodiazepines have the same working mechanism. The only differences are the half-life and the peak time. So, when studying benzodiazepines, it is allowed to make an equivalent dose of one specific benzodiazepine).

Table 2. List of tranquillizers considered in this study, along with the multipliers used for scaling the doses of those tranquillizers to a diazepam-equivalent dose. The last column is the inverse of the centre column.

Tranquillizer	Multiplier	mg/(mg Diazepam)
Diazepam	1.0	1.00
Alprazolam	10.0	0.10
Bromazepam	1.0	1.00
Brotizolam	40.0	0.03
Chlordiazepoxide	0.5	2.00
Clobazam	0.5	2.00
Clorazepate potassium	0.75	1.33
Flunitrazepam	0.1	10
Flurazepam	0.33	3.03
Lorazepam	5.0	0.20
Lormetazepam	10.0	0.10
Midazolam	1.33	0.10
Nitrazepam	1.0	1.00
Oxazepam	0.33	3.03
Temazepam	1.0	1.00
Zolpidem	1.0	1.00
Zopiclone	1.33	0.75

For each admission, we obtained the age of the patient at the start of the dossier from the patient table. The gender is reported in the admissions table; only the gender assigned at birth is included in this dataset. We counted the number of violence incidents before admission and the number of violence incidents during the first 14 days of admission. The main diagnosis groups were converted to binary values, where 1 means that this diagnosis was present for that admission, and that it took place during the first 14 days of admission. Other binary variables derived from the diagnoses table were "Multiple problem" and "Personality disorder". For all diagnoses present for a given admission, we computed the maximum and minimum "levels of care demand", and saved them as two new variables. Matching the administered medication to the admissions by patient ID and date, we computed the total amount of diazepam-equivalent benzodiazepines administered in the first 14 days of admission, and the total administered in the remainder of the admission. The former is one of the predictor variables. The target variable is binary, i.e., whether benzodiazepines were administered during the remainder of the admission or not.

The final dataset consists of 3192 admissions. Of these, 1724 admissions correspond to men, while 1468 correspond to women. A total of 2035 admissions had some benzodiazepines administered during the first 14 days of admission, while 1980 admissions had some benzodiazepines administered during the remainder of the admission. Table 3 shows the final list of variables included in the dataset.

Table 3. List of variables in the final dataset.

Variable	Type
Patient ID	Numeric
Emergency	Binary
First admission	Binary
Gender	Binary
Age at admission	Numeric
Duration in days	Numeric
Age at start of dossier	Numeric
Incidents during admission	Numeric
Incidents before admission	Numeric
Multiple problem	Binary
Personality disorder	Binary
Minimum level of care demand	Numeric
Maximum level of care demand	Numeric
Past diazepam-equivalent dose	Numeric
Future diazepam-equivalent dose	Numeric
Nursing ward: Clinical Affective and Psychotic Disorders	Binary
Nursing ward: Clinical Acute and Intensive Care	Binary
Nursing ward: Clinical Acute and Intensive Care Youth	Binary
Nursing ward: Clinical Diagnosis and Early Psychosis	Binary
Diagnosis: Attention Deficit Disorder	Binary
Diagnosis: Other issues that may be a cause for concern	Binary
Diagnosis: Anxiety disorders	Binary
Diagnosis: Autism spectrum disorder	Binary
Diagnosis: Bipolar Disorders	Binary
Diagnosis: Cognitive disorders	Binary
Diagnosis: Depressive Disorders	Binary
Diagnosis: Dissociative Disorders	Binary
Diagnosis: Behavioural disorders	Binary
Diagnosis: Substance-Related and Addiction Disorders	Binary
Diagnosis: Obsessive Compulsive and Related Disorders	Binary
Diagnosis: Other mental disorders	Binary
Diagnosis: Other Infant or Childhood Disorders	Binary
Diagnosis: Personality Disorders	Binary
Diagnosis: Psychiatric disorders due to a general medical condition	Binary
Diagnosis: Schizophrenia and other psychotic disorders	Binary
Diagnosis: Somatic Symptom Disorder and Related Disorders	Binary
Diagnosis: Trauma- and stressor-related disorders	Binary
Diagnosis: Nutrition and Eating Disorders	Binary

2.3. Evaluation Metrics

The performance of the model is to be evaluated by the use of the balanced accuracy (average of true positive rate and true negative rate) and the F1 score. (As seen in Section 2.2, the distribution of data points across classes is almost balanced. With that in mind, we could have used accuracy instead of balanced accuracy. However, we had decided on an evaluation procedure before looking at the data, based on previous experience in the field.

We find no reason to believe that our choice should affect the results significantly.) As for quantifying bias, we used four metrics:

- *Statistical Parity Difference:* Discussed in [26] as the difference between the correctly classified instances for the privileged and the unprivileged group. If the statistical parity difference is 0, then the privileged and unprivileged groups receive the same percentage of positive classifications. Statistical parity is an indicator for representation and therefore a group fairness metric. If the value is negative, the privileged group has an advantage.
- *Disparate Impact:* Computed as the ratio of the rate of favourable outcome for the unprivileged group to that of the privileged group [31]. This value should be close to 1 for a fair result; lower than 1 implies a benefit for the privileged group.
- *Equal Opportunity Difference:* The difference between the true positive rates between the unprivileged group and the privileged group. It evaluates the ability of the model to classify the unprivileged group compared to the privileged group. The value should be close to 0 for a fair result. If the value is negative, then the privileged group has an advantage.
- *Average Odds Difference:* The difference between false positives rates and true positive rates between the unprivileged group and privileged group. It provides insights into a possible positive biases towards a group. This value should be close to 0 for a fair result. If the value is negative, then the privileged group has an advantage.

2.4. Machine Learning Methods

We used AI Fairness 360, a package for the discovery and mitigation of bias in machine learning models. The protected attribute in our dataset is gender, while the favourable class is "man". We employ two classification algorithms implemented in ScikitLearn [50]: logistic regression and random forest (We consider these models because they are simple, widely available and widely used within and beyond the clinical field). For logistic regression, we use the "liblinear" solver. For the random forest classifier, we use 500 estimators, with min_samples_leaf equal to 25.

There are three types of bias mitigation techniques: *pre-processing, in-processing,* and *post-processing* [23]. Pre-processing techniques mitigate bias by removing the underlying discrimination from the dataset. In-processing techniques are modifications to the machine learning algorithms to mitigate bias during model training. Post-processing techniques seek to mitigate bias by equalizing the odds post-training. We used two methods for bias mitigation. As a *pre-processing* method, we used the reweighing technique of [32], and retrained our classifiers on the reweighed dataset. As an *in-processing* method, we added a discrimination-aware regularization term to the learning objective of the logistic regression model. This is called a *prejudice remover*. We set the fairness penalty parameter eta to 25, which is high enough that prejudice will be removed aggressively, while not too high, such that accuracy would be significantly compromised [33]. Both of these techniques were seamlessly implemented in AI Fairness 360. To apply *post-processing* techniques in practice, one needs a training set and a test set; once the model is trained, the test set is used to determine how outputs should be modified in order to limit bias. However, in clinical applications, datasets tend to be small, so we envision a realistic scenario in which the entire dataset is used for development, making the use of post-processing methods impossible. For this reason, we did not study these methods further. The workflow of data, models, and bias mitigation techniques is shown in Figure 1.

To estimate the uncertainty due to the choice of training data, we used 5-fold cross-validation, with patient IDs as group identifiers to avoid using the same sample for development and testing. Within each fold, we again split the development set into 62.5% training and 37.5% validation, once again with patient IDs as group identifiers, to avoid using the same sample for training and validation. We trained the model on the training set, and used the validation set to compute the optimal classification threshold, which is the threshold that maximizes the balanced accuracy on the validation set. We then retrained the model on the entire development set, and computed the performance and fairness metrics on the test set. Finally, we computed the mean and standard deviation of all metrics across the 5 folds.

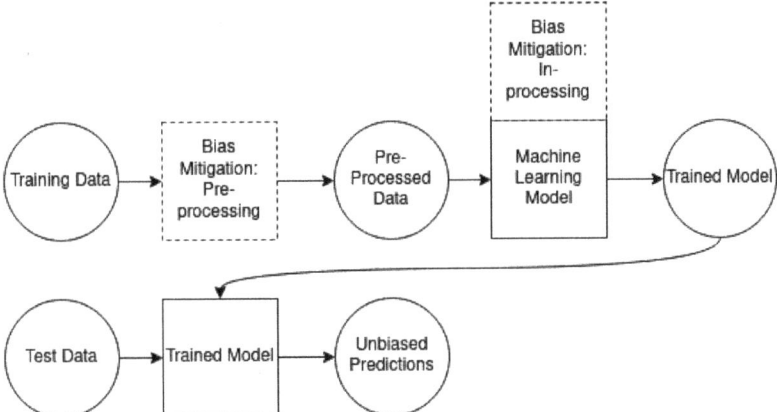

Figure 1. Workflow of data, machine learning models, and bias mitigation techniques used in this research.

The code used to generate the dataset and train the machine learning models is provided as a GitHub repository (https://github.com/PabloMosUU/FairnessForPsychiatry, accessed on 16 February 2022).

3. Results

Each of our classifiers output a continuous prediction for each test data point. We converted these to binary classifications by comparing with a classification threshold. Figures 2–7 show the trade-off between balanced accuracy and fairness metrics as a function of the classification threshold. Figures 2 and 3 show how the disparate impact error and average odds difference vary together with the balanced accuracy as a function of the classification threshold of a logistic regression model with no bias mitigation, for one of the folds of cross-validation. The corresponding plots for the random forest classifier show the same trends. The performance and fairness metrics after cross-validation are shown in Tables 4 and 5, respectively. Since we observed bias (see Section 4 for further discussion), we implemented the mitigation strategies detailed in Section 2.4. Figures 4 and 5 show the validation plots for a logistic regression classifier with reweighing for one of the folds of cross-validation; the plots for the random forest classifier show similar trends. Figures 6 and 7 show the validation plots for a logistic regression classifier with prejudice remover.

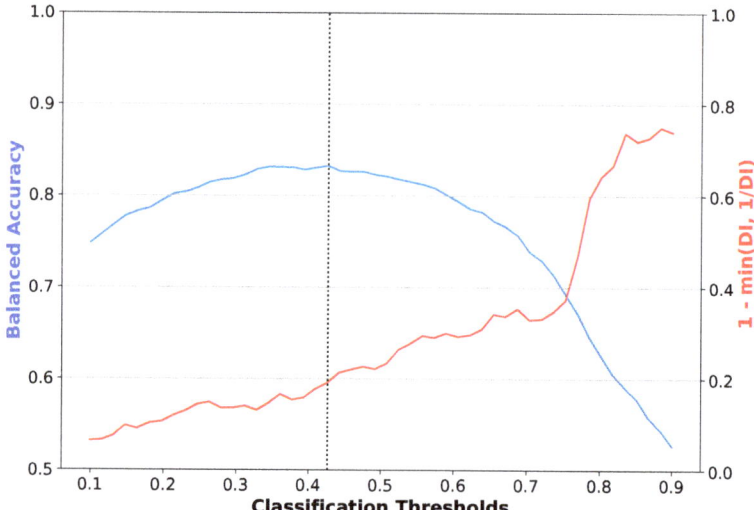

Figure 2. Balanced accuracy and disparate impact error versus classification threshold for a logistic regression classifier with no bias mitigation. The dotted vertical line is the threshold that maximizes balanced accuracy. The plot shown corresponds to one of the folds of cross-validation. Disparate impact error, equal to 1-min(DI, 1/DI), where DI is the disparate impact, is the difference between disparate impact and its ideal value of 1.

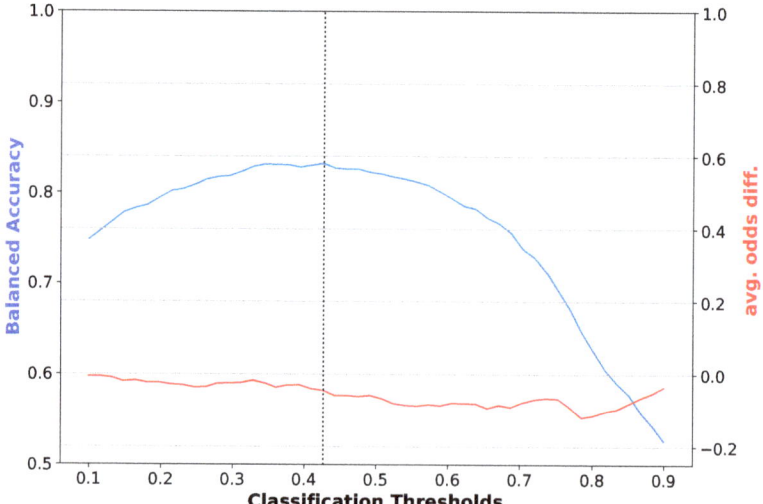

Figure 3. Balanced accuracy and average odds difference versus classification threshold for a logistic regression classifier with no bias mitigation. The dotted vertical line is the threshold that maximizes balanced accuracy. The plot shown corresponds to one of the folds of cross-validation.

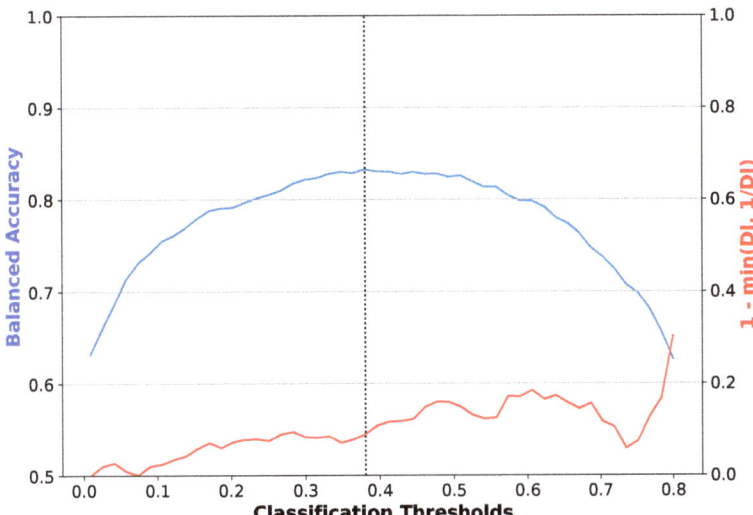

Figure 4. Balanced accuracy and disparate impact error versus classification threshold for a logistic regression classifier with reweighing. The dotted vertical line is the threshold that maximizes balanced accuracy. The plot shown corresponds to one of the folds of cross-validation. Disparate impact error, equal to 1-min(DI, 1/DI), where DI is the disparate impact, and the difference between disparate impact and its ideal value of 1.

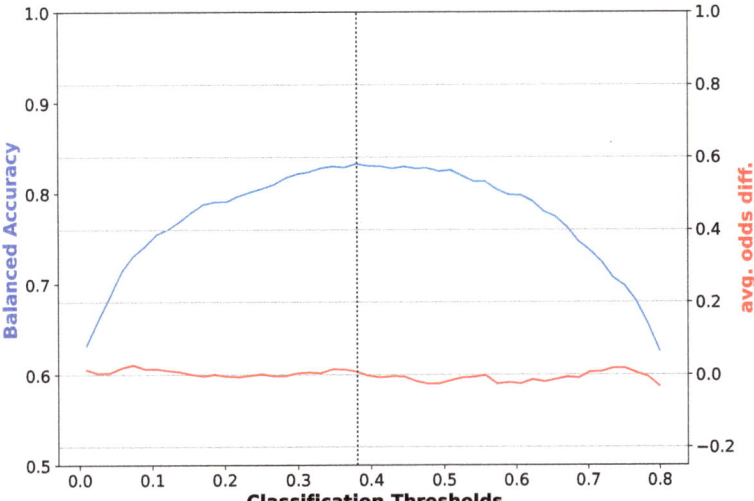

Figure 5. Balanced accuracy and average odds difference versus classification threshold for a logistic regression classifier with reweighing. The dotted vertical line is the threshold that maximizes balanced accuracy. The plot shown corresponds to one of the folds of cross-validation.

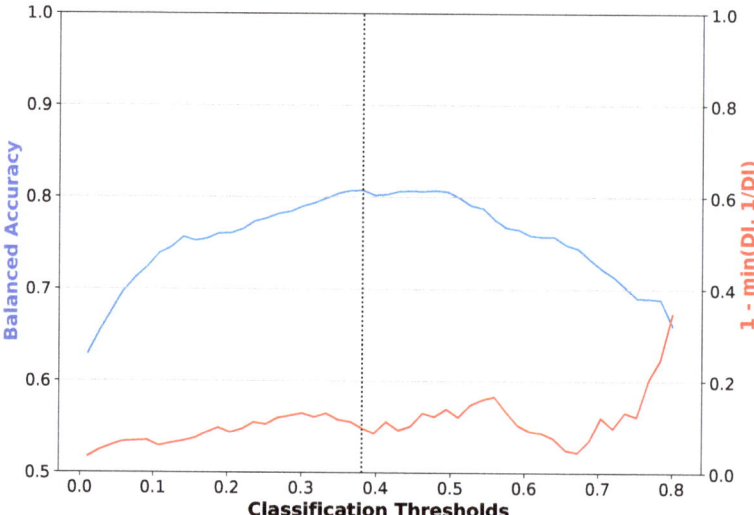

Figure 6. Balanced accuracy and disparate impact error versus classification threshold for a logistic regression classifier with prejudice remover. The dotted vertical line is the threshold that maximizes balanced accuracy. The plot shown corresponds to one of the folds of cross-validation. Disparate impact error, equal to 1−min(DI, 1/DI), where DI is the disparate impact, and the difference between disparate impact and its ideal value of 1.

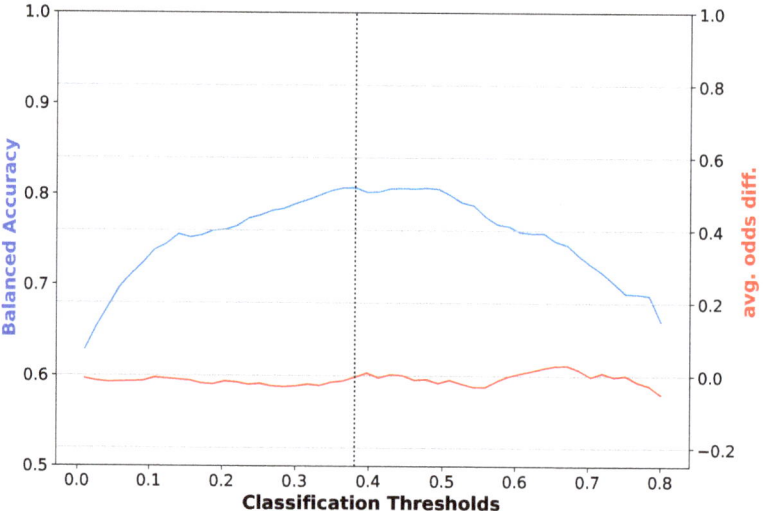

Figure 7. Balanced accuracy and average odds difference versus classification threshold for a logistic regression classifier with prejudice remover. The dotted vertical line is the threshold that maximizes balanced accuracy. The plot shown corresponds to one of the folds of cross-validation.

Table 4. Classification metrics for logistic regression (LR) and random forest (RF) classifiers including bias mitigation strategies reweighing (RW) and prejudice remover (PR). The classification metrics are balanced accuracy (Acc_{bal}) and F1 score. The errors shown are standard deviations.

Model		Performance	
Clf.	Mit.	Acc_{bal}	F1
LR		0.834 ± 0.015	0.843 ± 0.014
RF		0.843 ± 0.018	0.835 ± 0.020
LR	RW	0.830 ± 0.014	0.839 ± 0.011
RF	RW	0.847 ± 0.019	0.840 ± 0.020
LR	PR	0.793 ± 0.020	0.802 ± 0.029

Table 5. Fairness metrics for logistic regression (LR) and random forest (RF) classifiers including bias mitigation strategies reweighing (RW) and prejudice remover (PR). The fairness metrics are disparate impact (DI), average odds difference (AOD), statistical parity difference (SPD), and equal opportunity difference (EOD). The errors shown are standard deviations.

Model		Fairness			
Clf.	Mit.	DI	AOD	SPD	EOD
LR		0.793 ± 0.074	−0.046 ± 0.021	−0.110 ± 0.038	−0.038 ± 0.028
RF		0.796 ± 0.071	−0.018 ± 0.017	−0.083 ± 0.031	−0.013 ± 0.035
LR	RW	0.869 ± 0.066	−0.003 ± 0.013	−0.066 ± 0.035	0.004 ± 0.034
RF	RW	0.830 ± 0.077	−0.004 ± 0.023	−0.070 ± 0.034	0.001 ± 0.043
LR	PR	0.886 ± 0.056	−0.008 ± 0.003	−0.060 ± 0.034	−0.020 ± 0.045

4. Discussion

4.1. Analysis of Results

As reported in Table 5, all fairness metrics show results favourable to the privileged group (see Section 2.3 for a discussion of the fairness metrics we use). Reweighing improved the fairness metrics for both classifiers. The prejudice remover also improved the fairness metrics, albeit at a cost in performance. There was no big difference in performance between the logistic regression and random forest classifiers. If fairness is crucial, then the logistic regression classifier gives more options in terms of the mitigation strategies. The better mitigation strategy is the one closest to the data, for it requires less tinkering with the model, which can lead to worse explainability.

In addition, we computed, for each fold of cross-validation, the difference for each performance and fairness metric between a model with a bias mitigator and the corresponding model without bias mitigation. We then took the mean and standard deviation of those differences, and report the results for performance and fairness metrics on Tables 6 and 7, respectively. We can see that differences in performance for reweighing are mostly small, while the gains in fairness metrics are statistically significant at a 95% confidence level. Meanwhile, the prejudice remover incurs a greater cost in performance, with no apparent greater improvement to the fairness metrics.

Table 6. Classification metric differences of models with bias mitigators reweighing (RW) and prejudice remover (PR) compared to a baseline without bias mitigation, for logistic regression (LR) and random forest (RF) classifiers. The classification metrics are balanced accuracy (Acc_{bal}) and F1 score. The errors shown are standard deviations. Differences significant at 95% confidence level are shown in **bold**.

Model		Performance	
Clf.	Mit.	ΔAcc_{bal}	$\Delta F1$
LR	PR	**−0.040 ± 0.013**	**−0.041 ± 0.025**
LR	RW	−0.003 ± 0.013	−0.005 ± 0.013
RF	RW	0.003 ± 0.002	**0.005 ± 0.001**

Table 7. Fairness metric differences of models with bias mitigators reweighing (RW) and prejudice remover (PR) compared to a baseline without bias mitigation, for logistic regression (LR) and random forest (RF) classifiers. The fairness metrics are disparate impact (DI), average odds difference (AOD), statistical parity difference (SPD) and equal opportunity difference (EOD). The errors shown are standard deviations. Differences significant at 95% confidence level are shown in **bold**.

Model		Fairness			
Clf.	Mit.	ΔDI	ΔAOD	ΔSPD	ΔEOD
LR	PR	**0.092 ± 0.036**	0.038 ± 0.021	**0.050 ± 0.019**	0.018 ± 0.042
LR	RW	**0.075 ± 0.021**	**0.043 ± 0.017**	**0.043 ± 0.014**	0.042 ± 0.034
RF	RW	**0.034 ± 0.013**	**0.014 ± 0.006**	**0.013 ± 0.006**	0.014 ± 0.011

4.2. Limitations

Some diagnoses did not have a diagnosis date filled out in the raw dataset. In those cases, we used the treatment end date. Some data points did not have a value for that variable either, and in those cases, we used the treatment start date. This leads to an inconsistent definition of the diagnosis date, and hence to inconsistencies in the variables related to diagnoses during the first 14 days of admission. However, we carried out the analysis again with only the diagnoses for which the diagnosis dates were present in the raw data, and the results followed the same trends.

On a similar note, we removed a few medication administrations that did not have an administering date. A better solution would have been to remove all data corresponding to those patients, albeit at the cost of having fewer data points. We carried out the analysis again in that configuration, and obtained similar results.

Finally, this work considered only the diagnoses that took place within the first 14 days of admission. It might have been interesting to also consider diagnoses that took place *before* admission. We leave this option for future work.

4.3. Future Work

The present work considered benzodiazepine prescriptions administered during the remainder of each patient's admission. To make the prediction task fairer for the computer, we could consider predicting benzodiazepines administered during a specific time window, for example, days 15–28 of an admission.

Previous work noted a possible bias between the gender of the *prescriber* and the prescriptions of benzodiazepines [16,17]. It would be interesting to look into this correlation in our dataset as well; one could train a model to predict, on the basis of patient and prescriber data, whether benzodiazepines will be prescribed. If there are correlations between the gender of the prescriber and the prescription of benzodiazepines, we could raise a warning to let the practitioner know that the model thinks there might be a bias.

Finally, there are other medications for which experts suspect there could be gender biases in the prescriptions and administrations, such as antipsychotics and antidepressives. It would be beneficial to also study those administrations using a similar pipeline as the one developed here.

As a final note, [51] warned against the use of blind applications of fairness frameworks in healthcare. Thus, the present study should be considered only as a demonstration of the importance of considering bias and mitigation in clinical psychiatry machine learning models. Further work is necessary to understand these biases on a deeper level, and what course of action should be taken.

5. Conclusions

Given our results (Section 3) and discussion thereof (Section 4.1), we can conclude that a model trained to predict future administrations of benzodiazepines based on past data is biased by the patients' genders. Perhaps surprisingly, reweighing the data (a pre-processing step) seems to mitigate this bias quite significantly, without loss of performance. The in-processing method with a prejudice remover also mitigated this bias, but at a cost to performance.

This is the first fairness evaluation of a machine learning model trained on real clinical psychiatric data. Future researchers working with such models should consider computing fairness metrics and, when necessary, adopt mitigation strategies to ensure patient treatment is not biased with respect to protected attributes.

Author Contributions: Conceptualization, F.S. and M.S.; methodology, P.M. and M.S.; software, P.M and J.K.; validation, P.M.; formal analysis, P.M.; investigation, J.K. and F.S.; resources, F.S.; data curation, P.M., J.K. and F.S.; writing—original draft preparation, P.M.; writing—review and editing, P.M.; visualization, J.K.; supervision, P.M. and J.M.; project administration, F.S. and M.S.; funding acquisition, F.S. and M.S. All authors have read and agreed to the published version of the manuscript.

Funding: This research was funded by the COVIDA project, which in turn is funded by the Strategic Alliance TU/E, WUR, UU en UMC Utrecht.

Institutional Review Board Statement: The study was approved by the UMC ethics committee as part of PsyData, a team of data scientists and clinicians working at the psychiatry department of the UMC Utrecht.

Informed Consent Statement: Not applicable.

Data Availability Statement: The datasets generated for this study cannot be shared, to protect patient privacy and comply with institutional regulations.

Acknowledgments: The core content of this study is drawn from the Master in Business Informatics thesis of Jesse Kuiper [52].

Conflicts of Interest: The authors declare that the research was conducted in the absence of any commercial or financial relationships that could be construed as a potential conflict of interest.

References

1. Pestian, J.; Nasrallah, H.; Matykiewicz, P.; Bennett, A.; Leenaars, A. Suicide Note Classification Using Natural Language Processing: A Content Analysis. *Biomed. Inform. Insights* **2010**, *3*, BII.S4706. [CrossRef] [PubMed]
2. Menger, V.; Spruit, M.; van Est, R.; Nap, E.; Scheepers, F. Machine Learning Approach to Inpatient Violence Risk Assessment Using Routinely Collected Clinical Notes in Electronic Health Records. *JAMA Netw. Open* **2019**, *2*, e196709. [CrossRef] [PubMed]
3. Le, D.V.; Montgomery, J.; Kirkby, K.C.; Scanlan, J. Risk prediction using natural language processing of electronic mental health records in an inpatient forensic psychiatry setting. *J. Biomed. Inform.* **2018**, *86*, 49–58. [CrossRef] [PubMed]
4. Suchting, R.; Green, C.E.; Glazier, S.M.; Lane, S.D. A data science approach to predicting patient aggressive events in a psychiatric hospital. *Psychiatry Res.* **2018**, *268*, 217–222. [CrossRef] [PubMed]
5. van Mens, K.; de Schepper, C.; Wijnen, B.; Koldijk, S.J.; Schnack, H.; de Looff, P.; Lokkerbol, J.; Wetherall, K.; Cleare, S.; O'Connor, R.C.; et al. Predicting future suicidal behaviour in young adults, with different machine learning techniques: A population-based longitudinal study. *J. Affect. Disord.* **2020**, *271*, 169–177. [CrossRef] [PubMed]
6. Kalidas, V. Siamese Fine-Tuning of BERT for Classification of Small and Imbalanced Datasets, Applied to Prediction of Involuntary Admissions in Mental Healthcare. Master's Thesis, Eindhoven University of Technology, Eindhoven, The Netherlands, 2020.

7. Delgado-Rodriguez, M.; Llorca, J. Bias. *J. Epidemiol. Community Health* **2004**, *58*, 635–641. [CrossRef]
8. Kim, H.B.; Myung, S.K.; Park, Y.C.; Park, B. Use of benzodiazepine and risk of cancer: A meta-analysis of observational studies. *Int. J. Cancer* **2017**, *140*, 513–525. [CrossRef]
9. Quaglio, G.; Pattaro, C.; Gerra, G.; Mathewson, S.; Verbanck, P.; Des Jarlais, D.C.; Lugoboni, F. High dose benzodiazepine dependence: Description of 29 patients treated with flumazenil infusion and stabilised with clonazepam. *Psychiatry Res.* **2012**, *198*, 457–462. [CrossRef]
10. Federatie Medisch Specialisten. Angststoornissen. Available online: https://richtlijnendatabase.nl/richtlijn/angststoornissen/gegeneraliseerde_angststoornis_gas/farmacotherapie_bij_gas/benzodiazepine_gegeneraliseerde_angststoornis.html (accessed on 18 November 2021).
11. Vinkers, C.H.; Tijdink, J.K.; Luykx, J.J.; Vis, R. Kiezen voor de juiste benzodiazepine. *Ned. Tijdschr. Geneeskd.* **2012**, *156*, A4900.
12. Bjorner, T.; Laerum, E. Factors associated with high prescribing of benzodiazepines and minor opiates. *Scand. J. Prim. Health Care* **2003**, *21*, 115–120. [CrossRef]
13. Peters, S.M.; Knauf, K.Q.; Derbidge, C.M.; Kimmel, R.; Vannoy, S. Demographic and clinical factors associated with benzodiazepine prescription at discharge from psychiatric inpatient treatment. *Gen. Hosp. Psychiatry* **2015**, *37*, 595–600. [CrossRef] [PubMed]
14. Cook, B.; Creedon, T.; Wang, Y.; Lu, C.; Carson, N.; Jules, P.; Lee, E.; Alegría, M. Examining racial/ethnic differences in patterns of benzodiazepine prescription and misuse. *Drug Alcohol Depend.* **2018**, *187*, 29–34. [CrossRef] [PubMed]
15. Olfson, M.; King, M.; Schoenbaum, M. Benzodiazepine Use in the United States. *JAMA Psychiatry* **2015**, *72*, 136–142. [CrossRef] [PubMed]
16. McIntyre, R.S.; Chen, V.C.H.; Lee, Y.; Lui, L.M.W.; Majeed, A.; Subramaniapillai, M.; Mansur, R.B.; Rosenblat, J.D.; Yang, Y.H.; Chen, Y.L. The influence of prescriber and patient gender on the prescription of benzodiazepines: Evidence for stereotypes and biases? *Soc. Psychiatry Psychiatr. Epidemiol.* **2021**, *56*, 1433–9285. [CrossRef] [PubMed]
17. Lui, L.M.W.; Lee, Y.; Lipsitz, O.; Rodrigues, N.B.; Gill, H.; Ma, J.; Wilkialis, L.; Tamura, J.K.; Siegel, A.; Chen-Li, D.; et al. The influence of prescriber and patient gender on the prescription of benzodiazepines: Results from the Florida Medicaid Dataset. *CNS Spectrums* **2021**, *26*, 1–5. [CrossRef] [PubMed]
18. Maric, N.P.; Latas, M.; Andric Petrovic, S.; Soldatovic, I.; Arsova, S.; Crnkovic, D.; Gugleta, D.; Ivezic, A.; Janjic, V.; Karlovic, D.; et al. Prescribing practices in Southeastern Europe—Focus on benzodiazepine prescription at discharge from nine university psychiatric hospitals. *Psychiatry Res.* **2017**, *258*, 59–65. [CrossRef]
19. Bellamy, R.K.E.; Dey, K.; Hind, M.; Hoffman, S.C.; Houde, S.; Kannan, K.; Lohia, P.; Martino, J.; Mehta, S.; Mojsilović, A.; et al. AI Fairness 360: An extensible toolkit for detecting and mitigating algorithmic bias. *IBM J. Res. Dev.* **2019**, *63*, 4:1–4:15. [CrossRef]
20. Baer, T. *Understand, Manage, and Prevent Algorithmic Bias*; Apress: Berkeley, CA, USA, 2019.
21. Ellenberg, J.H. Selection bias in observational and experimental studies. *Stat. Med.* **1994**, *13*, 557–567. [CrossRef]
22. Barocas, S.; Selbst, A. Big Data's Disparate Impact. *Calif. Law Rev.* **2016**, *104*, 671. [CrossRef]
23. d'Alessandro, B.; O'Neil, C.; LaGatta, T. Conscientious Classification: A Data Scientist's Guide to Discrimination-Aware Classification. *Big Data* **2017**, *5*, 120–134. [CrossRef]
24. Lang, W.W.; Nakamura, L.I. A Model of Redlining. *J. Urban Econ.* **1993**, *33*, 223–234. [CrossRef]
25. Chouldechova, A.; Roth, A. A Snapshot of the Frontiers of Fairness in Machine Learning. *Commun. ACM* **2020**, *63*, 82–89. [CrossRef]
26. Dwork, C.; Hardt, M.; Pitassi, T.; Reingold, O.; Zemel, R. Fairness through Awareness. Available online: https://arxiv.org/abs/1104.3913 (accessed on 18 November 2021).
27. Zemel, R.; Wu, Y.; Swersky, K.; Pitassi, T.; Dwork, C. Learning Fair Representations. In Proceedings of the 30th International Conference on Machine Learning, PMLR, Atlanta, GA, USA, 17–19 June 2013; Volume 28, pp. 325–333.
28. Joseph, M.; Kearns, M.; Morgenstern, J.; Roth, A. Fairness in Learning: Classic and Contextual Bandits. Available online: https://arxiv.org/abs/1605.07139 (accessed on 18 November 2021).
29. Friedler, S.A.; Scheidegger, C.; Venkatasubramanian, S. On the (Im)Possibility of Fairness. Available online: https://arxiv.org/abs/1609.07236 (accessed on 18 November 2021).
30. Saleiro, P.; Kuester, B.; Hinkson, L.; London, J.; Stevens, A.; Anisfeld, A.; Rodolfa, K.T.; Ghani, R. Aequitas: A Bias and Fairness Audit Toolkit. Available online: https://arxiv.org/abs/1811.05577 (accessed on 18 November 2021).
31. Feldman, M.; Friedler, S.; Moeller, J.; Scheidegger, C.; Venkatasubramanian, S. Certifying and Removing Disparate Impact. Available online: https://arxiv.org/abs/1412.3756 (accessed on 18 November 2021).
32. Kamiran, F.; Calders, T. Data preprocessing techniques for classification without discrimination. *Knowl. Inf. Syst.* **2012**, *33*, 1–33. [CrossRef]
33. Kamishima, T.; Akaho, S.; Asoh, H.; Sakuma, J. Fairness-Aware Classifier with Prejudice Remover Regularizer. In *Machine Learning and Knowledge Discovery in Databases*; Flach, P.A., De Bie, T., Cristianini, N., Eds.; Springer: Berlin/Heidelberg, Germany, 2012; pp. 35–50.
34. Scheuerman, M.K.; Wade, K.; Lustig, C.; Brubaker, J.R. How We've Taught Algorithms to See Identity: Constructing Race and Gender in Image Databases for Facial Analysis. *Proc. ACM Hum.-Comput. Interact.* **2020**, *4*, 1–35. [CrossRef]

35. Xu, T.; White, J.; Kalkan, S.; Gunes, H. Investigating Bias and Fairness in Facial Expression Recognition. In Proceedings of the Computer Vision—ECCV 2020 Workshops, Glasgow, UK, 23–28 August 2020; Bartoli, A., Fusiello, A., Eds.; Springer International Publishing: Cham, Switzerland, 2020; pp. 506–523.
36. Yucer, S.; Akcay, S.; Al-Moubayed, N.; Breckon, T.P. Exploring Racial Bias Within Face Recognition via Per-Subject Adversarially-Enabled Data Augmentation. In Proceedings of the IEEE/CVF Conference on Computer Vision and Pattern Recognition (CVPR) Workshops, Seattle, DC, USA, 14–19 June 2020; pp. 18–19.
37. Liu, H.; Dacon, J.; Fan, W.; Liu, H.; Liu, Z.; Tang, J. Does Gender Matter? Towards Fairness in Dialogue Systems. Available online: https://arxiv.org/abs/1910.10486 (accessed on 18 November 2021).
38. Kizilcec, R.F.; Lee, H. Algorithmic Fairness in Education. Available online: https://arxiv.org/abs/2007.05443 (accessed on 18 November 2021).
39. Geneviève, L.D.; Martani, A.; Shaw, D.; Elger, B.S.; Wangmo, T. Structural racism in precision medicine: Leaving no one behind. *BMC Med. Ethics* **2020**, *21*, 17. [CrossRef]
40. Tripathi, S.; Fritz, B.A.; Abdelhack, M.; Avidan, M.S.; Chen, Y.; King, C.R. (Un)Fairness in Post-Operative Complication Prediction Models. Available online: https://arxiv.org/abs/2011.02036 (accessed on 18 November 2021).
41. Singh, H.; Mhasawade, V.; Chunara, R. Generalizability Challenges of Mortality Risk Prediction Models: A Retrospective Analysis on a Multi-center Database. *medRxiv* **2021**. [CrossRef]
42. Amir, S.; van de Meent, J.W.; Wallace, B.C. On the Impact of Random Seeds on the Fairness of Clinical Classifiers. Available online: https://arxiv.org/abs/2104.06338 (accessed on 18 November 2021).
43. Jasuja, G.K.; Reisman, J.I.; Weiner, R.S.; Christopher, M.L.; Rose, A.J. Gender differences in prescribing of zolpidem in the Veterans Health Administration. *Am. J. Manag. Care* **2019**, *25*, e58–e65. [CrossRef]
44. Nam, S.K.; Chu, H.J.; Lee, M.K.; Lee, J.H.; Kim, N.; Lee, S.M. A Meta-analysis of Gender Differences in Attitudes Toward Seeking Professional Psychological Help. *J. Am. Coll. Health* **2010**, *59*, 110–116. [CrossRef]
45. Strakowski, S.M.; McElroy, S.L.; Keck, P.E.; West, S.A. Racial influence on diagnosis in psychotic mania. *J. Affect. Disord.* **1996**, *39*, 157–162. [CrossRef]
46. Rumshisky, A.; Ghassemi, M.; Naumann, T.; Szolovits, P.; Castro, V.M.; McCoy, T.H.; Perlis, R.H. Predicting early psychiatric readmission with natural language processing of narrative discharge summaries. *Transl. Psychiatry* **2016**, *6*, e921. [CrossRef]
47. Tang, S.X.; Kriz, R.; Cho, S.; Park, S.J.; Harowitz, J.; Gur, R.E.; Bhati, M.T.; Wolf, D.H.; Sedoc, J.; Liberman, M.Y. Natural language processing methods are sensitive to sub-clinical linguistic differences in schizophrenia spectrum disorders. *NPJ Schizophr.* **2021**, *7*, 25. [CrossRef] [PubMed]
48. Kaczmarek-Majer, K.; Casalino, G.; Castellano, G.; Hryniewicz, O.; Dominiak, M. Explaining smartphone-based acoustic data in bipolar disorder: Semi-supervised fuzzy clustering and relative linguistic summaries. *Inf. Sci.* **2022**, *588*, 174–195. [CrossRef]
49. Nederlands Huisartsen Genootschap. Omrekentabel Benzodiazepine naar Diazepam 2 mg Tabletten. 2014. Available online: https://www.nhg.org/sites/default/files/content/nhg_org/images/thema/omrekentabel_benzodiaz._naar_diazepam_2_mg_tab.pdf (accessed on 22 March 2022).
50. Pedregosa, F.; Varoquaux, G.; Gramfort, A.; Michel, V.; Thirion, B.; Grisel, O.; Blondel, M.; Prettenhofer, P.; Weiss, R.; Dubourg, V.; et al. Scikit-learn: Machine Learning in Python. *J. Mach. Learn. Res.* **2011**, *12*, 2825–2830.
51. Pfohl, S.R.; Foryciarz, A.; Shah, N.H. An empirical characterization of fair machine learning for clinical risk prediction. *J. Biomed. Inform.* **2021**, *113*, 103621. [CrossRef] [PubMed]
52. Kuiper, J. Machine-Learning Based Bias Discovery in Medical Data. Master's Thesis, Utrecht University, Utrecht, The Netherlands, 2021.

Article

Explainable AI for Psychological Profiling from Behavioral Data: An Application to Big Five Personality Predictions from Financial Transaction Records

Yanou Ramon [1,*], R.A. Farrokhnia [2], Sandra C. Matz [3] and David Martens [1]

1. Department of Engineering Management, University of Antwerp, 2000 Antwerp, Belgium; david.martens@uantwerp.be
2. Columbia Business & Engineering Schools, New York, NY 10027, USA; farrokhnia@gsb.columbia.edu
3. Department of Management, Columbia Business School, New York, NY 10027, USA; sm4409@gsb.columbia.edu
* Correspondence: yanou.ramon@uantwerp.be

Abstract: Every step we take in the digital world leaves behind a record of our behavior; a digital footprint. Research has suggested that algorithms can translate these digital footprints into accurate estimates of psychological characteristics, including personality traits, mental health or intelligence. The mechanisms by which AI generates these insights, however, often remain opaque. In this paper, we show how Explainable AI (XAI) can help domain experts and data subjects validate, question, and improve models that classify psychological traits from digital footprints. We elaborate on two popular XAI methods (rule extraction and counterfactual explanations) in the context of Big Five personality predictions (traits and facets) from financial transactions data ($N = 6408$). First, we demonstrate how global rule extraction sheds light on the spending patterns identified by the model as most predictive for personality, and discuss how these rules can be used to explain, validate, and improve the model. Second, we implement local rule extraction to show that individuals are assigned to personality classes because of their unique financial behavior, and there exists a positive link between the model's prediction confidence and the number of features that contributed to the prediction. Our experiments highlight the importance of both global and local XAI methods. By better understanding how predictive models work in general as well as how they derive an outcome for a particular person, XAI promotes accountability in a world in which AI impacts the lives of billions of people around the world.

Keywords: psychological profiling; predictive modeling; behavioral data; explainable artificial intelligence; rule extraction; counterfactual explanations

Citation: Ramon, Y.; Farrokhnia, R.A.; Matz, S.C.; Martens, D. Explainable AI for Psychological Profiling from Behavioral Data: An Application to Big Five Personality Predictions from Financial Transaction Records. *Information* **2021**, *12*, 518. https://doi.org/10.3390/info12120518

Academic Editors: Gabriele Gianini and Pierre-Edouard Portier

Received: 29 October 2021
Accepted: 7 December 2021
Published: 13 December 2021

Publisher's Note: MDPI stays neutral with regard to jurisdictional claims in published maps and institutional affiliations.

Copyright: © 2021 by the authors. Licensee MDPI, Basel, Switzerland. This article is an open access article distributed under the terms and conditions of the Creative Commons Attribution (CC BY) license (https://creativecommons.org/licenses/by/4.0/).

1. Introduction

The information age is characterized by a wealth of user-generated data that is collected with every step a user takes in the digital environment. These digital footprints are increasingly available for academics, businesses and governments [1] and have been shown to provide highly intimate insights into people's lives as well as the ways in which they think, feel and behave. For example, digital footprints can be used to predict personality traits [2,3], mental health [4], sexual and political orientation [2,5] or intelligence [2]. The process of translating digital footprints into meaningful psychological profiles with the help of machine learning has been termed 'psychological profiling', and drives applications in a variety of areas ranging from marketing to employment to mental health (see Figure 1 for a conceptual overview). As Matz et al. [6] define it, psychological profiling is "the automated assessment of psychological traits from digital footprints". Over the past decade, researchers have been tapping into a broad variety of data sources for psychological profiling, including social media data (e.g., Facebook likes and status updates [2,7]), mobile sensing data [8], music listening preferences [9,10], mobility behaviors [11] as well as financial transaction records [12,13].

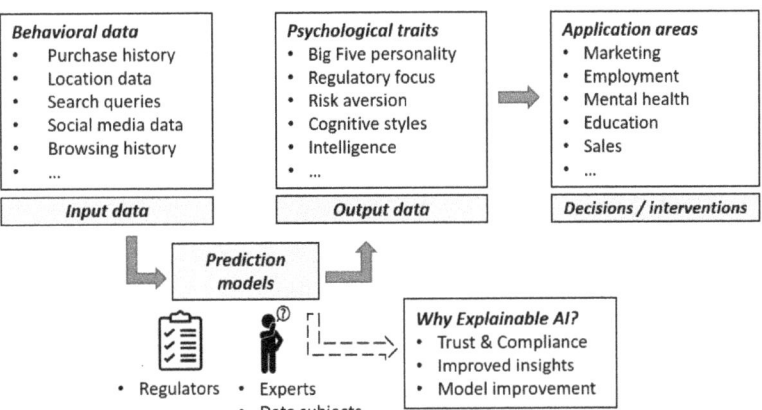

Figure 1. Explainable AI in applications that leverage behavioral data for psychological profiling.

1.1. AI as a Black Box

Machine learning models that classify psychological traits from behavior can be highly accurate. However, at the same time, their structure can be very complex, which has earned them the reputation of being a 'black box' that is difficult to penetrate. The complexity arises from either the learning technique (e.g., Random Forest models), the data, or both. Consequently, it is often difficult—if not impossible—to understand how classifications were made when using nonlinear models without relying on interpretation techniques like the ones we use in this study. Even for linear models or decision trees, it can be challenging to gain meaningful insights into how classifications are made, because of the high dimensional and sparse nature of behavioral data [14–17]. For example, if we want to predict people's personality based on the Facebook pages they 'like', a user is represented by a binary feature for every page, which results in an enormous feature space. Linear models trained on these data end up having a large number of features (i.e., every Facebook page becomes a separate feature in the model), each of which is assigned a corresponding weight. Alternatively, only the features with the largest weights can be inspected. Because the data is sparse, however, only a small fraction of the classified instances is 'explained'. Kosinski et al. [2], for example, predicted personal traits using over 50,000 Facebook pages and interpreted the models by listing the pages that are most related to a trait of interest. Amongst the top predictors for high intelligence were pages like 'Science' and 'Curly Fries'. Due to the data sparsity, however, these pages are only relevant ('liked') by a small fraction of all users predicted as intelligent, which leaves a substantial part of the classifications unexplained (on average, a user liked 170 pages out of a total of 55,814 pages that were used by the model).

In addition to the outlined challenges associated with the high dimensionality and sparsity of digital footprint data, the non-redundancy of the data also impacts the ability to meaningfully interpret model predictions. Given that many behavioral features are relevant for the classification task, applying feature input selection or dimensionality reduction generally results in worse predictive performance, and makes a detailed interpretation of the model impossible [14,18,19]. Taken together, the high dimensionality and sparsity of digital footprint data in combination with the explosion in potentially relevant features, drive the complexity of models developed from behavioral data, making them difficult to interpret.

1.2. Why the Interpretability of AI Matters

The lack of transparency and inability to explain decisions of AI systems for psychological profiling from digital traces creates challenges for their adoption. We distinguish three main reasons for the need of interpretability: (1) trust and compliance, (2) insights and (3) model improvement.

1.2.1. Trust and Compliance

Explaining model outputs helps validate and justify the relations learned from the data and compare this with theoretical assumptions and domain knowledge. This can increase trust of experts to eventually accept these systems [20,21]. Trusting a model implies believing its reliability or truth [21]. Next to the model's out-of-sample predictive performance, the explanation needs to provide evidence that the model learned a meaningful pattern that is not only useful in specific circumstances. The need for trust and validation also stems from increasing regulatory pressure. Both the United States (US) and European Union (EU) are pushing toward a regulatory framework for transparent and accountable AI, and global organizations like OECD and G20 aim for a more human-centric approach. Especially for systems deemed as high-risk (defined in the EU's recent AI Act, and referring to every system that can negatively impact the life of a human), explainability has emerged as a key business and regulatory challenge. For example, systems that regulate access to financial services, educational opportunities or employment fall in this category. Psychological profiling can also be part of such applications. Think of talent acquisition and management systems that assess job-relevant characteristics (In the last decade, many companies have been created that leverage AI for more fair, efficient and effective talent acquisition and management, for example, advertising online job vacancies or measuring the fit of job seekers with open roles in a company using behavioral data (game-based assessments or video interviews). Examples are pymetrics (https://www.pymetrics.ai/ (accessed on 2 November 2021)) and Humantic AI (https://humantic.ai/ (accessed on 2 November 2021))), or systems to prioritize medical aid (e.g., to people who display early signs of depression [1,4]).

Appropriate human-machine interface tools should be put in place that allow experts to interpret the model outputs and overrule them when necessary. This is also important to guarantee safe and fair AI systems that do not exhibit differential effects on subgroups or underrepresented groups [22], which can open up organizations to legal entanglements or cause reputational damage [23,24]. In HR analytics, for example, when predicting which persons to invite for an interview, based on resumes and behavioral assessments, it is important to know why a model makes decisions, to ensure there is no unfair treatment of certain groups like women or immigrants (for example, think of the algorithmic discrimination in Amazon's male-biased hiring tool [23] or Uber running job ads targeted exclusively at men [24]). Interpretability techniques might not directly solve these issues, but can be used as a tool to audit models and detect sources of bias that can arise from skewed data collection or real human bias hidden in the data. In addition, regulatory requirements and increasing customer expectations push companies to provide transparency to those affected by the data-driven decisions (hereafter 'data subjects'). For example, the General Data Protection Regulation (GDPR) notes the 'right to explanation' for those affected by decisions of AI systems.

1.2.2. Improved Insights

A second reason for model explainability stems from a broader goal of predictive modeling: to learn something about a domain. Interpretability allows researchers and domain experts to verify knowledge encoded in the models, which can be useful for building on prior research, or for theory building and exploratory work. For example, businesses might ask: what are the main reasons we are inviting job applicants to an interview based on their resumes and motivations? Psychologists might wonder: what are the behavioral manifestations of people on social media who suffer from burn-outs?

Explaining AI systems helps explore new insights, that, in turn, can inspire new hypotheses to be tested with more traditional, statistical methods [25]. Insights into personality predictions from behavior can also lay groundwork for (research on) interventions targeting specific behavior (e.g., to promote well-being [11]).

In addition, improved insights might translate into a competitive advantage when companies are able to *share* these insights with consumers. In targeted marketing and sales efforts relying on the prediction of psychological profiles [1], for example, explainability could be used to validate the models predictions and meet the needs of demanding customers who want both control and service [6,26]. As Matz et al. [6] argue, insight into not just the data that is collected but also the inferences that are derived from it, can help data consumers make more informed decisions that are based on trade-offs between improved service and privacy. In line with this, non-profit initiatives like mePrism (https://www.meprism.com/ (accessed on 4 November 2021)) and Digita (https://www.digita.ai/ (accessed on 4 November 2021)) aim to give insight to online users on the data that's collected about them and how companies use this information, and support them to be in charge over their digital footprints. The European Commission's Digital Services Act (DSA) further emphasizes this by noting that recipients of online advertisements should get "meaningful explanations of the logic used" for "determining that specific advertisement is to be displayed to them" (paragraph 52). Another example of giving insights to data subjects is providing personalized feedback to job candidates on data-driven insights about their strengths, development needs and organizational fit, that can in turn guide them in future job search endeavors. Moreover, this can improve the candidate experience and the overall quality of the recruiting process, and eventually benefit the company as well [27].

1.2.3. Model Improvement

Explanations can be used to improve prediction models and identify weaknesses that arise from models overfitting to the data and/or perpetuating historical biases. When modeling human behavior, monitoring the important predictors of a model is crucial, for example, to identify reasons for drops in performance over time, that can be caused by changing behavior; a phenomenon known as 'concept drift' (for example changing spending behavior in times of a pandemic [28]; we refer to Stachl et al. [22] and Lu et al. [29] for more examples). Technology and culture are evolving at a rapid pace which means that the purpose of technical devices and the way we interact with them are constantly changing. The information captured by online behavior can thus change over time and lead the model's performance to drop [29]. Although a number of control mechanisms can be put into place (e.g., online learning [29,30]), understanding which behavioral features have a (large) impact on a model's classifications through explanations can help domain experts make sound statements on the expected lifetime of a model and its sensitivity to rapidly changing technological indicators and digital behavior. For example, the type of mobile phone applications that people use might change more rapidly compared to the genres of movies people watch or the type of places they visit on the weekend, which reflect more 'stable' behavior.

Explanations can also help understand the generalization ability of a model beyond the sample data or improve overall troubleshooting. For example, some behavior can be specific to populations located in geographical regions. If the model picks up these specific behaviors and gives them a large weight in the decisions, this might limit the usability of that model in other contexts.

1.3. Using Explainable AI to Overcome Black Box Approaches: Research Overview

Over the last decade, a growing body of research has been dedicated to the field of Explainable Artificial Intelligence (XAI). The aim of this research area is to develop and apply algorithms to explain prediction models and individual predictions. The desire to have both predictive and interpretable models resulted in an explosion of new methods to extract useful information from black box models. (A detailed overview of all XAI methods proposed in the literature is beyond the scope of this study, so we point readers interested in learning more about all different techniques to recent overviews, for example, Arrieta et al. [31], Guidotti et al. [32], or Molnar [33]. In this study, we select methods that we believe are particularly suitable to explain classifications of models from large-scale behavioral data).

In this study, we build on this research to address the challenge of model interpretability. We contribute to the literature in different ways: (1) first, this study presents, to the best of our knowledge, the first application of rule-based XAI methods (rule extraction and counterfactual explanations) to the field of computational psychology, in which model interpretability has been overlooked up to now; (2) second, using a case study of personality predictions from real-world consumer spending data, we apply XAI to provide global insight into why a model makes classifications of interest (e.g., when does the model typically classify someone as Neurotic based on their behavior?) and generate more granular, local explanations for why a particular decision was made (e.g., why does the model classify this person as Neurotic?); (3) third, we empirically demonstrate the importance of both global and local XAI for different use cases (model acceptance, validation, insights and improvement), on the basis of concrete examples from the case study; and, (4) lastly, we elaborate on the practical implications of the use of XAI, and the difference between local and global methods, for domain experts and researchers interacting with, and data subjects being targeted by the model.

The remainder of this paper is structured as follows: in Section 2, we describe the XAI techniques and motivate why we select these methods in this paper. Next, in Section 3, we describe the data and methods used in our case study. We apply XAI in the context of Big Five personality predictions from real-world financial transactions data collected by a non-profit organization in the United States (N = 6408). To bring in an angle that goes beyond the prediction task in related work, we model personality hierarchically: we model both traits and their underlying facets (e.g., Extraversion can be broken down in facets: Assertivism, Energy and Sociability). In Section 3.5, we first discuss the classification performance of the models, and then go over the observations from the model interpretability analysis. In Section 4, we summarize the main findings and their implications, and point at a good deal of room for further research at the intersection of XAI and computational psychology. Finally, Section 5 sets out the conclusions of this study.

2. Introduction to the Field of Explainable AI (XAI)

As described in Section 1, models that classify psychological traits from behavioral data are often considered 'black box' approaches. That is, it is generally difficult to determine why and under which conditions a class of interest (hereafter also referred to as the 'positive class') was predicted. In an attempt to open the black box, the field of XAI field has started to develop tools and frameworks that provide insights into how models work, providing human experts with the ability to understand the logic that goes into the algorithm's decisions. A large body of work has focused on post hoc explanations to extract information about a model's behavior without addressing details of their inner workings. Instead, these methods only use the input data and the model's predicted outputs. One of the most prominent advantages of post hoc explainability is that interpretations can be provided after developing complex models without needing to sacrifice predictive performance [33].

Explanation methods can have a global or local scope. Global explanations give insight into models at an aggregate level, over all the model's classifications. Local explanations explain individual classifications. In this study, we use both *global* and *local* XAI methods to explain *classifications* (There exists a subtle yet important distinction between explanation methods that explain (discrete) classifications vs. (continuous) predicted scores (we refer to Fernandez et al. [34] for a full discussion). In this study, we focus on explaining classifications that drive concrete decisions and/or actions to be taken) of a model C_M, that predict a psychological trait $\mathbf{Y}$ (i.e., *target variable*) from behavioral data $X \subset \mathbb{R}^{N \times M}$, where N and

M, respectively, indicate the number of data subjects (i.e., *instances*) and features. Note that we solely focus on classification tasks in this study. Although prior work on psychological profiling has predominantly focused on predictive performance [22,35], there have been attempts at explaining the underlying mechanisms. Some studies have highlighted the face validity of predictive models by showing the most related predictors to the target (based on univariate correlations prior to modeling that do not necessarily reflect what the model learned from the data [2]), or by providing a list of important features [8,13,36]. While such approaches offer initial insights, they do not reflect how the (combination of) feature values impact(s) the predicted classes, nor the extent to which the classifications are explained. Understanding the latter is particularly valuable when modeling very sparse data where one feature might only be relevant to a small number of instances (e.g., liking 'Curly Fries' on Facebook might be predictive of IQ, but only a small fraction of the population likes 'Curly Fries' on Facebook). In this paper, we therefore move beyond what has previously been suggested by the literature. Our selection of methods is based on the following criteria: we exclude methods that might not be suitable when modeling high-dimensional behavioral data. For example, visualizations of feature effects are mentioned in Stachl et al. [22] as a way to increase interpretability in personality computing applications, by tracing how the outcome variable changes as the value of a feature changes (e.g., score on Extraversion). However, we argue that this approach is not appropriate for models with hundreds to thousands of features, where many features might be relevant for the task, and for which the important features may vary substantially between classifications (as we will demonstrate in Section 3.5). Users who want to understand how a specific variable relates to the predicted outcome (either at an aggregate or local level) might still benefit from using this approach; however, it is impractical to show how classifications come about by showing the effect of just one or two features (i.e., interaction plot).

As a *global* XAI method, we therefore use rule extraction to capture under which conditions a class of interest is predicted, and discuss how these explanation rules can be used to validate learned relations, generate new hypotheses, and identify weaknesses of the model. To explain predictions at the *local* level, we use counterfactual explanations that reveal which features contributed to a single classification, or more precisely, point to changes of the feature values that lead the model to make another decision. In the following subsections, we go over rule extraction and counterfactual explanations in more detail.

2.1. Rules as Global Explanations

We use rule extraction as a global method to gain insight into the classification models. Rule extraction has been proposed in the literature to generate explanations by distilling a comprehensible set of rules (hereafter 'explanation rules') from a complex classification model C_M [15,37–39]. Rule extraction is based on surrogate modeling of which the goal is to use an interpretable model to approximate the predictions of a more complex model $\hat{Y}$. The interpretable model used as surrogate can be a concise set of if-then-else rules (in which case it's called 'rule extraction') or a linear model with a small number of features. The complexity of the rules is restricted so that the final explanations are comprehensible to humans. (Rule extraction can be challenging for high-dimensional, sparse data, as the black box model needs to be replaced by many rules to explain a substantial fraction of the classifications, which leaves the user again with an incomprehensible explanation. To address this, Ramon et al. [15] proposed a technique based on metafeatures (i.e., clusters of the original features) to extract a concise set of rules that more accurately approximates the model's behavior. In this study, however, we apply rule extraction on the original data, because the dimensionality and sparsity of the data used in the case study are still manageable). A main motivation for the use of rule extraction is to combine the desirable predictive behavior of complex classification techniques with the comprehensibility of decision trees and/or rules.

We use rule extraction for different reasons. First, an important advantage of rule extraction is that the learned relations between features and predicted classes are not lost.

Another advantage is that it approximates *classification* behavior of a model. This is in contrast to other XAI methods, like feature relevance methods, that do not reflect how features impact predicted classes, but merely provide a list of important features [34]. Moreover, using rule extraction—or surrogate models in general—we can quantify the extent to which the model is explained using a metric called *Fidelity*. (If we use a linear model as surrogate to approximate the model's behavior, we can also compute *Fidelity* of the explanation. However, the same limitations as for feature relevance lists hold. The information about the interaction between features and their correspondence to the class gets lost. Moreover, it gets more difficult to grasp the classification behavior. There will exist a very large number of conditions that explain when the model predicts a particular output, rendering the explanation less comprehensible). *Fidelity* can be operationalized in different ways. Here, we refer to the metric that computes the overlap between the predicted classes of the model $\hat{Y}$ and the classes predicted by the explanation rules $\hat{Y}_{rules}$ as *Fidelity*. (Essentially, you can compare *Fidelity* to *Accuracy* that is used as a performance metric in a traditional machine learning context. *Accuracy* measures to what extent the model's predictions $\hat{Y}$ overlap with the ground-truth classes Y. In contrast, *Fidelity* measures to what extent the explanation rules' predicted classes $\hat{Y}_{rules}$ overlap with the model's predicted classes $\hat{Y}$). The goal is to extract rules that have high *Fidelity*, i.e., approximate the patterns learned in the original model to the best possible extent. For imbalanced problems, it is often more insightful to use the $Fscore_f$ of predicting the output of the model to measure the quality of the explanation, which we refer to as $Fscore_f$. $Fscore_f$ is measured by the harmonic mean between $Recall_f$ and $Precision_f$, and reflects how well the 'positive class' is explained by the rules. $Recall_f$ measures the proportion of positives predicted by the model that are retrieved, and $Precision_f$ measures the proportion of correct classifications among the instances predicted as a class of interest (a 'positive') by the rules. All else equal, we prefer an explanation rule set that results in a higher $Fscore_f$, because this explanation reflects the original model's predictions more accurately. We measure the quality of rules on an out-of-sample test set, as we want the explanation to reflect the model's prediction behavior on *new* data, not just on the training data. (The same challenges of overfitting in machine learning hold in the surrogate modeling context. As an extreme example, consider a decision table as an explanation that memorizes when the model predicts a class of interest. For new data, the table would never classify someone as a class of interest (the persons' identifiers will never match an identifier in the table). We would get a high in-sample, but a low out-of-sample *Fidelity*, because the decision table does not reflect how the model is actually making classifications from the data).

2.2. Counterfactual Rules as Local Explanations

For explaining model classifications at the local level, we compute counterfactual rules [16,17,40]. Compared to local feature relevance methods, such as Local Interpretable Model-agnostic Explanations (LIME) [41] and SHapley Additive exPlanations (SHAP) [42], counterfactual rules explain the model's predicted class instead of the score [17,34]. Following Martens & Provost (2014), who defined counterfactuals for document classifications, we define counterfactual rules for a classification as a set of features from the instance that is causal: changing the value of the features causes the system's decision to change. In other words, the decision would have been different if not for the presence of this set of features. There are multiple ways of defining changes of the feature values. A common approach is to simulate the 'missingness' of a feature by replacing the value by the mean value of the feature (for continuous features), or the median or mode value (for sparse numerical, binary or categorical data). In essence, we are asking ourselves the question if the model would make the same decision if a feature in question would be missing [34]. It is important, both in research and practice, that the choice on how to define 'changes' is clearly mentioned, because, depending on this, slightly different explanations may arise.

We use counterfactual explanations, first of all, because they point at a set of features without which the AI system would have made a different decision. They help us understand how features affect *decisions* of AI systems, rather than predicted scores, in terms of domain knowledge, rather than in terms of modeling techniques. Providing a concrete justification for a decision gives data subjects insight into changes to receive a desired result in the future, based on their current behavior, and is consistent with requirements specified in regulatory frameworks [40]. Another advantage is that the explanation only comprises a (small) fraction of all features used in a model, which makes it a particularly interesting approach to explain decisions of models with high-dimensional feature dimensions. Prior work showed cases where these explanations can be obtained only in seconds for models on large-scale data, and that explanations typically consisted of a handful to a few dozen of features [16,17,26]. Moreover, in contrast to local feature relevance methods, where it is non-trivial to choose the complexity setting (i.e., how many features to show), the answer for counterfactuals is clear-cut: those features are shown that allow for the creation of a counterfactual rule [17].

3. Case Study: Predicting Personality Traits from Financial Transaction Records

We use a case study on the prediction of Big Five personality traits from real-world transactions data to demonstrate how global and local XAI methods can help shed light on the ways by which the prediction model learns and makes decisions about the target individual.

Figure 2 depicts the methodology used in our case study. We describe (i) how the data was collected (Section 3.1), (ii) how the data was prepared for the analyses (Section 3.2), (iii) the model specifications (Section 3.3), as well as (iv) the ways in which XAI can help understand and validate the models (Section 3.4). (This methodology can be applied more generally to psychological profiling applications that mine other types of behavioral data, such as social media data, GPS location data and web browsing histories). In what follows, we go over each step in more detail. In Section 3.5, the results of the case study are discussed.

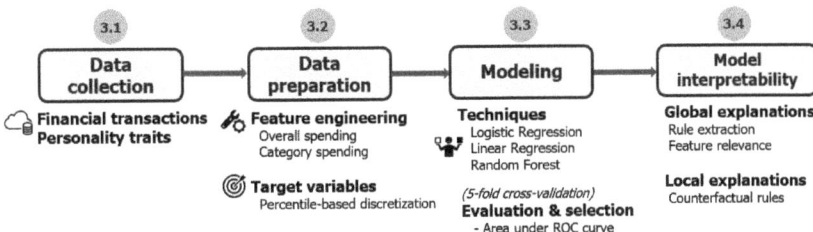

Figure 2. Methodology of the case study to develop models that classify people's personality from financial transactions (Sections 3.1–3.3) and gain insight into the final models by means of global and local XAI methods (Section 3.4).

3.1. Data Collection

3.1.1. Financial Transactions

We use financial transactions data collected by a non-profit based in the US. The organization offers a money management application to help people manage their savings more effectively. Individuals can join the platform by linking their bank accounts, including checking, savings and credit card accounts. Using these data, the organization provides people with financial decision-making aid and motivates them to achieve savings objectives by offering rewards and lotteries. As part of their onboarding experience, users can voluntarily complete a personality questionnaire. For the purpose of our case study, we use de-identified historical transactions between January and December 2019. We subset the data to active accounts to guarantee a sufficient amount of data per person: we discard individuals with fewer than five transactions or less than $100 spent on a monthly basis, or fewer than five distinct spending categories. (The users of the money management application have relatively large financial constraints. For this reason, we set more flexible criteria compared to related studies (see for example Tovanich et al. [13])). This exclusion procedure leaves us with $N = 6408$ data subjects of whom we have transactions data (linked to their self-reported personality profiles) that can be fed into the prediction models. The transactions data include a time stamp indicating when the transaction was made, the amount of the transaction (in US Dollar), and the category of the transaction. Each transaction belongs to one of the 285 spending categories.

Table 1 shows summary statistics of the sample data. The individuals observed in the data generally have a low-income profile, i.e., they spend, on average, about $15,000 over the course of one year. In the US, a household has on average $63,036 of expenditures per year [43]. With an average household consisting of 2.5 adults, this is equivalent to annual expenditures of $25,214 per capita. The average amount of yearly expenditures for low-income households with a total income before taxes less than $15,000 is lower, and equals $15,745 per capita [43].

Table 1. Summary statistics of the transactions data. The data contains 4,539,634 spending records between January and December 2019 of 6408 data subjects. Only individuals with at least five transactions and $100 spent in each month, and at least five distinct spending categories are selected. There are 285 spending categories and the average household consists of 3 people.

Per Customer	Mean (Std)	Median
Total amount transactions	$47,236.26 ($58,441.34)	$33,649.78
Amount per transaction	$66.77 ($53.94)	$16.71
Number of transactions	708.43 (441.49)	621
Unique number of spending categories	43.66 (16.12)	43
Per Spending Category	**Mean (Std)**	**Median**
Total amount transactions	$1,062,070 ($4,142,055)	$29,256.64
Rel. total amount transactions	0.0035 (0.014)	9.7×10^{-5}
Number of transactions	15,928.54 (51,812.71)	544
Rel. number of transactions	0.0035 (0.011)	1.2×10^{-4}
Customer support	981.79 (1494.70)	240
Rel. customer support	0.15 (0.23)	0.04

3.1.2. Personality Traits

Personality traits are conceptualized as relatively stable characteristics that explain and predict differences in cognition, affect and behavior. Decades of research have suggested that there are five dimensions that explain these individual differences across a broad variety of contexts, including different cultures or language. These five dimensions are known as the Big Five (BF) Model of Personality [44]. The BF model proposes five traits that capture individual differences in the way people think, feel and behave [44]: (1) *Extraversion*, the tendency to seek stimulation in the company of others, to be outgoing and energetic; (2) *Agreeableness*, the tendency to be warm, compassionate and cooperative; (3) *Conscientiousness*, the tendency to show self-discipline, aim for achievement, and be organized; (4) *Neuroticism*, the tendency to experience unpleasant emotions easily; and (5) *Openness to Experience* (or simply *Openness*), the tendency to be intellectually curious, creative and open to feelings [13,44]. Personality theory specifies that traits are hierarchically organized [44,45]: each domain subsumes more specific facets that have a unique variance not entirely explained by the higher order Big Five. (Adaptations of the original Big Five Inventory (BFI) questionnaire (e.g., BFI-2-S)—that was not intended as hierarchical measure—allow to simultaneously assess someone's personality at the trait and facet level). The facets vary slightly across models and measures, but for the purpose of this case study we leverage the Big Five Inventory (BFI-2) questionnaire which suggests the following facets:

- Extraversion: Sociability, Assertiveness, Energy
- Agreeableness: Compassion, Respectfulness, Trust

- Conscientiousness: Organization, Productivity, Responsibility
- Neuroticism: Anxiety, Depression, Emotional Volatility
- Openness: Intellectual Curiosity, Aesthetic Sensitivity, Creative Imagination

Our sample data contains the (self-reported) BF personality traits of the data subjects at the trait (5) and facet (15) level. All 6408 individuals completed a personality survey and provided their consent to have their transactions history matched with their survey responses for the purpose of this study. The traits were measured by the established BFI-2-S questionnaire [45], in which participants indicate their agreement with 30 statements using a five-point Likert scale (1 = 'Disagree strongly' to 5 = 'Agree strongly'). For example, in the survey, one of the statements that belongs to the Extraversion trait is "I am someone who is full of energy" (see Figure A1 for a full snapshot of the survey). Each trait (resp., facet) was measured using a six-item (resp., two-item) scale and the final (averaged) scores range between 1 and 5, respectively, indicating a low or high score. With Cronbach's alpha being larger than 0.7 across all Big Five traits (Extraversion = 0.80, Agreeableness = 0.79, Conscientiousness = 0.82, Neuroticism = 0.85, Openness = 0.72), internal consistencies were found to be good. Figure 3 shows the distribution of the traits. Neuroticism follows a normal distribution, whereas Extraversion and Openness are approximately normally distributed. The distributions of Conscientiousness and Agreeableness are skewed to the left, indicating that the majority of individuals in the sample perceive themselves as highly agreeable and conscientious. Table A1 shows the mean and standard deviation of the traits in the sample under investigation and compares this against a reference sample of 1000 American individuals (i.e., the Internet sample in Soto & John [45]).

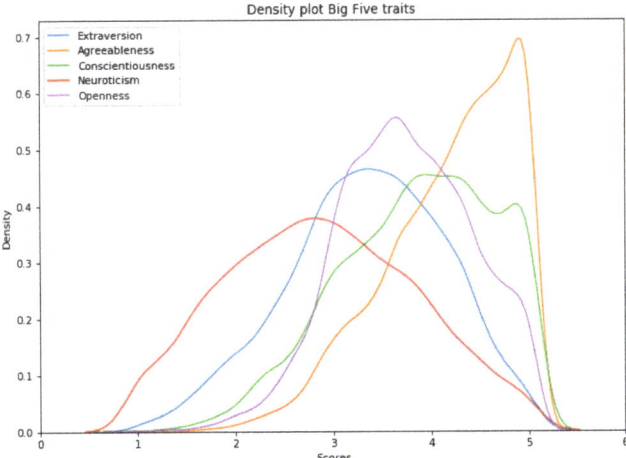

Figure 3. Distribution of scores on the Big Five traits in our sample of 6408 individuals.

3.2. Data Preparation

3.2.1. Feature Engineering

The spending data reflect a wide range of behavioral patterns, which we organize into two broad categories of features based on related work [12,13]: (1) *overall spending* that comprises summary statistics of spending aggregated over time and features that enrich the aggregated measures with finer-grained, time-dependent information (e.g., how much does the daily amount someone spends vary over time?) and (2) *category spending* that reflects a person's spending category profile and relative spending per category. In total, we extract 578 features from the raw transactions data. Calculations and definitions of the features are detailed in Table A2.

Overall spending. For every individual, we compute the total number of transactions n_{tot} and the total amount someone spent a_{tot} aggregated over the 12-month period. We also compute the average amount spent per transaction a_{avg} and the (relative) variability of the transaction amount a_{cv} defined as the ratio between the standard deviation and the mean of the transaction amount. (We use the coefficient of variation because it is a more robust measure when comparing the variance of two variables with different means, i.e., the average amount of money spent per transaction varies between individuals). A low variability indicates that a person spends money equally over different transactions. Lastly, we measure the average daily amount spent $a_{avg,daily}$ and the (relative) variability of the daily transaction amount $a_{cv,daily}$ which is computed similar to a_{cv} but then on a daily basis. A low value for $a_{cv,daily}$ indicates that someone spends their money equally over different days.

Category spending. For every individual, we compute their spending proportions in each category: we calculate both the relative amount of transactions n_c and the relative amount of money a_c that a person spent in each category c. Their transactions are mapped to the 285 spending categories, then aggregated and normalized to get the percentage of spending in each category. We also compute the number of unique spending categories C_{tot} and the diversity of spending over different categories $C_{entropy}$. A high value of $C_{entropy}$ indicates that someone equally distributed their transactions over the spending categories in which they made transactions. A low value indicates that a person has transactions that are distributed over a few categories.

3.2.2. Target Variables

Each person in the data is characterized by a set of historical financial transactions and a (self-reported) score for each of the traits. Following prior work [8,13,22], we define a multi-class classification task for each of the traits by splitting the data into three classes (High vs. Middle vs. Low), where we create discrete classes in the continuous scale scores using a percentile-based approach [8,13]. (Classes of personality can also be constructed using a central tendency estimate [46], however, this can result in a high rate of misclassifications. Big Five traits tend to be normally distributed [22,47], which means that many scores lie close to the central tendency estimate of the scale (see Figure 3). Consequently, the artificial 'Low vs. High' distinction results in a greater separation between subjects than actually exists. Further, this approach likely results in a large number of misclassifications due to measurement error, i.e., the true scores on BF traits of each individual may be close to, but not exactly equal to, the measured values). We specifically focus on the High and Low classes. This decision was driven by the fact that the higher and lower classes are often those of interest in applied contexts, where it is useful, for example, to know which individuals are highly extraverted and therefore have certain behavioral tendencies. For example, companies might want to adjust their marketing message to the outgoing and social nature of extraverts or select the most conscientious candidates for a job interview.

We use min-max normalization to transform the raw scores into a decimal between 0 and 1. The normalized scores are used to develop the regression models (e.g., Logistic Regression), which can in turn be used to make classifications using a threshold (an approach known as regression-based classification). Second, we use percentile-based discretization to map the scores to personality buckets. To construct a binary target that indicates if someone scores High on a trait, we transform the scores that exceed the 66th percentile to 1, else 0. In a similar fashion, we construct another binary variable that indicates if someone scores Low on a trait using the 33rd percentile.

3.3. Modeling

3.3.1. Modeling Techniques

Machine learning algorithms can be used to make classifications of psychological traits about new individuals. These algorithms are suitable for large-scale data, such as behavioral data, and allow to model complex relationships. Moreover, the algorithms can pick up on subtle patterns of which humans are unaware or cannot perceive [22]. We test both linear and nonlinear models from the data and select the final classification model using a five fold cross-validation procedure to test out-of-sample performance. For linear models, we train regularized Linear and Logistic Regression models. (We use both lasso and ridge regularization). We also train Random Forest models that account for possible nonlinearities between the behavioral features and the target personality classes. Random Forest classifiers (resp., regressors) are ensemble learners that fit a number of decision tree classifiers (resp., regressors) on various subsamples of the data and use averaging to improve the out-of-sample accuracy.

We train all models using the same financial transactions data to predict High and Low levels on the traits. Figure 4 depicts the pre-processed financial transactions data and binary target. For each trait, we construct two separate models, in line with a one-vs.-rest approach for multi-class problems: (1) a model that decides if someone scores High on a trait and (2) one that decides if someone scores Low on a trait. For example, for Extraversion, we train a model that predicts High Extraversion and another that predicts Low Extraversion.

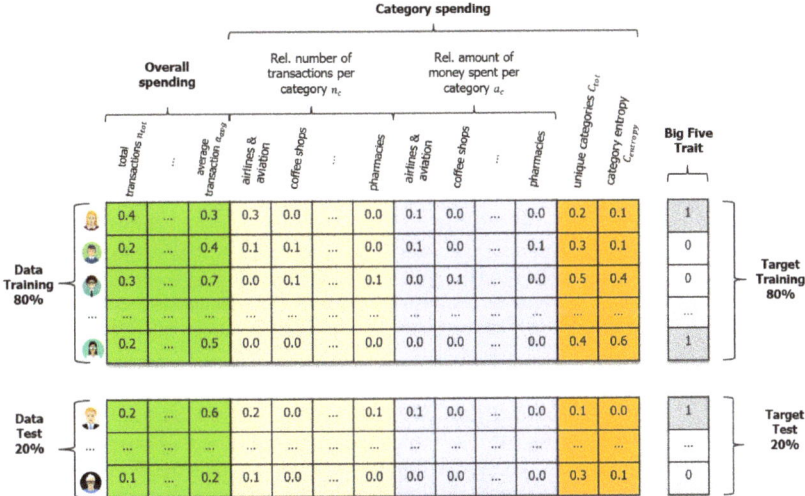

Figure 4. Pre-processed financial transactions data and binary target variable (Big Five trait).

3.3.2. Evaluation & Selection

The final classification system consists of a (continuous) scoring function f that can be used to assign a score s to every instance x. Given a threshold k, explicit class predictions can be assigned to instances x using a binary indicator function $\hat{Y} = I(s > k)$, with $f(x) = s$, which, in turn, can be linked to a decision. After selecting the final model for each trait (see *Linear vs. Nonlinear Models* in Section 3.1), we obtain class label predictions using the final model and setting the threshold k so that the fraction of individuals predicted as positive (i.e., belonging to a personality class) equals the fraction of positives in the data (approximately one-third of the data).

We use the *Area under the Receiver Operating Curve (AUC)* to measure the general performance of the models. It reflects the model's ability to rank a true positive instance (e.g., a true extrovert) higher than a true negative instance (e.g., a true introvert) [48]. The AUC value does not depend on a classification threshold, but only on the score ranking of the instances that the model returns [48]. Moreover, AUC is not influenced by the underlying distributions of the personality classes (i.e., imbalance of the target variable). AUC is useful to summarize the model's performance in one metric and decouples classifier performance from the specific conditions under which the classifier will be used. Also, AUC allows for an easy comparison with random predictions, since a random classifier should result in a AUC value of 50%. We use AUC to compare the predictive accuracy of linear vs. nonlinear models and the predictability of different traits from the financial transactions data [47]. We report the average AUC across the five folds (see Figure A2).

3.4. Model Interpretability

3.4.1. Global Explanations: CART to Extract Rules

We use the *CART* decision tree algorithm of the Scikit-learn library (https://scikit-learn.org/stable/modules/tree.html (accessed on 2 December 2021)) in *Python* to extract global explanation rules. The algorithm extracts a set of if-then-else rules using the behavioral features together with the predicted classes $\hat{Y}$ of the classification model. We set the maximum tree depth to 3, to limit the complexity of the explanation rules and make them easily understandable by humans. Depending on the setting, however, a user can increase the maximum complexity and get more granular explanations, possibly with additional insights. For the other parameters of the *CART* algorithm, we use the default settings (e.g., as a splitting criterion it uses the Gini impurity).

3.4.2. Local Explanations: SEDC to Compute Counterfactual Explanations

We use the SEDC algorithm to compute (local) counterfactual rules (*Python* code available (https://github.com/yramon/edc (accessed on 2 December 2021))), that is based on a best-first heuristic search strategy [16,17,40]. We define counterfactuals as the set of features that need to change so that the predicted class changes, where a 'change' is defined as replacing the original feature value with the median value of that feature computed over the training data. To use SEDC, the decision-making (i.e., assignment of a person to a personality bucket) should be based on comparing a predicted score (i.e., the model's output) to a threshold. The scoring function is used by the SEDC algorithm so that it first considers features that, when replacing their value with the mean, reduce the predicted score the most in the direction of the opposite class (i.e., the 'best-first' feature).

3.5. Results

In the following sections we will outline how XAI methods can be used to validate predictive models that compute personality from real-world transactions data. We first discuss the extent to which personality traits and facets can be predicted using both linear and non-linear models (Section 3.5.1). Next, we show how rule extraction explains classifiers at an aggregate level and describe practical use cases of global interpretability on the basis of concrete examples from the case study (Section 3.5.2—Global explanations). Lastly, we provide empirical support for why local explanations are important—especially when modeling behavior—and elaborate on the implications of our observations (Section 3.5.2—Local explanations).

3.5.1. Classification Performance Analysis

Linear vs. Nonlinear Techniques

First, we focus on the performance of linear vs. nonlinear techniques to model personality. We compare the performance of linear models (LR and Logit) vs. nonlinear models (RF), measured by the difference in AUC. The goal here is to provide a sound statement regarding the superiority of more flexible techniques for modeling personality from spending data. For the majority of traits and facets, nonlinear models outperform linear models (see Figure A3). On average, traits could be predicted with 58.14% accuracy in the linear models (min = 53.13%, max = 61.82%), and 59.31% in the nonlinear models (min = 53.35%, max = 63.98%). Since we find that RF models—capable of finding nonlinear patterns— generally outperform the linear models, we select RF as the final technique and report all following results based on the outputs of the RF models.

Predictability of Personality Traits and Underlying Facets

Figure 5 shows the prediction accuracy of the selected models that classify personality. There is a wide variation in the models' performances, ranging from moderate (e.g., AUC = 53.4% for Low Aesthetic Sensitivity) to decent performance (e.g., AUC = 63.9% for High Productivity). The best classification performance is achieved when predicting High levels of Productiveness, Depression and Neuroticism. Overall, individuals can be classified substantially above chance level for the majority of traits, which is in line with prior work that explored the value of spending data to segment people based on their personalities. The performances we find are comparable with, and even slightly better than, accuracies reported in related studies that use machine learning to predict BF traits from spending data [12,13].

A second observation is that (the facets in) Conscientiousness and Neuroticism are the most predictable traits from the data, while Agreeableness and Openness characteristics are the least predictable. One possible explanation for this observation is that implicit behavioral residues—like the transaction records in this study—are particularly useful to predict *intrapersonal* characteristics (Conscientiousness and Neuroticism), while other types of digital footprints that constitute more explicit identity claims, like social media data, are more valuable for recognizing *interpersonal* traits [46,49] (Openness, Extraversion and Agreeableness). Our results suggest that the spending patterns differ more between those groups scoring different on intrapersonal traits, allowing for a better classification compared to interpersonal traits.

Further, the facets that underlie the same trait are not always equally predictable. For example, it is easier to predict Energy levels from financial transactions than Sociability and Assertiveness (all facets of Extraversion). Similarly, high levels of Productivity are easier to predict than Low levels, and Emotional Volatility as part of Neuroticism is less predictable from these data than Anxiety and Depression.

3.5.2. Model Interpretability Analysis

In the next sections we explore the explainability of the models at the global and local level and discuss use cases of interpretability on the basis of examples from our case study. For simplicity, we only explain predictions of the Random Forest models that predict High levels of a trait which are more frequently used in applied contexts. However, the analysis would follow a similar pattern for the models that predict Low levels. Our goal is to demonstrate the value and different use cases of XAI by means of a realistic case study. We aim to provide compelling evidence to academics and practitioners for the importance of XAI methods in *any* application that leverages behavioral data to assess psychological traits, making the implications of our findings relevant beyond the examples presented in this case study.

Global Explanations: Rule Extraction

Tables 2 and 3 respectively show the explanation rules that approximate the classification behavior of the models that predict personality and their quality. The predictions of the rules substantially overlap with the model predictions (*Fidelity* ranges from 72.07% to 81.59%) and the rules that explain when a trait is predicted achieve high levels of reliability (see the *Precision$_f$* column in Table 3). When comparing the rules and the feature relevance lists (shown in Figure 6), we observe a considerable amount of overlap of the top features identified as important in the black box model. However, the feature relevance lists do not explain how the feature values lead to a classification of interest, and cannot account for interactions of features or shed light onto the directionality of the effects. In contrast, the extracted rules displayed in Table 2 capture associations between features and personality classes that the model learned and utilized in the prediction task.

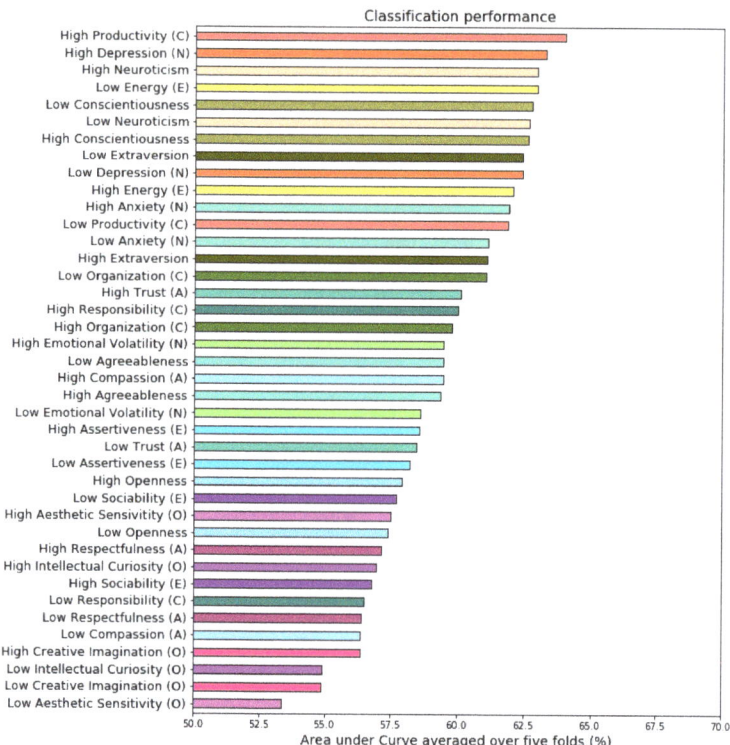

Figure 5. Prediction accuracy of models that classify High or Low levels of personality traits and facets expressed by the AUC averaged over five folds. The personality trait to which each facet belongs, is shown in parentheses (e.g., 'E' stands for Extraversion).

To make the decision rules more tangible, we discuss a number of face-valid examples that are representative of these global explanations (see Table 2). Focusing on the personality trait of Conscientiousness, for example, the explanation shows that individuals with high transaction volumes in Discount stores are more likely to be classified as conscientious by the algorithm. This rule aligns with the general description of conscientiousness as the tendency to exercise self-control and to be less impulsive. In addition, the model identified the association between Conscientiousness and high transaction volumes in Clothing & Accessories and Beauty products, which is consistent with research showing that conscientious individuals demonstrate a stronger interest in clothing and physical appearance than individuals scoring low on Conscientiousness [13,50,51]. Moreover, the rules provide insight into specific model behavior, such as trade-offs made by the model to make personality classifications which cannot be identified in the feature relevance list (see Figure 6). More precisely, the rules show that the model classifies someone as conscientious when there are many transactions in the categories Square Cash and Beauty products, irrespective of spending volumes in other categories. However, when a person's relative spending in the Beauty products category drops below a certain threshold (0.3%), then a substantial amount of spending in the category Clothing & Accessories needs to be observed to still classify the person as conscientious.

Gaining insight into how predictors impact personality classifications at a global level can also help explore new hypotheses about the relationship between spending behavior and psychological traits. In our case study, it is notable that, within the money transactions space, there are different payment services that are predictive for different personalities. This can trigger new research questions, such as, why a specific group of people—homogeneous in terms of personality— would develop their own distinct taste in payment services (e.g., see research on brand personality). More precisely, an important category in the models to predict personality is Square Cash, a mobile payment application that allows users to easily transfer money to friends and family. Since this mobile application is identified as important for explaining classifications of the algorithm (Square Cash appears in almost all explanations in Table 2), future research might investigate this relationship to understand what makes Square Cash users uniquely conscientious or not depending on its interaction with other spending features.

Table 2. Global explanation rules. If-then-else rules that explain when the algorithm classifies High levels of personality traits based on financial transactions. The Default class comprises Low to Medium levels of the same trait. Note: Discount stores and Discount stores ($), respectively, indicate the relative number of transactions in vs. the amount of money spent in a category. 'Square Cash' and 'Venmo' are mobile payment applications to transfer money to friends and family.

Trait	Explanation Rules

Neurotic	if (Square cash($) $\leq$ 0.3%) and (Average transaction $\leq$ $57.08) and (Clothing & Accessories $\leq$ 0.7%) $\to$ Model predicts High Neuroticism
	if (Square cash($) > 0.3%) and (Subscription($) > 0.5%) and (Loans & Mortgages($) $\leq$ 3.9%) $\to$ Model predicts High Neuroticism
	else: Model predicts Default

Conscientious	if (Square cash > 0.4%) and (Beauty Products > 0.3%) $\to$ Model predicts High Conscientiousness
	if (Square cash > 0.4%) and (Beauty Products $\leq$ 0.3%) and (Clothing & Accessories($) > 0.8%) $\to$ Model predicts High Conscientiousness
	if (Square cash $\leq$ 0.4%) and (Discount Stores > 0.8%) and (Shops > 0.5%) $\to$ Model predicts High Conscientiousness
	else: Model predicts Default

Extroverted	if (Square cash $\leq$ 0.7%) and (Clothing & Accessories ($) > 0.7%) and (Hotels & Motels > 0.1%) $\to$ Model predicts High Extraversion
	if (Square cash > 0.7%) and (Variability transaction amount $\leq$ 0.31) $\to$ Model predicts High Extraversion
	if (Square cash > 0.7%) and (Variability transaction amount > 0.31) and (Service > 0.3%) $\to$ Model predicts High Extraversion
	else: Model predicts Default

Agreeable	if (Square cash $\leq$ 0.5%) and (Discount Stores($) > 0.1%) and (Shops $\leq$ 0.6%) $\to$ Model predicts High Agreeableness
	if (Square cash > 0.5%) and (Discount Stores > 0.7%) $\to$ Model predicts High Agreeableness
	if (Square cash > 0.5%) and (Discount Stores $\leq$ 0.7%) and (ATM > 5.7%) $\to$ Model predicts High Agreeableness
	else: Model predicts Default

Open	if (Venmo($) > 0.1%) $\to$ Model predicts High Openness
	if (Venmo($) $\leq$ 0.1%) and (Square cash($) > 0.5%) and (Digital purchase > 2.5%) $\to$ Model predicts High Openness
	if (Venmo($) $\leq$ 0.1%) and (Square cash($) $\leq$ 0.5%) and (Taxi($) > 0.4%) $\to$ Model predicts High Openness
	else: Model predicts Default

Table 3. Out-of-sample performance of rules that explain the model's classifications. The performance of a random explanation is shown in parentheses.

Personality Class	Fidelity (%)	$Fscore_f$ (%)	$Precision_f$ (%)	$Recall_f$ (%)
Neuroticism	79.02 (58.16)	62.48 (29.79)	66.87 (29.79)	58.64 (29.79)
Conscientiousness	75.82 (58.74)	52.45 (29.09)	61.29 (29.09)	45.84 (29.09)
Extraversion	78.47 (55.57)	58.43 (33.31)	81.86 (33.31)	45.43 (33.31)
Agreeableness	81.59 (60.95)	63.35 (26.59)	67.33 (26.59)	59.82 (26.59)
Openness	72.07 (56.78)	50.82 (31.59)	57.28 (31.59)	45.68 (31.59)

Lastly, global model interpretability can help identify problems or weaknesses of the model, for example, related to the data quality or the generalizability of the model. When modeling human behavior, monitoring the performance of a model and understanding the contribution of individual (behavioral) features can be crucial. For example, changes in the meaning of certain behaviors can result in sudden drops in performance over time, a phenomenon termed 'concept drift' (described in Section 1). Returning to the the mobile application Square Cash, for example, it is conceivable that such a mobile applications might at first be niche product that is only used by specific groups with similar psychological profiles, but over time becomes more widespread and used by a wider population. As a result, the spending feature might lose its predictive power, challenging the expected lifetime of the prediction model.

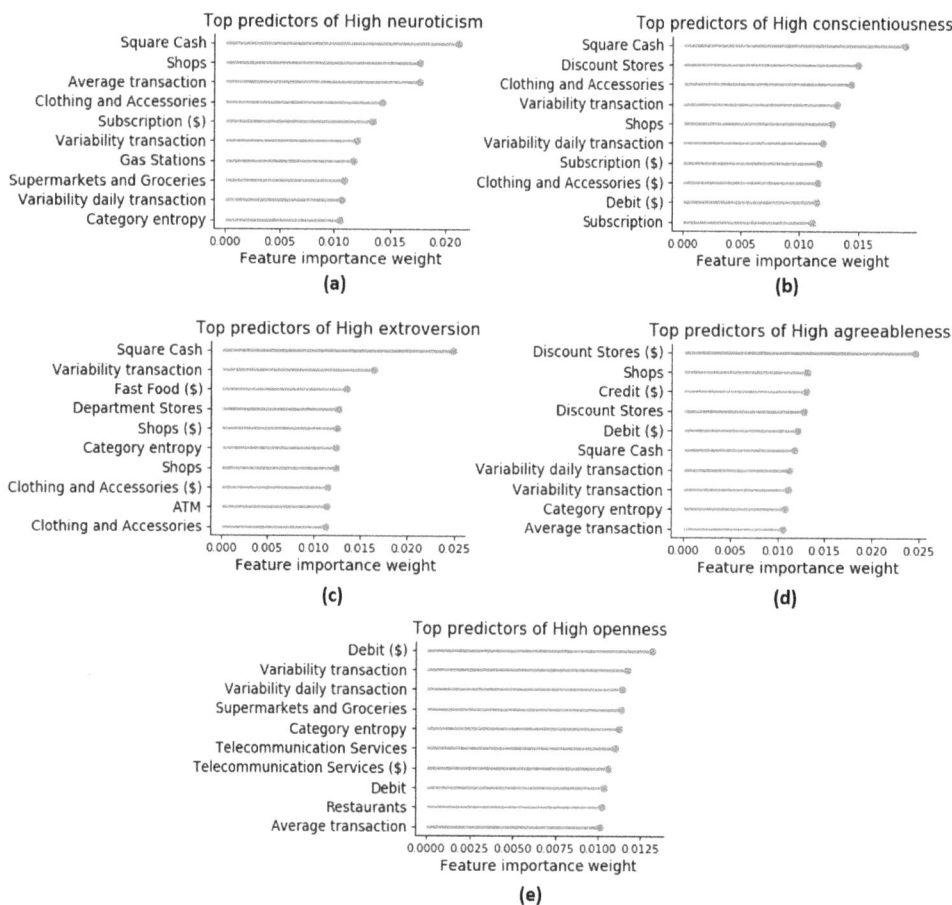

Figure 6. Feature relevance lists that show top features in the model that predicts High levels of (**a**) Neuroticism, (**b**) Conscientiousness, (**c**) Extraversion, (**d**) Agreeableness, and (**e**) Openness. The importance weights are computed as the average impurity reduction over the trees in the Random Forest.

Local Explanations: Counterfactual Explanations

In addition to global model interpretability, we compute local explanations to identify important features for individual classifications. In Table 4, local explanations are shown for why individuals who are predicted to be highly neurotic. For example, the explanation for why Person E was predicted to be neurotic can be interpreted as follows: "if Person E had spent *less money* in Department Stores, but *more frequently* in Square Cash → then Person E would not have been predicted to be neurotic". There are some interesting observations when looking at the counterfactuals in Table 4. First, our experiments show that the explanations are generally concise (on average, explanations consist of 0.3% of the full feature space).

Second, the explanations vary tremendously in nature: people are assigned to the same personality class based on vastly different behaviors. In other words, there is a lot of uniqueness in the explanations associated with each individual. This is visually depicted by Figure 7 which plots the distribution of pairwise similarities between counterfactual explanations. We observe that the majority of explanations has no overlap. This observation is consistent with prior work on local explanations for models on behavioral data demonstrating the variety of local explanations [16,17,26].

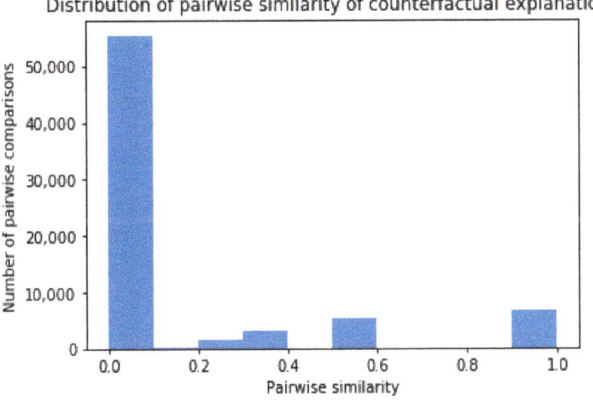

Figure 7. Distribution of pairwise similarity between counterfactual explanations for predicting Neuroticism. A value of 0 (resp., 1) indicates no (resp., perfect) overlap.

When explaining the predictions for the personality trait of Neuroticism, 91.1% of the explanations are unique. This implies that people will receive different explanations most of the time. As a result, the local explanations provide insights into the specific behavior of a person that led the model to make a decision, making the explanation more granular and personally relevant than the global explanation rules. To illustrate this more clearly, consider two female individuals in our sample, both classified as neurotic by the model. Examining the global explanations in Table 2, they are both explained by the first explanation rule, that includes the features Square Cash, Average transaction amount and Clothing & Accessories. (Note that the global explanation shows which combination of feature values likely leads the model to predict a Neurotic person, however, it does not give an exhaustive ($Recall_f$ is not 100%) nor perfectly reliable ($Precision_f$ is not 100%) rule set that explains when the model predicts a Neurotic person. Moreover, changing the features' values such that the rule would no longer apply to the person, does not guarantee that the predicted class flips to the Default, because there might be other combinations of feature values—not captured by the incomplete global explanation—that lead to the prediction of a Neurotic person). However, going a level deeper to the local explanations, we get a more granular notion of which features contributed to the classification of each of the two women. For the first woman, the predictors Gas Stations, Square Cash and Taxi are part of the explanation for being classified as neurotic. In contrast, the second woman would receive an explanation that comprises the features Average transaction amount, Clothing & Accessories, Fast Food and Public Transportation Services.

Third, local explanations not only vary in the specific features and feature combinations they use, but also in the complexity of the counterfactual rules to explain decisions. Depending on someone's set of historical transactions (their 'financial behavior profile'), it can become harder to flip the model's predicted class. Generally, in the results, we observe a trend that the number of features that counterfactually explain the predicted class positively relates to the prediction confidence of a model as depicted by Figure 8. Moreover, the number of feature changes needed to flip the predicted class is generally larger for True Positives compared to False Positives. This finding provides some intuitive satisfaction and is in line with prior work on counterfactual explanations [26]. When explaining why individuals are predicted as neurotic, the average number of features in the explanations for True Positives and False Positives is, respectively, 2.09 and 1.79. This difference suggests that a person who is incorrectly classified as neurotic needs to change fewer features to receive a different classification than someone who was accurately classified to be neurotic.

Finally, the explanations in Table 4 provide another interesting insight. For example, Person A was predicted as neurotic due to two features: "if Person A had spent *more frequently* in Clothing & Accessories and Restaurants, but *less frequently* in Computers & Electronics, Insurance and Shops → then Person A would not have been predicted as neurotic". The rule highlights that it is not always the behavior that people exhibit that are most predictive for a psychological characteristic. The behavior that people do not or only rarely exhibit might also drive the model's classification.

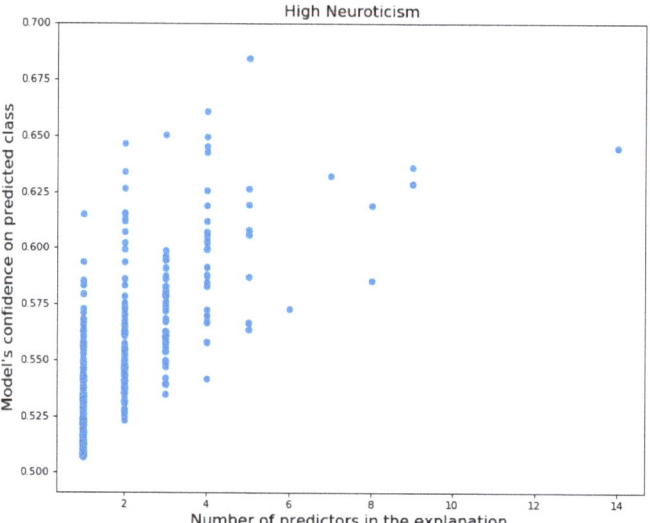

Figure 8. Model's predicted scores vs. number of predictors in the explanation to counterfactually explain the predicted class High Neuroticism. The correlation between the scores and explanation sizes is 0.68.

Table 4. Local explanations that show the features that (counterfactually) explain the predicted class High Neuroticism. A selection of explanations is shown for instances i with highest predicted scores s_i.

Instance i	Counterfactual Explanation for Instance i
Person a (s_a = 0.69) $size_{CF,a} = 5$	If you had spent *less frequently* in Computers & Electronics, Insurance and Shops, and *more frequently* in Clothing & Accessories and Restaurants → then you would not have been predicted as Neurotic
Person b (s_b = 0.66) $size_{CF,b} = 4$	If you had spent *less frequently* in Pets, Shops and Veterinarians, and spent *less money* on Subscription → you would not have been predicted as Neurotic
Person c (s_c = 0.65) $size_{CF,c} = 3$	If you had spent *less frequently* in Shops, *less money* on Internal Account Transfer and Subscription → then you would not have been predicted as Neurotic
Person d (s_d = 0.65) $size_{CF,d} = 2$	If you had spent *less frequently* in Shops, and *less money* on Subscription → then you would not have been predicted as Neurotic
Person e (s_e = 0.65) $size_{CF,e} = 4$	If you had spent *less frequently* in Food & Beverage, PayPal and Shops, and *less money* on Subscription → then you would not have been predicted as Neurotic
Person f (s_f = 0.65) $size_{CF,f} = 4$	If you had spent *less frequently* in Check, Department stores and Shops, and *more frequently* in Supermarkets & Groceries → then you would not have been predicted as Neurotic
Person g (s_g = 0.64) $size_{CF,g} = 4$	If you had spent *less frequently* in Shops and Tobacco, and *less money* on Subscription and Tobacco → then you would not have been predicted as Neurotic
Person h (s_h = 0.64) $size_{CF,h} = 8$	If you had spent *less frequently* in Food & Beverage, Vintage & Thrift, *less money* on Department stores, Shops, Tobacco and Vintage & Thrift, *more frequently* in Clothing & Accessories, *more money* in Arts & Entertainment, and the variability of your spending amount was *lower* → then you would not have been predicted as Neurotic

4. Discussion

In this paper, we demonstrated the value of XAI in the context of psychological profiling that translates innocuous digital footprints into psychological traits. Our case study highlights the importance of both global and local methods to address interpretability challenges when working with high-dimensional, sparse behavioral data.

4.1. Importance of Global Explanations and Implications

Global rules provide general insights into the decisions a model makes about a target based on what it has learned from the the full (training) data set. Global rules hence provide an explanation of the decision model that is comprehensible to the individuals making predictions and the individuals who are the target of predictions [21]. While other global XAI methods exist (e.g., feature relevance scores), we argue that rule extraction— and surrogate explanations in general—is a particularly useful tool to understand how a (combination of) feature(s) impact(s) model *decisions*, and to provide an estimate of how well the classifications can be explained (measured by *Fidelity*). Insight into the *Fidelity* of an explanation is important in the context of behavioral data. If the most important features in a model are extremely sparse, an explanation with few rules and/or few conditions per rule will fail to make accurate predictions for most people, as reflected by a low *Fidelity* or $Fscore_f$. When this is the case, novel rule extraction approaches can be used to replace features with metafeatures (groups of individual behavioral features—e.g., 'fast food' purchases that are made up of individual merchants) to increase the *Fidelity* of the extracted rules [15].

Our experiments demonstrate how global rules can be used to validate what the model learned at an aggregate level. This additional understanding can add a layer of trust to the out-of-sample performance measures by testing the face validity of the global rules (i.e., compare them with related work and existing knowledge). Not only could global rules be used to validate models before they are deployed in practice, but they could also be used to continuously audit the functionality of a model (i.e., does it use information that we do not *want* it to use?). For example, when verifying if a model exhibits algorithmic bias toward a certain protected group (e.g., minorities), we can use post hoc explanations to audit the model. Importantly, global rule extraction calls for the inclusion of domain experts. In our case study, for example, personality psychologists can help determine whether the extracted rules make sense in the context of the vast body of literature on the correlates of personality traits.

Our case study also shows how XAI at a global level can be used to generate novel hypotheses that would have been impossible to derive deductively (e.g., different preferences for mobile payment services). As Stachl et al. [22] note, researchers should "invest time and effort to finding persistent and stable digital behavioural dimensions when working on theoretical models". A future direction that is worth exploring is how higher-level, less-sparse metafeatures can help construct more 'stable' behavioral profiles that can be used for (bottom-up) theory building and hypothesis generation. This is especially interesting when modeling very high-dimensional and sparse behavioral data, for example, modeling the fine-grained places people visit [11], web pages they browse or pages they 'like' on Facebook [2]. While individual places, websites and Facebook pages might be highly predictive at any given point in time, they are also likely to change (e.g., the same coffee shop, website or Facebook page might only survive for a certain period of time). Using metafeatures for modeling is likely to lead to worse predictive performance in the moment [14,18,19]. However, they might prove valuable when extracting insights from high-performing models and generating hypotheses that are more stable over time. In sum, global rule extraction methods provide researchers and practitioners with a tool to validate their models, create a more robust foundation for future investigations of the relationship between human behavior and psychological constructs, and facilitate replication efforts in computational social sciences research [52].

4.2. Importance of Local Explanations and Implications

Next to global insights, our experiments highlight the importance of local counterfactual rules to address interpretability issues of models on behavioral data. While global rule extractions have partially found their way into social science research, local counterfactuals (and other types of local explanations) have largely been overlooked so far. The value of local rule extractions is manifold. First, they are concise: Only a small fraction of features of the full feature space is part of the explanations. We might worry providing users with explanations that are unnecessarily large, especially in the context of behavioral data. In our experiments, we see that the explanations generally have a small size, especially relative to the total number of features present in the model. This concurs with findings of Chen et al. [26], Fernandez et al. [34] and Martens & Provost [16].

Second, they are specific to the individual's behavior: Explanations point at *unique* behavior of the person that contributed most to the classification. Counterfactual explanations have the additional advantage that they are consistent with requirements currently described in regulation [40]. For example, the advisory organ of the EU on GDPR, Working Party 29, provided additional details on meaningful information that data subjects should receive when subject to automated decisions: "The company should find simple ways to tell the data subject about the rationale behind, or the criteria relied on in reaching the *decision*, ... The information should be sufficiently comprehensive for the data subjective to understand the reasons for the *decision*." Local rule extractions satisfy these requirements.

Third, local explanations could be used by companies that chose to be transparent about the ways by which they target individuals. In addition to mandated regulations, Facebook's 'Why Am I Seeing This Ad' initiative or the AdChoices program [26], for example, could provide their users with a clearer and more personalized explanation for why they are seeing a given ad. Notably, prior work has suggested that contrary to most people's intuition, transparency and control in the context of online advertising can indeed result in higher engagement levels [53,54]. Similarly, local rule extraction might solve a problem many companies are facing when sharing global rules with users. Especially when the stakes are high, there is a concern that individuals will use these insights to 'game the system'. In the context of hiring or lending for example, companies often do not want to disclose the exact working of the predictions they make, because they are worried that their models will be rendered inadequate as soon as individuals have the ability to strategically update their records in a certain direction. Local explanations are inherently relevant to one individual, but not per se useful for other people. This greatly reduces the risk of 'gaming' the system.

Finally, for experts interacting with a model (e.g., psychologists or HR managers), local explanations can be useful to understand how a particular prediction was made, and what to focus their attention on: either to overrule the decision (when domain knowledge or context outweighs the explanation for the decision), or to understand a misclassification to guide error analysis. For example, consider the (fictitious) example of predicting mental health problems from online web searches. When a person is identified as depressed by the algorithm, it is useful for experts to validate the decision based on the (words in) searches that contributed most to this decision, instead of going through the hundreds of searches of this person. Further, knowing why the classification was made can be used to overrule the decision: say a person was identified as depressed because of searching for 'symptoms of depression', but, when looking at queries in the same time window, it turns out the person logged in multiple times on the web page of the Department of Psychology at Columbia University. A user seeing this explanation would better understand why the prediction was made, and in this case, likely identify it as a false positive prediction, as this might not be an unusual search query for Psychology students.

4.3. Limitations

Our study has a number of limitations. The first limitation stems from the use of a case study as the experimental method. Future research should validate the rule-based XAI methods discussed in this paper in other applications on psychological profiling, i.e., with different behavioral data and/or psychological characteristics to predict. Next, we do not conduct a user study to estimate the impact of XAI on behavior and attitudes of the experts interacting with the model or the data subjects being targeted. It is essential to further investigate, for example, the extent to which trust and/or acceptance of experts are impacted by increased (post-hoc) interpretability or how effective these XAI methods can be as auditing tools. Moreover, future work can study the impact on attitudes of data subjects (e.g., regarding privacy) when they are provided with local explanations of how their data is turned into information about their psychological traits. Lastly, the case study is based on a data sample that consists of low-income households in the US, which might not be representative for the general population. However, our main focus is on the demonstration of XAI for different use cases, and from this point of view, it is actually interesting how XAI can help detect if a final model 'picks up' sample-specific patterns, and how this tells us something about the generalizability of the model.

5. Conclusions

Psychological profiling from digital footprints has attracted considerable interest from researchers and practitioners alike who study and apply the methodology across a wide variety of applications, ranging from marketing to employment to healthcare. Given that the underlying models can become very complex, they have earned the reputation of being a 'black box' that is difficult to penetrate. Most of the research in this area has focused on the predictive accuracy of models, without much effort being dedicated to explaining how the classifications come about. However, the explainability of these systems—central in the field of Explainable AI—is becoming an essential requirement to generate trust and increase the acceptance of predictive technologies as well as generate better insights from these systems.

In this study, we showed how global and local XAI techniques can help domain experts and data subjects validate, question and improve models that classify psychological traits from digital footprints. Using real-world financial transactions data to predict

Big Five personality traits, we demonstrated how global rule extraction can be used to understand a model's classification behavior at an aggregate level, and discussed use cases of global model interpretability (validation, insights and improvement). Furthermore, we empirically showed how local counterfactual rules can reveal more granular insights into why classifications are made (i.e., individuals are classified as exhibiting a personality trait for reasons that reflect their unique financial spending behavior), and discussed implications of this uniqueness for experts and data subjects. We hope this study encourages researchers and practitioners in the field of psychological profiling to implement XAI as a tool to develop more human-centric, interpretable psychological profiling systems that support decision-making.

Author Contributions: Conceptualization, Y.R., R.A.F., S.C.M. and D.M.; Data acquisition, R.A.F.; Data curation, Y.R.; Formal analysis, Y.R.; Funding acquisition, Y.R. and R.A.F.; Investigation, Y.R., R.A.F., S.C.M. and D.M.; Methodology, Y.R., R.A.F., S.C.M. and D.M.; Project administration, Y.R.; Resources, Y.R. and R.A.F.; Software, Y.R.; Supervision, R.A.F., S.C.M. and D.M.; Visualization, Y.R.; Writing—original draft, Y.R.; Writing—review & editing, Y.R., R.A.F., S.C.M. and D.M. All authors have read and agreed to the submitted version of the manuscript.

Funding: This research was funded by Research Foundation—Flanders grant number 11G4319N.

Institutional Review Board Statement: The study was conducted according to the guidelines of the Declaration of Helsinki, and approved by the Institutional Review Board of Columbia Business School (AAAT0788-M00Y01, 31 July 2020) and University of Antwerp (SHW2076, 4 September 2020).

Informed Consent Statement: Informed consent obtained from all subjects involved in the study.

Data Availability Statement: With explicit permission, the non-profit SaverLife collects financial transactions data to provide their services to platform users. The data is collected through an API developed by Plaid, a company that allows people to share their personal financial data with applications and developers. Because of the sensitive nature of the data and the agreements the authors signed with the data provider and are subject to its provisions, it is not possible to publicly share the data.

Acknowledgments: The authors wish to express their gratitude to SaverLife for providing data access and support, with special thanks to Leigh Phillips, David Derryck, Tim Lucas, Grace Boorstein, and Xiao Bi. The authors are also thankful to 'Advanced Projects and Applied Research in Fintech' at Columbia Business School for general, technical, and data support as well as Suwen Ge for his excellent and exemplary contributions as a senior research assistant and Sandra Navalli for her indispensable facilitation and comments. R.A. Farrokhnia is particularly grateful to Sharon Sputz at the Data Science Institute at Columbia University and, in alphabetical order, to Thomas Brown, Jessica Brucas, Melody Brumfield, Binu Nair, Anna Marie O'Neill, Anna Wojnarowska, and Michelle Zern of Columbia Business School for their invaluable administrative and departmental support.

Conflicts of Interest: The authors declare no conflict of interest.

Abbreviations

The following abbreviations are used in this manuscript:

AI	Artificial Intelligence
BB	black box
BF	Big Five
BFI	Big Five Inventory
DSA	Digital Services Act
EU	European Union
G20	Group of Twenty
GDPR	General Data Protection Regulation
LIME	Local Interpretable Model-agnostic Explanations
OECD	Organisation for Economic Co-operation and Development
SHAP	SHapley Additive exPlanations
US	United States
XAI	Explainable Artificial Intelligence

Appendix A

The Big Five Inventory–2 Short Form (BFI-2-S)

Here are a number of characteristics that may or may not apply to you. For example, do you agree that you are someone who *likes to spend time with others*? Please write a number next to each statement to indicate the extent to which you agree or disagree with that statement.

1	2	3	4	5
Disagree strongly	Disagree a little	Neutral; no opinion	Agree a little	Agree strongly

I am someone who...

1. ___ Tends to be quiet.
2. ___ Is compassionate, has a soft heart.
3. ___ Tends to be disorganized.
4. ___ Worries a lot.
5. ___ Is fascinated by art, music, or literature.
6. ___ Is dominant, acts as a leader.
7. ___ Is sometimes rude to others.
8. ___ Has difficulty getting started on tasks.
9. ___ Tends to feel depressed, blue.
10. ___ Has little interest in abstract ideas.
11. ___ Is full of energy.
12. ___ Assumes the best about people.
13. ___ Is reliable, can always be counted on.
14. ___ Is emotionally stable, not easily upset.
15. ___ Is original, comes up with new ideas.
16. ___ Is outgoing, sociable.
17. ___ Can be cold and uncaring.
18. ___ Keeps things neat and tidy.
19. ___ Is relaxed, handles stress well.
20. ___ Has few artistic interests.
21. ___ Prefers to have others take charge.
22. ___ Is respectful, treats others with respect.
23. ___ Is persistent, works until the task is finished.
24. ___ Feels secure, comfortable with self.
25. ___ Is complex, a deep thinker.
26. ___ Is less active than other people.
27. ___ Tends to find fault with others.
28. ___ Can be somewhat careless.
29. ___ Is temperamental, gets emotional easily.
30. ___ Has little creativity.

Please check: Did you write a number in front of each statement?
BFI-2 items copyright 2015 by Oliver P. John and Christopher J. Soto.

Scoring Key

Item numbers for scoring the BFI-2-S domain and facet scales are listed below. Reverse-keyed items are denoted by "R." Due to the limited reliability of the two-item facet scales, we only recommend using them in samples with approximately 400 or more observations. For more information about the BFI-2, visit the Colby Personality Lab website (http://www.colby.edu/psych/personality-lab/).

Domain Scales
Extraversion: 1R, 6, 11, 16, 21R, 26R
Agreeableness: 2, 7R, 12, 17R, 22, 27R
Conscientiousness: 3R, 8R, 13, 18, 23, 28R
Negative Emotionality: 4, 9, 14R, 19R, 24R, 29
Open-Mindedness: 5, 10R, 15, 20R, 25, 30R

Facet Scales
Sociability: 1R, 16
Assertiveness: 6, 21R
Energy Level: 11, 26R
Compassion: 2, 17R
Respectfulness: 7R, 22
Trust: 12, 27R
Organization: 3R, 18
Productiveness: 8R, 23
Responsibility: 13, 28R
Anxiety: 4, 19R
Depression: 9, 24R
Emotional Volatility: 14R, 29
Aesthetic Sensitivity: 5, 20R
Intellectual Curiosity: 10R, 25
Creative Imagination: 15, 30R

Citations for the BFI-2 and BFI-2-S
Soto, C. J., & John, O. P. (2017). The next Big Five Inventory (BFI-2): Developing and assessing a hierarchical model with 15 facets to enhance bandwidth, fidelity, and predictive power. *Journal of Personality and Social Psychology, 113*, 117-143.

Soto, C. J., & John, O. P. (2017). Short and extra-short forms of the Big Five Inventory–2: The BFI-2-S and BFI-2-XS. *Journal of Research in Personality, 68*, 69-81.

Figure A1. Snapshot of the Big Five Inventory–2 Short Form that was filled out by the participants.

Table A1. Mean and standard deviation of the BF traits and facets in this study vs. the Internet sample [45]. The fourth column shows the mean-level difference d between the two samples. The last column represents the Cronbach's alpha of each item scale that measures a BF trait.

Domain or Facet	This Study	Internet Sample [45]	d	Cronbach's Alpha
Extraversion	3.35 (1.08)	3.23 (0.80)	0.12	0.8012
Sociability	3.21 (1.08)	2.95 (1.05)	0.26	
Assertiveness	3.58 (1.02)	3.28 (0.93)	0.30	
Energy	3.25 (1.13)	3.47 (0.89)	−0.22	
Agreeableness	4.19 (0.67)	3.68 (0.64)	0.51	0.7868
Compassion	4.34 (0.83)	3.84 (0.78)	0.50	
Respectfulness	4.40 (0.76)	3.98 (0.71)	0.42	
Trust	3.84 (0.92)	3.23 (0.82)	0.61	
Conscientiousness	3.87 (0.79)	3.43 (0.77)	0.44	0.8153
Organization	3.52 (1.17)	3.42 (1.01)	0.10	
Productivity	3.89 (0.96)	3.37 (0.90)	0.52	
Responsibility	4.18 (0.82)	3.48 (0.81)	0.70	
Neuroticism	2.88 (0.96)	3.07 (0.87)	−0.19	0.8533
Anxiety	3.34 (1.07)	3.43 (0.93)	−0.09	
Depression	2.61 (1.13)	2.85 (1.02)	−0.24	
Emotional volatility	2.67 (1.17)	2.93 (1.05)	−0.26	
Openness	3.75 (0.68)	3.92 (0.65)	−0.17	0.7219
Intellectual curiosity	3.83 (0.79)	4.10 (0.70)	−0.27	
Aesthetic sensitiy	3.57 (0.96)	3.80 (0.92)	−0.23	
Creative imagination	3.83 (0.94)	3.85 (0.81)	−0.02	
	$N = 6408$	$N = 1000$		

Table A2. Summary of features capturing spending behavior.

Type	Feature Notation	Feature Name	Description
Overall	n_{tot}	Total transactions	Total number of transactions over 12 months
	a_{tot}	Total amount transactions	Total amount of money spent over 12 months
	a_{avg}	Average transaction	Average amount of money spent per transaction
	a_{cv}	Variability transaction	Variability of amount of money spent per transaction
	$a_{avg,daily}$	Average daily transaction	Average amount of money spent on a daily basis
	$a_{cv,daily}$	Variability daily transaction	Variability of amount of money spent on a daily basis
Category	n_c	Category c	Relative number of transactions in category c (e.g., Fast Food)
	a_c	Category c (\$)	Relative amount of money spent in category c (e.g., Fast Food (\$))
	C_{tot}	Unique categories	Number of distinct spending categories
	$C_{entropy}$	Category entropy	Diversity of spending in different categories

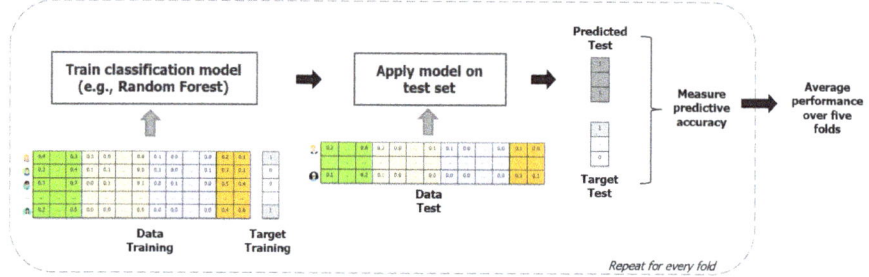

Figure A2. Five fold cross-validation procedure to develop classification models to predict BF traits.

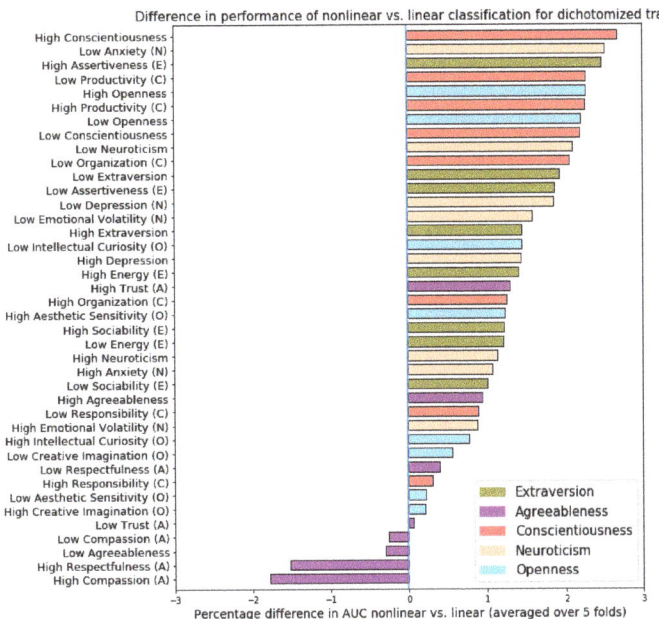

Figure A3. Percentage difference in predictive accuracy of nonlinear vs. linear classification models for dichotomized personality traits, expressed by the difference in Area under the Curve (AUC), and ranked by decreasing difference in AUC. Positive values indicate that the best nonlinear model outperformed the best linear model.

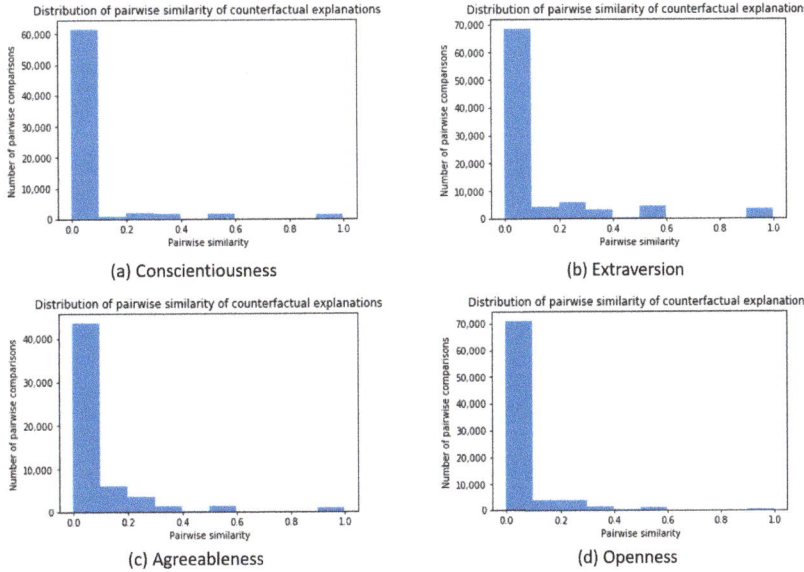

Figure A4. Distribution of pairwise similarity between counterfactual explanations for predicting (**a**) Conscientiousness, (**b**) Extraversion, (**c**) Agreeableness and (**d**) Openness. A value of 0 (resp., 1) indicates no (resp., perfect) overlap.

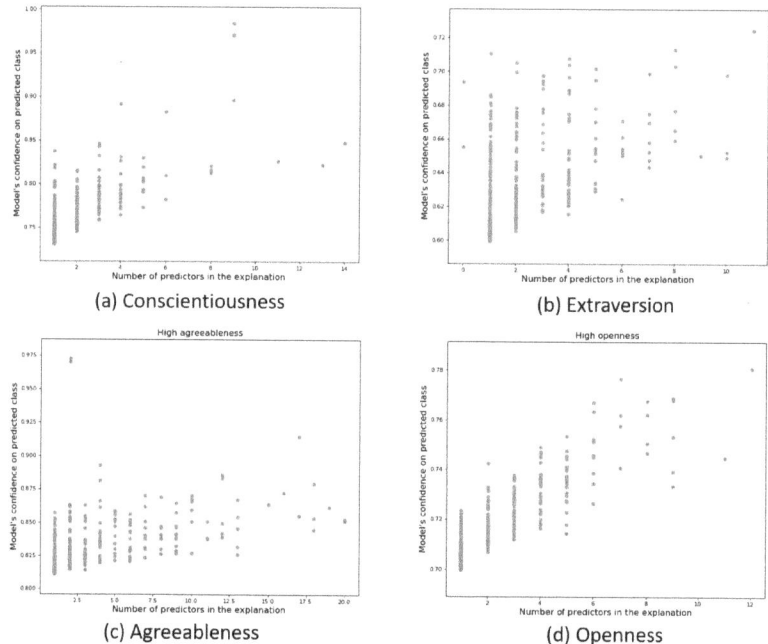

Figure A5. Model's predicted scores vs. number of features in the explanation to counterfactually explain the predicted class. The correlations between the confidence scores and explanation sizes are 0.72 (Conscientiousness), 0.52 (Extraversion), 0.44 (Agreeableness), 0.87 (Openness).

References

1. Matz, S.C.; Netzer, O. Using Big Data as a window into consumers' psychology. *Curr. Opin. Behav. Sci.* **2017**, *18*, 7–12. [CrossRef]
2. Kosinski, M.; Stillwell, D.; Graepel, T. Private traits and attributes are predictable from digital records of human behavior. *Proc. Natl. Acad. Sci. USA* **2013**, *110*, 5802–5805. [CrossRef] [PubMed]
3. Matz, S.C.; Kosinski, M.; Nave, G.; Stillwell, D. Psychological Targeting as an Effective Approach to Digital Mass Communication. *Proc. Natl. Acad. Sci. USA* **2017**, *114*, 12714–12719. [CrossRef]
4. Moshe, I.; Terhorst, Y.; Opoku Asare, K.; Sander, L.B.; Ferreira, D.; Baumeister, H.; Mohr, D.C.; Pulkki-Råback, L. Predicting Symptoms of Depression and Anxiety Using Smartphone and Wearable Data. *Front. Psychiatry* **2020**, *12*, 625247. [CrossRef]
5. Praet, S.; Van Aelst, P.; Martens, D. Predictive modeling to study lifestyle politics with Facebook likes. *EPJ Data Sci.* **2021**, *10*, 50. [CrossRef]
6. Matz, S.C.; Appel, R.; Kosinski, M. Privacy in the Age of Psychological Targeting. *Curr. Opin. Psychol.* **2020**, *31*, 116–121. [CrossRef] [PubMed]
7. Youyou, W.; Kosinski, M.; Stillwell, D. Computer-based personality judgements are more accurate than those made by humans. *Proc. Natl. Acad. Sci. USA* **2015**, *112*, 1–5. [CrossRef]
8. de Montjoye, Y.-A.; Quoidbach, J.; Robic, F.; Pentland, A.S. Predicting people personality using novel mobile phone-based metrics. In Proceedings of the Social Computing, Behavioral-Cultural Modeling and Prediction, SBP 2013, Lecture Notes in Computer Science, Washington, DC, USA, 2–5 April 2013; Volume 7812, pp. 48–55.
9. Rentfrow, P.J.; Gosling, S.D. The do re mi's of everyday life: The structure and personality correlates of music preferences. *J. Personal. Soc. Psychol.* **2003**, *84*, 1236–1256. [CrossRef] [PubMed]
10. Nave, G.; Minxha, J.; Greenberg, D.M.; Kosinski, M.; Stillwell, D.; Rentfrow, J. Musical Preferences Predict Personality: Evidence from Active Listening and Facebook Likes. *Psychol. Sci.* **2018**, *29*, 1145–1158. [CrossRef]
11. Müller, S.R.; Peters, H.; Matz, S.C.; Wang, W. Investigating the Relationships Between Mobility Behaviours and Indicators of Subjective Well-Being Using Smartphone-Based Experience Sampling and GPS Tracking. *Eur. J. Personal.* **2020**, *34*, 714–732. [CrossRef]
12. Gladstone, J.J.; Matz, S.C. Can Psychological Traits be Inferred from Spending? Evidence from Transaction Data. *Psychol. Sci.* **2019**, *30*, 1087–1096. [CrossRef]

13. Tovanich, N.; Centellegher, S.; Seghouani, N.B.; Gladstone, J.; Matz, S.; Lepri, B. Inferring Psychological Traits from Spending Categories and Dynamic Consumption Patterns. *EPJ Data Sci.* **2021**, *10*, 1–30. [CrossRef]
14. Clark, J.; Provost, F. Unsupervised dimensionality reduction versus supervised regularization for classification from sparse data. *Data Min. Knowl. Discov.* **2019**, *33*, 871–916. [CrossRef]
15. Ramon, Y.; Martens, D.; Evgeniou, T.; Praet, S. Can metafeatures help improve explanations of prediction models when using behavioral and textual data? *Mach. Learn.* **2021**, 1–40. [CrossRef]
16. Martens, D.; Provost, F. Explaining data-driven document classifications. *MIS Q.* **2014**, *38*, 73–99. [CrossRef]
17. Ramon, Y.; Martens, D.; Provost, F.; Evgeniou, T. A Comparison of Instance-level Counterfactual Explanation Algorithms for Behavioral and Textual Data: SEDC, LIME-C and SHAP-C. *Adv. Data Anal. Classif.* **2020**, *14*, 801–819. [CrossRef]
18. De Cnudde, S.; Martens, D.; Evgeniou, T.; Provost, F. A benchmarking study of classification techniques for behavioral data. *Int. J. Data Sci. Anal.* **2020**, *9*, 131–173. [CrossRef]
19. Junqué de Fortuny, E.; Martens, D.; Provost, F. Predictive Modeling With Big Data: Is Bigger Really Better? *Big Data* **2014**, *1*, 215–226. [CrossRef]
20. PwC. 22nd Annual Global CEO Survey. Available online: https://www.pwc.com/gx/en/ceo-survey/2019/report/pwc-22nd-annual-global-ceo-survey.pdf (accessed on 27 September 2021).
21. Martens, D. *Data Science Ethics: Concepts, Techniques, and Cautionary Tales*; Oxford University Press: Oxford, UK, 2022.
22. Stachl, C.; Pargent, F.; Hilbert, S.; Harari, G.M.; Schoedel, R.; Vaid, S.; Gosling, S.D.; Bühner, M. Personality Research and Assessment in the Era of Machine Learning. *Eur. J. Personal.* **2020**, *34*, 613–631. [CrossRef]
23. Dastin, J. Amazon Scraps Secret AI Recruiting Tool That Showed Bias against Women. Available online: https://www.reuters.com/article/us-amazon-com-jobs-automation-insight-idUSKCN1MK08G (accessed on 29 September 2021).
24. Murgia, M. Algorithms Drive Online Discrimination, Academic Warns. Available online: https://www.ft.com/content/bc959e8c-1b67-11ea-97df-cc63de1d73f4 (accessed on 27 September 2021).
25. Shmueli, G. To explain or to predict? *Stat. Sci.* **2010**, *25*, 289–310. [CrossRef]
26. Chen, D.; Fraiberger, S.P.; Moakler, R.; Provost, F. Enhancing Transparency and Control When Drawing Data-Driven Inferences About Individuals. *Big Data* **2017**, *5*, 197–212. [CrossRef]
27. Dattner, B.; Chamorro-Premuzic, T.; Buchband, R.; Schettler, L. The Legal and Ethical Implications of Using AI in Hiring. Available online: https://hbr.org/2019/04/the-legal-and-ethical-implications-of-using-ai-in-hiring (accessed on 27 September 2021).
28. Baker, S.R.; Farrokhnia, R.A.; Meyer, S.; Pagel, M.; Yannelis, C. How Does Household Spending Respond to an Epidemic? Consumption During the 2020 COVID-19 Pandemic. *Natl. Bur. Econ. Res. Work. Pap.* **2020**, *10*, 834–862. [CrossRef]
29. Lu, J.; Liu, A.; Dong, F.; Gu, F.; Gama, J.; Zhang, G. Learning under concept drift: A review. *IEEE Trans. Knowl. Data Eng.* **2018**, *31*, 2346–2363. [CrossRef]
30. Mittal, V.; Kashyap, I. Online Methods of Learning in Occurence of Concept Drift. *Int. J. Comput. Appl.* **2015**, *117*, 18–22.
31. Arrieta, A.B.; Díaz-Rodríguez, N.; Del Ser, J.; Bennetot, A.; Tabik, S.; Barbado, A.; Garcia, S.; Gil-Lopez, S.; Molina, D.; Benjamins, R.; et al. Explainable Artificial Intelligence (XAI): Concepts, taxonomies, opportunities and challenges towards responsible AI. *Inf. Fusion* **2020**, *58*, 82–115. [CrossRef]
32. Guidotti, R.; Monreale, A.; Ruggieri, S.; Turini, F.; Giannotti, D.; Pedreschi, A. A survey of methods for explaining black box models. *ACM Comput. Surv. (CSUR)* **2018**, *51*, 1–42. [CrossRef]
33. Molnar, C. *Interpretable Machine Learning*, 1st ed.; Lulu: Morrisville, NC, USA, 2019. Available online: https://christophm.github.io/interpretable-ml-book/ (accessed on 3 December 2021).
34. Fernandez, C.; Provost, F.; Han, X. Explaining data-driven decisions made by AI systems: The counterfactual approach. *arXiv* **2020**, arXiv:2001.07417.
35. Settani, M.; Azucar, D.; Marengo, D. Predicting individual characteristics from digital traces on social media: A meta-analysis. *Cyberpsychol. Behav. Soc. Netw.* **2018**, *21*, 217–228. [CrossRef]
36. Stachl, C.; Au, C.; Schoedel, R.; Buschek, D.; Völkel, S.; Schuwerk, T. Behavioral patterns in smartphone usage predict big five personality traits. *OSF* **2019**, 1–24. [CrossRef]
37. Andrews, R.; Diederich, J. Survey and critique of techniques for extracting rules from trained artificial neural networks. *Knowl.-Based Syst.* **1995**, *8*, 373–389. [CrossRef]
38. Huysmans, J.; Baesens, B.; Vanthienen, J. Using Rule Extraction to Improve the Comprehensibility of Predictive Models. *SSRN Electron. J.* **2006**. [CrossRef]
39. Martens, D.; Baesens, B.; Van Gestel, T.; Vanthienen, J. Comprehensible credit scoring models using rule extraction from support vector machines. *EJOR* **2007**, *183*, 1466–1476. [CrossRef]
40. Wachter, S.; Mittelstadt, B.; Russell, C. Counterfactual Explanations without Opening the Black Box: Automated Decisions and the GDPR. *Harv. J. Law Technol.* **2018**, *31*, 841. [CrossRef]
41. Ribeiro, M.T.; Singh, S.; Guestrin, C. "Why Should I Trust You": Explaining the Predictions of Any Classifier. In Proceedings of the 22nd ACM SIGKDD International Conference on Knowledge Discovery and Data Mining, San Francisco, CA, USA, 13–17 August 2016; pp. 1135–1144.
42. Lundberg, S.M.; Lee, S.-I. A Unified Approach to Interpreting Model Predictions. In *Advances in Neural Information Processing Systems*; Guyon, I., Luxburg, U.V., Bengio, S., Wallach, H., Fergus, R., Vishwanathan, S., Garnett, R., Eds.; Curran Associates Inc.: New York, NY, USA, 2017; Volume 30.

43. US Bureau of Labor Statistics. Available online: https://www.bls.gov/cex/tables/calendar-year/mean-item-share-average-standard-error/cu-income-before-taxes-2019.pdf (accessed on 17 September 2021).
44. Costa, P.; McCrae, R. Normal personality assessment in clinical practice: The NEO personality inventory. *Psychol. Assess.* **1992**, *4*, 5–13. [CrossRef]
45. Soto, C.S.; John, O.P. Short and extra-short forms of the Big Five Inventory-2: The BFI-2-S and BFI-2-XS. *J. Res. Personal.* **2017**, *68*, 69–81. [CrossRef]
46. Pianesi, F.; Mana, N.; Cappelletti, A.; Lepri, B.; Zancanaro, M. Multimodal recognition of personality traits in social interactions. In Proceedings of the International Conference on Multimodal Interfaces (ICMI), Chania, Greece, 20–22 October 2008.
47. Phan, L.V.; Rauthmann, J.F. Personality Computing: New frontiers in personality assessment. *Soc. Personal. Psychol. Compass* **2021**, *15*, e12624. [CrossRef]
48. Provost, F.; Fawcett, T. *Data Science for Business: What You Need to Know about Data Mining and Data-Analytic Thinking*, 1st ed.; O'Reilly Media, Inc.: Newton, MA, USA, 2013.
49. Chittaranjan, G.; Blom, J.; Gatica-Perez, D. Who with Big-Five: Analyzing and Classifying Personality Traits with Smartphones. In Proceedings of the 15th Annual International Symposium on Wearable Computers, San Francisco, CA, USA, 12–15 June 2011; pp. 29–36.
50. Aiken, L.R., Jr. The relationships of dress to selected measures of personality in undergraduate women. *J. Soc. Psychol.* **1963**, *59*, 119–128. [CrossRef]
51. Darden, L.A. Personality Correlates of Clothing Interest for a Group of Non-Incarcerated and Incarcerated Women Ages 18 to 30. Ph.D. Thesis, University of North Carolina, Greensboro, NC, USA, 1975.
52. Open Science Collaboration. Estimating the reproducibility of psychological science. *Curr. Opin. Behav. Sci.* **2015**, *349*, aac4716. [CrossRef]
53. Aaker, J.L. Dimensions of Brand Personality. *J. Mark. Res.* **1997**, *34*, 347–356. [CrossRef]
54. Tucker, C.E. Social Networks, Personalized Advertising, and Privacy Controls. *J. Mark. Res.* **2014**, *51*, 546–562. [CrossRef]

Article

Learnable Leaky ReLU (LeLeLU): An Alternative Accuracy-Optimized Activation Function

Andreas Maniatopoulos and Nikolaos Mitianoudis *

Department of Electrical and Computer Engineering, Democritus University of Greece, 67100 Xanthi, Greece; amaniato@ee.duth.gr
* Correspondence: nmitiano@ee.duth.gr; Tel.: +30-25410-79572

Abstract: In neural networks, a vital component in the learning and inference process is the activation function. There are many different approaches, but only nonlinear activation functions allow such networks to compute non-trivial problems by using only a small number of nodes, and such activation functions are called nonlinearities. With the emergence of deep learning, the need for competent activation functions that can enable or expedite learning in deeper layers has emerged. In this paper, we propose a novel activation function, combining many features of successful activation functions, achieving 2.53% higher accuracy than the industry standard ReLU in a variety of test cases.

Keywords: activation function; ReLU family; activation function test

1. Introduction

Activation functions originated from the attempt to generalize a linear discriminant function in order to address nonlinear classification problems in pattern recognition. Thus, an activation function is a nonlinear, monotonic function that transforms a linear boundary function to a non-linear one. The same principle was used in perceptrons in order to allow the perceptron to classify the inputs. The most straightforward activation function is the identity function ($y = x$), along with the binary activation function in Equation (1) that resembles an activation/classification switch.

$$y = 1 \ if \ x > 0 \ or \ y = 0 \ if \ x \leq 0 \qquad (1)$$

This is the first nonlinearity used in perceptrons and multilayer perceptrons and made its way to more complex neural networks later on. Despite its simplicity, the discontinuity at $x = 0$, which rendered the calculation of the corresponding derivative rather difficult, encouraged the search for new monotonic and continuous activation functions. The first continuous, nonlinear activation function that was used was the sigmoid, also called the logistic or the soft-step activation function, and is described by Equation (2).

$$\sigma(x) = \frac{1}{1 + e^{-x}} \qquad (2)$$

This allowed the computation of nonlinear problems by using a low number of neurons. The sigmoid was used in the hidden layers of common neural networks and enabled the training and inference of these systems for years. A similar function can arise from the sigmoid function through a linear transformation of the input and the output is the Hyperbolic tangent (Tanh) presented in Equation (3).

$$\tanh(x) = \frac{e^x - e^{-x}}{e^x + e^{-x}} \qquad (3)$$

Again, this was widely used in neural networks for years, and it was generally accepted that the Tanh function favored faster training convergence, compared to the sigmoid function. However, the computation of these activation functions is rather expensive, since it entails look-up table solutions; thus, they are non-optimal choices for neural networks. The emergence of deeper architectures and deep learning, in general, has also highlighted another deficit of the two traditional activation functions. Their bounded output restricted the dissipation of derivatives in back-propagation when the network was deep. In other words, deeper layers received almost zero updates to their weights; that is, they were able to learn during the training process. This phenomenon is also known as the vanishing gradient problem.

The difficulty in computational calculation and deep learning is partially solved with the introduction of the rectified linear unit (ReLU) [1] in Equation (4).

$$y = \max\{0, x\} = x \mid x > 0 \tag{4}$$

The ReLU achieves great performance, while being computationally efficient. Since it poses no restriction on positive inputs, gradients have more chances to reach deeper layers in back-propagation, thus enabling learning in deeper layers. In addition, the computation of the gradient in backpropagation learning is reduced to a multiplication with a constant, which is far more computationally efficient. Thus, a whole new era in learning and inference with neural networks has emerged, dominating the last decade.

One drawback of the ReLU is that it does not activate for non-positive inputs, causing the deactivation of several neurons during training, which can be viewed again as a vanishing gradient problem for negative values. The non-activation for non-positive numbers is solved with the introduction of the Leaky rectified linear unit (Leaky ReLU) [2], which activates slightly for negative values, as expressed in Equation (5).

$$y = \begin{cases} 0.01x & \text{if } x < 0 \\ x & \text{if } x \geq 0 \end{cases} \tag{5}$$

One can encounter a number of other variations of ReLU in the literature. One basic variation of the ReLU is the Parametric Rectified Linear Unit (PReLU) [3], which has a learnable parameter, α, controlling the leakage of the negative values, presented in Equation (6). In other words, PReLU is a Leaky ReLU; however, the slope of the curve for negative values of x is learnt through adaptation instead of being set at a predetermined value.

$$y = \begin{cases} \alpha x & \text{if } x < 0 \\ x & \text{if } x \geq 0 \end{cases} \tag{6}$$

Moving away from the family of ReLU, we see that there is the Gaussian Error Linear Unit (GELU) [4] in Equation (7). This activation function is non-convex and non-monotonic and features curvature everywhere in the input space. The authors in Reference [4] claim that GELU can offer a regularization effect on the trained network, since the output is determined on both the input and the stochastic properties of the input. Thus, neurons can be masked off the network, based on the statistical properties of x, which resembles the batch normalization [5] and the Drop-out [6] mechanisms.

$$y = \frac{1}{2}x(1 + \text{erf}(\frac{x}{\sqrt{2}})) = x\Phi(x) \tag{7}$$

Another nonlinear activation function is the Softplus [7,8], as described by Equation (8). The Softplus function features smooth derivatives and less computational complexity, as compared to the GELU; however, it is still more complex compared to the ReLU family.

$$y = \ln(1 + e^x) \tag{8}$$

The exponential linear unit (ELU) [9] in Equation (9) is another smooth, continuous and differentiable function that tackles the vanishing gradient problem for negative values through an exponential function. This function saturates for great negative values; however, the degree of saturation is controlled by the learnable parameter, α.

$$y = \alpha(e^x - 1) \text{ if } x \leq 0 \text{ or } y = x \text{ if } x > 0 \tag{9}$$

The scaled exponential linear unit (SELU) [10] is another version of the ELU with controllable parameters that induce self-normalizing properties.

$$y = \lambda\alpha(e^x - 1) \text{ if } x \leq 0 \text{ or } y = \lambda x \text{ if } x > 0 \tag{10}$$

where the values of $\alpha = 1.6733$ and $\lambda = 1.0507$.

These last activation functions act similar to the ReLU family, providing slightly higher accuracy in complex problems, while having higher computational cost due to the exponential/logarithmic part in the computation and the more complicated implied derivatives at back-propagation.

In Reference [11], Courbariauxet et al. introduced a stricter version of the original sigmoid function, coined "hard sigmoid", which is given by the formula:

$$y = \max(0, \min(1, \frac{x+1}{2})) \tag{11}$$

The proposed function was less computationally expensive as compared to the original sigmoid and yielded better results in its experiments [11].

Another derivative from the original sigmoid function is the Swish activation function, which was introduced in Reference [12] and is described by the following formula:

$$y = \text{swish}(x) = x \text{ sigmoid}(\beta x) = \frac{x}{1 + e^{-\beta x}} \tag{12}$$

where β can be a fixed or a trainable parameter. Swish can be regarded as a smooth function that serves as an intermediate between a linear function and a ReLU.

Finally, the Mish activation function [13] is a self-regularized non-monotonic activation function that was inspired by the Softplus function and Swish and is described by the following:

$$y = x \tanh(\ln(1 + e^x)) \tag{13}$$

There is no trainable/adjustable parameter here, nonetheless, it seems to outperform Swish and other functions in a study [13]. The computational complexity of estimating the function is noteworthy in this case.

More complicated activation functions have also recently been proposed. In Reference [14], Maguolo et al. propose the Mexican ReLU, which is described by the following equation:

$$y = PReLU(x) + \sum_{j=1}^{k-1} c_j \varphi_{aj,\lambda j}(x) \tag{14}$$

where $\varphi_{a,\lambda}(x) = \max(\lambda - |x - a|, 0)$ is a Mexican-hat-type function, and a and λ are learnable parameters. In Reference [15], the concept of reproducing activation functions is introduced, where a different activation function is applied to each neuron. The applied activation function is a weighted combination of a set of known activation functions with learnable parameters and weights for each neuron. In Reference [16], Zhou et al. define the activation function as a trainable piecewise linear unit with five learnable parameters for each neuron. In Reference [17], Shridhar et al. introduce the concept of a stochastic activation function, where $y = \mu(x) + \sigma\varepsilon$, where ε is drawn randomly from a Gaussian pdf with N(0,1), σ is a trainable or static parameter and $\mu(x)$ can be a static or learnable function, usually initialized by the ReLU. In Reference [18], Bingham and Miikkulainen propose a genetic algorithm to create customized activation functions from a family of well-known activation functions. The evolution begins with a parent activation function that evolves through four evolutionary operations (insert, remove, change and regenerate). Each function that is generated is parameterized, and a fitness score is estimated. The functions that yield the best fitness scores are added to the population of activation functions to be used in the NN.

The objective of the paper is to propose a novel activation function that (a) expands the ReLU family by adding support to the negative values; (b) the degree of saturation for the negative values is controlled by a learnable parameter, α; (c) this parameter α simultaneously controls a learning boost for positive values; (d) in the case of $\alpha \to 0$, the learning at these nodes ceases, leading to a regularization of the network, similar to Drop-out, which eliminates the need of such techniques; (e) the accuracy performance gain of the proposed activation function over ReLU increases with the information complexity of the dataset (i.e., the difficulty of the problem); and it (f) remains a simple function with a single learnable/adaptive parameter and a simple update rule, in contrast to far more complicated adaptive activation functions.

2. The Proposed Activation Function

In this paper, we propose a novel activation function combining the best qualities of the ReLU family, while having low computational complexity and more adaptivity to the actual data. The equation that describes the Leaky Learnable ReLU (LeLeLU) is as follows:

$$y = \alpha \max(x, 0) + 0.1\alpha \min(0, x) \tag{15}$$

$$y = \begin{cases} 0.1\alpha x & if\ x < 0 \\ \alpha x & if\ x \geq 0 \end{cases} \tag{16}$$

where α is a learnable parameter that controls the slope of the activation function for negative inputs, but what is different here is that it simultaneously controls the slope of the activation function for all positive inputs. There is a constant multiplier, 0.1, that reduces the slope for negative input values in a similar manner to the Leaky ReLU, which seems to work well in our experiments. LeLeLU is depicted in Figure 1 for various values of α.

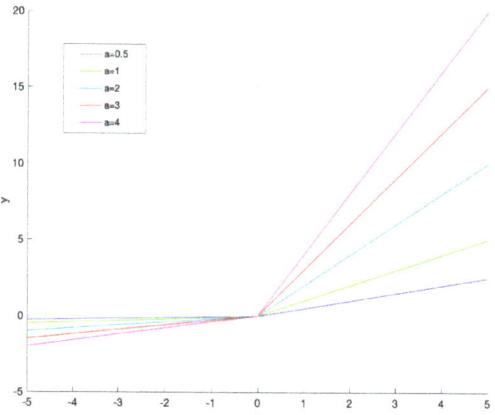

Figure 1. Proposed activation function LeLeLU for various values of α.

The derivative of LeLeLU can simply be calculated by the following:

$$\frac{dy}{dx} = \begin{cases} 0.1\alpha & if\ x < 0 \\ 0 & if\ x = 0 \\ \alpha & if\ x > 0 \end{cases} \tag{17}$$

The update formulations of the parameter α can be derived by using the chain rule. The gradient of α for one layer for each neuron, i, can be given by the following:

$$\frac{\partial L}{\partial \alpha_i} = \sum_{y_i} \frac{\partial L}{\partial f(y_i)} \frac{\partial f(y_i)}{\partial \alpha_i} \tag{18}$$

where $L(\bullet)$ denotes the neural network's loss function, and y_i denote the output of the i-th neuron.

In order to reduce the computational cost in demanding situations, one can choose to keep the parameter α the same for a number of neurons, i.e., for a layer. For the layer-shared variant, the gradient of α is as follows:

$$\frac{\partial L}{\partial \alpha} = \sum_i \sum_{y_i} \frac{\partial L}{\partial f(y_i)} \frac{\partial f(y_i)}{\partial \alpha} \tag{19}$$

where the summation Σ_i sums over all neurons of the layer. The complexity overhead of α, the learnable parameter, is negligible for both forward and backward propagation, while gradient descent with the momentum method was used during training.

$$\alpha_i^+ \leftarrow \mu \alpha_i - \eta \frac{\partial L}{\partial \alpha_i} \tag{20}$$

where η is the learning rate, and μ denotes momentum.

The parameter α is learnable per filter during training, and during testing, we observed a correlation between dataset complexity, depth-wise position of respective filter in the neural network topology and training phase.

It is obvious in Figure 1 that, for $\alpha = 1$, our proposed activation function turns into the leaky ReLU activation function. The strong point of the proposed activation function is that the learnable parameter influences both the negative and the positive values. This implies that the adaptation of α can accelerate training in certain parts of the network during certain epochs of the training procedure, when α gets values that are larger than 1. In contrast, when α gets lower than 1 values, learning slows down for certain parts of the network.

In the special case that α gets values close to zero, not only learning is halted for these neurons, but their output is close to zero, which implies that these neurons are severed from the network. Hence, by de-activating several neurons, the network is automatically regularized during training in a similar manner to the popular Drop-out technique [6]. The difference is that, by using the proposed activation function, network regularization is performed by the adaptation of the activation function and network training, whereas a Drop-out is a mechanism that works as an extra step during network training. The adaptation of the parameter α is investigated in more detail in the next section.

3. Parameter Adaptation and Network Regularization

In this section, we investigate the role and behavior of parameter α during training. As a testbed, we used the Fashion MNIST dataset and the corresponding network architecture in Figure 2. The programming environment was MATLAB 2020a on a Haswell i7 4770 s, 16 GB DDR3 RAM, NVidia GTX 970 4 GB PC, running Windows 10. The code for implementing LeLeLU can be found here (https://github.com/ManiatopoulosAA/LeLeLU, accessed on 10 October 2021).

In the proposed network architecture, we included the use of Batch Normalization [5], which is a form of network regularization that keeps the mean and variance of neurons' output normalized. The use of Drop-out is often complementary to Batch Normalization; therefore, we can see in the literature that they can be used in parallel. Since the proposed activation function is similar to PReLU, we would like to compare the performance of the proposed activation function with PReLU on the previously described testbed. In addition, since the proposed activation function is performing regularization in the same manner as Drop-out, we would like to compare its performance with a combination of PReLU, using Drop-out on each layer.

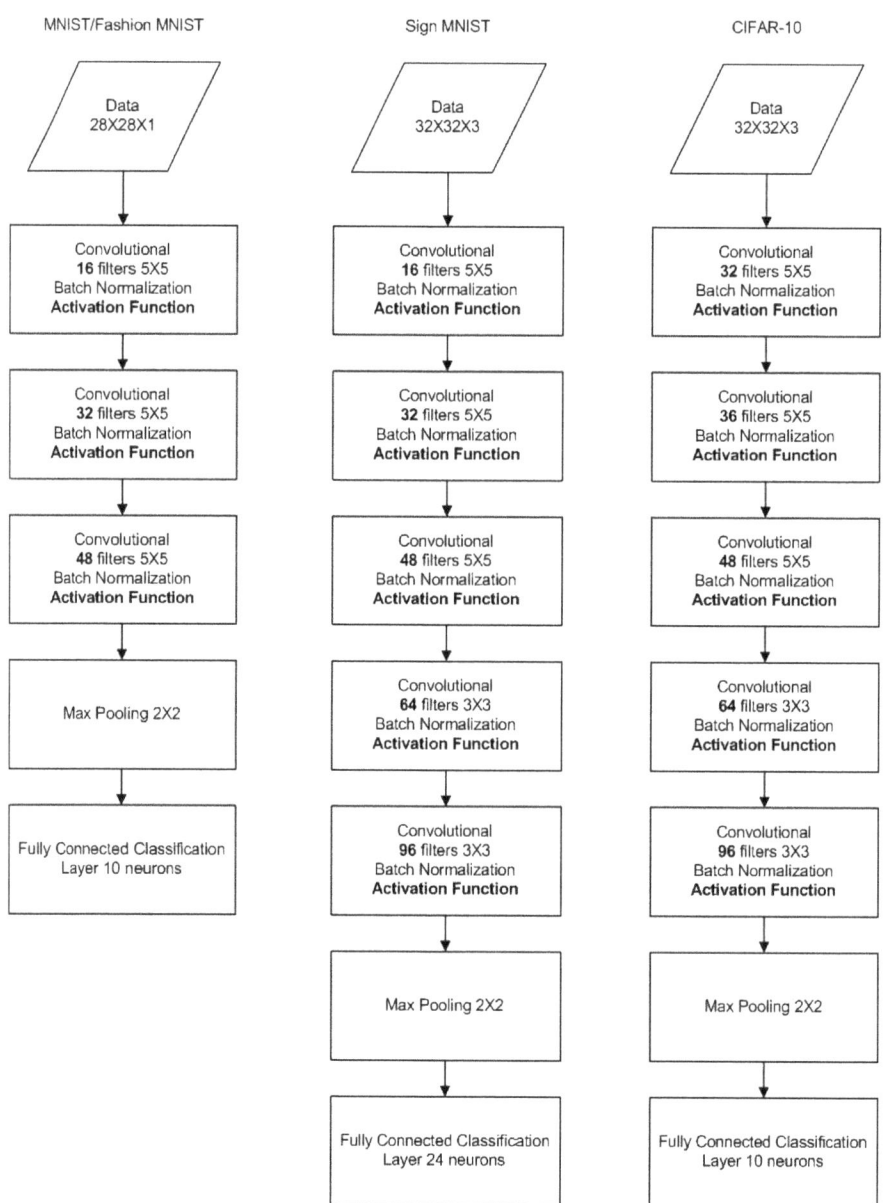

Figure 2. Neural networks' topologies that were employed for each dataset (MNIST, Fashion MNIST, Sign MNIST and CIFAR-10).

The results are very conclusive. The architecture using PReLU only yields classification accuracy of 0.82, with notably slower convergence. The architecture using PReLU and Drop-out yields a classification accuracy of 0.829, whereas the proposed activation function with batch normalization but without Drop-out achieves an accuracy of 0.912. Thus, at first, LeLeLU performed better than PReLU itself. At the same time, LeLeLU is performing better than PReLU with a regularizer (Drop-out). This implies that the adaptation of LeLeLU is regularizing the network itself and even works better than Drop-out by 8.8%. There is an extra computational cost for the adaptation of parameter α. Based on the previous testbed, the runtime of the proposed scheme is marginally longer by 2.56%, compared to the PReLU+Drop-out combination. We reckon that this might be due to the fact that Drop-out completely removes and does not process some neurons from the network, whereas, in our case, the network continues to process these neurons, even in the case that $\alpha \to 0$ in their LeLeLU.

In Figure 3, we visualized the adaptation of parameter α for a random neuron/filter as it changes for every epoch. It is obvious that there is an active Drop-out-like behavior at least twice for every neuron during the training process, while there are instances where the parameter α is near 1, accelerating the learning of the neuron in question.

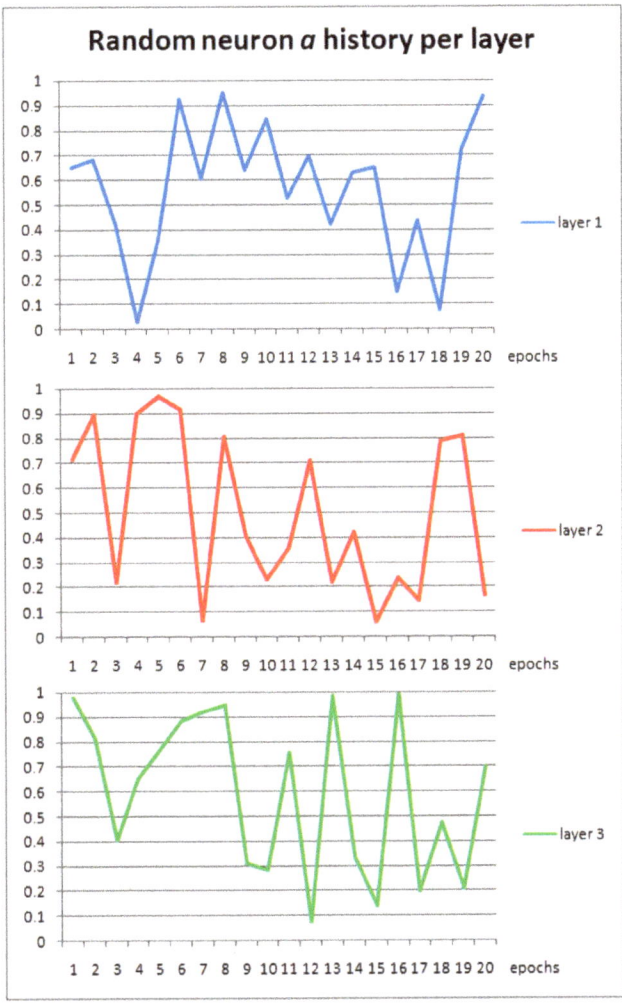

Figure 3. Values of parameter a during training for 3 neurons in different layers.

4. Results

In this section, we perform a more thorough comparison between the various activation functions for various different datasets.

4.1. Datasets and Network Topologies

The topology of all networks used to compare the four activation functions is displayed in Figure 3.

More specifically, MNIST and Fashion MNIST run on a three-hidden-layer convolutional neural network with 16, 32 and 48 5×5 filters, while the last layer was a 10-neuron classification layer. The Sign MNIST runs on a five-hidden-layer convolutional neural network with 16, 32 and 48 5×5 filters, while the last two hidden layers have 64 and 96 3×3 filters, respectively. The last layer is a 24-neuron fully connected classification layer. Lastly, the CIFAR-10 classification dataset runs on a five-hidden-layer convolutional neural network with 32, 36 and 48 5×5 filters, while the last two hidden layers have 64 and 96 3×3 filters respectively, with the last layer being a 10 neuron classification layer.

The MNIST topology was trained for 15 epochs, the Fashion MNIST for 20 epochs, the Sign Language dataset for 20 and the CIFAR-10 dataset for 60 epochs. Since the scope of this paper is the comparison of different activation functions, and since the ReLU activation function is the most widely known and used, all results presented were normalized to the accuracy obtained used by the ReLU activation.

All testing was conducted with five-fold validation, and the results presented in the next section are the mean of the three median values. In other words, from the five accuracy results of five-fold validation, the largest and lowest values were dropped, and the three median values were averaged to give a more balanced score that is less prone to outliers. In our experiments, we benchmarked the following activation functions: Tanh, ReLU, PReLU, ELU, SELU, HardSigmoid, Mish, Swish and the proposed LeLeLU. These activation functions were chosen as representative examples of each category of baseline activation functions, as described earlier in the introduction. We preferred to compare with simple activation functions with minimal computational cost or adaptation, such as the proposed one, avoiding those mentioned earlier with great adaptation complexity and many trainable parameters.

4.2. Numerical Results

Here, we evaluate all experiments, using accuracy, i.e., the number of correctly classified examples over the total number of examples in the testing dataset. As stated previously, the overall accuracy is estimated via five-fold validation. Then, we consider the accuracy achieved by ReLU as the baseline result, and we calculate normalized accuracy as the ratio (in percentage) of the new activation function accuracy over the accuracy achieved by ReLU.

In Table 1, we can see the accuracy and normalized accuracy on the MNIST dataset, using the nine activation functions. All activation functions perform well, with the LeLeLU giving a small boost of 0.23% over the baseline ReLU. The proposed LeLeLU outperforms current state-of-the-art activation functions, including Swish and Mish. The MNIST dataset contains a well-studied and easy-to-classify dataset, and therefore the improvement is minimal but existent. It should be noted that PReLU slightly underperforms in this experiment, but this is minimal.

In Table 2, we can see the accuracy and normalized accuracy on the Fashion MNIST dataset, using the nine activation functions. All activation functions perform relatively well. The LeLeLU gives a significant boost of 1.8% over the baseline ReLU, whereas PReLU improves slightly by 0.06%, with the ELU giving the second best improvement of 1.2%. Mish and Swish outperform the traditional ReLU, but they are well below the proposed LeLeLU.

Table 1. Test accuracy in the MNIST dataset of the activation functions in question, using the corresponding neural network, and accuracy normalized to that attained by ReLU activation function.

Activation Function	Accuracy	Normalized Accuracy
ReLU	0.9875	100%
PReLU	0.9861	99.9%
Tanh	0.9835	99.6%
ELU	0.9879	100%
SELU	0.9878	100.04%
HardSigmoid	0.9756	98.79%
Mish	0.9881	100.06%
Swish	0.9878	100.04%
LeLeLU	**0.9897**	**100.23%**

Table 2. Test accuracy in the Fashion MNIST dataset of the activation functions in question, using the corresponding neural network, and accuracy normalized to that attained by ReLU activation function.

Activation Function	Accuracy	Normalized Accuracy
ReLU	0.8956	100%
PReLU	0.8961	100.06%
Tanh	0.8979	100.2%
ELU	0.9071	101.2%
SELU	0.8959	100.03%
HardSigmoid	0.8704	97.19%
Mish	0.9037	100.9%
Swish	0.9019	100.7%
LeLeLU	**0.912**	**101.8%**

In Table 3, we can see the accuracy and normalized accuracy on the Sign Language dataset, using the nine activation functions. Here, the results are more impressive. All other activation functions clearly underperform, as compared to the baseline ReLU, with the LeLeLU giving the only improved performance with a significant boost of 3.2% over the baseline. Here, again, we witness the superiority of the proposed LeLeLU, compared to Mish and Swish, which are the only ones that offer an improvement to ReLU, but their improvement is less impressive than that of the LeLeLU. This experiment clearly demonstrated the significant ability of LeLeLU to adapt over the dataset and improve both positive and negative values learning, as compared to the stationary ReLU.

In Table 4, we can see the accuracy and normalized accuracy on the CIFAR-10 dataset, using the five activation functions. Here, the LeLeLU is again scoring the best improvement over the baseline, with a significant boost of 4.9%. PReLU and ELU have demonstrated improvement in this example of 3.5% and 3.4% respectively, with the Tanh underperforming, as expected. Mish and Swish offer less significant improvement, whereas, SELU is the second runner-up, offering an improvement of 4%.

Overall, LeLeLU shows a consistent tendency to improve classification accuracy over the baseline ReLU, which is not the case for the other tested activation function. PReLU, which is very close to LeLeLU, shows very unstable performance with cases of serious underperformance. It is evident that the performance of all competing tested activation functions depends on the dataset used. Some might underperform or overperform the original ReLU function. Only the proposed LeLeLU seems to consistently offer an improvement in all tested cases. This clearly demonstrates that the addition of a controllable slope (parameter α) in the positive values area of the activation function has improved classification performance. This parameter also controls the speed of adaptation of positive values and seems to improve performance by either accelerating or slowing down learning, in contrast to the fixed slope for positive values of ReLU and PReLU.

Table 3. Test accuracy in the Sign Language dataset of the activation functions in question, using the corresponding neural network, and accuracy normalized to that attained by ReLU activation function.

Activation Function	Accuracy	Normalized Accuracy
ReLU	0.9073	100%
PReLU	0.8815	97.2%
Tanh	0.8522	93.9%
ELU	0.8721	96.1%
SELU	0.8196	93%
HardSigmoid	0.8586	97.4%
Mish	0.8974	101.8%
Swish	0.8947	101.5%
LeLeLU	**0.9353**	**103.2%**

Table 4. Test accuracy in the CIFAR-10 dataset of the activation functions in question, using the corresponding neural network, and accuracy normalized to that attained by ReLU activation function.

Activation Function	Accuracy	Normalized Accuracy
ReLU	0.6829	100%
PReLU	0.7094	103.5%
Tanh	0.6785	99.3%
ELU	0.7065	103.4%
SELU	0.7103	104%
HardSigmoid	0.6652	97.4%
Mish	0.6938	101.6%
Swish	0.6890	100.9%
LeLeLU	**0.7166**	**104.9%**

4.3. LeLeLU Performance in Larger Deep Neural Networks

In this section, we evaluate the performance of the proposed LeLeLU in more real-life deep network architectures, such as the VGG-16 and the *ResNet-v1-56*.

4.3.1. VGG-16 with LeLeLU

The first large neural network in our experimentation is the VGG-16, used to classify Cifar-10 and Cifar-100 datasets. The topology of the network and the results for different activation functions are also presented in Reference [17].

The CIFAR-100 dataset is an expansion of the Cifar-10. It has 100 classes, containing 600 images per class. From those 600 images per class, 500 are considered training images and 100 test images per class. The resolution of the images is also 32 by 32 pixels, the same as with Cifar-10.

The VGG-16 topology used in our work is the same with Reference [17], with two convolutional layers with 64 filters, followed by max pooling; two convolutional layers with 128 filters, followed by max pooling; three convolutional layers with 256 filters, followed by max pooling; and two similar blocks of three convolutional layers with 512 filters each, followed by max pooling, one after the other. The final layer is a classification layer. Figure 4 depicts the VGG-16 topology.

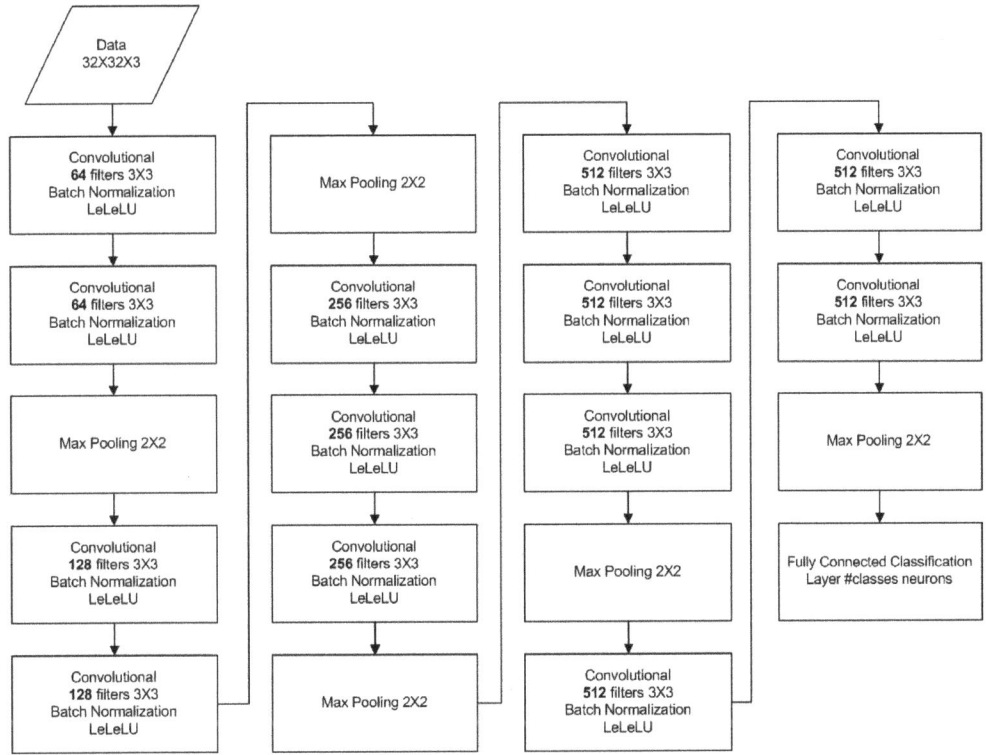

Figure 4. Neural networks VGG-16 topology that was employed for Cifar-10 and Cifar-100.

In Tables 5 and 6, we depict the performance of VGG-16 for Cifar10 and Cifar100 for various activation functions. We can easily see that the proposed function LeLeLU offers the best or the second best classification accuracy among the competing activation functions and a clear improvement over the widely used ReLU. More specifically, it offers the best performance for Cifar-10 and the second best for Cifar-100, behind ELU. However, it outperforms the more state-of-the-art Swish function, which is more prominent in the modern deep-learning literature. We preferred again to compare against simple activation functions with minimal computational complexity and adaptation. The ProbAct function that is proposed in Reference [17] yields a maximum of 0.8892 for Cifar10 and 0.5583 for Cifar100 for an element-wise bound trainable parameter σ (comparable to ours). Their score is better than LeLeLU in Cifar10, but far worse in Cifar100; however, it should also be noted that the parameter σ should be bound by another sigmoid function during adaptation (i.e., computational complexity) in order to stabilize the performance, which is far more complicated than our simple unbound adaptation rule.

4.3.2. ResNet-v1-56 with LeLeLU

In Reference [18], there is an extensive comparison of various activation functions, using the ResNet-v1-56 architecture for the classification of the Cifar-100 dataset. Here, we use the same topology and training methods as in Reference [18], along with the published results, to compare our proposed activation function. Again, in our comparison, we prefer baseline activation function with minimal complexity, such as the one proposed in this paper.

Table 7 contains the classification accuracy for CIFAR-100, along with the proposed function. The proposed LeLeLU activation function enables the network to better adapt to the complex dataset, having the highest classification accuracy in this test. Again, LeLeLU seems to perform better, as compared to modern counterparts, including Mish and Swish. It is also noteworthy that the complicated activation function produced by the genetic algorithm in Reference [18] for the ResNet-v1-56 architecture does not exceed accuracy of 0.7101.

Table 5. Test accuracy in the CIFAR-10 dataset of the activation functions in question, using the VGG-16 neural network, and accuracy normalized to that attained by ReLU activation function.

Activation Function	Accuracy	Normalized Accuracy
Sigmoid	0.1	11.46%
Tanh	0.1	11.46%
ReLU	0.8727	100%
Leaky ReLU	0.8649	99.1%
PReLU	0.8635	98.94%
ELU	0.8765	100.44%
SELU	0.8665	99.29%
Swish	0.8655	99.17%
LeLeLU	**0.8792**	**100.74%**

Table 6. Test accuracy in the CIFAR-100 dataset of the activation functions in question, using the VGG-16 neural network, and accuracy normalized to that attained by ReLU activation function.

Activation Function	Accuracy	Normalized Accuracy
Sigmoid	0.01	1.99%
Tanh	0.01	1.99%
ReLU	0.5294	100%
Leaky ReLU	0.4944	93.39%
PReLU	0.4630	87.46%
ELU	**0.5660**	**106.91%**
SELU	0.5152	97.31%
Swish	0.5401	102.02%
LeLeLU	0.5632	106.38%

Table 7. Test accuracy in the CIFAR-100 dataset of the activation functions in question, using the ResNet-v1-56 neural network, and accuracy normalized to that attained by ReLU activation function.

Activation Function	Accuracy	Normalized Accuracy
Sigmoid	0.3647	52.37%
HardSigmoid	0.3255	46.74%
ReLU	0.6964	100%
Leaky ReLU	0.6978	100.2%
GELU	0.7019	100.79%
PReLU	0.7223	103.72%
ELU	0.6967	100.04%
SELU	0.6852	98.39%
Mish	0.6988	100.34%
Swish	0.6968	100.06%
Softplus	0.6971	100.1%
Softsign	0.5838	83.83%
Tanh	0.6388	91.73%
LeLeLU	**0.7283**	**104.58%**

4.4. LeLeLU Performance vs. Dataset Complexity

In this section, we attempt to identify possible correlation between the gain in accuracy, offered by the proposed activation function LeLeLU, and the dataset used in the experiment.

We witnessed that in the previous experiments LeLeLU featured an increasing improvement in accuracy. Thus, we attempt to quantify the difference between the four datasets.

One feature of a dataset that we can identify is its complexity. We propose to estimate the complexity of the dataset by using an approximation of the Kolmogorov complexity theorem. Kolmogorov complexity can be defined for any information source. It can be shown [19–21] that, for the output of Markov information sources, Kolmogorov complexity is related to the entropy of the information source [22]. More precisely, the Kolmogorov complexity of the output of a Markov information source, normalized by the length of the output, converges most probably to the entropy of the source (since the output's length can be assumed to go to infinity) [23].

Based on this conclusion, we deduce that it is possible to evaluate the complexity of the dataset by using the product of the mean entropy of each sample and the bits required to represent every category (e.g., 7 for 80 classes). This method is very efficient, even in the case of large datasets. One could also employ only a representative amount of samples from each class and not the full dataset, without generally losing accuracy in the estimation of complexity. The following pseudocode (Algorithm 1) outlines the proposed procedure.

Algorithm 1 Dataset Complexity Estimation

Input: X_train data, number_of_classes
Output: Dataset_complexity
1   x_matrix is initialized to the X_train data
2   set number_of_classes to the number of classes of the classification problem
3   set number_of_training_files N to the number of training examples contained in the dataset
4   $T \leftarrow 0$
5   for each data sample in x_matrix
6   calculate the entropy E of the corresponding data sample
7       $T \leftarrow T + E$
8   end for
9   calculate mean entropy (ME): $ME \leftarrow T/N$
10 calculate the bits Q required to represent the number of classes
11 Dataset_complexity = ME × Q

We use the algorithm to estimate the complexity of each dataset used in our experiments. The findings are outlined in Table 8. It is clear that the complexity of each dataset correlates highly with the improvement offered by LeLeLU. Figure 5 depicts this finding in a logarithmic plot. We can clearly see that the more complex the dataset is, the bigger the improvement we can attain by using the proposed activation function. It also appears that the improvement is almost analogous to the logarithmic complexity of the dataset (see Figure 5. This implies that the adaptation of the parameter α for positive values helps the overall neural network to adapt faster to the complexity of the dataset, thus giving more improvement compared to the fixed non-adaptive baseline ReLU in more challenging problems.

Table 8. Complexity of each dataset of Section 4.2, given the above algorithm and the corresponding LeLeLU accuracy improvement.

Dataset	Complexity	LeLeLU Accuracy Improvement
MNIST	6.41	100.23%
Fashion MNIST	16.466	101.8%
Sign Language	33.584	103.2%
CIFAR-10	83.993	104.9%

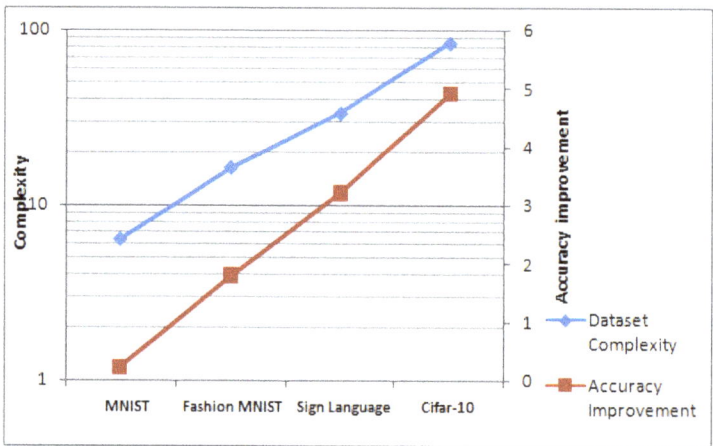

Figure 5. Correlation between the dataset's complexity and accuracy improvement.

In this section, we attempt to derive an empirical equation that provides an estimate of the accuracy improvement, offered by the LeLeLU over ReLU, given the complexity of the dataset. The equation that correlates the improvement over ReLU of the proposed function, based on our testing in small arbitrary topologies, is computed by finding the fit function of the two lines of Figure 5 and combining the two equations:

Let C denote the dataset complexity, and x the increasing integer identity of the dataset. The dataset complexity fit function can be estimated by exhaustive parameter search of an exponential function, as follows:

$$C = 3.159 e^{0.789x}$$
$$ln\left(\frac{C}{3.159}\right) = 0.789x \quad (21)$$
$$x = 1.267 ln\left(\frac{C}{3.159}\right)$$

Let *AccImpr* denote the accuracy improvement percentage. The accuracy improvement fit function can be estimated by linear fitting, as follows:

$$AccImpr = 1.54x - 2.018$$
$$x = \frac{AccImpr + 2.018}{1.54} \quad (22)$$

By combining Equations (20) and (21), we can conclude the following:

$$\frac{AccImpr + 2.018}{1.54} = 1.267 ln\left(\frac{C}{3.159}\right)$$
$$AccImpr = 1.54 * 1.267[ln(C) - ln(3.159)] - 2.018 \quad (23)$$
$$AccImpr = 1.951 ln(C) - 1.503 - 2.018$$

Thus, we end up with Equation (23), which yields the accuracy improvement offered by the proposed LeLeLU in terms of the dataset complexity. It is clear that Equation (23) is a monotonic rising function; that is, the more complex the dataset, the more accuracy improvement yielded the proposed LeLeLU.

$$AccImpr = 1.951 ln(C) - 3.521 \quad (23)$$

To verify the validity of Equation (23), we use the experiment of Cifar-100 with VGG-16, which was not used in the derivation of Equation (23). The Cifar-100 dataset has a complexity of 146.988, and the proposed function achieved an improvement of 6.38% over ReLU, as presented in Table 7. By substituting these figures in Equation (23), we can see that they verify Equation (23) very closely.

$$1.951 ln(146.988) - 3.521 = 6.215 \cong 6.38 \qquad (24)$$

In essence, Equation (23) provides a very good estimate of the LeLeLU's performance for any given dataset.

5. Discussion

The activation function is a core component in the neural network topology that affects both the behavior and computational complexity. By combining the best features of the ReLU family, we proposed the Learnable Leaky ReLU (LeLeLU), being linear and, thus, easily computable, while providing the parametric freedom to model the problem effectively. In our experiments, the proposed activation function consistently provided the best accuracy among the tested functions and datasets. It is very interesting that it features an almost analogous increase in accuracy gain to the complexity of the dataset. Thus, LeLeLU assists the network to adapt to the demands of challenging datasets, achieving almost analogous performance gain.

In the future, we will investigate methods to overcome the limitation of having to use batch normalization as a core component when implementing LeLeLU in a network. We will also investigate the effect of using higher-order polynomial versions of the original LeLeLU activation function and/or adding noisy perturbations in a similar manner to ProbAct [17].

Author Contributions: Conceptualization, A.M. and N.M.; methodology, A.M.; software, A.M.; validation, A.M.; formal analysis, A.M. and N.M.; writing—original draft preparation, A.M.; writing—review and editing, A.M. and N.M.; supervision, N.M. All authors have read and agreed to the published version of the manuscript.

Funding: This research received no external funding.

Institutional Review Board Statement: Not applicable.

Informed Consent Statement: Not applicable.

Data Availability Statement: The datasets used in this work can be found in the below publicly available links. MNIST dataset: http://yann.lecun.com/exdb/mnist/, accessed on 6 October 2021; Fashion MNIST dataset: https://github.com/zalandoresearch/fashion-mnist, accessed on 6 October 2021; Sign Language dataset: https://www.kaggle.com/datamunge/sign-language-mnist, accessed on 6 October 2021b; Cifar-10 dataset: https://www.kaggle.com/c/cifar-10, accessed on 6 October 2021; Cifar-100 dataset: https://www.kaggle.com/fedesoriano/cifar100, accessed on 6 October 2021.

Conflicts of Interest: The authors declare no conflict of interest.

References

1. Nair, V.; Hinton, G.E. Rectified Linear Units Improve Restricted Boltzmann Machines. In Proceedings of the 27th International Conference on International Conference on Machine Learning, 2010 ICML'10, Haifa, Israel, 21–24 June 2010; Omnipress: Madison, WI, USA; pp. 807–814, ISBN 9781605589077.
2. Maas, A.L.; Hannun, A.Y.; Ng, A.Y. Rectifier nonlinearities improve neural network acoustic models. In Proceedings of the 30th International Conference on Machine Learning, Atlanta, GA, USA, 16–21 June 2013; Volume 30.
3. He, K.; Zhang, X.; Ren, S.; Sun, J. Delving Deep into Rectifiers: Surpassing Human-Level Performance on ImageNet Classification. *arXiv* **2015**, arXiv:1502.01852.
4. Hendrycks, D.; Gimpel, K. Gaussian Error Linear Units (GELUs). *arXiv* **2016**, arXiv:1606.08415.
5. Ioffe, S.; Szegedy, C. Batch normalization: Accelerating deep network training by reducing internal covariate shift. *arXiv* **2015**, arXiv:1502.03167.

6. Srivastava, N.; Hinton, G.; Krizhevsky, A.; Sutskever, I.; Salakhutdinov, R. Dropout: A simple way to prevent neural networks from overfitting. *J. Mach. Learn. Res.* **2014**, *15*, 1929–1958.
7. Dugas, C.; Bengio, Y.; Bélisle, F.; Nadeau, C.; Garcia, R. Incorporating second-order functional knowledge for better option pricing. In *Advances in Neural Information Processing Systems*; The MIT Press: Cambridge, MA, USA, 2001; pp. 472–478.
8. Glorot, X.; Bordes, A.; Bengio, Y. Deep sparse rectifier neural networks. In Proceedings of the International Conference on Artificial Intelligence and Statistics, Fort Lauderdale, FL, USA, 11–13 April 2011.
9. Clevert, D.-A.; Unterthiner, T.; Hochreiter, S. Fast and Accurate Deep Network Learning by Exponential Linear Units (ELUs). *arXiv* **2015**, arXiv:1511.07289.
10. Klambauer, G.; Unterthiner, T.; Mayr, A.; Hochreiter, S. Self-normalizing neural networks. In Proceedings of the 31st International Conference on Neural Information Processing Systems, Long Beach, CA, USA, 4–9 December 2017; pp. 972–981.
11. Courbariaux, M.; Bengio, Y.; David, J.-P. BinaryConnect: Training deep neural networks with binary weights during propagations. In Proceedings of the NIPS'15: Proceedings of the 28th International Conference on Neural Information Processing Systems, Montreal, QC, Canada, 7–12 December 2015; Volume 2, pp. 3123–3131.
12. Ramachandran, P.; Zoph, B.; Le, Q.V. Swish: A Self-Gated Activation Function. *arXiv* **2017**, arXiv:1710.05941v1.
13. Misra, D.M. A self regularized non-monotonic neural activation function. *arXiv* **2019**, arXiv:1908.08681.
14. Maguolo, G.; Nanni, L.; Ghidoni, S. Ensemble of convolutional neural networks trained with different activation functions. *Expert Syst. Appl.* **2021**, *166*, 114048. [CrossRef]
15. Liang, S.; Lyu, L.; Wang, C.; Yang, H. Reproducing Activation Function for Deep Learning. *arXiv* **2021**, arXiv:2101.04844.
16. Zhou, Y.; Zhu, Z.; Zhong, Z. Learning specialized activation functions with the Piecewise Linear Unit. *arXiv* **2021**, arXiv:2104.03693.
17. Shridhar, K.; Lee, J.; Hayashi, H.; Mehta, P.; Iwana, B.K.; Kang, S.; Uchida, S.; Ahmed, S.; Dengel, A. ProbAct: A Probabilistic Activation Function for Deep Neural Networks. *arXiv* **2020**, arXiv:1905.10761v2.
18. Bingham, G.; Miikkulainen, R. Discovering Parametric Activation Functions. *arXiv* **2021**, arXiv:2006.03179v4.
19. Burgin, M. Generalized Kolmogorov complexity and duality in theory of computations. *Not. Russ. Acad. Sci.* **1982**, *25*, 19–23.
20. Kaltchenko, A. Algorithms for Estimating Information Distance with Application to Bioinformatics and Linguistics. *arXiv* **2004**, arXiv:cs.CC/0404039.
21. Vitányi, P.M.B. Conditional Kolmogorov complexity and universal probability. *Theor. Comput. Sci.* **2013**, *501*, 93–100. [CrossRef]
22. Solomonoff, R. *A Preliminary Report on a General Theory of Inductive Inference*; Report V-131; Office of Scientific Research, United States Air Force: Washington, DC, USA, 1960.
23. Jorma, R. *Information and Complexity in Statistical Modeling*; Springer: New York, NY, USA, 2007; p. 53, ISBN 978-0-387-68812.

Article

Interpreting Disentangled Representations of Person-Specific Convolutional Variational Autoencoders of Spatially Preserving EEG Topographic Maps via Clustering and Visual Plausibility

Taufique Ahmed and Luca Longo *

Artificial Intelligence and Cognitive Load Lab, The Applied Intelligence Research Centre, School of Computer Science, Technological University Dublin, D07 EWV4 Dublin, Ireland; taufique.ahmed@tudublin.ie
* Correspondence: luca.longo@tudublin.ie

Abstract: Dimensionality reduction and producing simple representations of electroencephalography (EEG) signals are challenging problems. Variational autoencoders (VAEs) have been employed for EEG data creation, augmentation, and automatic feature extraction. In most of the studies, VAE latent space interpretation is used to detect only the out-of-order distribution latent variable for anomaly detection. However, the interpretation and visualisation of all latent space components disclose information about how the model arrives at its conclusion. The main contribution of this study is interpreting the disentangled representation of VAE by activating only one latent component at a time, whereas the values for the remaining components are set to zero because it is the mean of the distribution. The results show that CNN-VAE works well, as indicated by matrices such as SSIM, MSE, MAE, and MAPE, along with SNR and correlation coefficient values throughout the architecture's input and output. Furthermore, visual plausibility and clustering demonstrate that each component contributes differently to capturing the generative factors in topographic maps. Our proposed pipeline adds to the body of knowledge by delivering a CNN-VAE-based latent space interpretation model. This helps us learn the model's decision and the importance of each component of latent space responsible for activating parts of the brain.

Keywords: electroencephalography; convolutional variational autoencoder; latent space interpretation; deep learning; spectral topographic maps

1. Introduction

Electroencephalography (EEG) is a method of recording brain activity (electrical potentials) using electrodes placed on the scalp [1]. It is generally known that EEG signals carry important information in the frequency, temporal, and spatial domains. EEG signals have been regularly used to diagnose a variety of mental disorders. However, analysis is difficult and decisions are tough to accept due to the low amplitude, complex collecting settings, and substantial noise [2]. EEG examines voltage variations in the order of microvolts caused by ionic currents within the neurons of the brain. Brain mapping is a neuroscience approach for exploring the advancement of understanding the structure and function of the human brain. EEG topography mapping (EEG topo-map) is a neuroimaging approach that uses a visual–spatial depiction to map the EEG signal. The EEG data from the electrodes is collected and processed into EEG topographical maps. The EEG topo-map visualises raw EEG data of voltage or power amplitude [3]. Some studies, for example, have converted EEG signals into topographic power head maps in order to preserve spatial information [4–6]. Topographic maps, on the other hand, are frequently redundant and contain significantly interpolated data between electrode locations. Many machine learning and deep learning algorithms have used temporal- and frequency-domain features to classify EEG signals. On the other hand, only a few studies combine the spatial and temporal dimensions of the

EEG signal. As a result, it is difficult to build efficient algorithms using features based on prior information. Therefore, the 2D convolutional neural network (CNN) is utilised to learn EEG features across diverse mental tasks without previous knowledge [7]. There are many techniques that have been employed to reduce their dimensionality and automatically learn essential features. The tensor-decomposition-based dimensionality reduction algorithm, transforms the CNN input tensor into a concise set of slices [8]. Another popular dimensionality reduction technique is spatial filtering. The performance of various spatial filtering techniques has been evaluated on the test set. These spatial filtering techniques extract EEG nonstationarity features that cause model accuracy to deteriorate even after 30 min of resting. These feature changes had varying effects on the spatial filtering algorithms chosen [9]. They also rely on a restricted number of channels because they restrict us from investigating the neural plausibility of the derived features in greater depth. EEG is referred to as a nonstationary signal since it fluctuates from subject to subject, and even from one recording session to the next for the same person [10,11]. The generative network accepts random noise from a certain distribution (e.g., Gaussian) and aims to generate synthetic data that is identical to real data. Since generative networks are sensitive to image generation, significant features from EEG signals are retrieved as images and used as the model's input [12]. An autoencoder (AE) is a deep learning neural network architecture that uses unsupervised learning to learn efficient features without using labelled input. These features, also known as latent spaces, are often lower in dimension than the original input and are utilised to reconstruct it with high fidelity [13]. During the encoding stage, a neural network uses a set of encoding parameters $\theta = \{W, b\}$ to translate the input x to a hidden representation $y = f_\theta(x) = s(Wx + b)$. Secondly, by using decoding parameters $\theta' = \{W', b'\}$, the hidden representation y is mapped to the reconstructed vector $z = g_{\theta'}(y) = s(W'y + b')$ [14].

A variational autoencoder (VAE) is a form of autoencoder that creates a probabilistic model of the input sample and then reconstructs it using that model. As a result, VAEs can be employed to generate synthetic data [15]. VAEs have shown a wide application with electroencephalographic (EEG) signals [16–18]. VAEs employ convolutional processes on input topographic maps to learn prominent high-level features that are lower in dimension, as shown in Figure 1. These high-level features are more portable because they do not require a large amount of digital memory to be stored. This lower level also includes useful and prominent representations of EEG data that can be used for a variety of reasons.

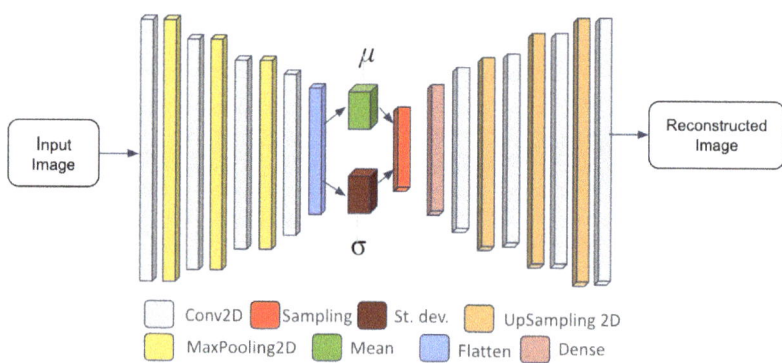

Figure 1. The structure of a variational autoencoder (VAE) leverages convolutional methods on input data that maps these data into the parameters of a probability distribution, such as the mean and the variance of a Gaussian distribution.

In the recent literature, the VAE has been employed for EEG data creation, augmentation, denoising, and automatic feature extraction. However, little research has been conducted into how the VAE model arrives at its conclusions.

The primary contribution of this study is to understand the significance of each latent space component of a convolutional variational autoencoder (CNN-VAE) trained with spatially preserved EEG topographic maps which influence the generative factors in EEG topographic maps. This can be achieved by interpreting the disentangled representation of a VAE by activating just one latent component at a time and setting the remaining components to zero, because it represents the distribution's mean. Disentangling the representation of CNN-VAE provides meaningful visualisations that aid in understanding which component of latent space is responsible for capturing which region of brain activation in EEG topographic maps. The learned CNN-VAE model is assessed by computing the SNR for actual and reconstructed EEG signals when the decoder network is trained with all latent components. Furthermore, it is also assessed by computing the average and channel-wise correlation values between the actual and the reconstructed signals with one active component at a time.

The proposed approach advances in the field of explainable artificial intelligence (XAI) by interpreting and disentangling the representation of VAE to understand the model's conclusion. In this study, the goal is to tackle the research problem of learning the importance of each latent component of VAE trained with spectral topographic EEG maps. Therefore, the research question being addressed is:

RQ: *Can a convolutional variational autoencoder (CNN-VAE) trained with spectral topographic maps and interpreting its disentangled representation disclose its decision?*

The rest of the work is organised as follows. Section 2 investigates related work on VAE latent space representation and interpretation, whereas Section 3 describes an empirical study and its methodology to answer the above research question. Section 4 presents the experimental results and findings. Section 5 represents the discussion. Finally, Section 6 concludes the manuscript by describing the contribution to the body of knowledge and highlighting future work directions.

2. Related Work

Traditional autoencoders (AEs) aim to learn prominent latent representations from unlabelled input while ignoring irrelevant features. As a result, the reconstructed data will be identical to the input data. Variational autoencoders (VAEs) were recently proposed as an effective extension of AEs, for modelling a dataset's probability distribution and learning a latent space, usually of a lower dimension, without explicit supervision [19]. In detail, this latent space is not composed of a fixed vector, but of a mixture of distributions. A VAE allows us to encode an input x to a latent vector $z = Encoder(x) \sim q(z \mid x)$ using an encoder network, and then use another network to decode this latent vector z back to a shape that is as close as possible to the original input data $\tilde{x} = Decoder(z) \sim p(x \mid z)$. In other words, the goal is to maximise the marginal log-likelihood of each observation in x, and the VAE reconstruction loss $\mathcal{L}_{rec}$ to the negative anticipated log-likelihood of the observations x [19], as in the following:

$$\mathcal{L}_{rec} = -\mathbb{E}_{q(z|x)}[\log p(x \mid z)] \qquad (1)$$

The performance of machine learning algorithms is often dependent on data representation because it can entangle and disguise many explanatory aspects of variations hidden beneath the data. VAE-based latent space analysis and decoding of EEG signals are important since they can precisely define and determine the relevant latent features [20]. Therefore, the VAE model gives a closed-form latent space representation of the distribution underlying the input data, which is ideal for unsupervised learning in order to understand the significance of each latent component in terms of capturing the number of true generative factors. In order to understand the VAE's decision, its disentangled representation must be interpreted and visualised. The following sub-section examines previous research on the interpretation of latent space representations.

2.1. Interpreting the VAE Disentangling Representations

This section includes a literature review on interpreting and disentangling the latent space of a VAE to understand its decision toward reconstruction capacity. The learned representation must be interpreted because the latent component is simple to understand. Therefore, the models based on latent representations, such as VAE, have recently emerged as powerful tools in this domain since their latent space can encode crucial hidden variables in the input data. A VAE requires the typical Gaussian distribution as a prior in the latent space; because all codes tend to follow the same prior they frequently suffer from posterior collapse [21]. The disentanglement is a condition of the latent space in which each latent variable is sensitive to changes in only one feature while being insensitive to changes in the others [13]. There are several ways to learn a disentangled latent space [13]. However, approaches that exploit the VAE structure are of special importance to our work. The disentangled latent variables have been applied successfully in a variety of applications, including face recognition [22], video prediction [23], and anomaly detection [24]. Another recent study uses VAE for anomaly detection, in which the latent space is partially disentangled and interpreted, with a few latent variables capturing the majority of the feature's information and others encoding little information. As a result, the degree to which the latent space representations are disentangled must be quantified [25]. The disentangled representation of the VAE is mostly interpreted to determine the components of latent space that influence the capture of artefacts in data. This method is based on determining the latent variable's out-of-order distribution (OOD). This can be accomplished by calculating the KL divergence of the images [26]. This is the difference between the generated latent distribution and the standard normal distribution ($\mu = 0, \sigma = 1$). The researcher provides one such definition, defining it as the degree to which a latent dimension $d \in D$ in a representation predicts a true generative component $k \in K$, with each latent dimension capturing no more than one generative factor [27]. Therefore, manually adjusting the latent space component of the VAE enables the user to examine how different latent values affected the outcome of the model [28]. The researcher also illustrated how a VAE model's latent space might be made more explainable by utilising latent space regularisation to force some selected dimensions of the latent space to map to meaningful musical qualities. Furthermore, a user interface feedback loop is provided to allow individuals to edit the parameters of the latent space and see the results of these changes in real time [29]. In another study, an attribute-regularized VAE (AR-VAE) is used, which employs a new supervised training method to generate structured latent spaces in which specified attributes are compelled to be embedded along specific dimensions of the latent space. The resulting latent spaces are simply interpretable and allow for the manipulation of individual properties via simple traversals along the regularised dimensions [30].

2.2. Interpretation of Latent Space for Cluster Analysis

Disentangling representations of generative adversarial networks (GANs) for clustering analysis have been intensively investigated to address the high-dimensionality issue associated with data. All latent components form a single large cluster, making them difficult to use for OOD or anomaly detection [26,31]. Therefore, the interpretation of latent space forms several smaller clusters of single latent variables if the features are independent. Such disentangled latent variables have been successfully used in several tasks such as face recognition [22] and anomaly detection. A new clustering approach called disentangling latent space clustering (DLS-clustering) directly learns cluster assignments using disentangled latent spacing without the use of extra clustering techniques. The latent space is split into two pieces by the disentangling process: discrete one-hot latent variables that are directly linked to categorical data and continuous latent variables that are linked to other sources of variation, which immediately results in clusters [32,33]. The researchers suggest an image-clustering method based on VAEs using a Gaussian mixture model (GMM) prior, with each component representing a cluster. The prior is learnt in conjunction with the posterior, which in turn learns a robust latent representation, resulting in an accurate clustering [34].

The interpretation of the VAE's disentangling representation is commonly utilised to improve the accuracy of classification tasks and a wide range of applications such as face recognition, video prediction, and anomaly detection. It is also used in cluster analysis to discover the OOD latent variable that drives the artefacts. The majority of the disentangled representation is examined in order to identify the single OOD latent variable. As a result, it will be useful for anomaly detection. Understanding the decision of the VAE, on the other hand, requires knowledge of the contribution of all latent variables to the VAE's reconstruction capacity. Understanding the significance of each latent component in spatially preserving EEG topographic maps via visual plausibility, clustering, and correlation values across the architecture's input and output remains a challenge.

3. Materials and Methods

In this study, if CNN-VAE is trained with spatially preserved EEG topographic maps, it provides a similar SNR for actual and reconstructed EEG signals and a higher and more positive correlation across the input and output of the architecture. Additionally, interpretation and visualisation of the learnt latent space representation provide knowledge of how well each latent component contributes to capturing the number of true generative factors in EEG topographic maps via clustering and visual plausibility. The detailed design of this research is illustrated in Figure 2, and the following sections describe its components.

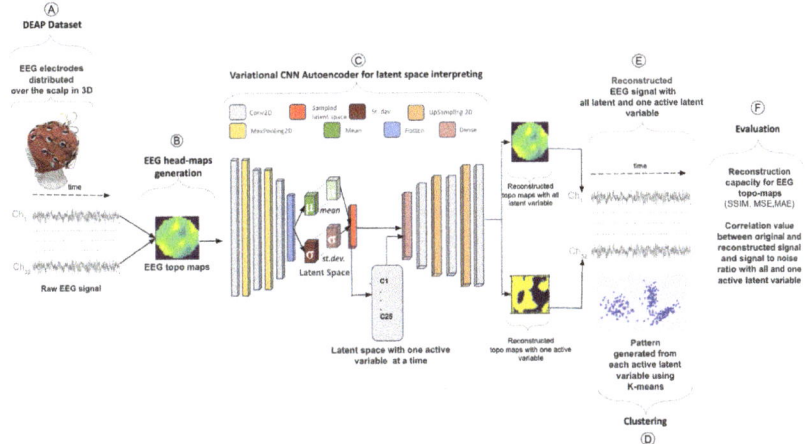

Figure 2. A pipeline for spatially preserving EEG topographic map generation and interpreting the latent space of CNN-VAE via clustering and visual plausibility. (**A**) The DEAP dataset was used to build a CNN-VAE from EEG signals. (**B**) EEG topographic head maps of size 40 × 40 generation. (**C**) A CNN-VAE model is learnt for a variable by variable interpretation of the latent space. (**D**) Clustering for visualising the learnt pattern from each active latent component. (**E**) Reconstruction of the signals from 32 electrode coordinate values of EEG topographic maps. (**F**) Evaluation of the model for reconstructed topographic maps as well as the signal.

3.1. Dataset

DEAP: The DEAP dataset was chosen because it contains multi-channel EEG recordings with a large number of participants and tasks. EEG data were collected from 32 persons who watched 40 one-minute music video clips [35]. Following a 60-s music clip, each participant was asked to rate a video. Each film was scored on a 1–9 scale for dominance, like/dislike, valence, familiarity, and arousal. The standard 10–20 systems were applied with the following 32 electrode positions: 'Fp1', 'AF3', 'F7', 'F3', 'FC1', 'FC5', 'T7', 'C3', 'CP1', 'CP5', 'P7', 'P3', 'Pz', 'PO3', 'O1', 'Oz', 'O2', 'PO4', 'P4', 'P8', 'CP6', 'CP2', 'C4', 'T8', 'FC6', 'FC2', 'F4', 'F8', 'AF4', 'Fp2', 'Fz', 'Cz'. Pre-processing comprised signal re-sampling at 128 Hz and a band-pass frequency filter that operated in the 1–50 Hz range.

3.2. EEG Topographic Head Maps Generation

Raw EEG signals were used in this stage to build spatially preserving EEG topographic maps. Before creating topographic maps, empirical tests were carried out to determine the best size of the topographic map that preserves spatial information about brain activation. This was performed by converting 3D to 2D polar to Cartesian coordinates and computing Euclidian distances between each channel in 2D polar to Cartesian coordinates as well as in 2D interpolated topographic map channel indexes. The results reveal that an image shape of 40×40 is the best form, with the smallest average difference between the electrode placements of 3D to 2D polar to Cartesian coordinates and 2D topographic map channel indexes. In addition, a 40×40 empty (with zeros) topographic map and a 2D edgeless image from the channel values are constructed. Finally, this 2D map is interpolated to produce maps of size 40×40, as illustrated in Figure 2B.

3.3. A Convolutional Variational Autoencoder

Following the creation of the topographic maps, a convolutional variational autoencoder (CNN-VAE) is built with the goal of converting input data into probability distribution parameters such as the mean and standard deviation of a Gaussian distribution. The CNN-VAE of the proposed pipeline can be considered general enough to be used in finding simpler representations of data for analysis because this method generates a continuous, organised latent space that provides salient features of the data without losing information [36]. The learnt latent space representation is the simple form of the data, its visualisation and interpretation help us to understand the model's decision. The CNN-VAE design consists of the following elements:

- The encoder is a neural network that takes a 40×40 tensor (as seen in Figure 2C) and defines the approximate posterior distribution $Q(Z \mid x)$, where x is the input tensor and Z is the latent space. The network will create the mean and standard deviation parameters of a factorised Gaussian with the latent space dimension of 25 by simply expressing the distribution as a diagonal Gaussian. This latent space dimension is the minimal dimension that leads to the maximum reconstruction capacity of the input EEG images. A similar experiment has been conducted on the EEG image shape of $32 \times 32 \times 5$, where the latent dimension 28 is considered as the minimal dimension that leads to the maximum reconstruction capacity of the input and maximum utility for classification tasks [5]. This architecture (Figure 2C) is made up of three 2D convolutional layers, each followed by a max pooling layer to minimise the dimension of the feature maps. In each convolutional layer, ReLU is employed as the activation function.
- The CNN-VAE decoder is a generative network that takes a latent space Z as input and returns the parameters for the observation's conditional distribution $P(x \mid Z)$ (as illustrated in the right side of Figure 2C). In this experiment, there are 2 different ways to train the decoder network. One is training it with latent space, utilising all variable values. The other way is to train with latent space where only one variable is active and has the latent sampled value, and all other variable values are set to zero, because zero is the mean of the distribution for each variable in the latent space. Similarly to the encoder network, the decoder is made up of three 2D convolutional layers, each followed by an up-sampling layer to reconstruct the data to the shape of the original input. In each convolutional layer, ReLU is employed as an activation function to regularise the neural network.

- By sampling from the latent distribution described by the encoder's parameters, the reparameterisation approach is utilised to provide a sample for the decoder. Because the backpropagation method in CNN-VAE cannot flow through a random sample node, sampling activities create a bottleneck. To remedy this, the reparameterisation technique is used to estimate the latent space Z using the decoder parameters plus one more, the ϵ parameter:

$$Z = \mu + \sigma \odot \epsilon \qquad (2)$$

where μ and σ are the mean and standard deviation of a Gaussian distribution, respectively, and ϵ is random noise used to maintain the stochasticity of Z. The latent space is now created using a function of μ, σ, and ϵ, allowing the model to backpropagate gradients in the encoder through μ and σ while retaining stochasticity through ϵ.

- A loss function is used to optimise the CNN-VAEs in order to ensure that the latent space is both continuous and complete, the same as in our previous experiment [5]. Traditional VAE employs the binary cross-entropy loss function in conjunction with the Kullback–Leibler divergence loss, which is a measure of how two probability distributions differ from one another [37]. In this experiment, a new type of divergence known as maximum mean discrepancy (MMD) is introduced. The notion behind MMD is that two distributions are similar if and only if all of their moments are the same. As a result, KL-divergence is used to determine how "different" the moments of two distributions, $p(z)$ and $q(z)$ are from one another [38]. MMD can achieve this effectively using the kernel embedding trick:

$$\text{MMD}(p(z) \| q(z)) = \mathbb{E}_{p(z),p(z')}\left[k(z,z')\right] + \mathbb{E}_{q(z),q(z')}\left[k(z,z')\right] - \\ 2\mathbb{E}_{p(z),q(z')}\left[k(z,z')\right] \qquad (3)$$

where $k(z, z')$ can be any universal kernel, such as Gaussian. A kernel can be thought of as a function that compares the "similarity" of two samples. It has a high value when two samples are similar and a low value when they are dissimilar.

This CNN-VAE architecture is trained using a randomly picked 70% of 200,000 data samples from a single person, with the remaining 30% divided into validation and testing. To avoid overfitting, an early stopping strategy with a patience value of ten epochs is used, which indicates that training is stopped if the validation loss does not improve for ten consecutive epochs.

3.4. Clustering for Generative Factor Analysis

As shown in Figure 2C, the decoder network is trained with all of the values in the latent space and also trained with only one component value of the latent space, and the remaining latent variable is set to zero to test the impact of each component on capturing the generative factors. To examine the number of generative factors captured from each active latent component, the reconstructed EEG topographic map from the decoder of CNN-VAE is passed as an input to the k-means algorithm. The silhouette score is calculated to determine how well the reconstructed EEG topographic maps cluster with other topo maps. This score allows us to see how many clusters were created and how many patterns were learnt from each latent component, as shown in Figure 2D.

3.5. Reconstructed EEG Signals

The reconstructed EEG topo maps produced by each latent component are converted into EEG signals by reading only the pixel values corresponding to the 32 electrodes. Following that, for each channel in the signal, the correlation values between the actual and raw signals are computed. Furthermore, the average SNR for the test data is calculated as shown in Figure 2E.

3.6. Models Evaluation

To assess the performance of CNN-VAE, evaluation metrics must be defined. The reconstruction capacity of CNN-VAE is considered in two stages.

3.6.1. Evaluation of Reconstructed EEG Topographic Maps

The reconstruction capacity of the learnt CNN-VAE models was assessed against previously unseen testing data using the structural similarity index (SSIM), mean absolute error (MAE), and mean squared error (MSE).

- **SSIM**: This is a perceptual metric that measures how much image quality is lost as a result of processing, including data compression. It is an index of structural similarity (in the real range [0, 1] between two topographic maps (images) [39]). Values close to 1 indicate that the two topographic maps are very structurally similar, whereas values close to 0 indicate that the two images are exceptionally dissimilar and structurally different.
- **MAE**: The average variance between the significant values in the dataset and the projected values in the same dataset is defined as the mean absolute error (MAE) [40].
- **MSE**: This is defined as the mean (average) of the square of the difference between the actual and reconstructed values: a lower value indicates a better fit. In this case, the MSE involves the comparison, pixel by pixel, of the original and reconstructed topographic maps [39].

3.6.2. Evaluation of Reconstructed EEG Signals

- **Correlation coefficient**: The correlation coefficient is a statistical measure of the strength of a two-variable linear relationship. Its values might range between -1 and 1. A positive correlation is represented by a number close to 1 [41].
- **Signal-to-noise ratio (SNR)**: An SNR is a measurement that compares the signal's real information to the noise in the signal. It is defined as the ratio of the signal power to noise power in a signal [42].

The formula for calculating an SNR is

$$SNR = 20 \log_{10} \left(\frac{S}{N} \right)$$

$$S = \sqrt{\frac{\sum (\text{signal})^{\wedge} 2}{\text{len(signal)}}} \quad N = \sqrt{\frac{\sum (\text{noise})^{\wedge} 2}{\text{len(noise)}}}$$

4. Results

This section presents the findings of the following empirical studies. First, investigating the appropriate size for EEG topographic maps. Second, the CNN-VAE model's performance in terms of reconstruction capacity for topographic images and EEG signals. Third, as indicated in Section 3.3, interpreting the disentangled representation of CNN-VAE utilising cluster analysis and coefficient of correlation across the input and output of the architecture.

All these empirical results help us find the impact of each VAE latent component on capturing the generative patterns of EEG signals.

4.1. Examining the Size of the EEG Topographic Maps

Figure 3 depicts the average Euclidian distances calculated between each channel in 2D polar to Cartesian coordinates as well as in 2D interpolated topographic map channel indexes ranging in size from 26×26 to 64×64. The results show that the image size 40×40 has the smallest average difference between electrode placements in 2D polar to Cartesian coordinates and 2D generated topo maps channel indexes. Additionally, increasing the image size has no effect on the average distance between the channels. These findings suggest that the image size of 40 × 40 retained the most spatial information of the EEG topo maps, which will be used as training data for the CNN-VAE in Section 3.3.

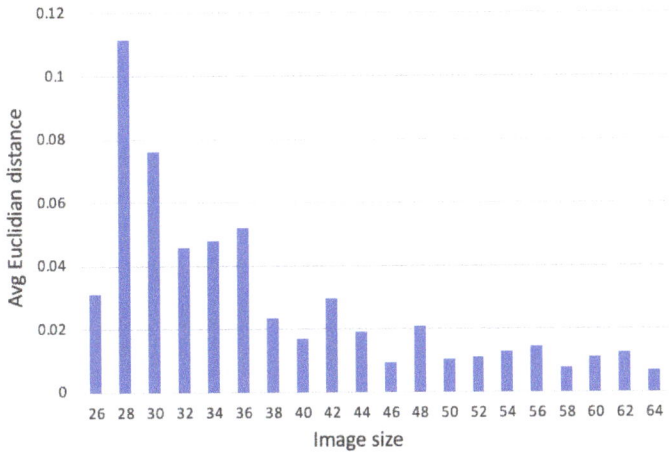

Figure 3. An example of average Euclidian distance computed from channel index of topographic maps ranging in size from 26 to 64.

4.2. Reconstruction Capacity of CNN-VAE Model

Two scenarios are used to describe the CNN-VAE model's reconstruction capabilities. One contains reconstructed EEG topography maps, while the other has reconstructed EEG signals. As described in Section 3.3, the decoder is trained with all latent variables as well as with only one active latent variable at a time, with the rest of the variables retained as zeros, because the empirical findings demonstrate that the mean of the latent space distribution for all latent components tends to be zero, shown in Figure A1, Appendix A. The distribution of the first four latent space components is depicted in Figure 4.

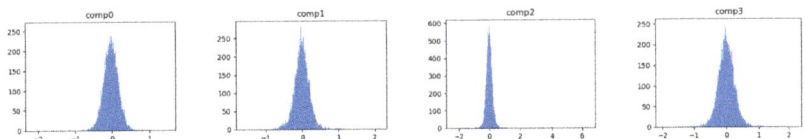

Figure 4. Distribution of the four latent spaces when one latent component is active at a time.

Table 1 shows the SSIM, MSE, MAE, and MAPE scores of the CNN-VAE models on unseen testing data, where this model was trained on 200,000 EEG topographic images with a latent space dimension of 25 and associated with one participant. It is feasible to observe that when all of the components in the latent space are used as input to the decoder, the SSIM value approaches one and the MSE, MAE, and MAPE values approach zero. This shows that CNN-VAE is functioning well in terms of topographic image reconstruction. Following that, the reconstructed EEG topo maps are transformed into EEG signals by reading only the pixel values corresponding to the 32 electrodes. The results demonstrate that all of the reconstructed signal channel data have a substantial positive correlation with the original raw data. Figure 5 depicts the signal from the T7 and P7 channels, as well as their correlation values with the original data's channel values. This finding strongly confirms that the reconstructed signals are semantically similar to the original signal. Subsequently, the signal-to-noise ratio (SNR) for each channel of the original and reconstructed test data is computed. The result also shows that the reconstruction capacity of CNN-VAE is performing well because the SNR values are identical to each other when the decoder is trained with all latent components, shown in Figure 6.

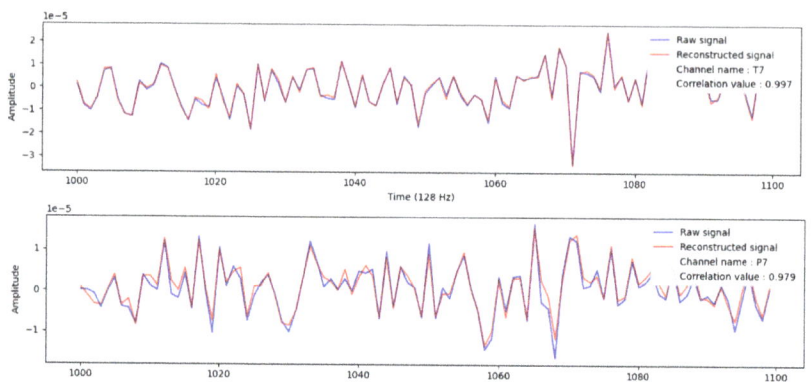

Figure 5. Signal from the T7 and P7 channels, as well as their correlation values with the original data's channel values.

Table 1. An example of the SSIM, MSE, MAE, MAPE, SNR, average correlation, and a number of clusters generated after interpreting the latent space of a one-person-specific convolutional variational autoencoder (CNN-VAE) on testing data.

Comp	SSIM	MSE	MAE	MAPE	SNR	AvgCorr	Cluster
C 1-25	1.0000	0.000000103	0.00019	0.00042	0.36697883	0.994	
C1	0.9969	0.0000375	0.00296	0.00484	0.108	0.107	2
C2	0.9970	0.0000369	0.00292	0.00478	0.092	0.134	3
C3	0.9969	0.0000374	0.00296	0.00484	0.107	0.119	2
C4	0.9969	0.0000376	0.00296	0.00485	1.241	0.095	3
C5	0.9973	0.0000309	0.00290	0.00474	0.114	0.267	2
C6	0.9971	0.0000341	0.00286	0.00467	0.117	0.236	2
C7	0.9970	0.0000353	0.00287	0.00470	0.096	0.283	2
C8	0.9969	0.0000373	0.00294	0.00481	0.153	0.118	2
C9	0.9969	0.0000374	0.00295	0.00482	0.112	0.14	2
C10	0.9971	0.0000352	0.00287	0.00470	0.099	0.231	2
C11	0.9969	0.0000373	0.00296	0.00483	0.103	0.116	2
C12	0.9969	0.0000376	0.00296	0.00484	0.088	0.09	2
C13	0.9971	0.0000351	0.00283	0.00463	0.11	0.278	2
C14	0.9969	0.0000377	0.00297	0.00486	0.058	0.089	2
C15	0.9974	0.0000295	0.00283	0.00463	0.115	0.294	2
C16	0.9970	0.000036	0.00285	0.00467	0.1	0.223	2
C17	0.9970	0.0000347	0.00280	0.00459	0.099	0.302	2
C18	0.9969	0.0000374	0.00296	0.00485	0.096	0.136	2
C19	0.9969	0.0000374	0.00295	0.00483	0.107	0.125	2
C20	0.9969	0.0000374	0.00295	0.00483	0.304	0.123	2
C21	0.9970	0.0000368	0.00294	0.00480	0.104	0.126	2
C22	0.9970	0.0000374	0.00296	0.00484	0.115	0.099	2
C23	0.9970	0.0000358	0.00291	0.00475	0.085	0.176	2
C24	0.9969	0.0000379	0.00298	0.00487	0.103	0.092	3
C25	0.9969	0.0000377	0.00297	0.00485	0.133	0.112	2

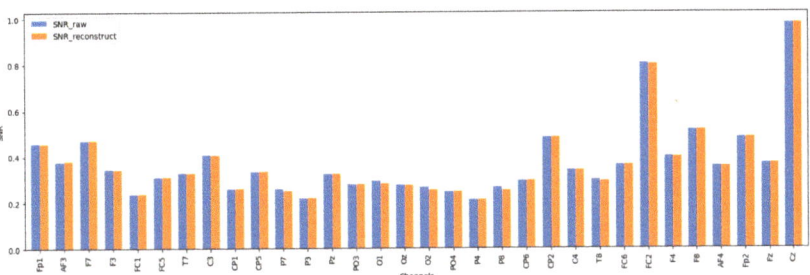

Figure 6. SNR for each channel of the original and reconstructed test data.

Similar to the first scenario, the reconstruction capacity of CNN-VAE, where its decoder network is trained only with one latent component alternatively and the remaining 24 components are set to zero, is also investigated to examine the impact of each latent variable on generating the patterns in the EEG topo maps. The results show that each latent variable contributes differently to capturing the generated aspects in topo maps. Furthermore, the reconstruction capacity of CNN-VAE is evaluated using metrics such as SSIM, MSE, MAE, and MAPE, where the SSIM value approaches one and the MSE, MAE, and MAPE values approach zero, as shown in Table 1.

4.3. Interpreting and Visualising the Latent Space

This section describes the results obtained from interpreting the disentangled representation of CNN-VAE via visual plausibility and cluster analysis (Section 4.2). An empirical experiment was carried out using test data, with 10 samples chosen at random to assess the impact of each latent component in capturing the number of true generative factors in spatially preserving EEG topographic maps. Figure 7 depicts ten images of test data and reconstructed images with active latent space components 0 and 1, with visual plausibility results clearly indicating that each component is learning two to three patterns from those EEG topographic maps. To validate these findings, k-means clustering with the silhouette visualiser is used to demonstrate the contribution of each latent component to capturing the patterns in EEG topographic maps, which provides the exact number of generated patterns from each active component. The results show that each component in the latent space is responsible for generating a minimum of two patterns in the EEG topographic maps shown in Figure 8.

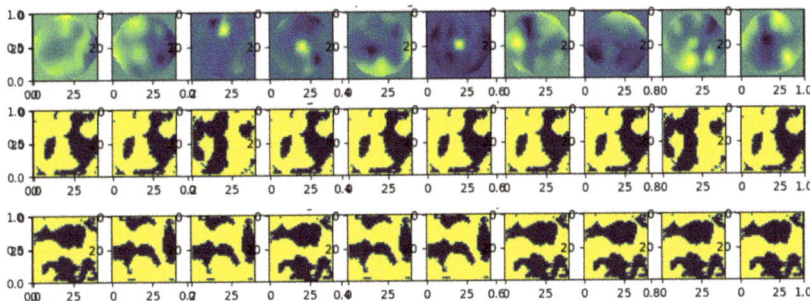

Figure 7. Randomly selected 10 samples of actual and reconstructed topo maps with active components 0 and 1 of the latent space.

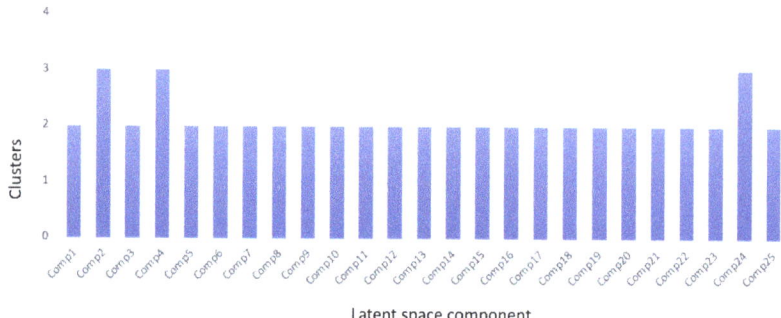

Figure 8. Cluster analysis on reconstructed test EEG topo maps generated from each latent space active component.

Finally, the reconstructed signal generated when setting up only one latent active component is transformed into EEG signals. In addition, 25 plots are generated to show the correlation values for each latent component grouped with all channels, shown in Figures A1 and A2. Similarly, 32 plots for the correlation value for each channel aggregated with all components are generated; however, because of space constraints, only the top 25 plots for each channel are given in Appendix A, Figure A3. To make the decision of CNN-VAE easier to understand, the critical analysis was performed by activating only one latent component at a time. The resultant reconstruction EEG topo maps with each active latent component are coloured blue and yellow, where blue indicates it has some value that indicates the particular region of the brain in the topographic map is captured, and yellow represents an image filled with zeros. With latent component 0, the findings show that channel 'FP1' has a negative correlation while channel 'AF4' has a positive correlation with the original data, as shown in Figure 9. According to these findings, shown in the second row of Figure 7, and referencing with the 10–20 system of electrode placement used to describe the location of scalp electrodes in Figure 10, it is clearly indicated that component 0 of the latent space is less significant for acquiring left and right frontal pole in EEG topo maps.

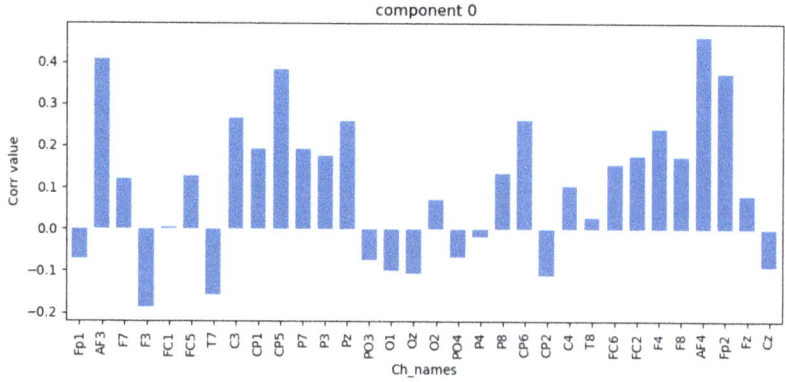

Figure 9. Correlation values computed between original and reconstructed signals generated with latent space component 0.

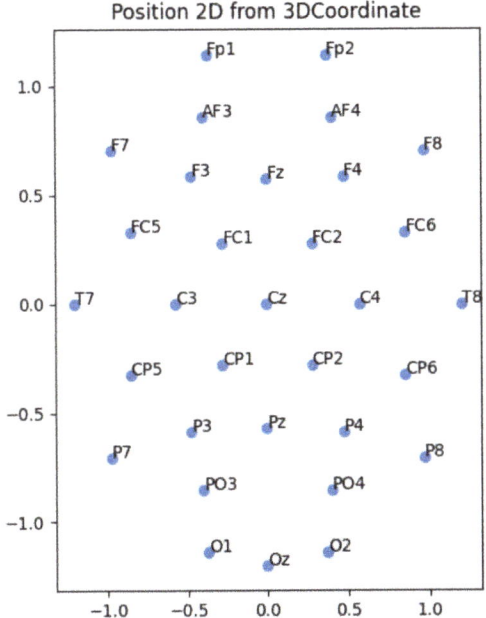

Figure 10. 10–20 system of electrode placement in EEG topographic maps of size 40 × 40.

5. Discussion

The results showed that when a CNN-VAE is trained with topographic maps of shape (40, 40) comprising 1600 overall values produced from 32 electrode values, the size of the maps can be reduced by up to 99% without losing salient information. In other words, each person-specific VAE may learn a latent space of up to 25 means and 25 standard deviations from a tensor of 1600 values without losing meaning, as measured by SSIM, MSE, MAE, and MAPE, between the original and reconstructed tensors.

The interpretation of CNN-VAE disentangled representation using visual plausibility and clustering analysis clearly shows that each component learns two to three patterns from those EEG topographic maps. These findings support the initial hypothesis, indicating that if CNN-VAE is trained with spatially preserved EEG topographic maps, it offers equivalent SNR and a stronger positive correlation between the architecture's input and output EEG signal. Furthermore, the interpretation and visualisation of the learnt latent space representation aid in understanding the model's choice.

The proposed pipeline for transforming EEG signals into a spatially preserved EEG topographic map, reconstructing EEG signals using CNN-VAE, and understanding the importance of each component in the latent space, as designed in Figure 2, has various advantages. To begin, convert the EEG signal into topographic maps that show the spatial distribution of the brain's electrical activity. This study used DEAP data to train our model because it contains multi-channel EEG recordings with a large number of participants and tasks with 32 channels. This pipeline may easily be applied with various numbers of electrodes and can generate topographic maps of any size with other emotion datasets such as SEED and DREAMER. Since our pipeline produces topographic maps of 40 × 40 with 32 channels, it can also produce maps of the same size with a larger number of electrodes. Secondly, training CNN-VAE with EEG topographic maps yields latent space, which is a set of prominent high-level features with a lower dimension. This bottom dimension provides useful and salient EEG data representations that can be used to generate synthetic EEG topographic head maps for data augmentation and employability in a variety of classification tasks. Third, interpreting their latent space allows us to create useful visualisations that aid in the analysis of outcomes obtained in training a CNN-VAE with EEG signals. Interpreting the learned latent space helps us to understand the decisions of CNN-VAE and find the artefactual component in the CNN-VAE of latent space. Therefore, this method can be used for any kind of anomaly detection task. Since our suggested pipeline supports disentangled representation interpretation, it enables us to construct the required region of the image by manually setting up the latent space component. As a result, users can generate various images based on a single input image. The findings obtained from this proposed pipeline can be used to gain the trust of stakeholders by demonstrating the visual plausibility of each latent component in capturing the generative components in EEG topographic maps.

Aside from the implications, our suggested pipeline has some constraints because human brains are complex nonlinear systems generating nonstationary nonlinear signals [10]. Therefore, generating factors from each component vary from subject to subject, as do the number of electrodes and shape of the topographic maps employed. This pipeline requires human intervention to analyse and interpret its latent space. In future work, the interpretation of latent space must be performed automatically without human intervention to analyse the data from all participants with varied numbers of channels and topographic map sizes.

6. Conclusions

Researchers have designed and implemented different methods for interpreting the latent space of VAE. Most of the methods are used to improve the accuracy of classification tasks in a wide range of applications such as face recognition, video prediction, and anomaly detection. In most of the studies, its latent space interpretation is used to detect only the OOD latent variable for cluster analysis. However, understanding the decision of VAE requires investigating the significance of each latent component in the model's decision. Therefore, interpreting its latent space via visual plausibility and clustering remains inadequate. The purpose of this study was to address this research challenge. An experiment has been conducted using an existing EEG dataset (DEAP) to understand the importance of each latent component of person-specific VAE. A CNN-VAE decoder network was trained with alternately one active latent component and the remaining components were set to zero because the mean value is close to zero in the distribution learnt from each latent component. Reconstructed EEG images generated from each latent active component were used as an input to k-means clustering to understand the number of generating factors learnt from each component. In addition, average and channel-wise correlation values with each component were computed to understand which component was responsible for activating which part of the brain. The results show that each component contributes differently to capturing and generating aspects in topographic maps, which are visualised using clustering techniques. Hence, this pipeline can be used to generate any size of EEG topo maps with any number of channels. This proposed pipeline is tested on only one participant's data. However, generating factors from each component may vary from participant to participant, as well as the number of electrodes and shape of the topographic maps employed. Future studies will include the automatic interpretation of the CNN-VAE latent space without human intervention to support the EEG data from all participants with varied numbers of channels and topographic map sizes. In addition, performing the interpretation of its latent representation reduces the artefacts by setting the specific component of the CNN-VAE latent space. Furthermore, a complete pipeline will be designed, which will automatically reduce the number of artefacts in EEG signals.

Author Contributions: Conceptualisation, Formal analysis, Investigation, Methodology, Project administration, Resources, Software, T.A. and L.L.; Supervision, L.L.; Validation, T.A. and L.L.; Visualization, T.A.; Writing—original draft, T.A.; Writing—review & editing, T.A. and L.L. All authors have read and agreed to the published version of the manuscript.

Funding: Technological University Dublin, Ireland, under grant PB04433.

Data Availability Statement: DEAP dataset: a dataset for emotion analysis using EEG, physiological, and video signals https://www.eecs.qmul.ac.uk/mmv/datasets/deap/ (accessed on 10 January 2021).

Conflicts of Interest: The authors declare no conflict of interest.

Abbreviations

The following abbreviations are used in this manuscript:

EEG	Electroencephalography
AE	Autoencoder
VAE	Varaiational autoencoder
CNN-VAE	Convolutional variational autoencoder
SNR	Signal-to-noise ratio
XAI	Explainable artificial intelligence
SVHN	Street-view house number
AR	Attribute-regularized
GAN	Generative adversarial network
DLS	Disentangling latent space
GMM	Gaussian mixture model
MMD	Maximum mean discrepancy
SSIM	Structural similarity
MSE	Mean squared error
MAE	Mean absolute error
MAPE	Mean absolute percentage error

Appendix A

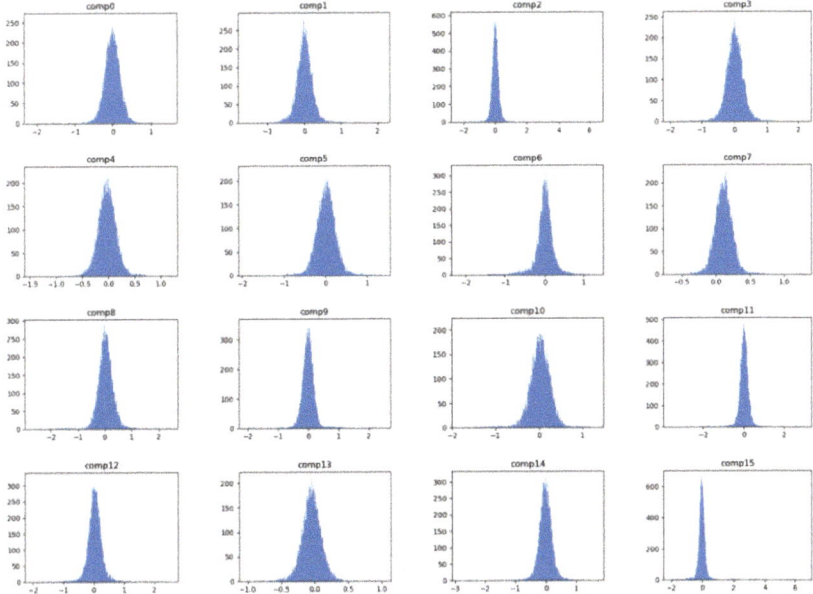

Figure A1. *Cont.*

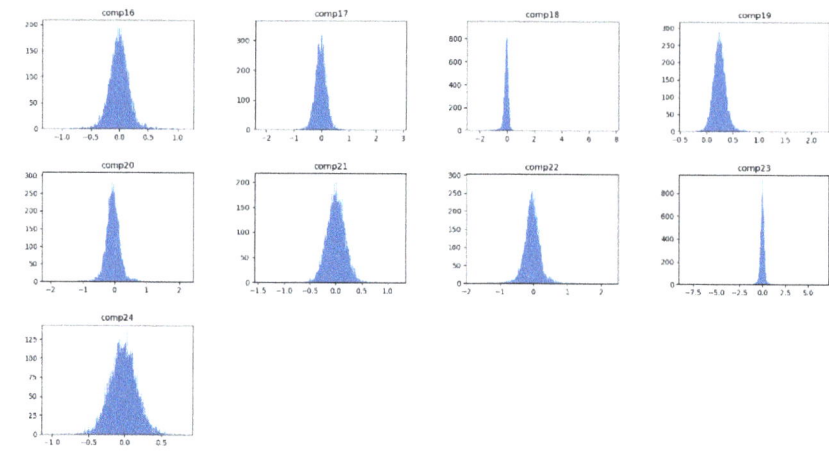

Figure A1. Distribution of all latent spaces when one latent component is active at a time.

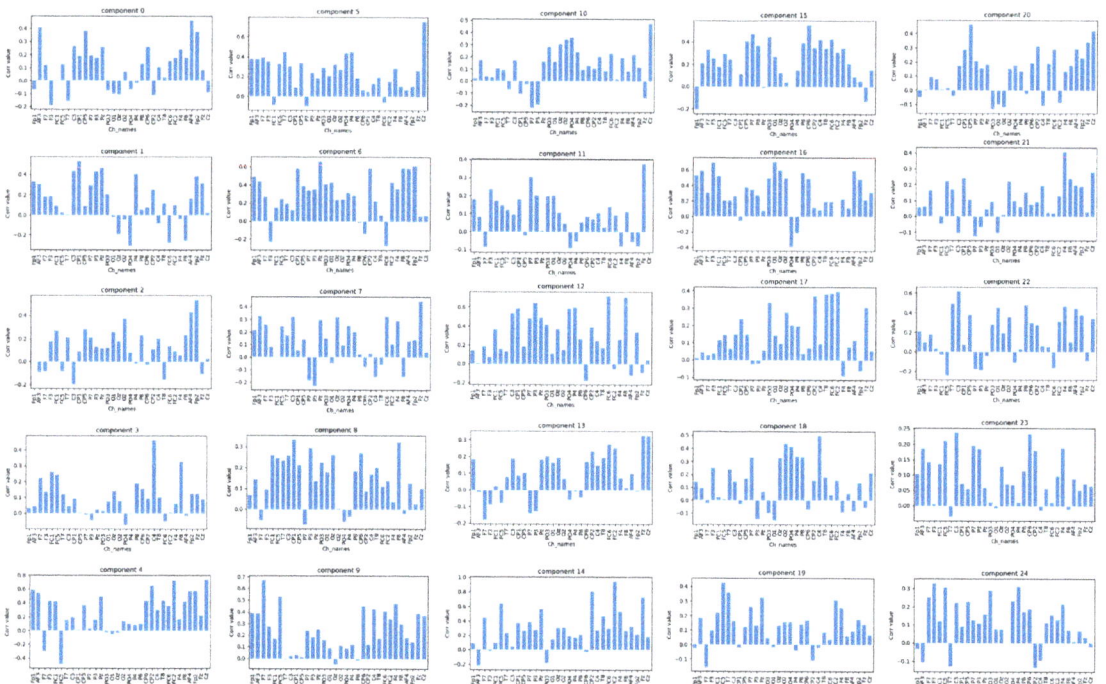

Figure A2. Correlation values between the original and reconstructed signal generated from each latent active component grouped with all channels.

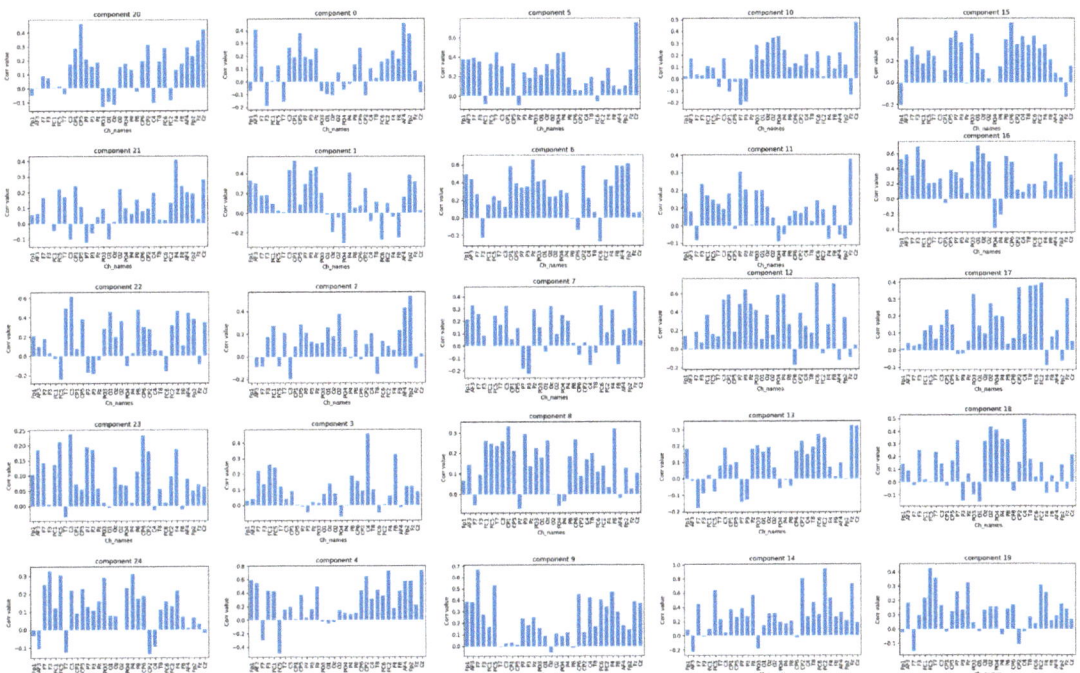

Figure A3. Correlation values between the original and reconstructed signal for each channel grouped with all latent components.

References

1. Binnie, C.; Prior, P. Electroencephalography. *J. Neurol. Neurosurg. Psychiatry* **1994**, *57*, 1308–1319. [CrossRef]
2. Khare, S.K.; March, S.; Barua, P.D.; Gadre, V.M.; Acharya, U.R. Application of data fusion for automated detection of children with developmental and mental disorders: A systematic review of the last decade. *Inf. Fusion* **2023**, *99*, 101898. [CrossRef]
3. Hooi, L.S.; Nisar, H.; Voon, Y.V. Comparison of motion field of EEG topo-maps for tracking brain activation. In Proceedings of the 2016 IEEE EMBS Conference on Biomedical Engineering and Sciences (IECBES), Kuala Lumpur, Malaysia, 4–8 December 2016; pp. 251–256.
4. Anderson, E.W.; Preston, G.A.; Silva, C.T. Using python for signal processing and visualization. *Comput. Sci. Eng.* **2010**, *12*, 90–95. [CrossRef]
5. Ahmed, T.; Longo, L. Examining the Size of the Latent Space of Convolutional Variational Autoencoders Trained With Spectral Topographic Maps of EEG Frequency Bands. *IEEE Access* **2022**, *10*, 107575–107586. [CrossRef]
6. Chikkankod, A.V.; Longo, L. On the dimensionality and utility of convolutional Autoencoder's latent space trained with topology-preserving spectral EEG head-maps. *Mach. Learn. Knowl. Extr.* **2022**, *4*, 1042–1064. [CrossRef]
7. Anwar, A.M.; Eldeib, A.M. EEG signal classification using convolutional neural networks on combined spatial and temporal dimensions for BCI systems. In Proceedings of the 2020 42nd Annual International Conference of the IEEE Engineering in Medicine & Biology Society (EMBC), Montreal, QC, Canada, 20–24 July 2020; pp. 434–437.
8. Taherisadr, M.; Joneidi, M.; Rahnavard, N. EEG signal dimensionality reduction and classification using tensor decomposition and deep convolutional neural networks. In Proceedings of the 2019 IEEE 29th International Workshop on Machine Learning for Signal Processing (MLSP), Pittsburgh, PA, USA, 13–16 October 2019; pp. 1–6.
9. Miladinović, A.; Ajčević, M.; Jarmolowska, J.; Marusic, U.; Colussi, M.; Silveri, G.; Battaglini, P.P.; Accardo, A. Effect of power feature covariance shift on BCI spatial-filtering techniques: A comparative study. *Comput. Methods Programs Biomed.* **2021**, *198*, 105808. [CrossRef] [PubMed]
10. Klonowski, W. Everything you wanted to ask about EEG but were afraid to get the right answer. *Nonlinear Biomed. Phys.* **2009**, *3*, 1–5. [CrossRef]
11. Lotte, F.; Congedo, M.; Lécuyer, A.; Lamarche, F.; Arnaldi, B. A review of classification algorithms for EEG-based brain–computer interfaces. *J. Neural Eng.* **2007**, *4*, R1. [CrossRef]
12. Bao, G.; Yan, B.; Tong, L.; Shu, J.; Wang, L.; Yang, K.; Zeng, Y. Data augmentation for EEG-based emotion recognition using generative adversarial networks. *Front. Comput. Neurosci.* **2021**, *15*, 723843. [CrossRef]

13. Bengio, Y.; Courville, A.; Vincent, P. Representation learning: A review and new perspectives. *IEEE Trans. Pattern Anal. Mach. Intell.* **2013**, *35*, 1798–1828. [CrossRef]
14. Vincent, P.; Larochelle, H.; Bengio, Y.; Manzagol, P.A. Extracting and composing robust features with denoising autoencoders. In Proceedings of the 25th International Conference on Machine Learning, Helsinki, Finland, 5–9 July 2008; pp. 1096–1103.
15. Bornschein, J.; Bengio, Y. Reweighted wake-sleep. *arXiv* **2014**, arXiv:1406.2751.
16. Abdelfattah, S.M.; Abdelrahman, G.M.; Wang, M. Augmenting the size of EEG datasets using generative adversarial networks. In Proceedings of the 2018 International Joint Conference on Neural Networks (IJCNN), Rio de Janeiro, Brazil, 8–13 July 2018; pp. 1–6.
17. Hwaidi, J.F.; Chen, T.M. A Noise Removal Approach from EEG Recordings Based on Variational Autoencoders. In Proceedings of the 2021 13th International Conference on Computer and Automation Engineering (ICCAE), Melbourne, Australia, 20–22 March 2021; pp. 19–23.
18. Li, K.; Wang, J.; Li, S.; Yu, H.; Zhu, L.; Liu, J.; Wu, L. Feature Extraction and Identification of Alzheimer's Disease based on Latent Factor of Multi-Channel EEG. *IEEE Trans. Neural Syst. Rehabil. Eng.* **2021**, *29*, 1557–1567. [CrossRef]
19. Kingma, D.P.; Welling, M. Auto-encoding variational bayes. *arXiv* **2013**, arXiv:1312.6114.
20. Li, X.; Zhao, Z.; Song, D.; Zhang, Y.; Pan, J.; Wu, L.; Huo, J.; Niu, C.; Wang, D. Latent factor decoding of multi-channel EEG for emotion recognition through autoencoder-like neural networks. *Front. Neurosci.* **2020**, *14*, 87. [CrossRef]
21. Zheng, Z.; Sun, L. Disentangling latent space for vae by label relevant/irrelevant dimensions. In Proceedings of the IEEE/CVF Conference on Computer Vision and Pattern Recognition, Long Beach, CA, USA, 15–20 June 2019; pp. 12192–12201.
22. Peng, X.; Yu, X.; Sohn, K.; Metaxas, D.N.; Chandraker, M. Reconstruction-based disentanglement for pose-invariant face recognition. In Proceedings of the IEEE International Conference on Computer Vision, Venice, Italy, 22–29 October 2017; pp. 1623–1632.
23. Hsieh, J.T.; Liu, B.; Huang, D.A.; Fei-Fei, L.F.; Niebles, J.C. Learning to decompose and disentangle representations for video prediction. *Adv. Neural Inf. Process. Syst.* **2018**, *31*. [CrossRef]
24. Wang, S.; Chen, T.; Chen, S.; Nepal, S.; Rudolph, C.; Grobler, M. Oiad: One-for-all image anomaly detection with disentanglement learning. In Proceedings of the 2020 International Joint Conference on Neural Networks (IJCNN), Glasgow, UK, 19–24 July 2020; pp. 1–8.
25. Siddharth, N.; Paige, B.; Desmaison, A.; Van de Meent, J.W.; Wood, F.; Goodman, N.D.; Kohli, P.; Torr, P.H. Inducing interpretable representations with variational autoencoders. *arXiv* **2016**, arXiv:1611.07492.
26. Ramakrishna, S.; Rahiminasab, Z.; Karsai, G.; Easwaran, A.; Dubey, A. Efficient out-of-distribution detection using latent space of β-vae for cyber-physical systems. *ACM Trans. Cyber-Phys. Syst. (TCPS)* **2022**, *6*, 1–34. [CrossRef]
27. Mathieu, E.; Rainforth, T.; Siddharth, N.; Teh, Y.W. Disentangling disentanglement in variational autoencoders. In Proceedings of the International Conference on Machine Learning, PMLR, Long Beach, CA, USA, 9–15 June 2019; pp. 4402–4412.
28. Spinner, T.; Körner, J.; Görtler, J.; Deussen, O. Towards an interpretable latent space: An intuitive comparison of autoencoders with variational autoencoders. In Proceedings of the IEEE VIS, Berlin, Germany, 27 October 2018.
29. Bryan-Kinns, N.; Banar, B.; Ford, C.; Reed, C.; Zhang, Y.; Colton, S.; Armitage, J. Exploring xai for the arts: Explaining latent space in generative music. *arXiv* **2022**, arXiv:2308.05496 2022.
30. Pati, A.; Lerch, A. Attribute-based regularization of latent spaces for variational auto-encoders. *Neural Comput. Appl.* **2021**, *33*, 4429–4444. [CrossRef]
31. Dinari, O.; Freifeld, O. Variational-and metric-based deep latent space for out-of-distribution detection. In Proceedings of the 38th Conference on Uncertainty in Artificial Intelligence, Eindhoven, The Netherlands, 1–5 August 2022.
32. Ding, F.; Yang, Y.; Luo, F. Clustering by directly disentangling latent space. In Proceedings of the 2022 IEEE International Conference on Image Processing (ICIP), Bordeaux, France, 16–19 October 2022; pp. 341–345.
33. Mukherjee, S.; Asnani, H.; Lin, E.; Kannan, S. Clustergan: Latent space clustering in generative adversarial networks. In Proceedings of the AAAI Conference on Artificial Intelligence, Honolulu, HI, USA, 27 January–1 February 2019; Volume 33, pp. 4610–4617.
34. Prasad, V.; Das, D.; Bhowmick, B. Variational clustering: Leveraging variational autoencoders for image clustering. In Proceedings of the 2020 International Joint Conference on Neural Networks (IJCNN), Glasgow, UK, 19 July 2020; pp. 1–10. [CrossRef]
35. Koelstra, S.; Muhl, C.; Soleymani, M.; Lee, J.S.; Yazdani, A.; Ebrahimi, T.; Pun, T.; Nijholt, A.; Patras, I. Deap: A database for emotion analysis; using physiological signals. *IEEE Trans. Affect. Comput.* **2011**, *3*, 18–31. [CrossRef]
36. Hwaidi, J.F.; Chen, T.M. A Novel KOSFS Feature Selection Algorithm for EEG Signals. In Proceedings of the IEEE EUROCON 2021—19th International Conference on Smart Technologies, Lviv, Ukraine, 6–8 July 2021; pp. 265–268.
37. Kingma, D.P.; Welling, M. Auto-encoding variational bayes in 2nd International Conference on Learning Representations. In Proceedings of the ICLR 2014-Conference Track Proceedings, Banff, AB, Canada, 14–16 April 2014.
38. Gretton, A.; Borgwardt, K.; Rasch, M.J.; Scholkopf, B.; Smola, A.J. A kernel method for the two-sample problem. *arXiv* **2008**, arXiv:0805.2368.
39. Sara, U.; Akter, M.; Uddin, M.S. Image quality assessment through FSIM, SSIM, MSE and PSNR—A comparative study. *J. Comput. Commun.* **2019**, *7*, 8–18. [CrossRef]
40. Schneider, P.; Xhafa, F. Chapter 3—Anomaly detection: Concepts and methods. In *Anomaly Detection and Complex Event Processing over IoT Data Streams*; Elsevier: Amsterdam, The Netherlands, 2022; pp. 49–66.

41. Asuero, A.G.; Sayago, A.; González, A. The correlation coefficient: An overview. *Crit. Rev. Anal. Chem.* **2006**, *36*, 41–59. [CrossRef]
42. Hanrahan, C. *Noise Reduction in Eeg Signals Using Convolutional Autoencoding Techniques*; Master's Thesis, Technological University Dublin, Germany, Ireland, 1 September 2019.

Disclaimer/Publisher's Note: The statements, opinions and data contained in all publications are solely those of the individual author(s) and contributor(s) and not of MDPI and/or the editor(s). MDPI and/or the editor(s) disclaim responsibility for any injury to people or property resulting from any ideas, methods, instructions or products referred to in the content.

Article

Revisiting Softmax for Uncertainty Approximation in Text Classification

Andreas Nugaard Holm, Dustin Wright * and Isabelle Augenstein

Department of Computer Science, University of Copenhagen, 1172 Copenhagen, Denmark; aholm@di.ku.dk (A.N.H.); augenstein@di.ku.dk (I.A.)
* Correspondence: dw@di.ku.dk

Abstract: Uncertainty approximation in text classification is an important area with applications in domain adaptation and interpretability. One of the most widely used uncertainty approximation methods is Monte Carlo (MC) dropout, which is computationally expensive as it requires multiple forward passes through the model. A cheaper alternative is to simply use a softmax based on a single forward pass without dropout to estimate model uncertainty. However, prior work has indicated that these predictions tend to be overconfident. In this paper, we perform a thorough empirical analysis of these methods on five datasets with two base neural architectures in order to identify the trade-offs between the two. We compare both softmax and an efficient version of MC dropout on their uncertainty approximations and downstream text classification performance, while weighing their runtime (cost) against performance (benefit). We find that, while MC dropout produces the best uncertainty approximations, using a simple softmax leads to competitive, and in some cases better, uncertainty estimation for text classification at a much lower computational cost, suggesting that softmax can in fact be a sufficient uncertainty estimate when computational resources are a concern.

Keywords: text classification; uncertainty quantification; efficiency

Citation: Holm, A.N.; Wright, D.; Augenstein, I. Revisiting Softmax for Uncertainty Approximation in Text Classification. *Information* **2023**, *14*, 420. https://doi.org/10.3390/info14070420

Academic Editors: Katsuhide Fujita and Ralf Krestel

Received: 19 May 2023
Revised: 3 July 2023
Accepted: 18 July 2023
Published: 20 July 2023

Copyright: © 2023 by the authors. Licensee MDPI, Basel, Switzerland. This article is an open access article distributed under the terms and conditions of the Creative Commons Attribution (CC BY) license (https://creativecommons.org/licenses/by/4.0/).

1. Introduction

The pursuit of pushing state-of-the-art performance on machine learning benchmarks often comes with an added cost of computational complexity. On top of already complex base models, such as transformer models [1,2], successful methods often employ additional techniques to improve the uncertainty estimation of these models, as they tend to be overconfident in their predictions. Though these techniques can be effective, the overall benefit in relation to the added computational cost is under-studied.

More complexity does not always imply better performance. For example, transformers can be outperformed by much simpler convolutional neural nets (CNNs) when the latter are pre-trained as well [3]. Here, we turn our attention to neural network uncertainty estimation methods in text classification, which have applications in domain adaptation and decision making, and can help make models more transparent and explainable. In particular, we focus on a setting where efficiency is of concern, which can help improve the sustainability and democratisation of machine learning, as well as enable use in resource-constrained environments.

Quantifying predictive uncertainty in neural nets has been explored using various techniques [4], with the methods being divided into three main categories: Bayesian methods, single deterministic networks, and ensemble methods. Bayesian methods include Monte Carlo (MC) dropout [5] and Bayes by back-prop [6]. Single deterministic networks can approximate the predictive uncertainty by a single forward pass in the model, with softmax being the prototypical method. Lastly, ensemble methods utilise a collection of models to calculate the predictive uncertainty. However, while uncertainty estimation can improve when using more complex Bayesian and ensembling techniques, efficiency takes a hit.

In this paper, we perform an empirical investigation of the trade-off between choosing cheap vs. expensive uncertainty approximation methods for text classification, with the goal of highlighting the efficacy of these methods in an efficient setting. We focus on one single deterministic and one Bayesian method. For the single deterministic method, we study the softmax, which is calculated from a single forward pass and is computationally very efficient. While softmax is a widely used method, prior work has posited that the softmax output, when taken as a single deterministic operation, is not the most dependable uncertainty approximation method [5,7]. As such, it has been superseded by newer methods such as MC dropout, which leverages the dropout function in neural nets to approximate a random sample of multiple networks and aggregates the softmax outputs of this sample. MC dropout is favoured due to its close approximation of uncertainty, and because it can be used without any modification to the applied model. It has also been widely applied in text classification tasks [8,9].

To understand the cost vs. benefit of softmax vs. MC dropout, we perform experiments on five datasets using two different neural network architectures, applying them to three different downstream text classification tasks. We measure both the added computational complexity in the form of runtime (cost) and the downstream performance on multiple uncertainty metrics (benefit). We show that by using a single deterministic method like softmax, instead of MC dropout, we can improve the runtime by 10 times while still providing reasonable uncertainty estimates on the studied tasks. As such, given the already high computational cost of deep-neural-network-based methods and recent pushes for more sustainable ML [10,11], we recommend not discarding efficient uncertainty approximation methods such as softmax in resource-constrained settings, as they can still potentially provide reasonable estimations of uncertainty.

Contribution In summary, our contributions are: (1) an empirical study of an efficient version of MC dropout and softmax for text classification tasks, using two different neural architectures, and five datasets; (2) a comparison of uncertainty estimation between MC dropout and softmax using expected calibration error; and (3) a comparison of the cost vs. benefit of MC dropout and softmax in a setting where efficiency is of concern.

2. Related Work
2.1. Uncertainty Quantification

Quantifying the uncertainty of a prediction can be performed using various techniques [4,12,13], such as single deterministic methods [14,15], which calculate the uncertainty on a single forward pass of the model. They can further be classified as internal or external methods, which describe if the uncertainty is calculated internally in the model or post-processing the output. Another family of techniques are Bayesian methods, which combine NNs and Bayesian learning. Bayesian neural networks (BNNs) can also be split into subcategories, namely variational inference [16], sampling [17], and Laplace approximation [18]. Some of the more notable methods are Bayes by backprop [6] and Monte Carlo dropout [5]. One can also approximate uncertainty using ensemble methods, which use multiple models to better measure predictive uncertainty, compared to using the predictive uncertainty given by a single model [9,19,20]. Recently, we have seen uncertainty methods being used to develop methods for new tasks [8,9], where mainly Bayesian methods have been used. We present a thorough empirical study of how uncertainty quantification behaves for text classification tasks. Unlike prior work, we do not only evaluate based on the performance of the methods, but perform an in-depth comparison to much simpler deterministic methods based on multiple metrics.

2.2. Uncertainty Metrics

Measuring the performance of uncertainty approximation methods can be performed in multiple ways, each offering benefits and downsides. Niculescu-Mizil and Caruana [21] explore the use of obtaining confidence values from model predictions to use for supervised learning. One of the more widespread and accepted methods is using expected calibration error (ECE, Guo et al. [22]), while ECE measures the underlying confidence of the uncertainty approximation, we have also seen the use of human intervention for text classification [8,9]. There, the uncertainty estimates are used to identify uncertain predictions from the model and ask humans to classify these predictions. The human-classified data are assumed to have 100% accuracy and to be suitable for measuring how well the model scores after removing a proportion of the most uncertain data points. Using metrics such as ECE, the calibration of models is shown, and this calibration can be improved using scaling techniques [22,23]. We use uncertainty approximation metrics like expected calibration error and human intervention (which we refer to as holdout experiments) to measure the difference in the performance of MC dropout and softmax compared against each other on text classification tasks.

3. Uncertainty Approximation for Text Classification

We focus on one deterministic method and one Bayesian method of uncertainty approximation. Both methods assume the existence of an already-trained base model, and are applied at test time to obtain uncertainty estimates from the model's predictions. In the following sections, we formally introduce the two methods we study, namely MC dropout and softmax. MC dropout is a Bayesian method which utilises the dropout layers of the model to measure the predictive uncertainty, while softmax is a deterministic method that uses the classification output. In Figure 1, we visualise the differences between the two methods and how they are connected to base text classification models.

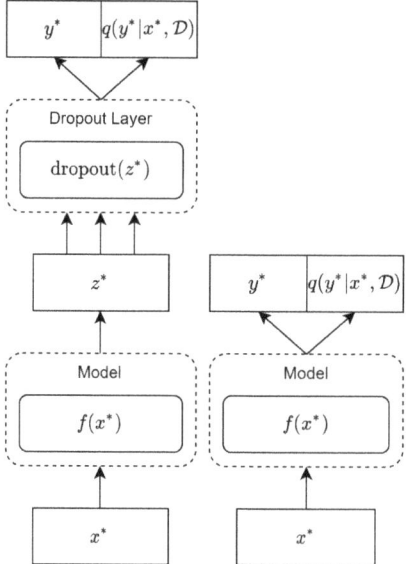

Figure 1. MC dropout (**left**) and softmax (**right**). In the version of MC dropout tested in this paper, a test input x^* is passed through model f to obtain a representation z^*, which is then subsequently passed through a dropout layer multiple times, and passed through the final part of the network to obtain prediction y^*. For softmax, dropout is disabled and a single prediction is obtained.

3.1. Bayesian Learning

Before introducing the MC dropout method, we quickly introduce the concept of *Bayesian learning*. We start by comparing Bayesian learning to a traditional NN. A traditional NN assumes that the network weights $\omega \in \mathbb{R}^n$ are real but of an unknown value and can be found through maximum-likelihood estimation, and the input data $(x,y) \in \mathcal{D}$ are treated as random variables. Bayesian learning instead views the weights as random variables, and infers a posterior distribution $p(\omega|\mathcal{D})$ over ω after observing $\mathcal{D}$. The posterior distribution is defined as follows:

$$p(\omega|\mathcal{D}) = \frac{p(\omega)p(\mathcal{D}|\omega)}{p(\mathcal{D})} = \frac{p(\omega)p(\mathcal{D}|\omega)}{\int p(\omega)p(\mathcal{D}|\omega)d\omega} \quad (1)$$

Using the posterior distribution, we can find the prediction of an input of unseen data x^* and y^* as follows:

$$p(y^*|x^*,\mathcal{D}) = \int p(y^*|x^*,\omega)p(\omega|\mathcal{D})d\omega. \quad (2)$$

However, the posterior distribution is infeasible to compute due to the marginal likelihood in the denominator, so we cannot find a solution analytically. We therefore resort to approximating the posterior distribution. For this approximation, we rely on methods such as Bayes by backpropagation [6] and Monte Carlo dropout [5].

3.2. Monte Carlo Dropout

At a high level, MC dropout approximates the posterior distribution $p(\omega|\mathcal{D})$ by leveraging the dropout layers in a model [5,24]. Mathematically, it is derived by introducing a distribution $q(\omega)$, representing a distribution of weight matrices whose columns are randomly set to 0, to approximate the posterior distribution $p(\omega|\mathcal{D})$, which results in the following predictive distribution:

$$q(y^* \mid x^*,\mathcal{D}) = \int p(y^*|x^*,\omega)q(\omega)d\omega. \quad (3)$$

As this integral is still intractable, it is approximated by taking K samples from $q(\omega)$ using the dropout layers of a learned network f, which approximates $p(y^*|x^*,\omega)$. As such, calculating $p(y^*|x^*,\omega)q(\omega)$ amounts to leaving the dropout layers active during testing, and approximating the integral amounts to aggregating predictions across multiple dropout samples. For the proofs, see Gal and Ghahramani [5].

MC dropout requires multiple forward passes, so its computational cost is a multiple of the cost of performing a forward pass through the entire network. As this is obviously more computationally expensive than the single forward pass required for deterministic methods, we provide a fairer comparison between softmax and MC dropout by using an efficient version of MC dropout which caches an intermediate representation and only activates the dropout layers of the latter part of the network. As such, we obtain a representation z^* by passing an input through the first several layers of the model, and pass only this representation through the latter part of the model multiple times, reducing the computational cost while approximating the sampling of multiple networks.

Combining Sample Predictions

With multiple samples of the same data point, we have to determine how to combine them to quantify the predictive uncertainty. We test two methods that can be calculated using the logits of the model, requiring no model changes. The first approach, which we refer to as mean MC, is averaging the output of the softmax layer from all forward passes:

$$u_i = \frac{1}{K}\sum_{k=1}^{K} \text{Softmax}\left(f(z_i^k)\right), \quad (4)$$

where z_i^k is a representation of the i'th data point of the k'th forward pass, and f is a fully-connected layer. The second method we use to quantify the predictive uncertainty is dropout entropy (DE) [8], which uses a combination of binning and entropy:

$$b_i = \frac{1}{K}\text{BinCount}(\text{argmax}(f(z_i))) \tag{5}$$

$$u_i = -\sum_{j=1}^{C} b_i(j) \log b_i(j) \tag{6}$$

where BinCount is the number of predictions of each class and b is a vector the probabilities of a class's occurrence based on the bin count. We show the performance of the two methods in Section 4.3.2.

3.3. Softmax

Softmax, a common normalising function for producing a probability distribution from neural network logits, is defined as follows:

$$u_i = \frac{e^{z_i}}{\sum_{j=1}^{C} e^{z_i(j)}}, \tag{7}$$

where z_i are the logits of the i'th data point. The softmax yields a probability distribution over the predicted classes. However, the predicted probability distribution is often overconfident toward the predicted class [5,7]. The issue of softmax's overconfidence can also be exploited [5,25]—in the worst case, this leads to the softmax producing imprecise uncertainties. However, model calibration methods like temperature scaling have been found to lessen the overconfidence to some extent [22]. As temperature scaling also incurs a cost in terms of runtime in order to find an optimal temperature, we choose to compare raw softmax probabilities to the efficient MC dropout method described previously, though uncertainty estimation could potentially be improved by scaling the logits appropriately.

4. Experiments and Results

We consider five different datasets and two different base models in our experiments. Additionally, we conduct experiments to determine the optimal hyperparameters for the MC dropout method, particularly the optimal amount of samples which affects the efficiency and performance of MC dropout. In the paper, we focus on the results of the 20 Newsgroups dataset; the results of the other four datasets are shown in the Appendices B and C. We further find the optimal dropout percentage in Appendix A.3.

4.1. Data

To test the predictive uncertainty of the two methods, we use five datasets for diverse text classification tasks. We use the following five datasets: The 20 Newsgroups dataset [26] is a text classification consisting of a collection of 20.000 news articles. The news articles are classified into 20 different classes. The Amazon dataset [27] is a sentiment classification task. We use the 'sports and outdoors' category, which consists of 272.630 reviews ranging from 1 to 5. The IMDb dataset [28] is also a sentiment classification task. However, compared to the Amazon dataset, this is a binary problem. The dataset consists of 50.000 reviews. The SST-2 dataset [29] is also a binary sentiment classification dataset, consisting of 70.042 sentences. Lastly, we also use the Wiki dataset [30], which is a citation needed task, i.e., we predict if a citation is needed. The dataset consists of 19.998 texts. For the 20 Newsgroups, Amazon, IMDb, and Wiki datasets, we use a split of 60, 20 and 20 for the training, validation and test data, the data in splits have been selected randomly. We used the provided splits for the SST-2 dataset, but due to the test labels being hidden, we used the validation set for testing. We select these datasets as they are large, the tasks are diverse, and they cover multiple domains of text. Additionally, they represent well-studied and standard benchmarks in the field of text classification, which helps with the reproducibility of the results and comparison with baselines.

4.2. Experimental Setup

We use two different base neural architectures with two different embeddings in our experiments. To recreate baseline results, the first model is the same model as proposed in [8], which is a CNN using pre-trained GloVe embeddings (Glove-CNN) with a dimension of 200 [31]. The second model uses a pre-trained BERT model [32] fine-tuned as a masked language model on the dataset under evaluation to obtain contextualised embeddings, which are then input to a CNN with 4 layers (BERT-CNN). The selection of these models allows us to compare the established baseline architecture from [8] with a more modern version of it which takes advantage of large language models. For both models, we use the final dropout layer for MC dropout. Both models are optimised using Adam [33] and are trained for 1000 epochs, with early stopping after 10 iterations if there have been no improvements, and we set the learning rate to 0.001.

MC Dropout Sampling

To make full use of MC dropout, we first determine the optimal number of forward passes through the model needed to obtain the best performance while maintaining high efficiency. This hyper-parameter search is imperative because the MC dropout performance and efficiency are correlated with the number of samples generated. To make a fair comparison against the already cheap softmax method, we want to find the minimum number of samples needed to approximate a good uncertainty. In Table 1, we show the performance, using the F1 score, of the MC dropout method with the BERT-CNN model on the 20 Newsgroups dataset for the following number of samples: $[1, 5, 10, 25, 50, 100, 1000]$. The table shows how the performance of the uncertainty approximation increases, given the number of samples. However, the performance gained by the number of samples falls off at 50. Given this, we use 50 MC samples in our experiments in order to balance good performance and efficiency.

Table 1. This table shows how the number of samples affect the performance of the MC dropout method, on the 20 Newsgroups dataset, using the BERT-CNN model. The results are reported using macro F1.

1	10	25	50	100	1000
0.8212	0.8623	0.8540	0.8591	0.8559	0.8573

4.3. Evaluation Metrics

We use complementary evaluation metrics to benchmark the performance of MC dropout and softmax. Namely, we measure how well each of the methods identify uncertain predictions as well as the runtime of the methods.

4.3.1. Efficiency

To quantify efficiency, we measure the runtime of each of the methods during inference and the calculation of the uncertainties. Since we do not calculate uncertainties during training, this is only performed on the test sets. Training the model is independent of the uncertainty estimation methods, since we only use them to quantify the uncertainty of the predictions of the model. We therefore only calculate the runtime of each of the methods based on the test data.

4.3.2. Performance Metrics

We use two main uncertainty metrics: test data holdout and expected calibration error (ECE). These metrics give us an estimation of the *epistemic* uncertainty of the model, i.e., the lack of certainty inherent in the model and its predictions. We do not cover metrics of *aleatoric* uncertainty in this paper, which focus on the inherent randomness of the data itself and which could be tested through the introduction of, e.g., label noise. For base model performance, we record the macro F1 score on the 20 Newsgroups, IMDb, Wiki, and SST-2 datasets, and the accuracy on the Amazon dataset.

Test data holdout: This metric ranks all samples based on the predictive uncertainty, and calculates the F1 and accuracy scores on a percentage of the samples by removing those which the model is least certain about. In other words, a method is better if it achieves a greater improvement in performance metrics (e.g., F1) when removing the most uncertain samples. As such, this metric expresses the relationship between model calibration and accuracy. We choose to remove 10%, 20%, 30% and 40% of the least certain samples for our experiments. This metric shows how well the two methods can identify uncertain predictions of the model, as reflected by improvements in performance when more uncertain predictions are removed [8]. In our experiments, we use the aforementioned mean MC, DE, and softmax method to calculate the uncertainties; we further add the penultimate layer variance (PL-Variance), where the PL-Variance utilises the variance of the last fully-connected layer as the uncertainty [34].

Expected calibration error: As a second uncertainty estimation metric, we use the expected calibration error (ECE, Guo et al. [22]), which measures, in expectation, how confident the predictions for both correct and incorrect predictions are. This tells us how well each of the MC dropout and softmax methods estimate the uncertainties at the level of probability distributions, as opposed to the holdout method which only looks at downstream task performance. ECE works by dividing the data into m bins, where each bin in B contains data that is within a certain range of probabilities, using the probability of the predicted class. Formally, ECE is defined as:

$$ECE = \sum_{m=1}^{M} \frac{|B_m|}{n} |acc(B_m) - conf(B_m)| \qquad (8)$$

where M is the size of the dataset and acc and $conf$ is the accuracy and mean confidence (i.e., predicted class probabilities) of the bin B_m.

Finally, to visualise the difference between the MC dropout and softmax, we create both confidence histograms and reliability diagrams [22]. The reliability diagrams show how close the models are to perfect calibration, where perfect calibration means that the models accuracy and confidence is equal to the bins confidence range. In all cases, we show reliability diagrams by comparing histograms of accuracy and confidence across confidence bins; as such, when confidence exceeds accuracy in a given bin, that indicates how overconfident the model is for that bin. The reliability diagrams help us visualise the ECE, by showing the accuracy and mean confidence of each bin, where each bin consists of the data which have a confidence within the range of the bin. To complement the reliability diagrams, we also use confidence histograms, which show the distribution of confidence.

4.4. Efficiency Results

In Table 2, we display the runtime of the different model and method combinations. The runtime for the forward passes is calculated as a sum of all the forward passes on the entire dataset, and the runtime for the uncertainty methods are calculated for the entire dataset. Observing the results, we see that softmax is overall faster, and is approximately 10 times faster when only looking at the forward passes, and using more complex aggregation methods in MC dropout, like DE, can be computationally heavy.

Table 2. Runtime measured in seconds for both MC dropout (top) and softmax (bottom). The times are on the full datasets split into the runtime of the forward passes and the runtime of calculating the uncertainty.

	Forward Passes	Mean MC	DE
20 Newsgroups	1.0876	0.0003	12.3537
IMDb	1.386	0.0018	216.11
Amazon	4.9126	0.0017	194.08
WIKI	1.1149	0.0010	15.8467
SST-2	1.0076	0.0003	3.4785
	Forward Passes	Softmax	PL-Variance
20 Newsgroups	0.0130	0.0002	0.0001
IMDb	0.0387	0.0003	0.0003
Amazon	0.4067	0.0004	0.0002
WIKI	0.0149	0.0002	0.0001
SST-2	0.0037	0.0002	0.0001

4.5. Test Data Holdout Results

Table 3 and the table in Appendix B show the performance of the two uncertainty approximation methods using the different datasets and models. The tables show the macro F1 score and accuracy (depending on the datasets), and the ratio of improvement from holding out data in parentheses. We observe that, in most cases, either dropout entropy (DE) or softmax has the highest score and improvement ratio. However, in most cases the two are close in performance and improvement ratio. We further observe that mean MC also performs well and is almost on par with DE; however, mean MC is a much more efficient method compared to DE, so the slight trade-off in performance could be beneficial in resource-constrained settings or non-critical applications.

Table 3. Macro F1 score and improvement rate for the 20 Newsgroups dataset.

BERT	0%	10%	20%	30%	40%
Mean MC	0.8591	0.8985 (1.0459)	0.9225 (1.0739)	0.9406 (1.0949)	0.9487 (1.1043)
DE	0.8591	0.9050 (1.0534)	0.9390 (1.0930)	0.9584 (1.1156)	0.9703 (1.1294)
Softmax	0.8576	0.9072 (1.0578)	0.9452 (**1.1021**)	0.9620 (**1.1216**)	**0.9742** (**1.1360**)
PL-Variance	0.8576	0.9006 (1.0501)	0.9246 (1.0781)	0.9403 (1.0964)	0.9484 (1.1058)
GloVe					
Mean MC	0.7966	0.8450 (1.0608)	0.8674 (1.0888)	0.8846 (0.1104)	0.8960 (1.1248)
DE	0.7966	**0.8469** (1.0631)	**0.8855** (**1.1116**)	0.9155 (1.1492)	**0.9416** (**1.1820**)
Softmax	0.7959	0.8465 (**1.0636**)	0.8846 (1.1115)	0.9149 (**1.1496**)	0.9402 (1.1813)
PL-Variance	0.7959	0.8436 (1.0599)	0.8667 (1.0891)	0.8848 (1.1118)	0.8966 (1.1266)

4.6. Model Calibration Results

To further investigate the differences between MC dropout and softmax, we utilise the expected calibration error (ECE) to observe the differences in the predictive uncertainties. In Table 4, we show the accuracy and ECE on the three datasets using the BERT embeddings.

The results from our holdout experiments in Table 3 and in Appendix B, combined with the results from our ECE calculations in Table 4, all point in the direction of the efficient MC dropout used in this study and softmax performing on par to each other, but with a large gap in runtime as shown in Table 2. To obtain a better understanding of if and where the two methods diverge, we plot the reliability diagrams and confidence histograms as described in Section 4.3.2.

Table 4. Accuracy and ECE of the two uncertainty approximation approaches on the three selected datasets.

	Accuracy	ECE
20 Newsgroups—Mean MC	0.8655	0.0275
20 Newsgroups—Softmax	0.8642	0.0253
IMDb—Mean MC	0.9354	0.0061
IMDb—Softmax	0.9364	0.0043
Amazon—Mean MC	0.7466	0.0083
Amazon—Softmax	0.7474	0.0097
WIKI—Mean MC	0.9227	0.0370
WIKI—Softmax	0.9230	0.0279
SST-2—Mean MC	0.7408	0.0535
SST-2—Softmax	0.7442	0.0472

Plot description: In Figures 2 and 3, we show the reliability diagrams and the confidence histograms on the 20 Newsgroups dataset using both our BERT-CNN and GloVe-CNN with both the MC dropout method and softmax. We create the reliability diagrams using 10 bins and the confidence histograms with 20. The reliability diagram's and confidence histogram's bins are an interval of confidence. We use 20 bins for the confidence histograms to obtain a more fine-grained view of the distribution. In the reliability diagram, the x-axis is the confidence and the y-axis is the accuracy. For the confidence histogram the x-axis is again the confidence and the y-axis is the percentage of the samples in the given bin.

Expectations: While ECE can quantify the performance of the models on a somewhat lower level than our other metrics, the metric can be deceived, especially in cases where models score high in accuracy. It will favour overconfident models; therefore, we expect the results to favour softmax. Looking at the ECE, we can observe that it will favour an overconfident method when the model achieves high accuracy. With this in mind, we expect the results to be skewed towards the softmax.

Observations reliability diagram: From the reliability diagram, we observe that the difference in confidence and outputs are small. The difference between the two uncertainty methods is also minimal, including both BERT and GloVe embeddings, suggesting minimal potential gains from using MC dropout in an efficient setting while still incurring a high cost in terms of runtime. We determine that there is minimal difference by visually inspecting the plots, and by observing the ECE displayed in Table 4. We further observe that in both MC dropout and softmax that the model worsens when we use the GloVe embeddings.

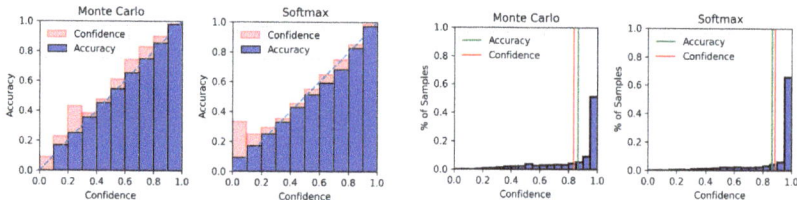

Figure 2. Reliability diagram (**left**, displayed as a stacked bar chart comparing accuracy and confidence) and confidence histogram (**right**) of 20 Newsgroups using BERT-CNN. Softmax and the efficient version of MC dropout tested in this paper are relatively similar in their calibration (a higher value for confidence than accuracy in any bin indicates overconfidence in that bin). At the same time, as indicated by the confidence histogram, softmax still produces more confident estimates on average.

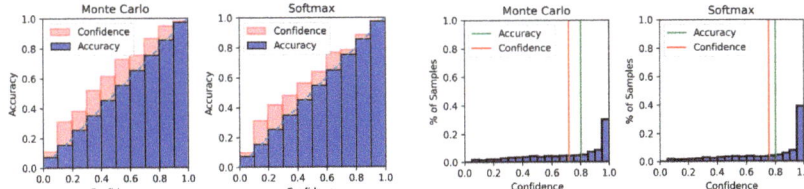

Figure 3. Reliability diagram (**left**, displayed as a stacked bar chart comparing accuracy and confidence) and confidence histogram (**right**) of 20 Newsgroups using GloVe-CNN. Comparing the plots of the figure to Figure 2, we see slight differences in both the reliability diagram and the confidence histogram. Most noticeably, we see slight differences in the reliability diagram, where we see more significant gaps between the confidence and the outputs, which indicates a less calibrated model due to the GloVe embeddings.

Observations confidence histogram: As mentioned earlier, we know that the softmax tends to be overconfident, which can be seen in the percentage of samples in the last bin. The MC dropout method, on the other hand, utilises the probability space to a greater extent. We include reliability diagrams and confidence histograms for the two other datasets in Appendix C.

Noise experiment: Inspecting both Table 4 showing the ECE values, and the performances in Tables 3, A2 and A3, we observe that using our two uncertainty estimation methods, we achieved very high F1 scores and accuracies and low ECEs. We hypothesised that high performance could lead to softmax achieving high ECE, due to naturally having high confidence, compared to MC dropout. We added zero-mean Gaussian noise to the 20 Newsgroups test embeddings and reperformed our ECE experiments to test our hypothesis. In Figure 4, we show the reliability diagram of the experiment with added noise, which shows the MC dropout outperforming softmax. To further build on the theory, we also inspect the confidence histogram, showing that softmax is still overconfident and the difference between the accuracy and mean confidence is high. This suggests that MC dropout is more resilient to noise and, in cases where the performance of a model is low, MC dropout could potentially obtain more precise predictive uncertainties.

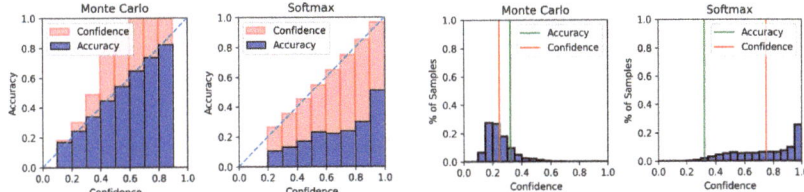

Figure 4. Reliability diagram of 20 Newsgroups dataset (displayed as a stacked bar chart comparing accuracy and confidence) using the BERT-CNN model, with added zero-mean Gaussian noise to the BERT embeddings. Softmax is highly overconfident compared to MC dropout (despite the efficient setting in this paper where only the final layers of the model are used for dropout), as indicated by the large gap between average confidence and accuracy in each bin of the histogram.

5. Discussion and Conclusions

In this paper, we perform an in-depth empirical comparison of using the MC dropout method in an efficient setting and the more straightforward softmax method. By doing a thorough empirical analysis of the two methods, shown in Section 4.3.2, using various metrics to measure their performance on both efficiency and performance levels, we see that in our holdout experiments in Table 3, the two methods perform approximately the same. Looking at the expected calibration error (ECE) experiments, the results again show that the MC dropout and softmax method perform somewhat equally, which we have shown in Section 4.6. We observe differences in the results as we observe a lower accuracy score, which we show in our noise experiment, which is also shown in Section 4.6. Prior research [7] investigated out-of-distribution analysis and found that softmax, both for sentiment classification and text categorisation tasks, can detect out-of-distribution data points efficiently. It further showcases that in these two tasks, the softmax can also, to some extent, perform well as a confidence estimator. While we show that the two methods perform almost equally, when comparing the predictive performance, the cost of using MC dropout is at a minimum 10 times that of running softmax, even in the efficient setting where only the final layer is dropped out, depending on the post-processing of the uncertainties, as we show in Section 4.4. The post-processing cost of MC dropout can quickly explode when used on larger datasets or if a more expensive method like dropout entropy is used instead of simpler approaches.

Given this, when could it be appropriate to use the more efficient softmax over MC dropout for estimating predictive uncertainty? Our results suggest that when the base accuracy of a model is high, the differences in uncertainty estimation between the two methods is relatively low, likely due to the higher confidence of the softmax method. In this case, if latency or resource efficiency is a concern such as on edge devices, it may be appropriate to rely on a quick estimate using softmax as opposed to a more cumbersome method. However, when model accuracy is expected to be low, softmax is still overconfident compared to MC dropout, so estimates using a single deterministic softmax may be unreliable. The downstream application may also impact this; in critical scenarios such as health care, it may still be more appropriate to use an inefficient method with better predictive uncertainty for improved decision-making. In low-risk applications where models are known to be accurate and efficiency is of concern, we have demonstrated that softmax can potentially be sufficient.

6. Limitations

We highlight a few key limitations of the study to further contextualise the work. First, we note that the study is restricted to neural-network-based methods, while other methods in ML may be useful to study for uncertainty estimation as well. Second, we note that we test a plain softmax method without temperature scaling—while calibrating a useful temperature could induce a cost in terms of time, it would potentially lead to better uncertainty estimation. Finally, we note that we also test an efficient form of MC dropout which only drops out a portion of the network; while this demonstrates that in an efficient setting, softmax can be as good or better at uncertainty estimation than MC dropout, full MC dropout still may have better uncertainty estimation when efficiency is not a concern.

Author Contributions: Conceptualisation, A.N.H., D.W. and I.A.; methodology, A.N.H.; software, A.N.H.; validation, A.N.H.; formal analysis, A.N.H.; investigation, A.N.H.; data curation, A.N.H.; writing—original draft preparation, A.N.H., D.W. and I.A.; writing—review and editing, A.N.H., D.W. and I.A.; supervision, I.A. All authors have read and agreed to the published version of the manuscript.

Funding: This research was funded by Innovation Fund Denmark grant number 9065-00131B.

Data Availability Statement: All data used is open-source and can be found in the referenced papers.

Conflicts of Interest: The authors declare no conflict of interest.

Appendix A. Reproducibility

Appendix A.1. Computing Infrastructure

All experiments were run on a Microsoft Azure NC6-series server. With the following specifications: 6 Inter Xeon-E5-2690 v3, NVIDIA Tesla K80 with 12 GB RAM and 56 GB of RAM.

Appendix A.2. Hyperparameters

We used the following hyperparameters for training our CNN model and CNN GloVe model: epochs: 1000; batch size: 256 for 20 Newsgroups, IMDb SST-2 and Wiki, and 128 for Amazon; early stopping: 10; learning rate: 0.001. For fine-tuning BERT, we used the following set of hyperparameters: epochs: 3; warm-up steps 500; weight decay 0.01; batch size 8; masked language model probability: 0.15. All hyperparameters are set without performing cross-validation.

Appendix A.3. Dropout Hyperparameters

The performance of the MC dropout method is correlated with the dropout probability. We therefore run our CNN model using BERT embeddings on the 20 Newsgroups dataset with the following dropout probabilities $[0.1, 0.2, 0.3, 0.4, 0.5]$. In Table A1, we show the results using the five different dropout probabilities, where we see that it stops improving at 0.4 and 0.5 percentage dropout. As such, we use a dropout of 0.5 for our experiments.

Table A1. We test how the dropout probabilities correlate with the performance of MC dropout, using the BERT-CNN model. The results are reported in terms of macro F1.

	0%	10%	20%	30%	40%
0.1	0.8598	0.9010	0.9255	0.9408	0.9483
0.2	0.8599	0.9005	0.9256	0.9408	0.9502
0.3	0.8596	0.9007	0.9245	0.9412	0.9491
0.4	0.8601	0.8996	0.9253	0.9425	0.9502
0.5	0.8591	0.8985	0.9225	0.9406	0.9487

Appendix B. Result Tables

Table A2. Macro F1 score and improvement rate for the IMDb dataset.

BERT	0%	10%	20%	30%	40%
Mean MC	0.9354	0.9668 (1.0335)	0.9829 (1.0508)	0.9901 (1.0585)	0.9930 (1.0616)
DE	0.9354	0.9679 (1.0347)	0.9789 (1.0465)	0.9787 (1.0463)	0.9798 (1.0475)
Softmax	**0.9364**	**0.9691 (1.0349)**	**0.9847 (1.0516)**	**0.9913 (1.0586)**	**0.9940 (1.0615)**
PL-Variance	**0.9364**	0.9678 (1.0335)	0.9837 (1.0506)	0.9901 (1.0574)	0.9933 (1.0608)
GloVe					
Mean MC	0.8825	0.9170 (1.0391)	0.9416 (1.0670)	**0.9614 (1.0894)**	0.9730 (1.1025)
DE	0.8825	**0.9183 (1.0406)**	**0.9430 (1.0686)**	0.9449 (1.0707)	0.9455 (1.0714)
Softmax	0.8824	0.9154 (1.0374)	0.9406 (1.0660)	0.9598 (1.0878)	0.9724 (1.1020)
PL-Variance	0.8824	0.9162 (1.0383)	0.9415 (1.0670)	0.9611 (1.0892)	**0.9736 (1.1034)**

Table A3. Accuracy score and improvement rate for the Amazon (Sports and Outdoors) dataset.

BERT	0%	10%	20%	30%	40%
Mean MC	0.7466	0.7853 (1.0518)	0.8137 (1.0898)	0.8392 (1.1240)	0.8605 (1.1526)
DE	0.7466	0.7850 (1.0513)	0.8191 (1.0871)	0.8492 (1.1374)	0.8684 (1.1631)
Softmax	**0.7474**	**0.7875 (1.0537)**	**0.8225 (1.1005)**	**0.8562 (1.1456)**	**0.8845 (1.1834)**
PL-Variance	**0.7474**	0.7856 (1.0510)	0.8144 (1.0896)	0.8404 (1.1244)	0.8610 (1.1520)
GloVe					
Mean MC	0.6979	0.7369 **(1.0559)**	0.7675 (1.0998)	0.7962 (1.1408)	0.8214 (1.1770)
DE	0.6979	0.7366 (1.0555)	0.7716 (1.1056)	0.8019 (1.1490)	0.8102 (1.1610)
Softmax	**0.6984**	**0.7374 (1.0559)**	**0.7730 (1.1068)**	**0.8067 (1.1550)**	**0.8359 (1.1969)**
PL-Variance	**0.6984**	0.7358 (1.0536)	0.7676 (1.0990)	0.7961 (1.1398)	0.8209 (1.1753)

Table A4. Macro F1 score and improvement rate for the Wiki dataset.

BERT	0%	10%	20%	30%	40%
Mean MC	0.9227	**0.9569 (1.0370)**	0.9742 (1.0557)	0.9824 (1.0646)	**0.9878 (1.0705)**
DE	0.9227	0.9566 (1.0367)	0.9743 (1.0559)	0.9767 (1.0585)	0.9762 (1.0579)
Softmax	**0.9230**	0.9561 (1.0358)	0.9745 (1.0558)	**0.9834 (1.0655)**	0.9869 (1.0692)
PL-Variance	**0.9230**	0.9566 (1.0364)	**0.9748 (1.0561)**	0.9827 (1.0647)	0.9869 (1.0693)
GloVe					
Mean MC	**0.8559**	0.8958 (1.0466)	0.9168 (1.0712)	**0.9325 (1.0896)**	0.9379 (1.0958)
DE	**0.8559**	0.8914 (1.0415)	0.9146 (1.0686)	0.9269 (1.0830)	0.9319 (1.0889)
Softmax	0.8539	0.8941 (1.0471)	0.9181 (1.0752)	0.9312 (1.0906)	**0.9393 (1.1001)**
PL-Variance	0.8539	**0.8958 (1.0491)**	**0.9209 (1.0785)**	0.9322 (**1.0918**)	0.9366 (1.0969)

Table A5. Macro F1 score and improvement rate for the SST-2 dataset.

BERT	0%	10%	20%	30%	40%
Mean MC	0.7407	0.7706 (1.0403)	0.7907 (1.0674)	0.8149 (1.1001)	0.8432 (1.1383)
DE	0.7407	**0.7744 (1.0454)**	**0.8008 (1.0811)**	**0.8265 (1.1158)**	**0.8472 (1.1437)**
Softmax	**0.7442**	0.7706 (1.0354)	0.8006 (1.0758)	0.8246 (1.1080)	0.8451 (1.1355)
PL-Variance	**0.7442**	0.7719 (1.0372)	0.7964 (1.0701)	0.8100 (1.0884)	0.8339 (1.1205)
GloVe					
Mean MC	0.7397	0.7658 (1.0354)	0.7853 (1.0354)	0.8013 (**1.0833**)	0.8202 (1.1088)
DE	0.7397	0.7648 (1.0339)	**0.7940 (1.0735)**	0.7998 (1.0812)	0.8204 (**1.1091**)
Softmax	**0.7442**	**0.7686 (1.0328)**	0.7918 (1.0639)	**0.8023 (1.0780)**	**0.8217** (1.0141)
PL-Variance	**0.7442**	**0.7686 (1.0328)**	0.7918 (1.0639)	**0.8023 (1.0780)**	0.8204 (1.1023)

Appendix C. Model Calibration Plots

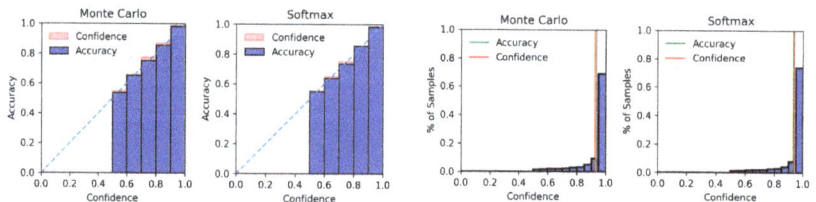

Figure A1. Reliability diagram (**left**) and confidence histogram (**right**) of IMDb using BERT-CNN.

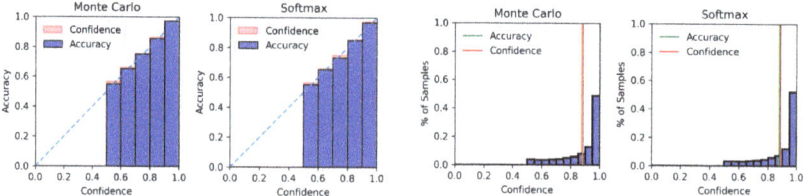

Figure A2. Reliability diagram (**left**) and confidence histogram (**right**) of IMDb using GloVe-CNN.

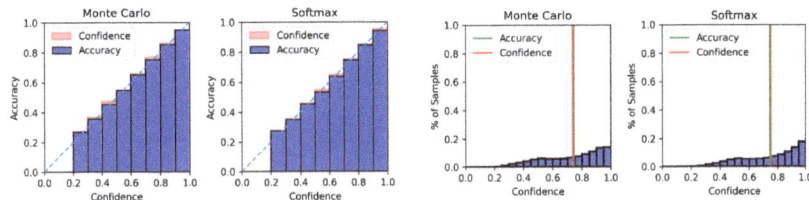

Figure A3. Reliability diagram (**left**) and confidence histogram (**right**) of Amazon using BERT-CNN.

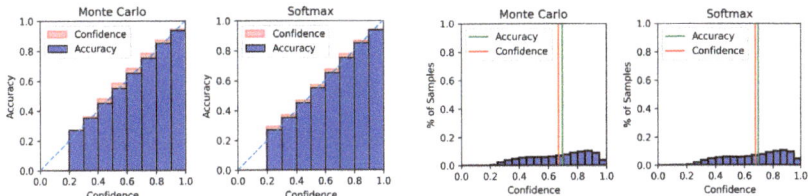

Figure A4. Reliability diagram (**left**) and confidence histogram (**right**) of Amazon using GloVe-CNN.

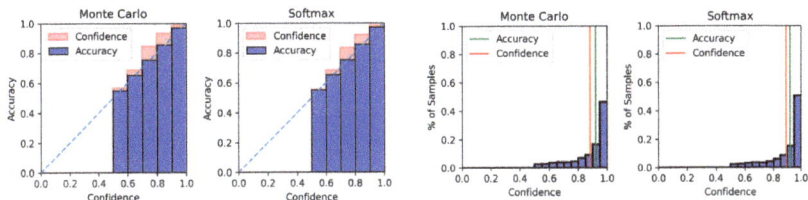

Figure A5. Reliability diagram (**left**) and confidence histogram (**right**) of WIKI using BERT-CNN.

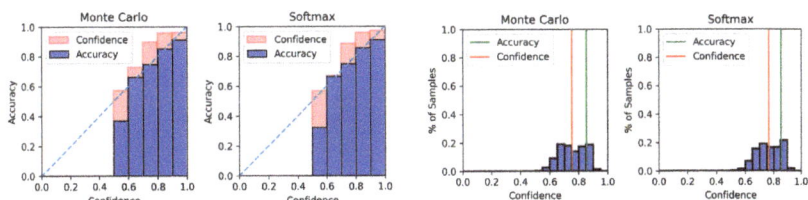

Figure A6. Reliability diagram (**left**) and confidence histogram (**right**) of WIKI using GloVe-CNN.

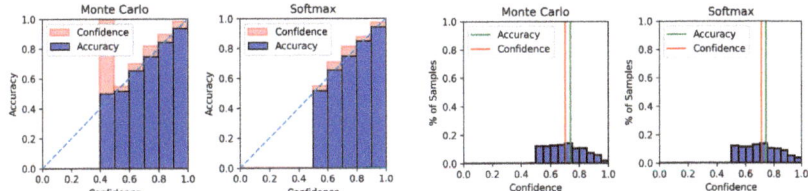

Figure A7. Reliability diagram (**left**) and confidence histogram (**right**) of SST-2 using BERT-CNN.

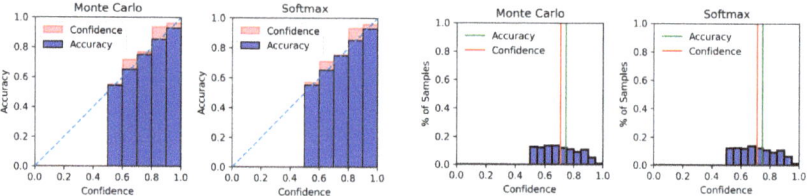

Figure A8. Reliability diagram (**left**) and confidence histogram (**right**) of SST-2 using GloVe-CNN.

References

1. Vaswani, A.; Shazeer, N.; Parmar, N.; Uszkoreit, J.; Jones, L.; Gomez, A.N.; Kaiser, L.; Polosukhin, I. Attention is All you Need. In Proceedings of the Advances in Neural Information Processing Systems 30, Long Beach, CA, USA, 4–9 December 2017; Guyon, I., Luxburg, U.V., Bengio, S., Wallach, H., Fergus, R., Vishwanathan, S., Garnett, R., Eds.; Curran Associates, Inc.: Red Hook, NY, USA, 2017; pp. 5998–6008.
2. Lin, T.; Wang, Y.; Liu, X.; Qiu, X. A Survey of Transformers. *arXiv* **2021**, arXiv:2106.04554.
3. Tay, Y.; Dehghani, M.; Gupta, J.P.; Aribandi, V.; Bahri, D.; Qin, Z.; Metzler, D. Are Pretrained Convolutions Better than Pretrained Transformers? In Proceedings of the 59th Annual Meeting of the Association for Computational Linguistics and the 11th International Joint Conference on Natural Language Processing (Volume 1: Long Papers), Online, 1–6 August 2021.
4. Gawlikowski, J.; Tassi, C.R.N.; Ali, M.; Lee, J.; Humt, M.; Feng, J.; Kruspe, A.; Triebel, R.; Jung, P.; Roscher, R.; et al. A Survey of Uncertainty in Deep Neural Networks. *arXiv* **2021**, arXiv:2107.03342.
5. Gal, Y.; Ghahramani, Z. Dropout as a Bayesian Approximation: Representing Model Uncertainty in Deep Learning. In Proceedings of the 33rd International Conference on Machine Learning, New York, NY, USA, 19–24 June 2016; pp. 1050–1059.
6. Blundell, C.; Cornebise, J.; Kavukcuoglu, K.; Wierstra, D. Weight Uncertainty in Neural Network. In Proceedings of the 32nd International Conference on Machine Learning, Lille, France, 6–11 July 2015; pp. 1613–1622.
7. Hendrycks, D.; Gimpel, K. A Baseline for Detecting Misclassified and Out-of-Distribution Examples in Neural Networks. In Proceedings of the 5th International Conference on Learning Representations, ICLR 2017, Toulon, France, 24–26 April 2017.
8. Zhang, X.; Chen, F.; Lu, C.T.; Ramakrishnan, N. Mitigating Uncertainty in Document Classification. In Proceedings of the 2019 Conference of the North American Chapter of the Association for Computational Linguistics: Human Language Technologies, Minneapolis, MN, USA, 2–7 July 2019; Long and Short Papers; Association for Computational Linguistics: Minneapolis, MN, USA, 2019; Volume 1, pp. 3126–3136. [CrossRef]
9. He, J.; Zhang, X.; Lei, S.; Chen, Z.; Chen, F.; Alhamadani, A.; Xiao, B.; Lu, C. Towards More Accurate Uncertainty Estimation In Text Classification. In Proceedings of the 2020 Conference on Empirical Methods in Natural Language Processing (EMNLP); Association for Computational Linguistics, Online, 16–20 November 2020; pp. 8362–8372. [CrossRef]
10. Strubell, E.; Ganesh, A.; McCallum, A. Energy and Policy Considerations for Deep Learning in NLP. In Proceedings of the 57th Annual Meeting of the Association for Computational Linguistics, Florence, Italy, 28 July–2 August 2019.
11. Patterson, D.A.; Gonzalez, J.; Le, Q.V.; Liang, C.; Munguia, L.; Rothchild, D.; So, D.R.; Texier, M.; Dean, J. Carbon Emissions and Large Neural Network Training. *arXiv* **2021**, arXiv:2104.10350.
12. Ovadia, Y.; Fertig, E.; Ren, J.; Nado, Z.; Sculley, D.; Nowozin, S.; Dillon, J.; Lakshminarayanan, B.; Snoek, J. Can you trust your model's uncertainty? Evaluating predictive uncertainty under dataset shift. In Proceedings of the Advances in Neural Information Processing Systems, Vancouver, BC, Canada, 8–14 December 2019; Curran Associates, Inc.: Red Hook, NY, USA, 2019; Volume 32.
13. Henne, M.; Schwaiger, A.; Roscher, K.; Weiss, G. Benchmarking Uncertainty Estimation Methods for Deep Learning with Safety-Related Metrics. In Proceedings of the Workshop on Artificial Intelligence Safety, Co-Located with 34th AAAI Conference on Artificial Intelligence, SafeAI@AAAI 2020, New York, NY, USA, 7 February 2020.
14. Mozejko, M.; Susik, M.; Karczewski, R. Inhibited Softmax for Uncertainty Estimation in Neural Networks. *arXiv* **2018**, arXiv:1810.01861.
15. van Amersfoort, J.; Smith, L.; Teh, Y.W.; Gal, Y. Uncertainty Estimation Using a Single Deep Deterministic Neural Network. In Proceedings of the 37th International Conference on Machine Learning, ICML Virtual Event, 13–18 July 2020; Volume 119, pp. 9690–9700. PMLR.
16. Hinton, G.E.; van Camp, D. Keeping the neural networks simple by minimizing the description length of the weights. In Proceedings of the Sixth Annual Conference on Computational Learning Theory, COLT'93, Santa Cruz, CA, USA, 26–28 July 1993; Association for Computing Machinery: New York, NY, USA, 1993; pp. 5–13. [CrossRef]
17. Neal, R. *Bayesian Training of Backpropagation Networks by the Hybrid Monte Carlo Method*; Technical Report; University of Toronto: Toronto, ON, Canada, 1993.
18. MacKay, D.J.C. A Practical Bayesian Framework for Backpropagation Networks. *Neural Comput.* **1992**, *4*, 448–472. [CrossRef]

19. Lakshminarayanan, B.; Pritzel, A.; Blundell, C. Simple and Scalable Predictive Uncertainty Estimation using Deep Ensembles. In Proceedings of the Advances in Neural Information Processing Systems, Long Beach, CA, USA, 4–9 December 2017; Guyon, I., Luxburg, U.V., Bengio, S., Wallach, H., Fergus, R., Vishwanathan, S., Garnett, R., Eds.; Curran Associates, Inc.: Red Hook, NY, USA, 2017; Volume 30.
20. Durasov, N.; Bagautdinov, T.; Baque, P.; Fua, P. Masksembles for uncertainty estimation. In Proceedings of the IEEE/CVF Conference on Computer Vision and Pattern Recognition, Nashville, TN, USA, 20–25 June 2021; pp. 13539–13548.
21. Niculescu-Mizil, A.; Caruana, R. Predicting good probabilities with supervised learning. In Proceedings of the 22nd international conference on Machine learning, ICML'05, Bonn German, 7–11 August 2005; Association for Computing Machinery: New York, NY, USA, 2015; pp. 625–632. [CrossRef]
22. Guo, C.; Pleiss, G.; Sun, Y.; Weinberger, K.Q. On Calibration of Modern Neural Networks. In Proceedings of the 34th International Conference on Machine Learning, Sydney, Australia, 6–11 August 2017; pp. 1321–1330.
23. Naeini, M.P.; Cooper, G.F.; Hauskrecht, M. Obtaining Well Calibrated Probabilities Using Bayesian Binning. In Proceedings of the AAAI conference on artificial intelligence, Austin, TX, USA, 25–30 January 2015; pp. 2901–2907.
24. Gal, Y.; Ghahramani, Z. Dropout as a Bayesian Approximation: Appendix. *arXiv* **2016**, arXiv:1506.02157.
25. Joo, T.; Chung, U.; Seo, M.G. Being Bayesian about Categorical Probability. In Proceedings of the 37th International Conference on Machine Learning, Virtual, 13–18 July 2020; pp. 4950–4961.
26. Lang, K. NewsWeeder: Learning to Filter Netnews. In Proceedings of the Twelfth International Conference on Machine Learning, Tahoe City, CA, USA, 9–12 July 1995; Prieditis, A., Russell, S., Eds.; Morgan Kaufmann: San Francisco, CA, USA, 1995; pp. 331–339. [CrossRef]
27. McAuley, J.; Leskovec, J. Hidden factors and hidden topics: Understanding rating dimensions with review text. In Proceedings of the 7th ACM conference on Recommender Systems, RecSys'13, Hong Kong, China, 12–16 October 2013; Association for Computing Machinery: New York, NY, USA, 2013; pp. 165–172. [CrossRef]
28. Maas, A.L.; Daly, R.E.; Pham, P.T.; Huang, D.; Ng, A.Y.; Potts, C. Learning Word Vectors for Sentiment Analysis. In Proceedings of the 49th Annual Meeting of the Association for Computational Linguistics: Human Language Technologies, Portland, OR, USA, 19–24 June 2011; Association for Computational Linguistics: Portland, OR, USA, 2011; pp. 142–150.
29. Socher, R.; Perelygin, A.; Wu, J.; Chuang, J.; Manning, C.D.; Ng, A.Y.; Potts, C. Recursive Deep Models for Semantic Compositionality Over a Sentiment Treebank. In Proceedings of the 2013 Conference on Empirical Methods in Natural Language Processing, EMNLP 2013, Grand Hyatt Seattle, Seattle, DC, USA, 18–21 October 2013.
30. Redi, M.; Fetahu, B.; Morgan, J.T.; Taraborelli, D. Citation Needed: A Taxonomy and Algorithmic Assessment of Wikipedia's Verifiability. In Proceedings of the WWW'19: The Web Conference, San Francisco, CA, USA, 13–17 May 2019.
31. Pennington, J.; Socher, R.; Manning, C.D. Glove: Global Vectors for Word Representation. In Proceedings of the 2014 Conference on Empirical Methods in Natural Language Processing, EMNLP 2014, Doha, Qatar, 25–29 October 2014.
32. Devlin, J.; Chang, M.W.; Lee, K.; Toutanova, K. BERT: Pre-training of Deep Bidirectional Transformers for Language Understanding. *arXiv* **2019**, arXiv:1810.04805.
33. Kingma, D.P.; Ba, J. Adam: A Method for Stochastic Optimization. In Proceedings of the 3rd International Conference on Learning Representations, ICLR 2015, Conference Track Proceedings, San Diego, CA, USA, 7–9 May 2015.
34. Zaragoza, H.; d'Alché Buc, F. Confidence Measures for Neural Network Classifiers. In Proceedings of the 7th Conference on Information Processing and Management of Uncertainty in Knowledge-Based Systems, Paris, France, 6–10 July 1998.

Disclaimer/Publisher's Note: The statements, opinions and data contained in all publications are solely those of the individual author(s) and contributor(s) and not of MDPI and/or the editor(s). MDPI and/or the editor(s) disclaim responsibility for any injury to people or property resulting from any ideas, methods, instructions or products referred to in the content.

Article

Exploring Neural Dynamics in Source Code Processing Domain

Martina Saletta [1,2,*] and Claudio Ferretti [2,*]

1 Department of Engineering and Architecture, University of Trieste, 34127 Trieste, Italy
2 Department of Informatics, Systems and Communication, University of Milano-Bicocca, 20126 Milan, Italy
* Correspondence: martina.saletta@unimib.it (M.S.); claudio.ferretti@unimib.it (C.F.)

Abstract: Deep neural networks have proven to be able to learn rich internal representations, including for features that can also be used for different purposes than those the networks are originally developed for. In this paper, we are interested in exploring such ability and, to this aim, we propose a novel approach for investigating the internal behavior of networks trained for source code processing tasks. Using a simple autoencoder trained in the reconstruction of vectors representing programs (i.e., program embeddings), we first analyze the performance of the internal neurons in classifying programs according to different labeling policies inspired by real programming issues, showing that some neurons can actually detect different program properties. We then study the dynamics of the network from an information-theoretic standpoint, namely by considering the neurons as signaling systems and by computing the corresponding entropy. Further, we define a way to distinguish neurons according to their behavior, to consider them as formally associated with different abstract *concepts*, and through the application of nonparametric statistical tests to pairs of neurons, we look for neurons with unique (or almost unique) associated concepts, showing that the entropy value of a neuron is related to the rareness of its concept. Finally, we discuss how the proposed approaches for ranking the neurons can be generalized to different domains and applied to more sophisticated and specialized networks so as to help the research in the growing field of explainable artificial intelligence.

Keywords: explainable AI; artificial neural networks; knowledge representation; source code analysis

Citation: Saletta, M.; Ferretti, C. Exploring Neural Dynamics in Source Code Processing Domain. *Information* **2023**, *14*, 251. https://doi.org/10.3390/info14040251

Academic Editors: Gabriele Gianini and Pierre-Edouard Portier

Received: 28 February 2023
Revised: 5 April 2023
Accepted: 17 April 2023
Published: 21 April 2023

Copyright: © 2023 by the authors. Licensee MDPI, Basel, Switzerland. This article is an open access article distributed under the terms and conditions of the Creative Commons Attribution (CC BY) license (https://creativecommons.org/licenses/by/4.0/).

1. Introduction

Research results on the use of deep learning systems show how the internal representation developed by a system during its training is of value, even for tasks different than those it was trained for. Techniques which exploit this fact are, for example, the methods for pretraining [1] or semisupervised learning, transfer learning [2], or internal interpretability [3]. The research that aims at characterizing such internal representation is active for the domains of image processing [4] and of natural language processing (NLP) [5], while fewer results are, however, available for the domain of source code processing.

In the specific field of source code static analysis, many neural systems have been presented (we refer the reader to [6,7] for surveys), especially for tasks related to the software engineering domain, such as bug detection or code completion, but also for more *semantic* purposes, e.g., automatic tagging or classification according to the functionality of the code snippet being examined.

Given the importance of understanding these neural networks for source code processing, which are becoming more and more common, we focus on examining the internal neurons of some given learning system in order to look for those which exhibit interesting behaviors in terms of classification performance or activation patterns.

The main goal is to define a general approach for discovering and exploiting *all* the knowledge learned by a given model. For instance, one can assume to have a neural model (trained on a main task) embedded in a code editor or in a software repository that also allows tapping into further parts of the internal representation developed while being trained. To this aim, this work provides the following contributions:

- A procedure for ranking neurons according to their ability in solving arbitrary binary classification tasks. With the experiments in this direction, we show how some neurons are able to autonomously build internal representations for different program properties.
- An information-theoretic approach for identifying neurons which exhibit interesting behaviours, with the aim to identify the most *informative* neurons in the network and to discriminate among neurons showing different activation patterns.
- A statistical measure for comparing the arbitrary binary tasks defined by single neurons (namely by simply establishing a threshold and by splitting the dataset according to the activation induced by each program instance) so as to identify neurons which recognize unique (or uncommon) *concepts*.

Related Work

Chasing the success achieved in a wide range of domains, such as those of images and NLP, systems based on machine learning (ML) are becoming popular also for dealing with source code (see, e.g., [6,7]) and, more in general, with software artifacts [8]. To this end, the recent literature features several examples of ML models trained in solving tasks related to the source code processing domain, including code completion [9], code summarization [10], and classification [11]. The choice of the input representation for feeding such models is, in general, a crucial aspect in this scope, since it is not always effective to use the pure textual representation as in classical NLP models. To this end, several works are focused in the design of program encodings or representations that are able to capture different properties so as to properly convey the seized information and to help in the solution of a specific task. An interesting approach in this direction is, for instance, the work described in [12], where a graph-based representation for programs derived from the abstract syntax tree (AST) is used for solving classical software engineering tasks such as predicting the name of a variable or if a variable has been misused. A similar idea is tackled in [13], where the authors propose a vector representation for programs, namely a source code *embedding*, for solving similar tasks, e.g., for predicting the name of a method.

Recently, besides the use of networks that need as input specific program representations, also the models commonly known as transformers [14], widely used for NLP applications, are becoming popular in the source code processing domain [15,16]. One of the advantages in using these kinds of networks is their flexibility: they can be trained once on generic and big corpora of data and then fine-tuned for solving several specific tasks.

The study of the internal behavior of neural models is becoming popular, and many research results in this direction show how the analysis of the activation patterns that a neuron exhibits is of interest, both in terms of the internal representations it develops and when considered only for its inherent dynamics. A recent work [17], for instance, proposes a study of these dynamics from an information-theoretic perspective, while in the area of image analysis an interesting approach for studying the internal representations developed by the neurons is proposed in [4], where each neuron of an unsupervised trained network was evaluated with respect to a given image classification task, with insightful results. More recently, results have been obtained for evaluating single neurons for sentiment analysis tasks [18] or in networks trained to model natural languages [5].

More recently, groups of neurons have been devised to explain the decision processes of neural networks. For instance, *concept activation vectors* (CAVs) [19] have proven to be effective to model human-understandable concepts in the internal states of a network and have been effectively applied also in many different domains, such as that of chess [20] and of source code analysis [21,22].

2. Approach Description

In this section, we provide a high-level description of the approach we devised for analyzing the internal behavior of neural networks trained on source code, with the aim to express and reason about its dynamics in a measurable way.

We first trained a simple autoencoder (i.e., an artificial neural network trained in the reconstruction of the input, see [23] for a complete reference) on two different source code embeddings, and then we performed three categories of experiments:

1. Binary classification experiments, for ranking neurons considering their ability in solving specific tasks.
2. Analysis of the relevance of the neurons for the network itself, regardless of a given task.
3. Pairwise comparison of the neurons' dynamics, through the adoption of statistical techniques.

For all these experimental approaches, we first map the source code to feature vectors, namely via a neural embedding, and then we study the internal behavior of a neural network trained on such vectors by analyzing the activation values of the neurons on different program instances. In the first two cases, we are interested in assigning a score to each neuron, i.e., in ranking the neurons according to different criteria, while the aim of the third point is to possibly define a partition for the set of neurons in order to discriminate among different behaviors and to define an association among neurons sharing similar patterns in terms of statistical distribution of the activation values.

In the classification experiments, the score we assign to each neuron is represented by the accuracy obtained when used as a classifier for given binary problems, as will be detailed in Section 4. The basic concept is to consider, for each neuron, different activation thresholds and then to measure, for each threshold, the accuracy of the neuron in classifying program instances from a balanced labeled sample when predicting a program to be in class 0 if the activation yielded by that program is less than the threshold and to be in class 1 otherwise. The scoring mark for a neuron is the accuracy obtained while considering the threshold that leads to the highest accuracy.

In the second class of experiments, the score of each neuron is instead computed independently from any task. Similar studies, i.e., the definition of a scoring measure for evaluating the importance of single neurons in a network, have been already investigated in the literature [5,24]. While in the referred works the core idea is to use the correlation between activation values of neurons in distinct but isomorphic models (i.e., retraining on different training sets of the same model) for finding neurons that possibly capture properties that emerge in different models, in this paper we propose a ranking based on the concept of *entropy* used in information theory. The reason is that, while by means of the correlation analysis one is able to state which neurons are the most important with respect to the task the network is trained on, with the entropy-based measure we are proposing, the neurons are graded with regard to the importance they have according to their behavior in the network: since, by definition, the entropy in information theory is the average level of information emitted by a signaling system [25], computing the entropy of single neurons is equivalent to measuring how much each neuron is informative.

Finally, in the third class of experiments, we consider all the possible pairs of neurons and, for each pair, we perform a nonparametric statistical test for assessing which neurons share some activation patterns. This will also allow us, as it will be detailed and formalized in Section 5, to study if there exists a partition of the neurons based on their entropy levels such that (intuitively) activation patterns of the neurons belonging to the same part can be distinguished from those of neurons belonging to the other parts. Since, as it will be detailed in Section 5, we can associate with each neuron an arbitrary *concept*, being able to distinguish among different neurons' behaviors could be somehow comparable to detect different concepts that are autonomously learned by the network, regardless to the original task it is trained on.

3. Experimental Settings

This section describes the experimental setting we adopted in order to study both the ability of the hidden neurons of a generic neural network in building a high-level representation for some specific source code-related features, similar to what the authors of [4,18] did for images and natural language, and to characterize (and distinguish) the behavior of the neurons in terms of their entropy and their activation patterns.

3.1. Network Architecture

We chose to work in the context of a simple neural model, namely an autoencoder. Without any hyper-parameter optimization nor any in-depth study on the network design, we implemented a simple dense autoencoder having two hidden layers in the encoder, two symmetrical hidden layers in the decoder, and one code layer in the middle, as shown in Figure 1. We used the *ADADELTA* optimizer [26] and the mean squared error as a loss function. As the activation function for the hidden layers, we applied the Rectified Linear Unit (ReLU), defined for all $x \in \mathbb{R}$ as $\max(0, x)$. The model is implemented using the APIs provided by the Keras library [27].

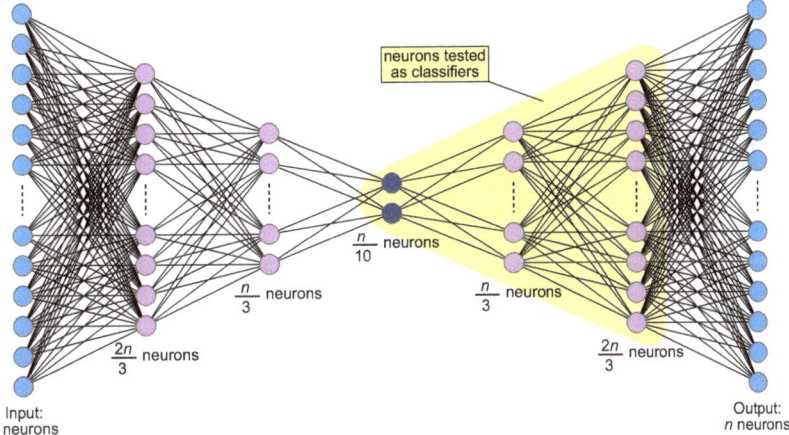

Figure 1. Network architecture. The sizes of the layers depend to the program vector dimensions. In all our experiments, we considered $n = 300$. Layers highlighted in yellow are those tested in the experiments.

3.2. Training

For the training phase, we used the dataset also adopted in [10], which is a collection of popular GitHub (https://github.com, accessed on 4 April 2023) Java projects that contains over 400,000 methods, while for all the experiments, we employed a subset of the Java-med dataset described in [28].

We performed two independent trainings of the autoencoder, using two different source code embedding algorithms for preprocessing all the methods in the dataset and computing the corresponding program vectors:

1. A 300-dimensional embedding obtained by simply applying the doc2vec model [29] to the methods in the dataset using the gensim framework [30]. To avoid inconsistencies related to formatting choices, such as the presence or absence of spaces between operands and operators, keywords and parentheses, we applied the doc2vec model to a pretty printed version of the methods obtained by using the Javaparser library [31].
2. The source code embedding proposed in [32], which we will refer to as ast2vec, consists of the application of the word2vec model [33] to words and sentences derived from the abstract syntax tree.

Notice that our approach can be applied to any neural network, from the most simple, to more sophisticated ones. In general, differently from the field of images, where the input of the network is exactly the object being studied, more often than with images, models for source code processing require a specific program representation as input, e.g., a numerical vector representation (embedding) or a stream of tokens, and each representation inherently preserves or emphasizes some program features to the detriment of others. Since in this work we are mostly interested in proposing and evaluating the approach rather than in studying the best input representation, the two sets of program vectors considered for our experiments have different underlying construction ideas: doc2vec embedding is built by applying a classical NLP technique to the pure source code, so it is not supposed to be particularly viable in this context, while ast2vec is developed by considering both structural (neighborhood of nodes in the AST) and lexical (identifiers chosen by the programmer) features, and thus it is assumed to be particularly suitable and flexible for general program comprehension applications.

We trained each autoencoder for 50 epochs using the hyper-parameters described in Section 3.1; due to the input vector dimensions, the layers in the encoder have, respectively, 300, 200, and 100 neurons, those in the decoder symmetrically have 100, 200, and 300 neurons, and the code layer has 30 neurons.

4. Experiments on Classification Tasks

For assessing the ability of the internal neurons in our networks to build internal representations for different program properties, we first tested each neuron in being used as a classifier for distinct binary classification problems, following the same approach of previous works [4,18].

4.1. Problems Definition

When dealing with images and product reviews as in the referred papers, the properties according to which to classify the input objects can be easily defined could be, for instance, the presence of particular patterns (e.g., cats or faces [4]) or positive and negative review sentiments [18], as in classical image recognition and sentiment analysis tasks. In the program comprehension context, however, such kinds of properties do not directly arise from the source code, or at least they are not immediately evident for a human being reading it. Therefore, we first defined different labeling policies for classification so as to capture properties having different natures:

- The first one, designed using the control flow graph (CFG) [34], addresses the syntactical structure of a method in terms of its **structural complexity**.
- The second one relies on the method's **identifiers** chosen by the programmers in order to target a task related to the functionality of a method.
- The third one is related to its **I/O relationship**, that is the relation between the input parameters and the returned object of a method.
- The last one is a **random** labeling strategy used as a baseline.

In the following, we formally describe these labeling policies with full details:

Structural Labeling Policy

We consider the *cyclomatic complexity* [35] of a program, defined starting from its CFG $\mathcal{G}$ having n vertices, e edges, and p connected components as:

$$V(\mathcal{G}) = e - n + p \qquad (1)$$

Dealing with Java methods, such metric can be easily calculated by counting 1 point for the beginning of the method, 1 point for each conditional construct and for each case or default block in a switch-case statement, 1 point for each iterative structure, and 1 point for each Boolean condition. Starting from this software metric, we define the problem as follows, for a given parameter c:

Problem 1. *Let M be a set of Java methods, let $c \in \mathbb{N}$, and let $h_c : M \to \{0,1\}$ be a binary classification rule for the methods. We define, for each $m \in M$:*

$$h_c(m) = \begin{cases} 0 & \text{if } V(\mathcal{G}_m) < c \\ 1 & \text{otherwise} \end{cases} \quad (2)$$

Identifiers-Based Labeling Policy

For the definition of the semantic labeling strategy, we adopted the same assumption that Allamanis et al. [10] and Alon et al. [36] made in their works, namely that the name a programmer gives to a method can be somehow considered as a summary of the method's operations, meaning that the name of a method shall provide some semantic information on the method itself. Starting from this premise, we define this semantic labeling considering the presence or absence of specific patterns, from a given set T, in the method name:

Problem 2. *Let M be a set of methods, let $N = \{lab_m : m \in M\}$ be the set of the names of the methods in M, and let T be a set of patterns. We write $r \leq s$ if r and s are strings and r is a substring of s. Let $h_T : M \to \{0,1\}$ be a binary classification rule for the methods. We define, for each $m \in M$:*

$$h_T(m) = \begin{cases} 1 & \text{if } \exists t \in T : t \leq lab_m \\ 0 & \text{otherwise} \end{cases} \quad (3)$$

I/O-Based Labeling Policy

The idea beyond this kind of labeling is that the relation between the input and the output of a program can suggest something about the functionality of a program. For example, a program that takes an array of integers as input, and that returns another array of integers, could possibly be a program that fulfills some kind of sorting or filtering operations, while a program that requires as input an array, no matter its type, and that returns an object of the same type, can possibly represent some kind of search operation.

For the definition of this class of binary problems, we only consider a subset of all the possible I/O relations, namely the presence or the absence of an array among the input arguments and whether the returned object is an array or a single element. For easing the discussion, we adopt the following binary notation to describe such possible relations:

00: many to many
01: many to one
10: one to many
11: one to one

Following this notation, this labeling strategy can be formalized as follows:

Problem 3. *Let M be a set of non-void methods, each having at least one input argument. Let $L = \{00, 01, 10, 11\}$ be the set of possible labels for each $m \in M$. We remark that it exists a function $l : M \to L$ that assigns a label to each method. Let $\mathcal{P}(L)$ be the power set of L. Let $h_P : M \to \{0,1\}$ be a binary classification rule. We define, for each $m \in M$ and for a given $P \in \mathcal{P}(L)$:*

$$h_P(m) = \begin{cases} 1 & \text{if } l(m) \in P \\ 0 & \text{otherwise} \end{cases} \quad (4)$$

Random Labeling Policy

We finally define a baseline labeling strategy for assessing our results by comparing them with the results obtained while solving an arbitrary task whose results should be only noise. We simply consider a random split of the methods:

Problem 4. *Let L be a randomly shuffled list of methods, and let $m_i \in L$ be the method having index i. Given a threshold $n \in \mathbb{N}$ and let $h_n : L \to \{0, 1\}$ be a binary classification function, we define, for each $m_i \in L$:*

$$h_n(m_i) = \begin{cases} 1 & \text{if } i \leq n \\ 0 & \text{otherwise} \end{cases} \quad (5)$$

4.2. Classification

We tested the performance of the hidden neurons in classifying methods according to different instances of the classes of problems described in the previous section. To this aim, we considered all the neurons in the code layer and in the two hidden layers in the decoder, as shown in Figure 1, and we tested their classification accuracy by considering the activation produced by a neuron for each method given as input. The reason why we tested only the decoding neurons lies in the nature of an autoencoder: in the encoder layers a progressive dimensionality reduction (and thus a compression of information) is performed, and this (likely) means that in the middle code layer only relevant features are encoded. Since in the decoder layers the dimension is symmetrically increased for reconstructing the input, we decided to test only those neurons since they are expected to hold more relevant features. We remark that the same approach have been proposed, with promising results, for images [4] and for natural language [18], but it is new, to the best of our knowledge, for source code processing applications.

In detail, for each of the selected neurons, we considered as possible thresholds 10 equally spaced values among the minimum and the maximum activation value of that neuron for methods in the training set. For each activation threshold, we computed the classification accuracy of the neuron on a given problem instance by considering, in a precomputed balanced sample of the test set, the activation value of the neuron for that method and by predicting the method to be in class 0 or in class 1 if the activation value is less or greater than the threshold, respectively.

This process, formally described in the algorithm outlined in Algorithm 1, gives us a procedure for ranking neurons according to a task: we assign to each neuron its highest accuracy score. Table 1 shows the accuracies obtained by the best neuron for the considered problem instances, while the complete results obtained with the classification experiments will be discussed with further details in Section 6.

Table 1. Best accuracy score for each of the problems defined in Section 4.

Class	Instance	doc2vec	ast2vec
Random	none	54%	52%
Structural	$c = 10$	81%	84%
Semantic	$T = \{\text{test}\}$	63%	71%
Semantic	$T = \{\text{daemon}\}$	70%	68%
I/O	$\{00\}$ vs. $\{01, 10, 11\}$	64%	65%
I/O	$\{00, 10\}$ vs. $\{01, 11\}$	59%	64%

Algorithm 1 Algorithm for finding the best neuron in classifying programs on binary problems. The accuracy is computed by considering two balanced classes, each having at least 300 examples.

1:	$bestAcc \leftarrow 0$	▷ accuracy of the best neuron
2:	**for all** neuron N **do**	
3:	$A \leftarrow$ activation values of N	
4:	$T \leftarrow$ activation thresholds	▷ 10 evenly spaced thresholds between 0 and $\max a \in A$
5:	$best_N \leftarrow 0$	▷ best accuracy for N
6:	**for all** $t \in T$ **do**	
7:	$pred \leftarrow$ empty list	▷ list of predictions
8:	**for all** $a \in A$ **do**	
9:	**if** $a \le t$ **then**	
10:	append 0 to $pred$	
11:	**else**	
12:	append 1 to $pred$	
13:	**end if**	
14:	**end for**	
15:	**if** ACCURACY($pred$) $\ge best_N$ **then**	
16:	$best_N \leftarrow$ ACCURACY($pred$)	▷ update best accuracy of N
17:	**end if**	
18:	**end for**	
19:	**if** $best_N \ge bestAcc$ **then**	
20:	$bestAcc \leftarrow best_N$	▷ update best neuron
21:	$bestNeuron \leftarrow N$	
22:	**end if**	
23:	**end for**	

5. Scoring Neurons Independently of any Task

In the previous section, we described our experiments for evaluating the ability of individual neurons in solving specific classification problems or, in other words, in recognizing predetermined program properties. In the following, we propose a scoring measure for neurons based on the concept of *entropy* used in information theory. Further, we use the Mann–Whitney U statistical test for comparing the behavior of two neurons, assessing whether they share similar activation patterns and thus whether they are able to approximately detect the same concept.

5.1. Entropy and Single Neurons

The method we propose for evaluating the importance of each neuron in the network is based on the information-theoretic concept of entropy [25]. As we will discuss in Section 6, the experiments performed for assessing the results obtained with this scoring approach proved the effectiveness of this ranking, since it can discriminate among neurons which exhibit very simple activation patterns (i.e., active on only very few instances and therefore with low entropy), from more elaborate ones (i.e., those having varied activation values on many instances, corresponding to medium or high entropy).

The baseline idea behind this approach is that each neuron can be seen as a signaling system whose symbols are its activation values. Formally, in information theory, the entropy is defined as the average information obtained from a signaling system S which can output q different symbols $s_1, \ldots, s_q$ with probability $p_i = P(s_i)$:

$$H(S) = \sum_{i=0}^{i \le q} p_i \log \frac{1}{p_i} \qquad (6)$$

Dealing with activation values, whose domain is continuous over $\mathbb{R}_0^+$, we constructed a discretization of that space by considering a set $R = \{r_1, \ldots, r_{1000}\}$ of 1000 evenly spaced intervals between 0 and the maximum activation value reached by a neuron for the vectors in the training set, and we considered those intervals as the possible symbols of the neurons' alphabet. More precisely, for each neuron N we computed the activation values yielded on a random sample of 10,000 vectors, and we determined the number of occurrences of each symbol by counting the activation values yielded in each interval r_i. We then considered the set $R_N \subseteq R$ of the occurring symbols in the neuron N and for each $r_i \in R_N$ we derived its occurring probability p_i using a softmax function over the set of countings. Then, we assigned to each neuron a score defined as the entropy computed over the set $P_N = \bigcup p_i$, where each p_i is the probability associated to the symbol r_i in R_N, as described by the algorithm reported in Algorithm 2.

Algorithm 2 Algorithm for computing the entropy of each neuron.

1: $R \leftarrow$ list of intervals
2: **for all** neuron N **do**
3:      $M \leftarrow$ random sample of 10000 methods
4:      $V \leftarrow$ activations of N for each $m \in M$
5:      SCORE_NEURON(N, R, V)
6: **end for**
7:
8: **procedure** SCORE_NEURON(N, R, V)
9:      $C \leftarrow$ empty list
10:     **for all** $r \in R$ **do**
11:         $c \leftarrow$ number of $v \in V$ such that $v \in r$
12:         append c to C
13:     **end for**
14:     remove all the 0s from C
15:     $P \leftarrow$ SOFTMAX(C)
16:     **return** $-\sum_{p_i \in P} p_i \log p_i$
17: **end procedure**

5.2. Pairwise Neuron Comparison

We now provide further considerations on how entropy distinguishes neurons. The main insight is that it is always is possible to associate, to each neuron, a *concept* by simply looking at the instances that produces the highest activation values for that neuron. In other words, the concept corresponds to the binary classification task obtained by fixing an activation threshold and then by predicting the instances as satisfying that concept if the yielded activation value is higher than the threshold. Given this premise, we can define an heuristic procedure for measuring the similarity of the concepts defined by two neurons, by applying the Mann-Whitney U test in the following way:

1. Choose two neurons N_{ref} and N_{cf}, representing the neuron that defines the concept and the neuron to compare it to, respectively.
2. Considering the neuron N_{ref}, for each program instance $m_i \in M = \{m_1, \ldots, m_n\}$, compute the set of activation values $A = \{a_1, \ldots, a_n\}$ and create the list $L = \langle m_1, a_1 \rangle, \ldots, \langle m_n, a_n \rangle$, sorted according to a_i.
3. After splitting the sorted list L in three equally sized parts, generate the sets M_0 and M_1 by grouping the instances from the first and last of those parts, respectively.
4. Select two equally sized random samples of instances from M_0 and M_1 and compute the corresponding two sets C_0 and C_1 of activation values for N_{cf}.
5. Perform the Mann-Whitney U test on the sets of values C_0 and C_1, with alternative hypothesis that the distribution underlying the first set is stochastically *less* than the distribution underlying the second one.

Notice that, in our procedure, the threshold is represented by a range of values instead of a single point. The reason is to make the definition of the binary classification problem more robust, since we are removing the points in the middle that could likely give rise to confusion.

As it will be discussed in Section 6, by applying this procedure to all the possible pairs of neurons we are able to assess that different entropy values correspond to different behaviors in terms of recognized concepts. Further, we show how the replicability of the concepts defined by the neurons varies when comparing neurons belonging to different entropy ranges.

6. Results Discussion

In this section, we introduce the results obtained with our experiments. We first analyze the performance of the neurons while solving different instances of the classification tasks described in Section 4, in the second part we look at the neurons from the information theoretic standpoint discussed in Section 5, while in the third part we compare pairs of neurons and we show how different entropy intervals clearly characterize specific behaviors.

6.1. Task-Based Experiments

A summary of the results obtained in the classification experiments is reported in Table 1. We considered different instances for the classification problems described in Section 4, and we evaluated the classification accuracy of each neuron. As can be seen in Figure 2, where we reported the accuracy distributions for some of the considered problem instances, for each problem most of the neurons reach an accuracy level between 0.5 and 0.55, while only a few neurons are indeed able to reach higher accuracies. This evidence is already interesting by itself since it means that single neurons perform differently when tested on a given task and also that some neurons are actually able to detect source-code-related properties. The accuracy varies a lot when considering different problem and different embeddings, but this is probably due to the features that are naturally seized by the vectors. Indeed, in our experiments this is confirmed by the good results obtained for the structural task with the ast2vec embedding (first diagram in Figure 2). Finally, the experiments on the baseline random problem confirm the validity of our results showing how the performance of the neurons on a randomly defined problem is far from being comparable to the one obtained on all the other tasks, hence good performances are not emerging by chance.

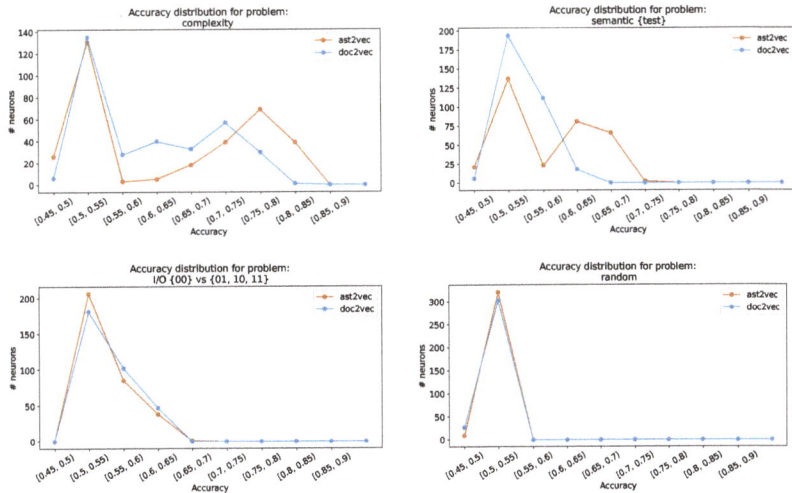

Figure 2. Classification accuracies reached by the neurons on different problem instances (see Section 4).

6.2. Task-Independent Experiments

We can start from the original goal of information theoretic entropy: it measures the average level of information of a source given its outcome. In our setting, each neuron can be considered a source of symbols, when we interpret its possible activation values as explained in Section 5.1.

Our measure of entropy allows us to distinguish (internal) neurons with respect to the variety of the activation values they output for each instance presented to the network. Eventually, each neuron's behavior in terms of output activation values is defined by the training process and, when considering internal neurons, also by its connectivity to the rest of the network.

Here we perform experiments aimed at showing how such a measure can be used to identify neurons that can be used to perform some interesting classifications of input instances. Previously, we identified interesting neurons by first specifying some classification problem, and then by measuring the performance of each neuron on it. Differently, the interest here is to specify what can characterize interesting classifications so as to look for corresponding behaviors among the internal neurons.

In this work, we firstly chose to understand how the behavior of neurons varies with different entropy values, and when operating on two different ways of embedding source code input instances.

To this aim, we first plotted the distribution of entropy values among the neurons of the autoencoder's section highlighted in Figure 1. The resulting distributions, in Figure 3, are qualitatively similar under both doc2vec and ast2vec embeddings, with a bimodal profile characterized by a peak of occurrences for very low values of entropy and an area of normally distributed frequencies for higher entropy values.

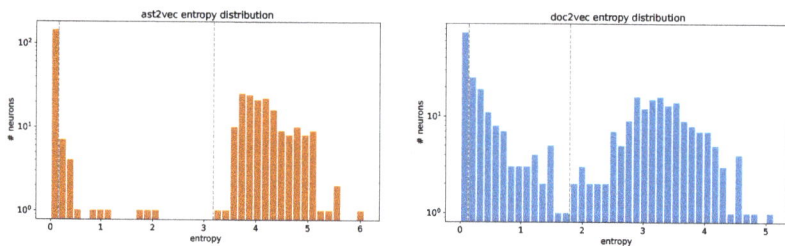

Figure 3. Distribution of the neurons' entropies in the ast2vec (**left**) and doc2vec (**right**) models. Vertical dashed lines separate the three classes of neurons described in Section 6.2.

Therefore, three classes of neurons having different entropy values can be roughly distinguished:

1. A big number of neurons (notice that the figure is in a logarithmic scale) having an entropy equals or very close to 0. These neurons are of no interest in this context since they are neurons that (almost) never activate. They could only be used for pruning the network in order to optimize the architecture, but it is out of the focus of this work.
2. Another big class of neurons having normally distributed high entropy values. Those neurons reach an high score since their activation values are distributed over a wide range. In addition, the probabilities of the occurring activation values to be in distinct intervals are relatively similar: this leads to an high score in terms of information theory.
3. A smaller set of neurons whose values are higher than 0 but that are out of the normal distribution of the majority of the values. The corresponding activation values are those between the dashed bars plotted in Figure 3. As it will be clear by the discussion in Section 6, those neurons are peculiar since they produce an activation higher than 0

only for a significant amount of vectors (i.e., >10%), while in all the other cases their activation is equal to 0.

For two neurons, one with low entropy and one with high entropy, we plotted their activation values for a set of input instances in Figure 4 (left). More related to our entropy measure, we show in the same Figure 4 (right) the distribution of symbols, defined on intervals of activation values, for the same two neurons.

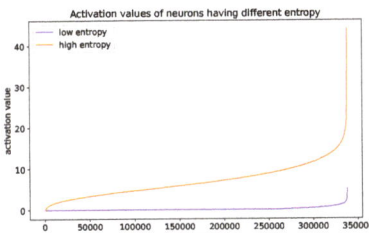 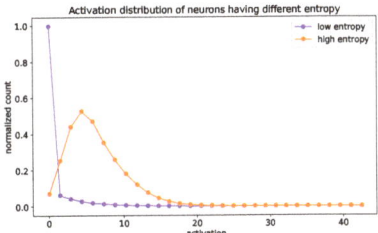

Figure 4. Activations of neurons having different entropies. In both the images, the purple line refers to a neuron having a low entropy score $H = 1.06$, while the orange line represents a neuron with an high entropy $H = 5.19$. The left figure is a simple plot of the sorted activation values for the two neurons, while the left figure reports the distribution of the activation values.

Moreover, even if in this analysis we consider the two embeddings systems as black boxes, the outcomes of these experiments, as presented by the data in Figure 3, are revealing something about how the ensembles of neurons of the two autoencoders are trained, with the two different vector datasets. The autoencoders eventually achieve their goals in different ways, with respect to the set of behaviors learned by their neurons. For ast2vec, Figure 3 tells us that only about half of the neurons have high entropy (above 3), while the others have a null or very small entropy value. It appears that the autoencoder is able to reconstruct the input with little contribution from many of its neurons. Instead, the autoencoder operating on the doc2vec instances eventually computes its output from the collective working of neurons with more diverse behavior in terms of their entropy, and with a smaller percentage of neurons with entropy of 0 or close to 0. The different training outcomes associated with the different datasets suggest further analysis of the datasets and of their distributional structures.

6.3. Pairwise Neuron Comparison Experiments

When exploring what neurons are representing, we experimented with the comparing measure introduced in Section 5. We take two neurons, N_{ref} and N_{cf}, and we assign to the first a reference role, and the second one will be compared to it in terms of how they can classify input instances. Preliminary findings show that experiments with ast2vec and doc2vec produce very similar results, and for this reason, all the following discussion is made by considering only the neurons in the ast2vec autoencoder.

As stated in Section 5.2, activations of a neuron on instances define its classifying behavior, and thus we will compare two neurons in terms of how a neuron can approximate the classification of another. For instance, looking at Figure 5 (right), we can see how a chosen neuron N_{cf} activates on negative instances (set M_0, bars in red) or positive (set M_1, bars in blue) for neuron N_{ref}. In this case, it appears that we can find a threshold on activation values good to classify most of the instances in the same way as the chosen N_{ref}.

Finally, we can see that in general such a threshold could be found when the medians of the two distributions, one from the activation values of N_{cf} on M_0 and the other from its activations on M_1, are separated, and we assess this with Mann–Whitney U test on those pairs of distributions.

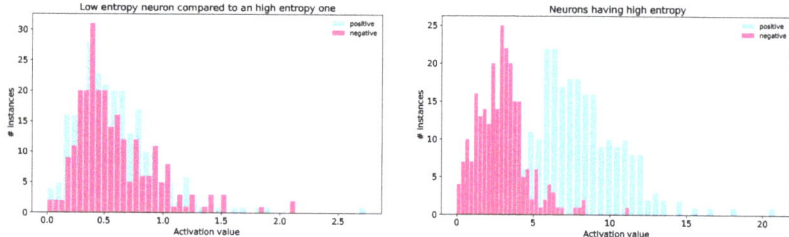

Figure 5. Activations of two high-entropy reference neurons, one compared against a low-entropy neuron (**left**) and one against a high-entropy neuron (**right**), both in the role of N_{cf}. Colors of bars correspond to the classes M_0 and M_1 defined by the reference neuron N_{ref}.

We remark that the results we will outline shortly still stay valid when considering the alternative hypothesis of having the first distribution stochastically *greater* than the second one. In fact, this would mean that instances producing a high activation level on the first neuron tend to produce a low activation level on the second one and vice versa. Therefore, in this case the binary classification produced by the first neuron could be approximated by the opposite of the classification produced by the second one.

Overall, we explored the reproducibility of a given classification, the one from a neuron N_{ref} by a second neuron N_{cf}, on every pair of neurons from the autoencoder section previously considered. Now we present the results and the insights of these experiments.

The first evidence is that there is a correlation between entropy of the two neurons we compare as described above. In Figure 6, we picture the success ratio of the test according to the entropy of the neurons being compared. When both the reference and the comparison neurons have high entropy, the Mann–Whitney U test favors the *less* hypothesis, with $p < \alpha$ where $\alpha = 0.01$ is the considered significance level.

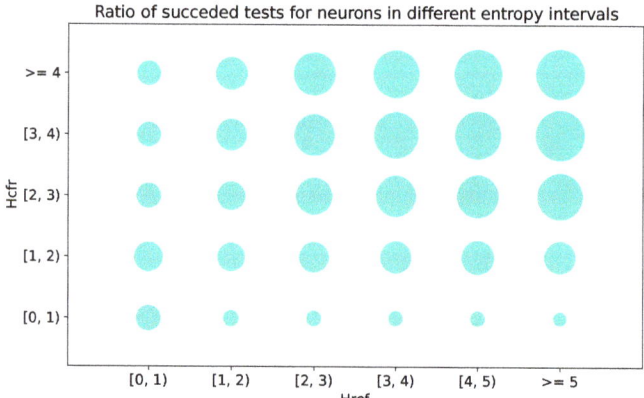

Figure 6. Ratio of successful Mann–Whitney U tests while comparing neurons belonging to different entropy ranges. When tests succeed the classification behavior of neuron N_{ref} can be approximated by defining a threshold on the activation levels of neuron N_{cf}.

For instance, we show in Figure 5 the details of two comparisons, one (left) where we compare a neuron with low entropy to a neuron with high entropy and another (right) where we compare two neurons having high entropy. The bars represent the distribution of the activation values for the instances in the two classes M_0 and M_1 defined by N_{ref}. Specifically, the colors of the bars are associated with the classification of instances of N_{ref}, while their position and height represent the activation levels produced by N_{cf} on the same instances. The two distributions on which the Mann–Whitney U test are performed are the activation values of the N_{cf} for instances associated to the two sets M_0 and M_1, respectively. In the first plot (left), we report the comparison of two neurons over which the test fails; that is, it is not possible to distinguish among the two distributions, and thus it is probable that the two medians are not one less than the other. We read this as evidence that no threshold is good enough to separate red and blue bars, while in the other one (right), this can be accomplished with some approximation.

Putting Things Together

The two measures we introduced, the entropy of each neuron and the similarity check between two neurons based on Mann–Whitney U test, are aimed at looking for (internal) neurons which can recognize interesting concepts. Therefore, we finally check how those measures apply on neurons which performed well in one of the specific tasks we presented in the previous section.

We took the neurons having accuracy above 0.8 on the task of estimating the cyclomatic complexity of source code. The evidence we gathered show that:

- Over the total 330 neurons, there are 39 under ast2vec embedding and only 1 for doc2vec,
- They all have entropy greater than 3.
- Some of the other neurons having high entropy perform badly on the task.
- Choosing a neuron performing well on the task, its comparison to low entropy neurons always fails (see Figure 7 left), and the outcome of its comparison to medium or high entropy neurons can be related to how good their accuracy is on the task (see Figure 7 right).

With our entropy measure and our comparison based on Mann–Whithey U test, we could first select and then group neurons which could be considered to be representative of specific learned concepts. In general, neurons having high entropy exhibit behaviors that appear to be the most interesting, and they can be compared, with respect to the concepts they can recognize, to neurons toward which our test succeeds.

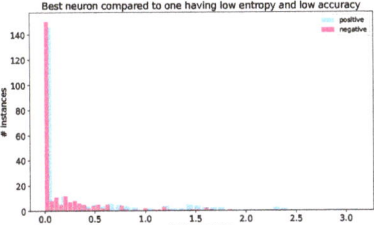 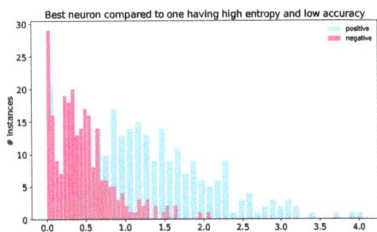

Figure 7. For the cyclomatic complexity classification, we show the outcome of our comparison between the best neuron in the task and two neurons not performing the same, with the first having low entropy (**left**) and the second one having high entropy (**right**).

7. Conclusions and Further Directions

This work aims at analyzing the dynamics of the internal parts of a neural network and at extracting knowledge from there. We approached this for a specific application domain, that of source code analysis, where what can be considered interesting knowledge cannot be defined as easily as when, for instance, recognizing objects in the natural domain of images.

Our approach is twofold. In the first part, we evaluate the performance of neurons belonging to an independently trained network when using them as classifiers for tasks related to properties of source code snippets. We then define when, in the same network, a neuron has a dynamics deemed interesting according to information-theoretic or statistical measures. We applied our methods to a simple autoencoder whose input was obtained from source code by using two different embeddings, one that just considers the linear sequence of words in the program lines (i.e., as if dealing with natural language) and another that also takes into account the formal parsing of the given programming language. We are able to show that:

- Several internal neurons perform well on tasks related to syntactic properties of code, such as its cyclomatic complexity, a common software engineering metric.
- The two embeddings we used performed differently when considering different tasks.
- Neurons can be algorithmically selected based on the richness of their activation dynamics.
- All the neurons that perform well on known tasks also reach high scores with our entropy measure.
- By choosing appropriate thresholds on activation values, in order to classify instances, neurons with high entropy are able to approximate each other's behavior.

Notice that the autoencoder operates on a "transformed" version of the source code (namely the program vectors), and thus the results obtained, which result from the information given by the data after the embedding process, are affected not only by the neural model under analysis but also by the chosen neural embedder.

Further work will be to apply our methods to explore the behavior of internal neurons of more sophisticated networks. For instance, recent works show how neural transformer models can be fruitfully used for source code [15,16]. The techniques we introduced could be employed to look for neurons which perform well on known tasks, even if belonging to a network trained while keeping in mind other goals. However, it would also be interesting to analyze how neurons classify with respect to the richness of their activation patterns and to group them by similarity, as allowed by our information-theoretic measures. Finally, we could study how to associate human-understandable concepts with the discovered internal activation patterns, similarly to what other authors did in the field of image understanding [19]. We expect that the more the neural model is structured and powerful, the more the measures we are introducing can prove their effectiveness in studying the internal representations and the developed knowledge of neural systems.

Author Contributions: Conceptualization, M.S. and C.F.; Software, M.S.; Investigation, M.S. and C.F.; Writing—original draft, M.S. and C.F.; Supervision, C.F. All authors have read and agreed to the published version of the manuscript.

Funding: This research received no external funding.

Data Availability Statement: Data is contained within the article.

Conflicts of Interest: The authors declare no conflicts of interest.

References

1. Erhan, D.; Courville, A.; Bengio, Y.; Vincent, P. Why does unsupervised pre-training help deep learning? In Proceedings of the 13th International Conference on Artificial Intelligence and Statistics, JMLR Workshop and Conference Proceedings, Sardinia, Italy, 13–15 May 2010; pp. 201–208.
2. Zhuang, F.; Qi, Z.; Duan, K.; Xi, D.; Zhu, Y.; Zhu, H.; Xiong, H.; He, Q. A comprehensive survey on transfer learning. *Proc. IEEE* **2020**, *109*, 43–76. [CrossRef]
3. Gilpin, L.H.; Bau, D.; Yuan, B.Z.; Bajwa, A.; Specter, M.; Kagal, L. Explaining explanations: An overview of interpretability of machine learning. In Proceedings of the IEEE 5th International Conference on data science and advanced analytics (DSAA), Turin, Italy, 1–3 October 2018; pp. 80–89.
4. Le, Q.V.; Ranzato, M.; Monga, R.; Devin, M.; Corrado, G.; Chen, K.; Dean, J.; Ng, A.Y. Building high-level features using large scale unsupervised learning. In Proceedings of the 29th International Conference on Machine Learning, ICML, PMLR, Edinburgh, Scotland, 26 June–1 July 2012; pp. 507–514.
5. Dalvi, F.; Durrani, N.; Sajjad, H.; Belinkov, Y.; Bau, A.; Glass, J.R. What Is One Grain of Sand in the Desert? Analyzing Individual Neurons in Deep NLP Models. In Proceedings of the 33rd AAAI Conference on Artificial Intelligence, Honolulu, HI, USA, 27 January–1 February 2019; pp. 6309–6317.

6. Le, T.H.M.; Chen, H.; Babar, M.A. Deep Learning for Source Code Modeling and Generation: Models, Applications, and Challenges. *ACM Comput. Surv.* **2020**, *53*, 62:1–62:38. [CrossRef]
7. Allamanis, M.; Barr, E.T.; Devanbu, P.T.; Sutton, C. A Survey of Machine Learning for Big Code and Naturalness. *ACM Comput. Surv.* **2018**, *51*, 81:1–81:37. [CrossRef]
8. Del Carpio, A.F.; Angarita, L.B. Trends in Software Engineering Processes using Deep Learning: A Systematic Literature Review. In Proceedings of the 46th Euromicro Conference on Software Engineering and Advanced Applications (SEAA), Portoroz, Slovenia, 26–28 August 2020; pp. 445–454. [CrossRef]
9. Liu, F.; Li, G.; Wei, B.; Xia, X.; Fu, Z.; Jin, Z. A Self-Attentional Neural Architecture for Code Completion with Multi-Task Learning. In Proceedings of the 28th International Conference on Program Comprehension, ICPC, ACM, Seoul, Republic of Korea, 13–15 July 2020; pp. 37–47.
10. Allamanis, M.; Peng, H.; Sutton, C.A. A Convolutional Attention Network for Extreme Summarization of Source Code. In Proceedings of the 33nd International Conference on Machine Learning, ICML, New York, NY, USA, 19–24 June 2016; pp. 2091–2100.
11. Mou, L.; Li, G.; Zhang, L.; Wang, T.; Jin, Z. Convolutional Neural Networks over Tree Structures for Programming Language Processing. In Proceedings of the Thirtieth AAAI Conference on Artificial Intelligence, Phoenix, AZ, USA, 12–17 February 2016; pp. 1287–1293.
12. Allamanis, M.; Brockschmidt, M.; Khademi, M. Learning to Represent Programs with Graphs. In Proceedings of the 6th International Conference on Learning Representations, ICLR 2018, Vancouver, BC, Canada, 30 April–3 May 2018.
13. Alon, U.; Zilberstein, M.; Levy, O.; Yahav, E. code2vec: Learning distributed representations of code. *Proc. ACM Program. Lang.* **2019**, *3*, 40:1–40:29. [CrossRef]
14. Vaswani, A.; Shazeer, N.; Parmar, N.; Uszkoreit, J.; Jones, L.; Gomez, A.N.; Kaiser, L.; Polosukhin, I. Attention is All you Need. In Proceedings of the Advances in Neural Information Processing Systems 30: Annual Conference on Neural Information Processing Systems (NIPS), Long Beach, CA, USA, 4–9 December 2017; pp. 5998–6008.
15. Kanade, A.; Maniatis, P.; Balakrishnan, G.; Shi, K. Learning and evaluating contextual embedding of source code. In Proceedings of the 37th International Conference on Machine Learning, ICML 2020, Virtual, 12–18 July 2020.
16. Ahmad, W.; Chakraborty, S.; Ray, B.; Chang, K.W. Unified Pre-training for Program Understanding and Generation. In Proceedings of the 2021 Conference of the North American Chapter of the Association for Computational Linguistics: Human Language Technologies, Online, 6–11 June 2021; pp. 2655–2668.
17. Yu, S.; Príncipe, J.C. Understanding autoencoders with information theoretic concepts. *Neural Netw.* **2019**, *117*, 104–123. [CrossRef] [PubMed]
18. Radford, A.; Jozefowicz, R.; Sutskever, I. Learning to Generate Reviews and Discovering Sentiment. *arXiv* **2017**, arXiv:1704.01444.
19. Kim, B.; Wattenberg, M.; Gilmer, J.; Cai, C.J.; Wexler, J.; Viégas, F.B.; Sayres, R. Interpretability beyond Feature Attribution: Quantitative Testing with Concept Activation Vectors (TCAV). In Proceedings of the 35th International Conference on Machine Learning, ICML 2018, Stockholm, Sweden, 10–15 July 2018; Volume 80, pp. 2673–2682.
20. McGrath, T.; Kapishnikov, A.; Tomašev, N.; Pearce, A.; Wattenberg, M.; Hassabis, D.; Kim, B.; Paquet, U.; Kramnik, V. Acquisition of chess knowledge in alphazero. *Proc. Natl. Acad. Sci. USA* **2022**, *119*, e2206625119. [CrossRef] [PubMed]
21. Saletta, M.; Ferretti, C. Towards the evolutionary assessment of neural transformers trained on source code. In Proceedings of the GECCO'22: Genetic and Evolutionary Computation Conference, Companion Volume, Boston, MA, USA, 9–13 July 2022; Fieldsend, J.E., Wagner, M., Eds.; ACM: 2022; pp. 1770–1778. [CrossRef]
22. Ferretti, C.; Saletta, M. Do Neural Transformers Learn Human-Defined Concepts? An Extensive Study in Source Code Processing Domain. *Algorithms* **2022**, *15*, 449. [CrossRef]
23. Goodfellow, I.J.; Bengio, Y.; Courville, A.C. *Deep Learning*; Adaptive Computation and Machine Learning; MIT Press: Cambridge, MA, USA, 2016.
24. Bau, A.; Belinkov, Y.; Sajjad, H.; Durrani, N.; Dalvi, F.; Glass, J.R. Identifying and Controlling Important Neurons in Neural Machine Translation. In Proceedings of the 7th International Conference on Learning Representations, ICLR, New Orleans, LA, USA, 6–9 May 2019.
25. Shannon, C.E. A mathematical theory of communication. *Bell Syst. Tech. J.* **1948**, *27*, 623–656. [CrossRef]
26. Zeiler, M.D. ADADELTA: An Adaptive Learning Rate Method. *arXiv* **2012**, arXiv:1212.5701.
27. Chollet, F. Keras. Available online: https://keras.io (accessed on 4 April 2023).
28. Alon, U.; Brody, S.; Levy, O.; Yahav, E. code2seq: Generating Sequences from Structured Representations of Code. In Proceedings of the 7th International Conference on Learning Representations, ICLR, New Orleans, LA, USA, 6–9 May 2019.
29. Le, Q.V.; Mikolov, T. Distributed Representations of Sentences and Documents. In Proceedings of the 31th International Conference on Machine Learning, ICML 2014, Beijing, China, 21–26 June 2014; pp. 1188–1196.
30. Řehůřek, R.; Sojka, P. Software Framework for Topic Modelling with Large Corpora. In Proceedings of the LREC 2010 Workshop on New Challenges for NLP Frameworks, Valletta, Malta, 22 May 2010; pp. 45–50.
31. Smith, N.; van Bruggen, D.; Tomassetti, F. *JavaParser: Visited*, Version Dated 5 February 2021; GitHub, Inc.: San Francisco, CA, USA, 2021.

32. Saletta, M.; Ferretti, C. A Neural Embedding for Source Code: Security Analysis and CWE Lists. In Proceedings of the 18th IEEE International Conference on Dependable, Autonomic and Secure Computing, DASC/PiCom/CBDCom/CyberSciTech, Calgary, AB, Canada, 17–22 August 2020; pp. 523–530.
33. Mikolov, T.; Sutskever, I.; Chen, K.; Corrado, G.S.; Dean, J. Distributed Representations of Words and Phrases and their Compositionality. In Proceedings of the Advances in Neural Information Processing Systems 26, Proceedings of NIPS, Lake Tahoe, Nevada, 5–10 December 2013; pp. 3111–3119.
34. Allen, F.E. Control Flow Analysis. *ACM Sigplan Not.* **1970**, *5*, 1–19. [CrossRef]
35. McCabe, T.J. A Complexity Measure. *IEEE Trans. Softw. Eng.* **1976**, *2*, 308–320. [CrossRef]
36. Alon, U.; Zilberstein, M.; Levy, O.; Yahav, E. A general path-based representation for predicting program properties. In Proceedings of the 39th ACM SIGPLAN Conference on Programming Language Design and Implementation, PLDI, Philadelphia, PA, USA, 18–22 June 2018; pp. 404–419.

Disclaimer/Publisher's Note: The statements, opinions and data contained in all publications are solely those of the individual author(s) and contributor(s) and not of MDPI and/or the editor(s). MDPI and/or the editor(s) disclaim responsibility for any injury to people or property resulting from any ideas, methods, instructions or products referred to in the content.

MDPI
St. Alban-Anlage 66
4052 Basel
Switzerland
www.mdpi.com

Information Editorial Office
E-mail: information@mdpi.com
www.mdpi.com/journal/information

Disclaimer/Publisher's Note: The statements, opinions and data contained in all publications are solely those of the individual author(s) and contributor(s) and not of MDPI and/or the editor(s). MDPI and/or the editor(s) disclaim responsibility for any injury to people or property resulting from any ideas, methods, instructions or products referred to in the content.

www.ingramcontent.com/pod-product-compliance
Lightning Source LLC
LaVergne TN
LVHW070732100526
838202LV00013B/1215